POLITICAL
ANTHROPOLOGY

POLITICAL ANTHROPOLOGY

edited by MARC J. SWARTZ, VICTOR W. TURNER *and* ARTHUR TUDEN

ALDINE Publishing Company / *Chicago*

Copyright © 1966 by Aldine Publishing Company
All rights reserved

First published 1966 by
ALDINE Publishing Company
320 West Adams Street
Chicago, Illinois 60606

Library of Congress Catalog Card Number 66–15210
Designed by David Miller
Printed in the United States of America

To
Audrey Swartz
Edie Turner
Agnes Tuden

CONTENTS

POLITICAL ANTHROPOLOGY

INTRODUCTION[1]

Marc J. Swartz, MICHIGAN STATE UNIVERSITY
Victor W. Turner, CORNELL UNIVERSITY
Arthur Tuden, UNIVERSITY OF PITTSBURGH

I

This book is the outgrowth of an experiment. Its editors, curious to explore current trends and styles of analysis in political anthropology, decided to ask a number of distinguished practitioners in this field to contribute papers for presentation at the 1964 Annual General Meeting of the American Anthropological Association. It was decided that the contributors were to be given considerable leeway in their choice and treatment of topics, for our aim was to find out whether "a wind of change" was invading political theory as it had invaded the actual politics of most societies that have been studied by anthropologists.

As the papers came in, it soon became clear that this is indeed the case. Since the last major bench mark in the anthropology of politics, *African Political Systems* (edited by Fortes and Evans-Pritchard, 1940), which has been both stimulus and model for several well-known anthologies, monographs, and articles, there has been a trend—at first almost imperceptible, then gaining momentum in the late 1950's and early 1960's—away from the earlier preoccupation with the taxonomy, structure, and function of political systems to a growing concern with the study of political processes. Professor Firth (1957, p. 294), with his flair for the detection of new theoretical tendencies, aptly characterized the new mood as one in which anthropologists would forsake "the well-trodden ground of conventional structural analysis for a type of inquiry which is from the outset an examination of 'dynamic phenomena.'"

Indeed, many of the papers we received centered their discussions on dynamic political phenomena and processes. They considered both re-

[1] The editors are indebted to Peter Worsley, Ralph Nicholas, and Moreau Maxwell for reading, and commenting on, this introduction. Professor Worsley made the interesting observation that we shifted from an economic metaphor when we were discussing legitimacy and support to a military metaphor when we took up the phases of overall political processes. Although we received much benefit from our colleagues' comments, the responsibility for the positions taken here is solely the editors'.

petitive and radical political change, the processes of decision-making and conflict resolution, and the agitation and settlement of political issues in a variety of cultural contexts. The papers were pervaded by a "becoming" rather than a "being" vocabulary: they were full of such terms as "conflict," "faction," "struggle," "conflict resolution," "arena," "development," "process," and so forth. It is true that this stress on the processual dimension of politics had been foreshadowed and prepared by a number of important books, some of which had first appeared soon after the publication of *African Political Systems*. Perhaps the most notable of these pioneer studies of political dynamics—although its major emphasis was on law rather than politics—was *The Cheyenne Way* by Llewellyn and Hoebel (1941), which focused attention on conflicts of interests and on the notion that "trouble cases lead us most directly to legal phenomena" (p. 37). The same outlook, applied to political behavior, clearly guides many of the contributors to this present volume. No fewer than five articles are directly concerned with the resolution of conflict and the settlement of disputes.

Few processes of political action run harmonious courses. It is not surprising, therefore, that processual studies tend also to study conflict, as well as its resolution. Several social philosophers have contributed to our vocabulary of concepts for the analysis of conflict; these include Hegel, with his "dialectic," Marx, with his "contradiction" and "struggle," and Simmel with his "conflict." More recently, Coser has done much to familiarize us with a more refined and systematic exposition of Simmel's theoretical standpoint (1956). But within the strictly anthropological tradition, the application of these and related concepts to the data of pre-industrial society is perhaps most fully exemplified by the work of Max Gluckman and the so-called "Manchester School."

These anthropologists, working with "the extended case method," have tended to lay emphasis on the processual aspect of politics in tribal societies, and even in certain sectors of complex societies. In Gluckman's words (1965, p. 235):

. . . they are now analyzing the development of social relations themselves, under the conflicting pressures of discrepant principles and values, as the generations change and new persons come to maturity. If we view these relations through a longish period of time, we see how various parties and supporters operate and manipulate mystical beliefs of various kinds to serve their interests. The beliefs are seen in dynamic process within day-to-day social life, and the creation and burgeoning of new groups and relationships.

This formulation, although it depends rather heavily upon the doctrine of the primacy of "interest" and underestimates the capacity of "mystical beliefs" to evoke altruistic responses from members of a social group, is nevertheless a good summary of the main characteristics of this nascent type of analysis. In this book, the articles by Middleton, Turner, Colson, and Nicholas are markedly influenced by the thinking of the Manchester School. These studies direct attention to conflicts of interests and values and to mechanisms for redressing conflicts and reconciling the parties to them.

The shift in emphasis from static and synchronic analyses of morphological types to dynamic and diachronic studies of societies in change was also evident in Evans-Pritchard's insistence, throughout the 1950's, that modern social anthropologists must consider the histories of the societies they study (1962), in Firth's notion of "organizational change" (gradual and cumulative rather than radical structural change [1959], and in the Cambridge University work on developmental cycles (Goody, 1958). But, in the main, these studies emphasized repetitive change that —at the end of a cycle of institutionally "triggered off" modifications in the pattern and content of social relations—brought about a regular return to the status quo ante. Again it was Gluckman who drew attention to radical change, or change in the social structure, for example, "in the size of a society, the composition or balance of its parts, or the type of organization" (as Ginsberg has defined such change [1956, p. 10]). Gluckman's fieldwork in the plural society of Zululand led him to reject the then dominant model of a social system as a set of functionally interconnected components, moving by graduated stages through culturally defined equilibria—or, at most, changing so slowly that no disruption of equilibrium or integration could occur.

From the viewpoint of the sociology of knowledge, it is no accident that this alteration of analytical focus from structure to process has developed during a period in which the formerly colonial territories of Asia, Africa, and the Pacific have been undergoing far-reaching political changes that have culminated in independence. Anthropologists who directed or undertook fieldwork during the 1950's and early 1960's found that they could not ignore or neglect the processes of change or resistance to change, whose concrete expressions were all around them. Many of these anthropologists worked in plural societies, characterized by ethnic diversity, sharp economic inequalities between ethnic groups, religious differences, political and legal heterogeneity—in short, major asymmetries of sociocultural scale and complexity between their ethnic constituents.

Such societies, studied by Furnivall (1948), Mitchell (1954), Gluckman (1954b, 1965), Wilson (1945), Kuper (1947), Epstein (1958), and M. G. Smith (1960b), have been conceptualized not so much as tightly integrated systems, modeled on either organic or mechanical analogues, but as social fields with many dimensions, with parts that may be loosely integrated, or virtually independent from one another, and that have to be studied over time if the factors underlying the changes in their social relationships are to be identified and analyzed. Probably because of the

magnitude of the new tasks confronting them, anthropologists have so
far generally eschewed the attempt to portray and analyze social fields
in anything like their full complexity or temporal depth. Rather, they
have attempted to isolate single sectors, or subsectors, within a single
dimension of such fields, and have then endeavored to say something
significant about the processes they have found there. Nevertheless, their
work is almost always impregnated by awareness of the wider context
and of its major properties—such as plurality, diversity, componential
looseness of fit, conflict, variations in degree of consensus (ranging to
complete lack of consensus), and the like.

II

The dimension that concerns us in this book is the political dimension, and within it we shall consider those relationships between personalities and groups that make up a "political field." Clearly, such concepts
depend on what is meant by "politics." "Politics," however, is almost as
difficult to define as it is easy to use as a description of occurrences
within societies and their constituent parts. It is easy to sympathize with
those who, like Fortes and Evans-Pritchard (1940), avoid defining the
term, for the concept has a wide range of useful application and the
great variety of data to which it is applied makes operational specifica-
tion difficult.

Still, we can hardly call this volume *Political Anthropology,* and bom-
bard the reader with political concepts and theoretical constructs, if we
do not provide a rather concise idea of what it is that we are talking
about.

Several qualities that lead us to consider a process as political are
readily noted and widely accepted as characteristic. First, a political
process is public rather than private. An activity that affects a neighborhood, a whole community, a whole society, or a group of societies is
unquestionably a public activity; whether it is *also* a political activity
depends upon other characteristics—in addition to its being public. A
religious ceremony may affect entire communities, societies, and even
groups of societies, but we may not wish to call it a "political activity"
(although—and now we begin to see some of the sorrow that is the lot
of the would-be definer of this concept—under some circumstances
and/or in certain respects we might want to call a religious ceremony
"political").

The second generally accepted quality of politics is that it concerns
goals. Combining the first characteristic with this second one, we can
go a bit further and say that politics always involves public goals. Although individual, private goals will always be importantly involved (see

Swartz's article in this volume), the emphasis will be upon goals desired for the group as a whole. These goals will include the achievement of a new relationship vis-à-vis some other group or groups: winning independence, fighting a war or making peace, gaining higher prestige than previously held, changing the relative standing of castes or classes within a group, etc.; a change in the relationship to the environment for all or most members of the group, such as building an irrigation project or clearing land for the whole village, etc.; and the allocation of offices, titles, and other scarce resources for which there is a group-wide competition.

From what has already been said about political goals, it will be clear that consciousness of a desired end is present, but this consciousness need be neither complete nor universal. Some of the members of a group may have little or no idea of what is being sought; only the leaders may have a clear idea of the end that is being pursued. The "goal" may be only a wish to escape a vaguely conceived dissatisfaction or to achieve a new state or objective that is not clearly formulated. Leaders may present their publics with goals that are, in a sense, only artifices for furthering a more distant or hidden end. Thus a trade union leader may call a strike over wages and working conditions, and the union members may believe these are the ultimate goals. The leader, however, may be using the strike to improve his position vis-à-vis other leaders and/or government officials. It is true that politics always concerns goals, but it is useful to recognize that "goal" is not a univocal concept and that all we are requiring here is that there be a striving for something for which there is competition. This competition, however, must be of a particular kind, and, to explain this, it is necessary to look briefly at what is meant by its being "group-wide."

In our society, money is competed for on a group-wide basis, but we would not say that this competition is necessarily political in character. What is meant here is that political allocations are those that require the consent of an entire group in order to be effectively made. Thus while every individual or unit in a society may be competing with every other individual or unit for an economic good, such as money, the results of these competitions do not require group-wide consent in order to be effective. However, competition for titles in, say, a West African society cannot be said to be settled unless the whole group consents to the allocation of the titles that results from the competition. Thus for allocation to be political in nature it must concern scarce goods, the possession of which depends upon a group's consenting to the allocation.

Another important end that is characteristic of politics is achieving settlements that are of public rather than only private concern. Settlements, to be public, must concern a group as a whole, in a rather direct and immediate way. Settling a quarrel between two friends—or between a man and wife—will be considered a public settlement if its accomplishment (or failure) affects, say, the immediate threat of a schism that would divide the whole group or realign the factions that exist within the group. Clearly, some settlements will be public and some will be private, and others will be hard to identify immediately. In this last (probably large) category, we can extract ourselves from vagueness by adhering to the "by-their-fruits-ye-shall-know-them" doctrine, considering all settlements as possibly political until the consequences of each case can be established by detailed investigation. If we find that a settlement or failure of settlement has implications for a group as a whole, we will call it "political" even though at its outset it did not appear to have group-wide consequences.

It is important to dwell a moment on "failure of settlement" and its implications for what is meant by "politics." Political activity is sometimes devoted to the prevention of settlements and to the subversion of the institutional framework by which settlements are reached. In this sort of situation we would not fail to note that a group, the "rebels," seeks a public goal—namely, the realignment of the resources and members of a larger group with which they were associated—and that this group carries out political activity as we have so far defined it.

The significance of this activity for the definition being presented is twofold. First, it must be made clear that politics does not consist entirely of activities that ultimately, or necessarily, promote the welfare and continued existence of a group, as constituted and organized at any particular time. Political activity includes all sorts of seeking-after-public-goals, which may be as concerned with the deracination of existing structures, mechanisms, and alignments as with their preservation.

Second, this consideration of disjunctive activity in politics provides an opportunity to clarify what is meant by goals and settlements that have consequences for a group. A "group" need not be a whole society, or even a major segment of a society; a number of individuals may join together in rejection of the goals and aims of the larger group of which they were formerly part. These individuals may constitute a faction (see Nicholas' paper) or a special interest group that devotes its energies to inducing conflict—rather than to promoting settlements—with the aim of overthrowing the organization of its parent body and/or changing the basic aims of that body. Such activities are clearly political, and the fact that the faction or special interest group uses noninstitutional means for seeking its ends (violence, for example) does not alter the political nature of its behavior.

A final major characteristic of "politics" is implicit in what has just been said: it involves some kind of focusing of power—using "power" in its broadest sense. This focusing need not entail the existence of a permanent hierarchy of power, but it will always involve the existence of differential behavior concerning public goals. Conceivably, the differential may be no more than that certain individuals announce group goals that have been jointly decided upon by all members of a group, participating equally—or it may be that a very few members determine a group's goals and that the others merely carry out the decisions. A differential will always be present.

We therefore have three characteristics that should serve to start our division of the universe into what is political and what is not. The adjective "political," as we have so far defined it, will apply to everything that is at once public, goal-oriented, and that involves a differential of power (in the sense of control) among the individuals of the group in question.

This tentative definition does not solve the sort of problem illustrated earlier by the example of the religious ceremony. A religious ceremony could have all the characteristics so far proposed: it could be public (everybody participates and is concerned with it), goal-oriented (it changes a group's relationship to the environment by ending a drought), and it could involve a differential possession of power (ritual experts could tell the others what to do), but we might be reluctant to say that the ceremony is primarily a political activity.

An obvious way out of this difficulty would be to overlook our reluctance and declare the ceremony a political activity on the entirely valid grounds that we can define things however we wish without any fear of our definitions being either true or false. But a more satisfying solution is available, which comes from our being able to look at an activity from different points of view. If we look at the religious ceremony from the point of view of the processes by which the group goals are determined and implemented (how it was decided that a ceremony was to be held, how the time and place were determined, how the things to be used in the ceremony were obtained, etc.) and by which power is differentially acquired (which ritual experts are successful in telling the "laity" what to do, how these experts marshal support for their power and undermine that of their rivals, etc.), we are studying politics. If, however, we look at the ritual from the perspective, say, of the way it relates the group to the supernatural and the way this relationship affects the relations among the constituent parts of the group, we are studying religion—or at least we are studying something other than politics.

The study of politics, then, is the study of the *processes* involved in determining and implementing public goals and in the differential achievement and use of power by the members of the group concerned with those goals.

In the remainder of this introduction a good deal will be said about the nature of political processes, so that (for the present) it is enough to point out that these processes are the key elements in politics. From the perspective of politics, processes such as marshaling support, undermining rivals, attaining goals, and achieving settlements are the prime foci of interest. The groups within which these processes occur are important because they constitute the "field" of political activity, but this activity moves across group boundaries without necessarily encountering hindrances, which is another way of saying the political field can expand and contract.

The important point here is that since politics is the study of certain kinds of processes, it is essential to center our attention on these processes rather than on the groups or fields within which they occur. This means, for example, that a political study follows the development of conflicts for power (or for acquiring support for proposed goals) into whatever groups the processes lead—rather than examining such groups as lineages, villages, or countries to determine what processes they might contain. To focus upon groups would be to credit them with a wholeness and a completeness that is not justified, for the understanding of what is happening in a village struggle for leadership may require an examination of the roots of the struggle in the national context.

To put this another way, political anthropology no longer exclusively studies—in structural-functionalist terms—political institutions of cyclical, repetitive societies. Its unit of space is no longer the isolated "society"; it tends to be the political "field." Its unit of time is no longer "structural time"; it is historical time. The combined unit is a spatial-temporal continuum.

A political field does not operate like clockwork, with all the pieces meshed together with finely tooled precision. It is, rather, a field of tension, full of intelligent and determined antagonists, sole and corporate, who are motivated by ambition, altruism, self-interest, and by desire for the public good, and who in successive situations are bound to one another through self-interest, or idealism—and separated or opposed through the same motives. At every point in this process we have to consider each unit in terms of its independent objectives, and we also have to consider the entire situation in which their *inter*dependent actions occur. This independence and this interdependence are emphatically not those of the parts of a machine or an animal. The institutionalization of political relationships may sometimes impose upon the observer the delusory appearance of mechanical or organic phenomena, but they are mere analogies that blind us to some of the most important qualities of political behavior. To understand such behavior, we have to know how the political "units" think, feel, and will in relation to their understanding of the issues that they generate or confront. As Parsons and Emmet have shown us (Parsons, 1937; Emmet, 1958), the factor of purposiveness is analytically crucial to the concept of political action.

III

Mention of Talcott Parsons reminds us of the impressive contribution that social philosophers and sociologists—Parsons himself, and Durkheim, Weber, Bierstedt, and Bales—and political scientists—such as Lasswell, Kaplan, Easton, M. Levy, and Banfield—to name only a few— have made to the study of political processes. Although anthropologists have tended to be extremely suspicious of the theories of political philosophers, as displayed in many ways—from the strictures in *African Political Systems* (Fortes and Evans-Pritchard, 1940)[2] to the less draconic pronouncements in current publications, we consider that the time is now ripe for dialogue, if not for marriage, between anthropology and other disciplines concerned with comparative politics.

From the sociologists and political scientists we hope to obtain a tool kit of concepts that, with some modification, will prove useful to anthropologists when they examine political behavior in real societies—but that will not unduly restrict assumptions about the nature of this behavior. Ideally, concepts for analyzing politics would be as applicable in societies that do not have centralized and/or permanent decision-making units as in societies that have such units; in societies where change is rapid and drastic, and in those where it is slow and gradual; in societies where the great bulk of the population has many important values, motivations, and relationships in common, and in societies where the population has little in common. In short, the purpose here is to present concepts of general applicability, which also allow recognition of the diversity of political systems.

FORCE AND COERCION

In most of the writing on political behavior, much attention has been paid to the role of coercion in general and force in particular. This is understandable in that some of the more obvious and striking types of political behavior involve the use, or threat, of force. Furthermore, the notion that politics has to do with decisions that apply to society as a whole quite naturally leads to an emphasis on the opposition between the interests of the individual and those of the group.

Despite its undeniable importance, insuperable difficulties confront the view that force is the sole, or even the major, basis of political behavior. These difficulties arise from the fact that force is a crude and

---

[2] The editors, in their introduction, remarked severely: "[The] conclusions [of political philosophers] have little scientific value; for they . . . are seldom formulated in terms of observed behavior or capable of being tested by this criterion" (p. 4). Yet their debt to Weber and Durkheim is now widely recognized.

expensive technique for the implementation of decisions. More importantly, force itself has to depend on interpersonal relationships that are
based on something *other* than force.

The crudity and essential inflexibility of force were intriguingly discussed by Talcott Parsons (1963b, p. 240) in the course of his extensive
analysis of parallels between politics and economics (1963a, 1963b). He
compared the role of force in politics to that of gold in a monetary system. Both have great effectiveness, and both may operate with a high
degree of independence from their institutional contexts, but excessive
dependence on either leads to rigidity and a reduction in the number
and type of things that the systems can do. A monetary system that
relies heavily on gold in its day-to-day transactions would be primitive
and clumsy, and the same would be true of a political system that is
heavily dependent on force.

The fact that force must rely on relationships based on something
other than force has been pointed out by Goldhamer and Shils (1939,
p. 178): the more that force is used in a system, the larger must be the
staff needed to apply it—and the greater the dependence of the users on
that staff. Although the relationship between those who apply force, on
the one hand, and those to whom it is applied, on the other, may be
based entirely on force, there must nevertheless be relationships *within
the force-using group* that are based on something else.

SUPPORT AND LEGITIMACY

If we understand "support" to mean anything that contributes to the
formulation and/or implementation of political ends, we can say that
although force (which is a form of support) may have an important part
to play in political systems, it can never be the only means of support in
the systems. Force as a mode of support must always be supplemented
by other modes of support.

"Legitimacy"[3] is a type of support that derives not from force or
its threat but from the values held by the individuals formulating, influencing, and being affected by political ends. Clearly, because decisions
are made on less than a group-wide scale, "legitimacy" is not limited in
its applicability to the area of politics. Here, however, our attention will
be reserved for the uses of legitimacy in a political context.

The derivation of legitimacy from values comes through the establishment of a positive connection between the entity or process having
legitimacy and those values. This connection can be established in a
number of different ways (some of which will be discussed below), but
in all cases it involves a set of expectations in the minds of those who
accept the legitimacy. These expectations are to the effect that the legiti-

[3] See Weber (1947, pp. 124-132, 324-329) for what is probably the most influential general discussion of legitimacy; and Parsons (1960, pp. 170-198).

mate entity or process will, under certain circumstances, meet certain obligations that are held by those who view it as legitimate. These obligations may be either specific (a legitimate chief will bring rain when it is needed) or general (a legitimate court will render a just decision), but it is important to note that they operate as predictions of what will happen in the future and not simply as accounts of what has happened in the past. Legitimacy is a type of evaluation that imputes future behavior of an expected and desired type (Parsons, 1963b, p. 238).

Legitimacy and all other types of support may be viewed most fruitfully in connection with various aspects of the political process rather than as applicable to total systems. That is, instead of trying to decide what kinds of support a whole political system may have, or whether the system as a whole is legitimate, increased analytic power can be gained by dividing the political system into a number of aspects or levels and examining each for the presence or absence of legitimacy, force, and other types of support. It is, of course, necessary to establish empirically the types of support that are decisive for political action on each level.

David Easton (1957, pp. 391-393; 1959, pp. 228-229) has suggested three aspects of the political system that are useful in an analysis of this sort. The first of these is what he calls "the political community." This is the largest group within which differences can be settled and decisions promoted through peaceful action. Clearly, force cannot be an important type of support for this entity, and legitimacy (that is, expectations of desirable sorts of settlements and decision implementations) will often, but not necessarily, be an important element. What Easton calls "the political community" and what we call "the political field" are distinct concepts. A "political field" may be coterminous with a "political community"; it may contain two or more political communities in relationships of cooperation or conflict; it may involve a political community and groups or individuals from outside that community; or it may not involve political communities.

Easton's second aspect is "the regime," which "consists of all those arrangements that regulate the way the demands put into the system are settled and the way in which decisions are put into effect" (1957, p. 392). Easton views these procedures as "the rules of the game" and as the criteria for legitimizing the actions of those involved in the political process. This, however, departs from the view of legitimacy taken here. Although the analytical usefulness of separating the procedures for reaching and implementing decisions is considerable, it is important to note that these procedures may or may not be viewed as legitimate. Thus it seems more fruitful to view "the rules of the game" or "regime" as the standard for *legality* and to leave the question unanswered whether the support of the rules or regime is derived from legitimacy or from some other source. As a product of these rules, legality will depend upon the status of the rules for its own status. Thus to the extent that the rules rest on force, legality will rest on force; to the extent that the rules rest on legitimacy, the difference between legality and legitimacy will be diminished. M. G. Smith has directed attention to the important distinction between legitimacy and legality, pointing out that whereas "law circumscribes legality, legitimacy is often invoked to sanction and justify actions contrary to existing law" (1960, p. 20).

Easton's final aspect is "government," and this in his view consists of both the political officials and the "administrative organization" of which they are part. For our purposes it is preferable to separate the officials from the "organization," so that "government" will here refer only to the interconnected series of statuses whose roles are primarily concerned with making and implementing political decision. Unlike a political community and regime, every society need not have a government, because making and implementing decisions can be (and often is) diffused among statuses whose roles include many duties other than (and sometimes more important than) making and implementing political decisions. As in the previous two analytic levels, however, a government, when it is present, may or may not have legitimacy as one of its major sources of support. The government of a group will be considered legitimate when the members of the group, its "public," believe—on the basis of experience—that the government will produce decisions that are in accord with the public's expectations.

POLITICAL STATUS, OFFICIAL, AND DECISION

Three further concepts may be usefully distinguished with reference to types of support: political status, official, and decision, none of which is dependent on the existence of government for its existence. A "political status," which is a position whose role is primarily that of making and/or implementing political decisions, may or may not be part of a network of political statuses, but in either case it may be examined for legitimacy or other types of support. Similarly, a "political official," although he must be the occupant of a political status, may or may not be part of a governmental structure; he may be the object of support of any or all types, independently of the types that are accorded his status. For example, an official may be considered legitimate or illegitimate independently of the legitimacy or absence of legitimacy of the government of which he is part, even if there is such a structure.

A "decision" is a pronouncement that concerns goals, allocations, or settlements that must ultimately originate from an entity (although the members of the group in question may not identify its source accurately) in the political system. However, the type of support, if any, that the decision receives may or may not be the same as the support accorded the sources of the decision. Among other things, this means that the decision may be legitimate even though the entity identified as its source is not, and that the decision may be illegitimate even though its source is legitimate. Indeed, the type of support discovered as operative at one level of analysis does not determine the type or types operative at another level. For example, although a political community and regime might be legitimate, this would not assure the legitimacy of the government, or of particular political statuses, officials, or decisions. As Easton put it: "It is always a matter for empirical inquiry to discover the degree to which support at one level is dependent upon support at the others" (1957, p. 393).

Just as different types of support can exist simultaneously at different levels of analysis, different types of support can operate at the same level at different times (as we will see in Section III of this introduction). This is true of all types of support, including legitimacy, which may fairly be regarded as a particularly stable attribute of political phenomena, relationships, and processes. For example, an official may begin his political career through a ritual that serves to establish positive expectations in the minds of those affected by him so that, at the beginning of his career in office, support is through legitimacy. (An example of this can be seen in Park's discussion of the role of the Kinga prince [pp. 229-237].) In the course of political activity, however, an official may consistently fail to meet these expectations and so lose the legitimacy gained through the ritual at the outset of his career. If he is to continue to fulfill his duties, he must have the support of some other type (or types), whether this be through force, the absence of alternatives, or some of the other types that will be discussed presently.

Similarly, legitimacy may not be associated with a political entity at the beginning of a career, but, through meeting expectations, the entity may come to achieve legitimacy, and to depend upon this type of support—more than (or even instead of) the type or types with which it began. Thus in Swartz's article we see that Bena headmen and village executive officers attain support (legitimacy) through their successful functioning as adjudicators. However, they do not begin their tenure in office with this sort of support, at least not necessarily. Instead, their early days in office are supported by extensions of personal support accorded their statuses and by supports deriving from the fact that they are appointed by the national government. In Turner's paper we observe how claimants for an important politico-ritual office assert their claims in terms of different criteria of legitimacy, so that their competition is at the same time a process of testing the contemporary validity of the rival criteria.

A particularly interesting example of the impermanence of a given type of support is provided by Cohen in his paper on the Kanuri. The Kanuri believe that success or failure by an individual is due to the amount of *arziyi*, which is a part of the individual's being, has provided for a self-legitimizing of officeholders. That they achieve office proves that they have more *arziyi* than others, but failure in office proves that their *arziyi* has decreased. Thus the belief in *arziyi* and in its variability among and within individuals can be viewed as an institutionalized means of estimating how well an officeholder will meet the expectations others have of him. When his *arziyi* is plentiful, he will be able to do what is required of him, but when it is not so bounteous he will not be able to do so. Thus his ability to gain office and to have retained it is proof of his ability to do what is or will be expected of him.

It will be clear from what has already been said that although legitimacy is only one member of the larger class of support, it is an important member. What must be examined now is whether it is fruitful to postulate the existence of legitimacy in all political systems.

POWER AND LEGITIMACY

Parsons (1963b) argues very stimulatingly that "power" should be understood to rest upon legitimacy. To simplify a highly ramified and complex position, he holds that power is the "generalized capacity to secure the performance of binding obligations—where in case of recalcitrance there is a presumption of enforcement by negative . . . sanctions" (p. 237). Despite the place occupied by negative sanctions (we will return to this in a moment), the essence of Parsons' position is seen in his view that the exercise of power is an interaction in which the power holder gains compliance with a decision concerning group goals in exchange for the understanding that the complying entity is entitled to invoke certain obligations in the future. In other words, obedience to the leader is conditioned upon his undertaking (tacitly or explicitly) to reciprocate later on with beneficial actions.

Power, in this context, is a symbolic medium whose functioning does not depend primarily upon its intrinsic effectiveness but upon the expectations that its employment arouses in those who comply with it. Among the Bena, as described by Swartz, the power of the village officials depends upon the expectations of the villagers that the officials will be successful settlers of disputes. Because power is symbolic, it is a generalized medium that operates independently of particular circumstances, sanctions, situations, or individuals. Power, in this sense. we propose to call "consensual power," to distinguish it from power based on coercion. In the sense in which we use it here, power may be regarded as the dynamic aspect of legitimacy, as legitimacy put to the test of social action.

Compliance based on consensual power is motivated by the belief (which may be only vaguely formulated) that at some time in the future the official, agency, government, etc., with which individuals comply will satisfy the compliers' positive expectations. This compliance may be with directives or regulations which are not congenial (for example, doing corvée labor), and when there is little or no prospect of a direct return from obeying the directives or regulations. However, if consensual power is present as an attribute of the source of the directives, compliance will result from the belief that in its overall operation the official, agency, or government will sooner or later bring about desired results or continue some desired state. Thus corvée labor may not be viewed by the workers as producing any desired result, but the official who orders it may be viewed as likely to do something desired. Because compliance based on consensual power is divorced from immediate dependence or gratification, consensual power allows much more flexibility than does compliance based on other types of support.

There may be little or even no consensual power in a given system, or there may be a great deal, but the amount of consensual power present will determine the flexibility of the system with respect to its ability to make and implement decisions in situations that are different from those previously encountered. This flexibility is in part the result of the element of legitimacy in consensual power that frees it from dependence upon particular sanctions, and in part it is the result of its being free from particular, concrete rewards.[4]

This is not to say that systems cannot operate without legitimacy (any more than it is true to say that any system is completely based upon legitimacy), but rather that as legitimacy in the imposing of obligations decreases, the suppleness of the system also decreases. Parsons (1963b, p. 238) puts this as follows:

. . . questioning the legitimacy of the possession and use of power leads to resort to progressively more "secure" means of gaining compliance. These must be progressively more effective "intrinsically," hence more tailored to the particular situation . . . and less general. Furthermore, insofar as they are intrinsically effective, legitimacy becomes a progressively less important factor of their effectiveness . . . at the end of this series lies resort, first to various types of coercion, eventually to the use of force as the most intrinsically effective of all means of coercion.

It should be noted that the element of legitimacy in consensual power has implications for both parties to an interaction that involves this kind of power. In other words, power in this sense has two sides. It involves obedience by those on whom it is exerted; nevertheless, it also implicates

---

[4] It should be emphasized that "consensual power" is a special concept, defined in terms of its dependence upon legitimacy for its effectiveness. "Power," as an unqualified term, here refers to a broader phenomenon, involving control of behavior through superior force and/or superior command of human and other resources. "Power" is more commonly used in the literature than "consensual power." For examples of definitions of the more usual usage, see Dahl (1957), Bierstedt (1950), and Goldhamer and Shils (1939). For a further discussion of the concept we refer to as "consensual power," see Parsons (1963b, pp. 237-238).

the wielder's power in the values he shares with the objects of power, values that take the form of the expectations of those who obey the powerful. Thus the connection with the value system that gives the power users the unique advantage of flexibility also gives the power objects the advantage of being able to invoke their legitimate expectations. Should these not be met on a regular basis, the legitimacy of the consensual power is thereby reduced and the system's flexibility undermined. In such a situation the system could go on operating, but compliance would be obtained mainly through an appeal to the coercion that serves as the "grounding" of the power system—but whose extensive use, in Parsons' analogy, would be similar to substituting the gold that is the grounding of a monetary system for the symbolic, paper money that has no intrinsic value.

In other words, a political system, in the absence of extensive legitimacy, is an extremely crude instrument for attaining group goals, settlements, and allocations because it does not have a "generalized capacity to secure performance." Indeed, if all legitimacy is removed, a political system is not analogous to a primitive monetary system based on an intrinsically valuable commodity (such as gold, which, though crude, has some general usefulness in exchange) but to a barter system with all the limitations such a system implies.

The answer to the question whether all political systems must be conceived as involving legitimacy is clearly a contingent one. If a system can achieve its group goals on a barter basis, exchanging (ultimately) force for compliance, there is no reason to assume that such a system must contain legitimacy in the form of political power—as that concept is defined here—although legitimacy may be present at some other focus. Among the Kuikuru (described by Dole in this volume) the only obvious locus for consensual power is the status of the shaman. However, in his role as agent of social control the shaman serves to bring coercion on deviants through a focusing of group opinion and a consequent mobilization of force against them. This is clearly not consensual power, as the concept is used here, but rather a "barter" in which conformity is exchanged for freedom from physical harm. This type of process fits within our view of political behavior because it involves decisions (in this case settlements) that affect the group as a whole; but there is no evidence to indicate that it entails the imposition of obligations through legitimacy.

It might be argued, however, that there is legitimacy in Kuikuru politics at the level of the political community. That is, although the processes by which settlements are achieved are not based on legitimacy, the political community *is* so based—in the sense that the members of the group believe that, by whatever means, their expectations concerning the settlement of disputes will at least sometimes be met within the confines of the group.

The general point of importance here is that the type of support at one level is not necessarily dependent upon the type found at another. The fact that a political community is supported through being legitimate does not mean that the means of gaining compliance within that community need be legitimate. An interesting consequence of taking the view that the types of support found at various levels are analytically independent is seen in the relationship between regime ("rules of the game") and power.

THE AUTHORITY CODE

We repeat that consensual power, and indeed *power* in all the senses in which it may be thought of, is the capacity to secure compliance with binding decisions. It will therefore be clear that if there is more than one locus of power in a system, the absence of a system of priorities among the obligations can lead to chaos. This will be the consequence of the simultaneous commitment of the group to different and possibly conflicting obligations (Parsons, 1963b, p. 246). It can further be envisioned that the same situation can result if there is only one power locus, if that locus is the source of more than a very few decisions and if there is no system whereby priorities are allocated. This system of priorities can be established, when it is required, by a hierarchy of power. Such a hierarchy may be thought of in terms of a differential assignment to particular statuses in the group of rights to use and acquire power. This system of assignment will be called "the authority code," and the rights assigned under it to statuses will be called "authority."

The authority code is one crucial part of what has been called the regime, and, in a regime based on legitimacy, this code will ordinarily be supported by a direct connection with the value system; for example, the divine right of kings, which establishes a connection between an authority code and a set of supernaturally supported values. In Middleton's article on conflict resolution among the Lugbara, for example, it is obvious that the supernatural basis of consensual power gives it legitimacy. More than this, the *assignment* of this power to individuals has its legitimacy unambiguously signaled in the sickness brought by ancestral ghosts to those who defy the power user. The elders who invoke the punitive dead are thus able to show they are in good standing with the ancestral source of legitimacy and can function as legitimate sources of consensual power. Interestingly, the possibility of claiming that sickness was the result of witchcraft rather than ghost invocation indicates one of the Lugbara devices for attacking or impugning an elder's claim to legitimacy.

In Section III, where these concepts are fed back into analyses of the phases of political developments, it is indicated how different types of support are manipulated by interested parties in sectional or factional struggles for positions of power and authority, and that an important part of this manipulation is the effort to establish the legitimacy of one's own ends and means and to throw doubt on those of one's opponents. However, the authority code need not be directly supported by common values, even when the obligations imposed by those holding power under the code are supported in this way. To put this rather differently, there is no analytic reason for viewing authority, or the procedure under which it is assigned to statuses, as necessarily legitimate even though the power that derives from this authority may be legitimate.

We argued earlier that it is fruitful to view legitimacy as an important basis for power in order to differentiate power so based from the less adaptable means for gaining compliance. This argument does not apply to the assignment of power to statuses. Analytically at least, there is no reason why the assignment of power to statuses on the basis of force should not work as well as assignment on the basis of values. The requirement for a hierarchy of obligation would be met in either way so long as the power was differentially assigned, and this is the crucial issue in authority codes. Empirically, it might work out that if the authority code is not based on legitimacy the authority it distributes to statuses might be less likely to operate through the exchange of compliance for the right to impose obligations at a later date ("consensual power"); but there is no analytic reason for assuming that this is the case. If, for example, a colonial government assigns rights to impose different obligations to various statuses, and these assignments are supported only by the superior force of the colonialists, there is no a priori reason to believe that the officials occupying the assigned statuses cannot gain compliance with the obligations allotted them through consensual power, as the term is used in this section, instead of through force alone.

The other side of this argument, of course, is that even though the authority code is supported through its connections with the value system, there is no reason to assume that its right to impose obligations need be exercised through anything other than the direct use of (or the threat or the possibility of the use of) force. Indeed, as we will see in Cohen's presentation of the Kuikuru case, this is precisely what often happens.

To summarize this part of the discussion, "power" can be usefully defined as involving legitimacy; it is one means of gaining compliance with obligations, and its most important difference from other means is that it allows for greater flexibility. "Power," used in this sense, is referred to as "consensual power." "Authority" is the right to use and acquire power vested in a status by a procedure based on the "authority code" (which is part of the regime). An authority code, and the authority resulting from its application, may or may not be based on legitimacy, but they will function to arrange the power that is present in a system in a hierarchy. Insofar as it is able to do this, a system will operate with minimal conflicts of obligations and interests. However, it must be understood that most systems contain unassigned power, both in its limited sense (defined here) and in its widest sense (defined as the ability to do what one wants to do, with or without the consent of the objects of power).

Our emphasis on the analytic independence of types of support at various foci should not be misinterpreted to mean that an empirical independence is being postulated. Important empirical regularities may well be discovered with reference to the types of relationships that exist among the various sources of support in given systems. For example, the discussion of power will have made it clear that if consensual power is to operate effectively, the objects of that power must have confidence that its users will meet their obligations. This psychological state might well be destroyed if the rights to use and acquire power were assigned on a basis that was not in accord with overall values and norms. In a highly complex political system, it seems particularly likely that this would be the case, but this matter can be established only by empirical investigation. Analytically, there is no reason for adopting a standpoint that asserts a necessary correspondence between these two levels of analysis—or, indeed, among any of the levels of analysis and the relationship of their sources of support.

INTRODUCTION AND MAINTENANCE OF DIFFERENT TYPES OF SUPPORT

So far, our discussion of support, legitimacy, power, and authority has focused mainly on obligations and the manner in which compliance is obtained. The discussion is now sufficiently advanced to take up two related questions: (1) How is support introduced and maintained within political systems? (2) How are we to classify and conceptualize different types of support?

"Demands," as the concept is used here, are desires of the members of a political community that political decisions of a particular sort be made, which ultimately concern the entire community. Demands may be made by individuals or by combinations of individuals, but in all cases the subject or subjects of the demands will be viewed by the demand makers as appropriate objects for political action. This last requirement of the definition arises from the fact that demands may be articulated statements or messages presented to the occupants of statuses having authority (Easton, 1965, p. 120), or they may be diffuse and loosely conceived states of mind that are only indirectly communicated. In the last case, it is necessary to differentiate demands from nonpolitical desires, although it should be noted that a desire is a demand even though other than political action is *also* thought appropriate. Thus the desire of a group of villagers to use village resources to build a bridge, when formulated in a meeting and presented to the appropriate official through an elected spokesman, is a demand—but so is the rather vaguely conceived and formulated desire that theft ought to be prevented, or punished. The latter may be regarded as a demand insofar as the holders of the desire believe that political action is an appropriate means of dealing with theft. It can operate as a demand through dissatisfaction with officials, statuses, and/or governments that fail to control theft, and, conceivably, it could become an important source of disaffection (withdrawal of support) without ever becoming clearly formulated.

Obviously, one means of bringing support into a political system is through the system's fulfilling the demands of its public. We have already seen that an official can achieve legitimacy through consistently meeting the demands of his "constituents," and can thus operate through the use of consensual power instead of less flexible means. However—disregarding for the moment the type of support gained in this way—it seems entirely likely that a system that consistently meets all the demands of those involved would be strongly supported; but it is also likely that no system can meet the demands of "all of the people, all of the time," since the things desired in all societies are necessarily scarce and desires may conflict. Political systems differ greatly both in type (including scope) and in the number of demands they contain at any particular moment, but they are similar in that—at least sometimes—some of the demands cannot be met.

If political systems are to survive, they must be able to weather the dissatisfaction that can arise from unmet demands. One way of doing this is to make extensive use of force, which, despite the limitations we have noted, can be a satisfactory means for dealing with noncompliance in some circumstances. Other techniques of survival include, of course, diplomacy, intrigue, the manipulation of interest groups, *divide et impera,* and other devices that will be discussed presently. Another means of insuring survival is to have at least some of the aspects of the political system firmly grounded in the value system; that is, to give them legitimate foundations. If officials, statuses, and so on are legitimate, they are in a position to implement their decisions through the use of consensual power, and thus, even if they do not satisfy a particular demand at a particular time, the presumption will be that eventually they will do so. How long this delay of satisfaction can go on before the legitimacy itself is undermined is an empirical question, to be answered by individual societies, but if legitimacy can be maintained despite a political system's failure to satisfy political demands, the absence of other types of support will present no serious problem. This is related to another means; namely, building a "reserve of support" (Easton, 1960, p. 122) through previously met demands. In more colloquial terms, the memory of many past satisfactions can cushion the shock of resentment caused by current unmet demands.

PERSUASION AND INFLUENCE

Still another means of gaining compliance with decisions, despite the absence of demand satisfaction, is persuasion. Persuasion can bring about compliance by bringing about changes in belief and attitude. An obvious example of how this can work is through bringing a dissatisfied group to believe either that their demands "actually" have been met or that they "really" don't want what they originally thought they did.

Persuasion can operate through inducements ("If you people will go along with this decision, I'll see that you all get 40 acres and a mule"), through threats, and through pointing out that noncompliance is a violation of commitments ("When we achieved independence we all agreed to work for the good of the country, but now you say you don't want to cooperate"). It can also operate on the basis that the individual or group is persuaded that behaving in a certain way is a "good thing" for him. If the process is based solely on an appeal that is independent of inducements, threats, and the "activation of commitments," it is called "influence" (Parsons 1963a, pp. 38, 48).

It is entirely possible for political decisions to be implemented by persuasion alone; thus officials can gain compliance with their decisions without the use of power either in its consensual or coercive forms. When this is done through the use of influence alone, none of the techniques for compliance so far discussed need be involved: By "leadership," Parsons (*ibid.*, p. 53) means gaining compliance through influence. In leadership, decisions are implemented, and support is won, through imparting the conviction that the decisions and support are in the best interests of those complying with the decisions and giving the support.

Without going into Parsons' elaborate discussion of the "influence" concept, we find it noteworthy that he views it as distinct from, but often involved with, power. This is particularly important for our theoretical purposes in that influence can be used to increase the amount of consensual power in a political system by increasing its scope. For example, some occupants of positions of authority try to convince their constituents that it would be a "good thing" for them to increase the demands they make upon the political system; then, through meeting these demands in a sufficiently reliable way, a new or further basis for legitimacy —and thus for consensual power—is established. The attempts of many new nation-states to eradicate tribalism and such tribal functions as the settlement of disputes can be looked upon as attempts to increase the consensual power of the national government and its officials through the process just indicated. One device that is utilized to this end is propaganda directed at convincing the citizens it would be better for them if the political functions they approve and desire were performed within the national rather than the tribal political community.

Of course, influence is not the only way in which the scope of a political system can be increased, since anything that brings new functions into a political system thereby increases its scope. However, increasing the scope of a system so as to add to its basis of consensual power is a more difficult task. To do this by means other than influence (for example, increasing the scope of the national government by eliminating tribal functions through coercion) is difficult, at least initially. This difficulty results because consensual power is based upon legitimacy, and, aside from the use of influence, it is not easy to increase the range of positive expectations (which form the base of legitimacy) without convincing the public that this increase is a "good thing" for them. As has been noted repeatedly, it is possible to operate on the basis of compliance-winning techniques that are divorced from legitimacy, but to do this is to decrease the flexibility and efficiency of a system. When increases in scope are won through influence, the decisions made in the new areas of operation will necessarily be supported by legitimacy, since by definition those affected by the decisions will have been brought to see that having decisions made in the remodeled system is a "good thing" for themselves.

The same basic argument obtains with respect to the use of influence to prevent dissatisfaction from arising from unmet demands. If, for example, those who are dissatisfied—feeling a decision was made that neglected their demands—can be brought to believe the decision was actually good for them, not only will general support be maintained in the system but also its legitimacy will not be called into question. These people could also be bribed or coerced into maintaining at least outward manifestations of support, but the effective use of influence would retain their positive evaluation of the system (or, at least, of some parts of the system.)

Before we begin a more systematic examination of the concept of support it will be well to take a moment to review the basic points that pertain to gaining compliance. Three different techniques have been presented, which can be differentiated according to the factors that constitute their bases. The first technique is *force and coercion*, and the basis of this technique is its *intrinsic effectiveness*. In other words, this system requires less in the way of complexity in shared values and expectations than the other two; it depends, instead, upon a limitation or reduction of alternatives, so that, in the last resort (force), the choice of those who are to comply is between suffering physical discomfort and acquiescence. The second technique for gaining compliance we have called *consensual power*, and its effectiveness depends upon legitimacy. Compliance is exchanged for the understanding that, at some future time, the compliers will be able to gain favorable decisions from the power holders. The third major technique is *persuasion*, and it rests upon convincing the compliers that the best course to follow is the course that has been proposed to them. One form of persuasion, *influence*, involves bringing those who comply to believe that the course proposed to them is genuinely for their benefit. Influence is closely related to legitimacy, but another form of persuasion is based upon threats and bribes, and, like the first technique, depends upon its intrinsic effectiveness more than upon shared values.

TYPES OF SUPPORT

"Support," it will be remembered, is defined here as anything that contributes to the formulation and/or implementation of political ends. This is a very broad concept, which might profitably be divided into two types. The simple division presented here is made with the understanding that a particular action or sequence of interactions may be classified under more than one heading. The main purpose of the classification is to indicate what is meant by "anything that contributes," and the suggested division will serve to organize discussion of the various means through which support can be brought into a political system. The processes discussed in each category are intended to be indicative rather than exhaustive.

Direct Support: This support is attached directly to some aspect of the political process, at any level; it is not mediated through an additional process or entity.

The most "primitive" type of support is that which is given to a decision for its own sake. Here the meeting of a demand leads to a positive evaluation of the decision that brought the fulfillment of the desire contained in the demand. This support does not *necessarily* lead to a more general type of support, and, when it does, the additional support belongs in the next category.

An official can acquire direct support in response to a decision or a series of decisions that he makes. This support may either be a very limited quid pro quo or a contribution to his positive evaluation, that is, legitimacy. Whether a particular decision leads to direct support for the maker of that decision, for the status he occupies, for the government or regime he represents, or even for the political community of which he is part, are empirical questions, to be established for each case. Support need not be attached directly to only one locus at a time, nor need it be attached directly to more than one.

Direct support need not arise only from a meeting of demands. It can result from identification, either in the psychological sense or in the sense of perceived identity of interests, and this process can be attached at one, or several, or all of the analytic levels. The same is true of legitimacy, which can be directly attached anywhere, but if it is to fit in this category it must result from the direct, positive evaluation of the locus in question. Viewing a status or government as legitimate because the occupants of the status or statuses meet one's expectations is direct support only for the officials who are positively evaluated, although this might lead to viewing other levels as legitimate.

Finally, coercion can be the source of direct support, bringing compliance with a decision through fear of the consequences of noncompliance or through eliminating the effective alternatives to compliance. Coercion, like the other bases for direct support, can be effective at all levels. It is perhaps most easily thought of as providing direct support for decisions, or officials, but there is no reason why this support cannot result from a realization of impotence in the face of the might of the authorities or from fear of the processes of the law (regime)—and thus attach directly to these loci.

Indirect Support: In this category, support is mediated through an intervening entity or process or through a number of such. This intervening component, in turn, is attached to the political system, at one or at several levels. The category of indirect support is very inclusive and, indeed, embraces much behavior that is sometimes denied entry to orthodox examinations of politics.

The most obvious kinds of indirect support are those that result from direct support. Support can be given to a decision, and this may lead to support being given to the official who made the decision, the status he occupies, and so on. As we have noted, these may all be direct supports, simultaneously given, but not necessarily. Individuals may be explicit in supporting, say, a headman *because* of the decisions he makes, but this is quite different from their direct support of both the decisions *and* the headman because, for example, both meet the individuals' values.

Indirect supports may result from involvement in nonpolitical processes and groups. For example, membership in a nonpolitical group may induce an individual to support a political official, decision, etc., in order to maintain his position in that group, and the same is true of subgroups (lineages, for example) in their relations with more inclusive groups (e.g., the tribe).

A related but perhaps less frequently considered source of indirect support is of a rather negative sort. Here involvement in a process originating in a nonpolitical group leads to demands on, and hence (under some circumstances) to support for the political system. For example, witchcraft accusations may arise within a nonpolitical group, a neighborhood, or a kin group, and this may result in the members' desire for a settlement. If a settlement is available only through political action, both the entire process behind the witchcraft accusations and the absence of a settlement procedure within the nonpolitical group provide indirect support for various levels of the political system. This support may be given only to the official who makes the settlement, but it may very well attach—simultaneously—to his status, the regime, and the political community.

Another important source of indirect support derives from the meanings and emotions that are associated with rites and symbols. The aroused feelings and beliefs can be associated with the various levels of the political system and can cause them to be positively evaluated. Clearly, the values and norms can themselves be viewed as sources of indirect support because it is through them that legitimacy is brought to politics. The same is true of the psychological processes by which evaluations are made, motivations focused, and desires formulated.

This, it might be objected, is casting too wide a net—including everything as a possible source of indirect support. While it can be argued that if everything is a possible source of support, there can be no analytic value in such a concept, it is difficult to see any harm in adopting such a permissive stance. Certainly, the disadvantages of a restricted outlook are obvious, and the wide scope of our position would commit the student of politics to an examination of virtually all aspects of behavior for their political implications, but there is nothing really new in this. Our hope is that we have provided those who wish to study politics with conceptual equipment of a type that may encourage them to undertake such a wide examination.

Salisbury's paper on politics and shell-money finance in New Britain is a particularly illuminating instance of the usefulness of having broadly applicable concepts of the types we have mentioned, for he is dealing with societies that have few relationships of superordination-subordination. He shows that persuasion plays a vital role in increasing shell money, and thus in gaining access to political control. He further indicates how persuasion appears as an indirect support of the polity inasmuch as it is a type of support for the process of acquiring the wealth that leads to political control. It might not be imprudent to argue that the economic system here appears as an indirect support for the political system, through the enrichment of the elite, even though the entire process is channeled through a democratic ideology.

Tuden shows, in the section of his article on the Swat Pathans, how the structural position of the saint can be a means of support, since he is able to influence disputes by virtue of the fact that he is not a member of any of the contending groups. Here, too, we see indirect economic support for political ends, in the khans' need for money to provide food and other goods for their followers.

Colson's description of the Tongan chief and headman provides an interesting example of a system that has more than one public that can provide support. The headman's status is closely enmeshed with the local community, and the occupant of this status depends upon the support of his local public. The chief, however, is not as deeply enmeshed in local affairs; he is, in fact, immune to strictly local pressures because his office is the creature of an extralocal administration, responsive only to the support and withdrawal of support of that (alien) administration. Not until the rise of national political parties did the chief become significantly concerned with achieving local support, for it was only through national parties that his public could affect him: these parties, dependent upon the favor of the local people, determined the appointment of chiefs.

The concepts we have discussed are intended to throw light on old issues and force their rethinking. One of the papers in this volume presents an example of how this might work, specifically, with the concept of support. In his paper on the economic activities of a Gilbertese chief, Berndt Lambert argues (against Sahlins, 1958), that the "tribute" of food made to chiefs in the smaller Oceanic societies may be thought of as "a confirmation of the chief's authority rather than a foundation of it." In other words, this redistributive process is a symbol of the legitimacy of the regime, and is at the same time a process of legitimizing the extant relationships between a particular chief and his kinsmen and their servants and followers. Not only chief-follower relationships but a variety of other relationships are legitimized in this way, such as those between aristocrats and commoners living in the same village as co-owners of an estate (who made a joint presentation), and the corporate links between members of a single village (who brought their taro together to the high chief). Lambert emphasizes the expressive and the instrumental aspects of a familiar economic process, and shows that this process is a type of "support" rather than an "economic basis."

IV

Much of the value of the concepts we have been discussing, consensual legitimacy, influence, types of support and the like, resides in their capacity to operate as conceptual tools for analyzing specific political behavior. To do this effectively, they have to relate to the conceptual frame already adumbrated, in which polities are regarded as spatial-temporal continua—not as harmoniously integrated and "timeless" systems. The course of political action, with its cumulative consequences, is by no means smooth from inception to terminus. Moreover, every terminus is a new beginning, though each beginning represents the result of an earlier phase of action or a set of linked and cumulating phases.

In the political process the concepts we have been examining—in their ideal purity and abstraction—become, as it were, fragmented and contaminated from their exposure to human interests, passions, and desires. Thus in the various studies of alien rule (Kupferer on the sub-Arctic Cree, Hughes on the St. Lawrence Island Eskimo, Gallin on Taiwanese villages, Colson on the Tonga of Zambia) we clearly see how conflicting expectations in sectors of changing societies, with varying degrees of pluralism, make "legitimacy" impossible for the total system. Conflicting criteria of legitimacy are manipulated by different groups to secure their goals.

The closer we come to the political grass roots the closer we have to consider such "motivations" as self-interest and ambition, and the more we are obliged to show, in terms of detailed and extended case histories, the working out of the courses of action that are set in train by these and like impulsions. But the course of personal or sectional ambition or aggrandizement, like that of true love, seldom runs smoothly. Among the barriers, obstacles, and hazards are the ideals, norms, values, and supernatural beliefs that are characteristic of the society, whose intersection with the political system at certain critical points provides the culturally constituted bases of legitimacy.

To make an adequate analysis of a political continuum over time we must begin by selecting a point in time; but where we begin is a matter of particular strategy or convenience, not of theoretical necessity. We may attempt to characterize the properties of our chosen field when its component entities are at peace with one another, or when intrigue is rife among them, or at any phase of open struggle. All these modes of political behavior are "normal," but it is perhaps tidier, and more convenient, to begin our study when the field components are at peace, or—in the popular mechanical analogy—in a state of rest or equilibrium. We must realize, when we do this, that the equilibrium we describe represents a temporary truce rather than a uniquely "natural" or a "healthy" political state. Thus into our preliminary characterization of the field we must be careful to build an abridged report of the history of the relationships between its parts that adequately accounts for the current absence of overt conflict between them. All politics, as most recent writers on the subject would agree, will at some time in their course involve processes of conflict over the distribution, allocation, and use of public power.

The territorial range and social scope of a political field are conditioned by the nature and intensity of the interests of the affected parties. This means that a field's social circumference is extremely fluid, expanding and contracting over time in response to changes of interests, or to policies in regard to interests. We stress the relative quality of the concept "field" to offset the absolute or rigid quality imputed to concepts that have often dominated political thinking hitherto: "political system," "political structure," and "the governmental process."

In the diachronics of political field analysis, it is possible to arrest the flow of events at any given point in time and abstract a "still." We are then confronted by a set of co-existing parts that can be conceptualized as structured, or as having positions relative to each other, and therefore as occupying a type of space—analogous to Kurt Lewin's notion of the *life-space* of an individual. Although such a "still" deprives us of the time dimension, it allows us to enumerate, with some accuracy, the political entities engaged and the type, kind, and intensity of their interrelations, and to attempt to estimate the sources of support held by them severally or in varying combinations.

But this creates an erroneous impression of stability and balance. In fact, the passage of time always reveals instability and imbalance in power relations, although the extent of instability and the speed with which it will be revealed is highly variable among political fields. Some of the sources of instability may be ecological and demographic variations that affect the size and wealth of political units, psychological factors, such as differences in the need-dispositions regnant in various groups within the population at various times, and the effects of pressures and influences that originate outside the political field. To the degree that there is consensus about beliefs, values, and norms throughout the field, and to the degree that the field contains efficient institutions for resolving conflict, instability can be confined within roughly predictable limits. There may be recurrent or oscillant change within the limits of the system—as Leach so memorably demonstrated for the Kachin in *Political Systems of Highland Burma* (1954)—but in certain fields, including some of those now being considered by political anthropologists, normative consensus hardly exists (hence neither does a common standard of legitimacy). Peace-keeping machinery therefore tends to be based on coercion and other intrinsically effective techniques rather than on consensual power.

The distinction made by M. G. Smith between "administration" and "politics" (1960, p. 15), which he regards as two aspects of the wider category of "government," is not readily applicable to political fields of an intersocietal type. For Smith, administrative action consists "in the authorized processes of organization and management of the affairs of a given unit," and political action seeks to influence the decision of policy. "Policy decisions define a program of action, implicitly or otherwise. The execution and organization of this program is an administrative process" (Smith, 1956, p. 42). Smith's view of "power" is close to our view of "influence" and "persuasion." He conceives politics as a struggle for power, as he uses the term, within a governmental framework.

Behind this view lie the tacit assumptions of the equilibrium theory, the view that a political system is in a steady state through the balance of complementary forces. We think the distinction between "influence" and "power" is worth making (whether this be regarded as consensual

power or as power based more directly on force) because power operates very differently from influence, both in how it is used (the means
of its application) and in the consequences of its use. For example, it
may be useful to distinguish interest groups that have influence but that
have to operate through others that have power from power groups
that need no intermediaries.

David Easton is closer to the empirical realities of politics when he
defines political life as "a set of social interactions on the part of individuals and groups" (1955, p. 49), but he seems to fall back into the
structuralist trap when he goes on to distinguish political interactions
from all other kinds of social interactions "in that they are predominantly
oriented toward the *authoritative* [our emphasis] allocation of values for
a society" (Easton, 1965, p. 50). Many political fields extend far beyond
the frontiers of "a society"; [5] and intersocietal struggles for power are
waged between political groups that recognize no common "authority"
and have little or no normative consensus. Furthermore, to equate "the
political" with societal politics is to deprive us of a crucial means of
understanding even the morphological distinctiveness of societal polities.
It is often through their co-membership in an intersocietal political field
that the societal components of that field, in ever shifting relationships
of conflict and alliance, assume their specific political form.[6]

In a well-known instance, that of the political field constituted by
the relationships between European and African societies involved in
various ways in the West-Central African slave trade from the sixteenth
to the nineteenth centuries, we think it can be shown, though with no
depth of historical evidence, that the "centralization" of some societies
was dynamically related to the "decentralization" of others (see, for
example, Gann, 1964, pp. 22-24). One dominant interest—material profit
—united a chain of societies of varying political types, but the differences between them were closely correlated with their economic and
military roles in the trade cycle. The Portuguese on the coast were
entrepreneurs, the Ovimbundu and Bangala were middlemen, the
Chokwe and Luvale were middlemen and marauders, the Lunda and
Luba, in the interior, were rulers and citizens of "gunpowder states," and
the scattered populations around them formed loose and uncentralized
polities, constantly raided by their centralized neighbors who made
treaties with the middlemen. Such treaties or "contracts" guaranteed that

[5] Many do not, and the societal units, which are "parts" of such fields, enjoy
varying degrees of independence within the field interdependence.

[6] We are aware, of course, that the field of "intersocietal" or "intertribal" or
"international" politics is only one of a number of ways in which single polities take
shape. Thus the resources of a whole society may be directed toward fulfillment of
an economic program and a religious command—and these will powerfully affect
the structures of administration and "policy-action" (as Southall refers to M. G.
Smith's "political action" [1965, p. 119]).

rulers of gunpowder states would supply the middlemen with slaves, ivory, beeswax, and rubber in exchange for guns, powder, cloths, beads, and other trade goods. Equipped with firearms, those chiefs who were fortunate enough to have priority in negotiating contracts with middlemen (supplied in the first instance with guns and goods by coastal entrepreneurs) rapidly conquered their neighbors, extended their domains, developed hierarchically organized political systems of some complexity (based on tribute and pillage), and reduced their neighbors—including those who had a measure of centralization—almost to the status of wandering bands or assemblages of villages whose members were instantly ready to take to the bush to avoid capture.

Other long-range trading systems embraced similar political fields in West, East, and East-Central Africa. The "structure" of the political system in each component society of the trade circle can be adequately studied only after the society's position in the total political field related to the trade circle has been analyzed. The political structure of a society acquires a special character if its role in the trade is that of raider rather than raided, or mobile trader rather than fixed provider of depots. Other kinds of political centralization appear to have developed in connection with the need to provide security to traders. As Vansina, Mauny, and Thomas recently argued, in *The Historian in Tropical Africa* (1964, p. 85):

While political centralization may not have been indispensable for trade to develop and flourish, the development of trade itself in some areas favored the creation of centralized political systems. And these in turn contributed in a large measure to the further development of trade by providing organization and security for markets and caravans.

Such considerations lead us to suggest that, despite its heuristic value during the period when anthropologists did fieldwork in societies under colonial and "indirect" rule, Radcliffe-Brown's synchronic frame of theory is no longer adequate. The appropriate field of anthropological study today is, in M. G. Smith's words, "a unit over time, not merely a unit at a particular point in time" (1962, p. 81). What we have called a political field is not necessarily a closely integrated system, but a spatial-temporal continuum with some systematic features. The parts of such a unit, under specified conditions, may exhibit varying degrees and kinds of interdependence, both institutionalized and contingent. Under different conditions, however, the same parts may operate, as it were, "out of mesh" with, and independently of, other parts of the continuum. When the parts of a single society are working with and against one another in regard to some policy issue, we may speak of "political behavior."

Behavior *within* the independent parts that relates to such processes as decision-making or conflict resolution, and that involves the use of or struggle for power (in its broadest sense), may be defined (in Easton's useful phrase) as "parapolitical behavior" (1965, pp. 49-56)—although there is a danger of introducing an overly static emphasis into our analysis if we do not do this with caution. Some types of intrasocietal behavior, which are oriented to conflicts of interests or competitions for power, can properly be described as "political" if they relate to the boundary-maintaining mechanisms of *whole* societies (for example, if the tribal council should be dissolved and all affairs handled by the national government), if they agitate issues that bear on the welfare (or even the survival) of *whole* societies, and if they provide sets of goals that involve all the parts of a society in coordinated action. Thus, viewed dynamically, and in terms of the spatial-temporal continuum model, "parapolitical behavior" may change into "political behavior," and vice versa—depending upon circumstances, upon the nature of the issues and goals situationally paramount, or upon the structural perspective employed.

Ideally, or properly speaking, we should not be studying a "field" (in Lewin's interpretation) because Lewin's field theory deals only with the *contemporaneous* situation as causative of behavior. For him, past events have only indirect influence as the origins of the present field, but, because they have ceased to exist, he holds that they cannot be considered active in the situation under study. This view closely resembles Radcliffe-Brown's notion of the synchronic analysis of a social system, conceptualized as "the network of actually existing social relationships."[7]

Our diachronic method of analysis, however, examines changes in the relationship between significant parts of the preliminary situation (which may be described as a field) over time, in a succession of phases. It is our view that these phases tend to follow one another in a processual pattern. Different kinds of political fields generate different kinds of patterns; nevertheless, one kind of pattern is of wide generality. Both at the level of intersocietal power struggles (for territory, monopoly of trade, or spheres of influence) and at the level of intrasocietal factional struggles, a patterned sequence of phases tends to occur, though it must be stressed that the course of action may be arrested during any of the phases. We indicate the full pattern below, though in specific instances it may never be completed.

[7] The synchronic view simply does not present an adequate conception of what is "past." If we say that we are interested in explaining state x, and if we grant that x is the result of a series of phases $a, b, c \ldots n$, it is difficult to argue against the view that insists that all we need is complete understanding of n to explain x, since a, b, c, etc., will have made their contributions to n, and need be examined only *there*. But if we conceptualize the causality not as merely linear but as cumulative (with the "accumulation" occurring in the personalities, structures, and meaning systems), x may be regarded as the result of $a', b', c' \ldots n'$, acting jointly to produce x. To explain a' (the "accumulation"), we must examine a, which is the past event itself, but even if we do not concern ourselves with the genesis of a' we will be led to examine the production of past x's to discern a pattern of x production, i.e., into "cross-temporal" studies.

(1) Mobilization of Political Capital

In this preliminary phase the groups and persons ("parts of the field") laying claim to leading roles in the anticipated struggle will attempt, during a period of external peace or truce, to maximize support of all types, or, in different terms, to mobilize their political capital. In pursuit of this goal they utilize such "internal" techniques as influence, intrigue, diplomacy, bluff, bribery, activation of commitments, threats of resort to force, and promises of rewards for support, and such "external" techniques as lobbying, present patronage, conspiracy, subversion, the acquisition of wealth, peaceful infiltration of the antagonists' ranks, espionage, and innumerable other devices, maneuvers, and intrigues (*a*) to build up their ranks and resources and (*b*) to deplete those of their anticipated adversaries. It seems to be characteristic of this phase that influence and the various other forms of persuasion are important within factions, and attempts to undermine the opposition's support through all available means are important externally. Middleton's paper on the Lugbara, Turner's on the Ndembu, and Miller's on the Chippewa provide adequate documentation of these techniques.

(2) The Encounter or "Showdown"

(*A*) *Breach of the Peace.* When one of the major parties to the conflict thinks it has acquired (whether realistically or delusorily) a decisive advantage in support, it decides to precipitate a crisis. Characteristically, it either provokes its antagonist to an intemperate action, or it takes the initiative in breaking the public peace. But perhaps this is stating the matter too strongly, for it is often sufficient if one party puts its rival in an embarrassing position, or puts itself in a favorable light at its rival's expense. In many cases the competitive accumulation of support is enough to produce multiple tensions in the relationships between parts of the field, of a sort and intensity that result in a spontaneous eruption of overt hostility between the rival parties.

Under favorable conditions the investigator will be able to make a crude assessment of the strength of support of the respective parties. This assessment would involve the investigation of the locus and extent of support, the mechanisms for obtaining control of resources, and such questions as "Who uses what mechanisms to get what support from where?" Robert Bierstedt's formulation (1950) that power "would seem to stem from three sources: (1) numbers of people, (2) social organization, and (3) resources" may be of help here, and his views should be related to the discussion of "support" in Section III.

Majorities, for Bierstedt, constitute "a residual locus of social power," and organization and discipline constitute another (so that an organized minority may control an unorganized majority); and access to the greater resources will confer superior power on a group otherwise equal in numbers and comparable in organization with its rivals. "Resources" are of many kinds, including part of the broader categories we would call direct and indirect support—"money, property, prestige, knowledge, competence, deceit, fraud, secrecy, and, of course, all of the things usually included under the term 'natural resources' . . . there are also supernatural resources in the case of religious associations, which, as agencies of a celestial government, apply supernatural sanctions as instruments of control" (Bierstedt, 1950).

The articles by Middleton, Turner, Friedrich, and Park illustrate how supernatural sanctions may be manipulated as power resources, and Swartz's article shows how one type of activity undertaken by an official can become a source of power to be used in other types of official activity. Bierstedt points out that although the factors just mentioned are not themselves "power," they may be considered "sources of power" in situations of conflict. We would prefer to call them "types of support," but, at any rate, their relative distributions can be plotted in relation to the alignment of factions at the outset of a struggle. It would also be useful to distinguish between "the inside view" of the contending parties—how they might estimate their chances of success—and the "outside view" of the investigator—whose aim is to make a construct of the total constellation of elements and their interrelations in the "field."

(*B*) *Crisis.* Breach of the peace is usually heralded or signaled by breaching a norm that is considered binding on *all* members of the political field. It may not be a political or legal norm; indeed, it is often an ethical norm that assumes political value as it is reinterpreted by the contending parties, especially with regard to "legitimacy." Examples of breaches of an ethical norm are failure to observe a critical caste or kinship rule, deliberate flouting of a religious interdiction, unauthorized trespass on another's territory, and the breaking of a marital norm (such as Henry VIII's divorce of Catherine of Aragon). The murder of Archduke Ferdinand at Sarajevo in 1914 by a Serbian fanatic was a breach of norm that precipitated the First World War—essentially a struggle between two blocs of major powers. Whatever the nature of the breach, it may serve as a pretext—at a given level of tension in a political field—to initiate an encounter between rival power-seekers.

Breach of such a norm leads more or less rapidly to "crisis"—which may be defined as a momentous juncture or turning point in the relations between components of a political field—at which apparent peace becomes overt conflict and covert antagonisms become visible. External crises may be used (through the internal employment of mechanisms of the types referred to above) to solidify support. Power crises sooner or later take a dichotomous form, and the field as a whole becames what Bailey (followed in this book by Nicholas and Hughes) has called an "arena," in which the contenders are ultimately arrayed in two camps or two factions.

Many subgroup rivalries may have existed prior to the crisis; afterwards, these rivalries are suspended until the resolution or denouement of the crisis, or they are "fed into" the alliances that are centered on the two major factions. In our terminology of Section III, it is frequently the function of persuasion and influence to involve these minor matters in the major matter.

(C) *Countervailing Tendencies.* Gluckman has argued, with much supportive documentation, that radical cleavage—especially within a society or community—is restrained and perhaps stopped before it really begins by the fact that "customary forms first divide and then reunite men."

Men quarrel in terms of certain of their customary allegiances, but are restrained from violence through other conflicting allegiances which are also enjoined on them by custom. The result is that conflicts in one set of relationships, over a wider range of society or through a longer period of time, lead to the reestablishment of social cohesion. Conflicts are a part of social life and custom appears to exacerbate these conflicts; but in doing so custom also restrains the conflicts from destroying the wider social order. (1956, pp. 1-4)

Gluckman's argument is particularly applicable to small-scale, weakly centralized or uncentralized societies in which subgroups are multifunctional and most relationships are multiplex; that is, in a "legitimate political community," especially where there is a "legitimate regime." In societies that are marked by a relatively high degree of division of labor and socioeconomic stratification, and by the development of many single-interest associational groups and complex hierarchical administrative bureaucracies, criss-crossing conflicts are less likely to prove eufunctional in terms of pansocietal cohesion. As Coser has noted:

Not *every* type of conflict is likely to benefit group structure, nor can conflict subserve such functions [of establishing unity or reestablishing unity and cohesion where it has been threatened by hostile and antagonistic feelings among the members] for *all* groups: whether social conflict is beneficial to internal adaptation or not depends on the type of issues over which it is fought as well as on the type of social structure within which it occurs. . . . Internal social conflicts which concern goals, values or interests that do not contradict the basic assumptions upon which the relationship is founded tend to be positively functional for the social structure. . . . Internal conflicts in which the contending parties no longer share the basic values upon which the legitimacy of the social system rests threaten to disrupt the structure. (1956, p. 151)

Consensus in small-scale societies, with what Durkheim calls "mechanical solidarity," tends to be religiously based and periodically reinforced by rites. Our examples of this are the articles on the Lugbara, Kinga, Ndembu, Tonga, Ila, Mexican peasants, and Kanuri. This is less likely to be the case in large-scale societies, with contracted religious domains, and it is even less likely in the political fields formed by inter-societal relations—especially where religious divisions exist. Relations are characterized by a major focus on the mobilization of internal support rather than by concern with such bases of common support as joint interests and shared values.

Nevertheless, multiple cross-cutting conflicts of loyalty and allegiance (if there is agreement on basic values) tend to inhibit the development of dichotomous cleavage. The role of many religious systems in relation to political struggles is to legitimate and posit the final mystical unity of *all* customs, however discrepant they may be, that control social relationships. Thus customs that thrust men into conflicting allegiances rest on common religious axioms and on the societal consensus these generate.[8] Where several societies, brought into political relationships in a single field by a crucial issue, share a single set of religious beliefs, the resultant situation is likely to be analogous to that within a single uncentralized society, and to share its crucial property of possessing conflicting customary allegiances. Religious authorities can here be appealed to as arbiters, as in medieval Europe, when pope and church played this role. But this leads us to the next phase in the progress of a power struggle.

(D) *Deployment of Adjustive or Redressive Mechanisms*. This process consists of the deployment of various redressive and adjustive mechanisms to seal off or heal the breach, and these mechanisms may range from "personal and informal arbitration to formal and legal machinery, and, to resolve certain kinds of crisis, to the performance of public ritual" (Turner, 1957, p. 98). Here, too, influence and other techniques for building a "legitimate case" are important. Turner has tried to classify some types of situations in which these and other procedures are brought into operation. He suggests that jural machinery (involving a judicial process) is employed when parties appeal to common norms, or, if norms are in conflict, when they can appeal to "a common frame of values which organize a society's norms in a hierarchy" (*ibid.*, p. 126). On the other hand, when a group feels itself to be in conflict with social norms, because of the working out of social processes that conflict with one another, this produces disputes where "judicial decision can condemn one or more of the disputants, but . . . cannot relieve the quarrels so as to preserve the threatened relationships" (*ibid*). These are, in fact, the conditions that in many parts of the primitive world provoke accusations of sorcery and witchcraft against one of the parties, or divinations of ancestral wrath, of breach of taboo, or of curses. These charges also

----

[8] See Gluckman (1954b), Kuper (1947), and Fortes and Evans-Pritchard (1940). In the last work, this comment by the editors is particularly noteworthy: "Myths, dogmas, ritual beliefs and activities . . . endow the social system with mystical values which evoke acceptance of the social order that goes far beyond the obedience exacted by the secular sanction of force" (p. 19).

follow the occurrence of natural misfortunes, especially in times of social crisis.

Gluckman has recently taken up this argument about the nature of the distinction between judicial and ritual-divinatory types of adjustive and redressive procedure. "It would also be better to keep these types distinct, even where we are dealing with tribes which do not have anything like an established judicial process" (1961, p. 13). A case in point is Middleton's article, which shows how leading Lugbara struggle to have it alleged that they are responsible when ancestral wrath harms a kinsman, because this validates their authority.

Redressive mechanisms may be further differentiated according to whether the crises they seek to resolve occur in intra- or intersocietal fields of political relationships. Where crises cannot be resolved in constituted courts of law, and where recourse cannot be made to ritual means of redress—as is frequently the case when conflict occurs between sovereign polities or highly autonomous subgroups within a polity—recourse may be made to the intervention of a third party, or group of parties, with the object of proposing a compromise. This often happens when there is approximate parity of political capital and resources between the contending parties.

If the decision of the third party *must* be accepted, we may speak of "arbitration," with the implication that the decision of the arbitrator is underwritten either by strong legal or strong religious sanctions. If negotiations are conditioned on voluntary acceptance by both contestants of the settlement proposed by the third party, we may speak of "mediation." Mediation involves the sustained intervention of the mediator, who must be concerned with more than the legal issues at stake and must utilize a variety of pragmatic techniques—ranging from friendly advice and pressure to formulations of new terms—to bring about a reconciliation of the interests of the opposed parties. (An example of this is seen in Swartz's description of the Bena *baraza*.) In intersocietal disputes, a mediator is often a person of high status or repute who frequently occupies a position in the political field of the contenders but has no direct interest in the issues that embroil them.

In other situations we may speak of "intermediaries" rather than mediators—when neither party will accept the third party's claim to be impartial. In such an instance the possibility of an outbreak of overt hostility is so strong that negotiation has to proceed between intermediaries who represent each party, since a face-to-face confrontation of the faction leaders is not possible or practical.

In this fourth phase of power struggles in political continua, various mechanisms of redress—jural, ritual, arbitrational, etc.—may be tried in order to produce a settlement or to restore the semblance of a peaceful state of relationships so that individuals and groups may once again pursue their ordinary lives and nonpolitical goals. In radically changing societies, however—as Siegel and Beals have shown (1960)—traditional redressive machinery may become inadequate for coping with new types of conflict in altered patterns of relationships; and society may remain in a state of "pervasive factionalism" that cannot be resolved. In less drastic situations of change, notably in societies under colonial control or with newly independent governments, traditional tribal mechanisms, unable to fulfill their conflict-resolving functions, may be gradually (sometimes rapidly) replaced by the formal administrative procedures of conflict resolution imposed or instituted by the central government.

(*E*) *Restoration of Peace.* When redressive mechanisms operate effectually, they lead either to a reestablishment of relations between the contending parties or to a social recognition of irreparable schism. But if the continuum is now analyzed synchronically, as a political field, and is compared with the political field that preceded the power struggle, many changes will usually be visible. As likely as not, the scope and range of the field will have altered; the number of its parts will be different; and their size will be different.

More importantly, the nature and intensity of the relations between parts, and the structure of the total field, will have changed. Oppositions will have become alliances, and vice versa. Asymmetric relations will have become symmetric relations. High status will have become low status and vice versa. New power will have been channeled into new authority and old authority defenestrated. Closeness will have become distance, and vice versa. Formerly integral parts will have segmented; formerly independent parts will have fused. Some parts will no longer belong to the field, and others will have entered it. Institutionalized relationships will have become informal; social regularities will have become irregularities. New norms will have been generated during the attempts to redress conflict; old norms will have fallen into disrepute.

The bases of support will be found to have altered. Some field components will have less support, others more, still others will have fresh support, and some will have none. The distribution of the factors of legitimacy will have changed, as have the techniques for gaining compliance.

Yet, through all these changes, certain crucial norms and relationships —and others less crucial—will persist. The explanation of both constancy and change can be found only by systematic diachronic analysis, by investigating the spatial-temporal continuum in terms not only of its synchronic divisions but also of its diachronic phases. Each phase has its specific properties, and each phase leaves its stamp on the structure of social relations in the political process.

The processual unit, and its phase structure, which we have just discussed, has affinities with Bales's "phase movement" (Bales and

Strodbeck, 1951), but it differs from the latter in that it is heavily
invested with institutionalized roles, relationships, and mechanisms; and
it is an inference from anthropological and sociological observational
data rather than from a series of controlled experiments. In specific
societies, moreover, such processual units may never reach the climax
posited here. Thus successful persuasion in phase A may result in one
party's securing the allegiance of the entire "public"—in which case
there will be no "encounter." And, very frequently, traditional redressive
and conciliatory machinery (phase D) prove inadequate in coping with
new kinds of issues and problems, and with new roles and statuses. Conflict becomes endemic (with, as one outcome, the "pervasive factionalism" discussed by Beals and Siegel), or recourse is made to new types
of machinery.

As a third alternative, in formerly tribal or village polities, the participants may (for the first time) invoke the legal institutions of the wider
political system: its courts, police, penal sanctions, judicial processes, etc.,
or, under certain circumstances, its ritual institutions. The paper by
Hughes, who shows how "contest" is replaced by "council" in the modern setting, and the paper by Gallin, who shows how Taiwanese villagers
have lost faith in traditional modes of mediation in disputes and are turning to the central government to seek redress, are examples of this third
alternative.

We propose to call the unit of political action a "political phase
development"—to bring out its cumulative character—or, in short, "phase
development." The unit's structure is such that it is equally applicable to
factional struggles in Indian and African villages and to major international "trouble cases," such as the Suez and the Cuban crises. Its temporal segmentation is highly flexible because each phase may vary considerably in duration vis-à-vis the others—though there is a tendency for
most political communities to act swiftly to seal off crises by the application of redressive machinery.

We are aware, of course, that the phase development is essentially
oriented to conflict, and that other types of political processes may lean
to cooperation, but we believe that only rarely does policy action escape
conflict. Conflict is covert if not open, and, in the pluralistic and changing societies now studied by anthropologists, even administrative action
tends to result in conflict.

Finally, phase developments are of variable duration and social span.
Moreover, some types lead to the restoration of the status quo. Although
this is true mostly for the smaller units in a political field, it must be
added that the relational structure observable at the climax of a small-
scale phase development is seldom the replica of the structure when the
breach occurred. Rather, the total development may be regarded as a
phase in a longer and broader development—that of the total political

community whose structure is cumulatively changed by the small climactic increments it receives from each small-scale development. Other types of phase development are signs and instruments of changes in basic social relations. By the use of this device or formula we believe that greater depth and clarity can be achieved in the study of changing systems, for each phase in a development has its own characteristics and each sociocultural system leaves its imprint on those characteristics. Thus each society has its cultural solutions to political crises—and indeed its own definition of what constitutes "crisis." Each society also has its own style of conflict resolution.

Processual studies of politics are still at an early stage—at the point of breach from earlier analytical norms! One aim of this book is to take tentative steps toward resolving the developing crisis by investigating the structure of political action revealed in empirical data. Within the general framework of political dynamics that we have used, subordinate processes—such as decision-making, the judicial process, the agitation and settlement of policy issues, the application of sanctions, the resolution of disputes, etc.—find their appropriate places as components of phases in the major sequence.

REFERENCES

BALES, R. F., and STRODBECK, F. 1951. Phases in group problem-solving. Journal of Abnormal and Social Psychology, XLVI, 485-495.

BIERSTEDT, ROBERT. 1950. An analysis of social power. American Sociological Review, XV, 6, 730-738.

COSER, LEWIS. 1956. The functions of social conflict. New York: Free Press of Glencoe.

DAHL, ROBERT A. 1957. The concept of power. Behavioral Science, 2, 201-215.

EASTON, DAVID. 1953. The political system: an inquiry into the state of political science. New York: Alfred A. Knopf.

———. 1957. An approach to the analysis of political systems. World Politics, 9, 383-400.

———. 1959. Political anthropology. In B. Siegel (ed.), Biennial Review of Anthropology. Stanford University Press.

———. 1965. A framework for political analysis. Englewod Cliffs, N.J.: Prentice-Hall.

EMMET, D. M. 1958. Function, purpose and powers. London: Macmillan.

EPSTEIN, A. L. 1958. Politics in an urban African community. Manchester University Press.

EVANS-PRITCHARD, E. E. 1963. Essays in social anthropology. London: Faber & Faber.

FIRTH, RAYMOND. 1957. Introduction to factions in Indian and overseas Indian societies. British Journal of Sociology, 8, 291, 295.

———. 1959. Social change in Tikopia. London: Allen & Unwin.

FORTES, M., and EVANS-PRITCHARD, E. E. (eds.). 1940. African political systems. Oxford University Press for the International African Institute.

FURNIVALL, J. S. 1948. Colonial policy and practice. Cambridge University Press.

GANN, LEWIS H. 1964. A history of Northern Rhodesia. London: Chatto & Windus.

GINSBERG, MORRIS. 1956. Factors in social change. In Transactions of the Third World Congress of Sociology, I, 10-19. London: International Sociological Association.

GLUCKMAN, MAX. 1954a. Political institutions. In Institutions of primitive society. Oxford: Basil Blackwell, pp. 66-81.

――――. 1954b. Rituals of rebellion in South East Africa. Manchester University Press.

――――. 1961. African jurisprudence, Presidential address to the Sociology Section of the British Association for the Advancement of Science. Advancement of Science, No. 74 (Nov., 1961).

――――. 1965. Politics, law and ritual in tribal society. Chicago: Aldine.

GOLDHAMER, H., and SHILS, E. 1939. Types of power and status. American Journal of Sociology, 45, 171-182.

GOODY, J. (ed.). 1958. The developmental cycle in domestic groups. Cambridge University Press.

KUPER, HILDA. 1947. An African aristocracy: rank among the Swazi. Oxford University Press for the International African Institute.

KUPER, LEO; WATTS HILSTAN; and RONALD DAVIES. 1958. Durban, a study in racial ecology. London: Jonathan Cape.

LEACH, EDMUND. 1954. Political systems of highland Burma. London: Bell.

LEWIN, K. 1951. Field theory in social science. New York: Harper & Row.

LLEWELLYN, K. N., and HOEBEL, E. A. 1941. The Cheyenne way. University of Oklahoma Press.

MITCHELL, J. C. 1954. African urbanization in Ndola and Luanshya. Rhodes-Livingstone communication, No. 6.

MITCHELL, J. C., and EPSTEIN, A. L. 1959. Occupational prestige and social status among Africans in Northern Rhodesia. Africa, 29, 22-39.

PARSONS, TALCOTT. 1937. Structure of social action. New York: McGraw-Hill.

――――. 1960. Structure and process in modern societies. New York: Free Press of Glencoe.

――――. 1963a. On the concept of influence. Public Opinion Quarterly, 27, 37-62.

――――. 1963b. On the concept of power. Proceedings of the American Philosophical Society, 107, 232-262.

RADCLIFFE-BROWN, A. R. 1952. Structure and function in primitive society. London: Cohen & West.

SAHLINS, MARSHALL. 1958. Social Stratification in Polynesia. Seattle: University of Washington Press.

SIEGEL, B., and BEALS, A. 1960. Conflict and factionalist dispute. Journal of the Royal Anthropological Institute, 90, 107-117.

SMITH, M. G. 1956. On segmentary lineage systems. Journal of the Royal Anthropological Institute, 86, pt. 2, 39-80.

――――. 1960a. Social and cultural pluralism. Annals of the New York Academy of Sciences, 83, 763-777.

――――. 1960b. Government in Zazzau. Oxford University Press for the International African Institute.

————. 1962. History and social anthropology. Journal of the Royal Anthropological Institute, 92, pt. 1, 73-85.

SOUTHALL, AIDAN. 1965. A critique of the typology of states and political systems. *In* Political systems and the distribution of power. London: Tavistock.

TURNER, V. W. 1957. Schism and continuity in an African society. Manchester University Press.

VANSINA, J.; MAUNY, R.; and THOMAS, L. V. (eds.). 1963. The historian in tropical Africa: studies presented and discussed at the Fourth International African Seminar, at the University of Dakar, Senegal, 1961. Oxford University Press for the International African Institute.

WILSON, G. and M. 1945. Analysis of social change. Cambridge University Press.

Part I

DIMENSIONS OF
CONFLICT IN POLITICAL ACTION

The articles in this section, for all their apparent diversity, all make direct or indirect reference to the concept of "conflict," a term that requires some preliminary scrutiny. We would be in general agreement with those authorities who would restrict its use to "oppositions compelled by the very structure of social organization" (Gluckman, *Politics, Law and Ritual in Tribal Society* [Chicago: Aldine, 1965, p. 109]). Gluckman has in fact proposed a clarifying refinement of the technical vocabulary for referring to different levels of phenomena and processes involving the collision or clashing of social variables, which includes the definition just given.

In addition, he suggests that

for surface disturbances of social life, depending on their nature, we can use competition, dispute, argument, strife, dissension, contention, fight, etc. "Struggle [should be] reserved for events with deeper and more fundamental roots, and "conflict" for discrepancies at the heart of the system . . . that set in train processes which produce alterations in the personnel of social positions, but not alterations in the pattern of positions. "Contradiction" [should be used] for those relations between discrepant principles and processes in the social structure which must inevitably lead to radical change in the pattern. (*ibid.*)

He defines the corresponding associative or conjunctive process as follows:

"Cooperation," "affiliation," "association," "ties," "bonds" refer to surface links between persons or combined activities; "solidarity" [refers] to a more deeply rooted interlinking; and "cohesion" to the underlying principles of structure that give unity to the system of a social field." (*ibid.*)

Three of the papers refer directly to the process of contradiction as it is manifested in political fields formed by the incorporation of formerly autonomous tribal or peasant communities in large-scale modern political systems. Nicholas, for example, shows how segmentary factional political systems are often found precisely where rapid social change is in train, "where the rules of political conflict [or as Gluckman might say, of "struggle"] are fluid and ambiguous." He indicates, too, how the kinds of bonds and solidarities that link faction leaders to their followers in

Indian village factional disputes rest on both traditional and modern criteria: kinship, caste, education, cash employment, landholding, political party membership, etc. Modes of interdependence that in the past formed systematic patterns have now become isolates—kinship, caste, and affinity need no longer necessarily constitute a cluster of political "supports"—and have been augmented by new modes, such as occupational ties, party affiliations, and the like.

The successful faction leader is the one who can best manipulate and exploit these modes to build up a following. Herein lies contradiction, for all loyalties are thus placed on an equal footing and traditional values are debased. Members of the same family, kin group, or caste may be split between different factions by cash inducements, political party affiliation, or voluntary associational links. The segmentary factional system is a temporary phenomenon of transition between traditional rivalries that are based on "oppositions compelled by the very structure of social organization" (Gluckman) and modern national party politics. Such a compromise formation may endure a long time, but ultimately it cannot resist the forces of industrialization, urbanization, and the increasing division of labor.

Other political outcomes of contradictory relations are illustrated in Harriet Kupferer's interesting comparison of the roles of the Cree chief and the New Guinea headman. She draws attention to a problem that has already been discussed in social structural terms by several anthropologists who have worked in African contexts (Mitchell, *The Yao Village* [Manchester University Press, 1956]; Fallers, *Bantu Bureaucracy* [Cambridge: Heffer, 1956]; and Gluckman, *Order and Rebellion in Tribal Africa* [New York: Free Press of Glencoe, 1963]). This problem is that of the role or office that lies at the bottom of the administrative hierarchy.

This "intercalary role," under conditions of alien rule, interlinks two disparate sets of political relations. On the one hand, it represents the state, with its bureaucratic techniques and ideology and its impersonal relationships; on the other, it is deeply enmeshed with the multiplex relationships of the local political community. A cross-cultural comparison of this type of role, under varying conditions of sociocultural homogeneity, heterogeneity, and pluralism, would provide valuable insights into the nature of the administrative process. Kupferer, working within the tradition of culture-personality studies, succeeds in showing us how the Cree band leader is rendered politically impotent because of a contradiction between the traditional Cree expectations associated with the role of the "good man" (who may counsel but cannot coerce) and the Euro-Canadian expectations of the role (here defined as that of a liaison between white authority and Cree subordinates).

Because the chief is appointed by aliens, a process that has no direct precedent in Cree culture and values, the Indians do not regard his authority as fully legitimate. His legitimacy is further called in question by his repeated failures to meet popular expectations, because the Euro-Canadians largely ignore the representations he makes on his people's behalf. Under the British colonial system of indirect rule, certain administrative, legislative, and judicial functions were reserved to African chiefs and headmen; under the Canadian government, the Cree leader is a chief only in title. The result is a tendency for the incumbent to "withdraw from the field," and not to act positively—either for or against the superior authority—unlike African chiefs under comparable circumstances.

Kupferer contrasts this ineffectual "modal role" behavior with that of the New Guinea headmen. In this culture area (before European overlordship) certain leaders—known in the literature as "big men"—acquired ephemeral influence through aggressive exchange relationships with other men; they were expected to aggrandize themselves at the expense of others. When Australian agents from government stations decided to appoint, as junior officials, "younger men [who were] less aware of tradition" than the former community headmen, their junior role was defined in terms of the "big man" model; and these officials exploited their new status (to advance their interests) even more ruthlessly than their archetypes had done. They were less concerned with representing and satisfying the interests of their fellows than either the Cree or the African headmen, and thus did not experience the conflict of authority and representation that rendered the Cree chief "impotent" and that removed many African headmen from their positions.

The impact of the modern world did not produce such direct contradictions in the structure of the political system of the Kuikuru Indians of central Brazil. Yet Gertrude Dole indicates that, even without European overlordship, European contact drastically altered the structure of tribal political relationships.

In the past few decades the Kuikuru, and other Upper Xingu tribes, have "suffered acute depopulation through epidemic diseases of European origin, to which the Indians have no natural immunity." This has had the demographic consequence of reducing the size of tribes below a viable threshold of structural continuity, so that several tribes have had to amalgamate. It has had the further political consequence that headmen have died before their oldest sons and heirs were mature. "The absence of a legitimate heir has made it necessary for an adult male in another family to assume the responsibility of leadership." The net result of depopulation and amalgamation has been that leadership has been distributed among several families instead of in a single patrilineage, as in the past, and claims to succession have been vested in rival patrilines. Because rigorous patriliny was formerly the legitimate mode of succession, this multiplication of criteria for candidacy has resulted in a dilution of the authority of leaders.

A contradiction now exists between the ideal of headmanship—which should be strongly authoritative, and based on patrilineal descent—and the reality—in which "a man who is quite unsuited finds himself recognized as headman but has not had the training necessary to provide leadership." Because succession is uncertain, Dole reports, there has been a tendency to neglect leadership training of boys in any one family.

The result is a power vacuum, which apparently has been partially filled by an ascription of greater-than-traditional authority to the role of the shaman. The shaman has acquired powers of social control that were formerly vested in headmen; for example, he can make a public indictment of "bad lots," persons who cause "resentment and anxiety" as sorcerers. Although ordinary Kuikuru may not thus accuse one another, after the shaman's indictment the accused may be hunted down and killed.

This situation reminds one of the new quasi-political role of Separatist church leaders in modern Zululand, as described by Bengt Sundkler (in *African Systems of Thought,* Fortes and Dieterlen [eds.] [Oxford University Press for the International African Institute, 1965]), who writes: "When chieftainship falls into limbo, there follows a vacuum of power and authority, and the Separatist church leader steps in" (pp. 280 f.).

Although Marc Swartz's paper lays dominant stress on the psychological bases for political compliance in Bena micropolitics, conflicts of value and interests in crucial sets of social relations are closely examined. He shows how the specifically Bena patterning of psychological characteristics—such as distrust, dependence, and hostility—are congruent with social interaction in a small-scale political community whose "vertebral" structural relationships are based on patrilineal descent and virilocal marriage. He shows how individuals are confronted by the almost insuperable task of allocating their scarce resources between the equally valid demands of a range of kinsmen so as to offend no one. On the one hand, community of interest in certain crucial relationships comes into conflict with a major value, which is attached to economic individualism, and, on the other hand, with customary allegiance to others. Each relationship is therefore divided by conflicts of loyalties and charged with ambivalent emotions.

It is in such a milieu that the relationship with the adjudicator acquires an extreme degree of political importance, for it appears to the Bena as relatively free from the dangers inherent in other kinds of social relationships. It is because the oppositions in these relationships are "compelled by the very structure of social organization" that they appear to be inevitable; and they tend to be hedged about by mystical beliefs. Ill feeling in them is thought to give rise to sorcery, if it is allowed to reach a certain threshold of intensity. Sorcery is believed to inhere espe-cially in the relationship between seminal brothers, and is not unknown between father and son.

These relationships link men closely, but at the same time set them at odds in matters of succession to office and inheritance of property. Sexual jealousies that arise in the marital and affinal contexts are also associated with sorcery beliefs. Thus there is little psychical security in the long-term operation of these ties.

But the adjudicator is thought to be above these tacit battles; he rep-resents, for Bena, "an agency for the emergence of objective truth." The village executive officer and his elders constitute a politico-jural agency in which trust may be reposed. In reaction to the ambivalence with which close kinship and affinal relationships are regarded and experi-enced, Bena seek recourse to their adjudicating agencies as their only hope. Indeed, "as ascension of the hierarchy progresses, the prestige of adjudicators increases." The reason for this is that the higher they are, the further removed they become from the intimate arenas of tacit con-flict, and the more prestige they have, the greater the likelihood that they can bring about acceptable resolution.

In other words, as people bring their disputes to higher and higher courts, these public forums make it increasingly less difficult to disclose matters that would be subject to concealment and dissimulation in rela-tions between close kin and affines. Nor is open speaking by plaintiff and defendant liable to mutual reprisal; there is, as it were, a privilege of the *baraza*. Openness is expected here, just as closeness—masked by a "pleasant and ingratiating demeanor"—is expected in extrajural relationships.

One of the politically significant effects of this emphasis on trust and truth in the adjudicative process is the effect upon the role of the politi-cal officials who adjudicate: the headmen and the village executive officers. Bena are strongly motivated to comply with their decisions, for they feel relatively secure in the knowledge that the adjudicators are disinterested. Moreover, because the Bena courts and moots (as else-where in Africa) see their major role as the reconciliation of persons rather than the strict administration of law and the imposition of sanc-tions on the lawbreaker, the adjudicators have the function of reintegrat-ing a disturbed social group. Success in this task enables the political official "not only to meet the expectations of the disputants that their difficulties be resolved, but also to contribute to the general expectation that he can bring about the resolution of significant disputes." In other words, an official's success in adjudication contributes directly to his legitimacy, "not only in the eyes of those actually involved in disputes but also for those who feel they might become involved in disputes—the entire Bena public.

Swartz's account throws light on one of the important ways in which a store of political credit is built up—and is an asset that can see the official through the "lean days" of imposing unpopular decisions upon his people. His article also puts into sharp forcus the role of the judicial process as an accumulator of legitimacy—in political systems in which judicial, administrative, and legislative functions are undertaken by the same sets of officials. Legitimacy acquired in the exercise of one function may be transferred to the exercise of another.

Finally, this set of papers exemplifies the current emphasis on process rather than structure, and enable us to relate such concepts as conflict, struggle, contradiction, power, support, legitimacy, and compliance to our process models.

SEGMENTARY FACTIONAL POLITICAL SYSTEMS [1]

Ralph W. Nicholas, MICHIGAN STATE UNIVERSITY

Social anthropology is generally vague about the relationship between "social structure," as an all-encompassing system, and subsystems of such pervasive importance as the political and economic systems. In "simple" societies, where a comprehensive picture of social relations can be drawn in terms of consanguinity and affinity, the question of discrete "components" of social structure is avoided: political, economic, kinship, and religious roles are ideally allocated by a single system of kinship statuses. Radcliffe-Brown, and his immediate heirs, recognized, of course, that no real society fulfills the ideal conditions. Their task—which is still the task of the field anthropologist—was finding order in the chaos of many people doing many things with many meanings.

One important means of reducing field observations to order is through the customary laws of the society. The work of the first structural anthropologists was to write systematic accounts of social rules. The most impressive fact about the relatively isolated, homogeneous societies that were the subjects of these rule-writing accounts was their stability. Not only were they relatively unaffected by what little outside contact they had, but they contained "tension-handling mechanisms" that, through ritual or other means, prevented internal forces from disrupting their equilibrium.

Professor Fortes worked with the Tallensi between 1934 and 1937, and it was on the basis of this research that he prepared his two monographs on Tallensi social structure. In a footnote to the foreword of the first book, he wrote: "In 1943, in the course of other duties, I had occasion to spend some time in the Northern Territories [of the Gold Coast]. I found that no social changes of significance had taken place among the Tallensi since 1937" (1945, p. xii). This comment raises a question: What would constitute a "social change of significance"?

Professor Fortes is perfectly clear about what is important in structural analysis; after his detailed examination of the segmentary structure

[1] I would like to express my gratitude to Professor William T. Ross, Director, and the Asian Studies Center at Michigan State University for the research support I have had while writing this paper. I am thankful to Professor F. G. Bailey, of the University of Sussex, and to my wife, Marta, who read and criticized an earlier version, saving me from a number of errors and obscurities.

49

of Tallensi clanship, he says (1945, p. 232): "This is an architectural way of looking at the structure of Tale society. . . . Our attention has been fixed mainly on the permanent edifice in which social relations and social activities are congealed rather than on their emergence in process." A "social change of significance" would obviously be an architectural change, an alteration in the form of the edifice.

The foreword to the second monograph contains a kind of warning to future students of social structure:

. . . I was able to pay a very short visit to the Tallensi in 1945. . . . I found that as far as their social structure was concerned there had been no appreciable change since . . . 1934. But there are many signs that they are on the threshold of a period of rapid change. The war has opened up wider horizons to many of the young men who saw active service. Native Administration has developed greatly; schools are being established; missionaries have started work inside Taleland (1949, p. viii).

Two points of importance are implied in Professor Fortes' statements: (1) It is possible (though presumably not easy) to analyze information about social relations and social activities from the point of view of their "emergence in process," as well as in terms of the architectural arrangements. (2) Changes that are occurring in the post-war world, and that affect even relatively isolated societies, may permanently unsettle the formerly solid architecture of a social structure.

Professor Evans-Pritchard (1940) opened a new realm of political structure with his explanation of the principle of complementary opposition in the Nuer political system. The architecture of the Nuer political structure is expressed in the fact that "each segment is itself segmented and there is opposition between its parts. The members of any segment unite for war against adjacent segments of the same order and unite with these adjacent segments against larger sections" (p. 142). However, Evans-Pritchard, like Fortes, has a warning for the pure structuralist: "These combinations are not always as regular and simple as they were explained to me and as I have stated them" (p. 144). He follows with an example of a feud that began with a conflict between Thiang and Yol divisions.

The dominant lineage in Thiang was not related to the dominant Yol lineage through ancestral brothers; the Thiang were "sister's sons" to the Yol. According to structural principles, they should not have been fighting at all; but they did, and the defeated Thiang fled for protection to the Leng section, who were "brothers" of the victorious Yol. "The Yol sent messages to the Leng telling them that they were not to receive their enemies or give them asylum." The Yol understood the structural principle here, at least, and wanted it put into operation. "The Leng replied that the ancestor of the Leng lineage was the maternal uncle of the ancestor of the Thiang lineage and that they could not refuse asylum to their sister's sons" (p. 144).

The Leng had a structural principle of their own to invoke. Why did they do it? Who was it who sent back the message saying "they are our sister's sons"? Perhaps it did not suit all members of the Leng section to reply thus to their brothers the Yol. Certainly, there was soon another fight, with Leng and Thiang against Yol. Was the Leng-Yol conflict "on the horizon"? Did the Leng take in the Thiang for the sake of extra spears in the upcoming fight? Or did the Thiang somehow persuade the Leng that it would be advantageous for them to fight the Yol? Perhaps the answers to these questions are not important if our object is an understanding of the architecture of the Nuer political system.

But perhaps, once we have a clear idea of the arrangement of parts in Nuer society, we are ready to examine the fine structure of the parts. Now that the Newtonian principles of "classical structuralism" are known (if indeed they are), we are prepared to have a look at the structure of the atoms and molecules of the social universe. I think we may find that the elementary components of the fine structure are in constant motion, and that they are related to one another by different principles than are the parts of a classical social structure.

It is significant that some of the major concerns of modern social anthropology focus on areas of "choice" in social structure. Students of kinship, for example, have begun to analyze in detail the "ego-centered kin group," the network of relatives that is peculiar to each individual in a society. Economic anthropology is built around the phenomenon of individual choice in the allocation of scarce resources among alternative ends. Political anthropology, which seems still to lag behind the rate of development in kinship and economic studies, may also focus on choice in the sphere of public affairs, beginning—where Professor Evans-Pritchard left off, in his ground-breaking account of politics—with an explanation of why the Leng gave asylum to the Thiang after their fight.

FACTIONAL POLITICS

No phenomenon in the field of political relations is less adapted to architectural analysis than that of factional political organization. Political parties, royal families, lineages, and clans—the kinds of groups involved in "conventional" political conflicts—are all corporate groups with continuity and fixed structural properties. At what point in a structural analysis should account be taken of factions? Redfield (1955) confronted this problem in trying to write about the social structure of the Maya village of Chan Kom:

> But what of factions? In the life of Chan Kom, as I knew it over a period of about twenty years, factions played so important a part that it is almost if not quite true to say that had there been no factions the form of the society would have been notably different. . . . The factions in Chan Kom for

at least a generation were a major assignment of personnel in connection with principal activities and decisions. . . .

On the other hand, I do not think that the people of Chan Kom, asked to describe their social institutions, would have included an account of the factions. . . . They did not think of factions as something that ought to be there, as no doubt they thought that families and kinship relationships ought to be there (pp. 41-42).

The problem of factionalism has been the subject of a good deal of recent theoretical treatment. The valuable papers of Siegel and Beals (1960a and 1960b), French (1962), Firth *et al.* (1957), and Fenton (1955)—as well as several detailed reports on specific cases—have been instrumental in shaping my views on factional politics, but the argument presented here is derived primarily from my own comparative study of factions.[2]

I regard factionalism as primarily a political activity or phenomenon. By "political activity" I mean organized conflict over public power. "Power" is control over resources, whether human or material. In every society some control over resources is private and some is public, applicable to the entire society and allocated according to a set of rules. Participants in political activity attempt to expand their control over resources; or, if they do not, they are not engaged in political action. No assumption need be made about what a political actor seeks power for; control over material resources and men may be used to attain a great variety of personal objectives.

Conflict or competition (rule-regulated conflict) for public power takes place in an "arena" (Bailey, 1960, pp. 243-248). Social anthropologists frequently regard an entire small society as a political arena. Increasingly nowadays, however, the villages and tribes that have been the usual subjects of anthropological research are becoming parts of independent national states. Large national societies may contain a number of distinct fields of political conflict: individual villages, and component units in federal states, and even political parties may have significant public power and so constitute arenas in their own right.

The arenas with which I deal in this essay are organized, during political conflict, by factions. Not all arenas in which factions are found can be said to be "organized" by factions. There are two politically significant factions in the West Bengal village of Chandipur, for example, but most public power lies with the autocratic village headman, and most adult villagers are not involved in factional politics (Nicholas,

[2] Some of the data and results of this comparative study are summarized in Nicholas (1965). In the following discussion I shall make frequent reference to the communities in which I have studied political organization: three villages in West Bengal, India, which I call Radhanagar, Govindapur, and Chandipur, and the Six Nations (Iroquois) Grand River Reserve near Brantford, Ontario. Further details on factionalism in these societies are available in the various articles listed in the references.

1963, pp. 25-26). Factions, in what I shall refer to as segmentary factional political systems, have three characteristics in common with the political conflict groups in segmentary societies, such as that of the Nuer: they are (1) exhaustive, (2) exclusive, and (3) functionally undifferentiated.

When I say that factions are exhaustive, I mean that they involve all members of a society who are eligible to participate in politics. Everyone in Nuer society is a member of a lineage; not everyone who lives in a society whose political system is factional need be a member of a faction. Children, however defined, are usually not eligible to participate in politics; and women are frequently excluded from the distribution of public power. In traditional Indian peasant villages, members of subordinate castes may be merely "human resources," not participants in the political system.

Segments are also exclusive: one may not be affiliated with two factions in the same arena at the same time. Unlike other kinds of exhaustive, exclusive social groups—lineages, clans, or castes, for example—factions do not have a permanent membership. In certain cases, persons may be persuaded to desert one faction in favor of another, so as to shift the balance of power in a particular conflict (see Barth, 1959).

Perhaps the most important notion contained in the idea of segmentation is that there is "structural equality" between segments. Factions are not functionally differentiated from one another. There may be many factions in a particular arena (there are nine in Govindapur village), or only two, but they are ideally equivalent to one another with respect to both structure and function.

Any of the ideal criteria for a segmentary system may be violated in a particular instance. The criterion of exhaustiveness may be violated, as when many eligible adults remain outside a factional conflict yet factions constitute the dominant mode of political organization. The criterion of exclusiveness may sometimes be violated: a prominent Govindapur villager claims to have voted for the headman's group while instructing his wife to vote for the opposition.

The criterion of lack of functional differentiation may also be violated. Factions occasionally take on characteristics of political parties: "progressive" and "conservative" factions purport to represent distinct interests within the public, rather than the interests of their leadership. To the extent that factions become means of "interest articulation," they become functionally differentiated from one another. (The taking of socially approved names by factions is often "window dressing," designed to create a favorable impression in polities where parties have an established position.) So long as an arena is organized by groups whose predominant characteristics are factional, I shall refer to it as having a "segmentary factional political system."

Before turning to an examination of the kinds of political arenas that are characteristically organized by factions, I should note that my use of "faction" does not imply a moral judgment. In many political systems, to accuse one's opponent of "factionalism" is to charge him with using unfair means in the pursuit of illegitimate goals. The view of factionalism implied in the rhetorical use of the term has evidently influenced some recent theories about this phenomenon.

ARENAS

Factional political systems are never found in large-scale arenas. The tie between leader and follower in a faction, as we shall see below, is based upon a personal transaction between them. As arenas grow larger, leader-follower ties dissolve into quasi-group networks; supporters may have only a second- or third-hand connection with the leader (Mayer, 1965). Political conflict groups, organized on a personal basis and used to obtain certain objectives set for them by leaders, may obviously be organized in an arena of any size, but they are not well adapted to competition in large arenas where manpower is essential.

The effectiveness of close-knit revolutionary "cells" is obviously great under certain circumstances. Such a group may "take over" a local trade union group, town council, larger political organization, etc. (though in so doing they invite their opponents to organize in the same way to combat them). Such "take-overs" will never make a revolution, however; a revolution depends not so much on well-disciplined individual cells as on the organization among them. Thus a cell, which is sometimes called a "faction" in a trade union meeting, is in fact only a constituency party group with respect to its leadership.

One characteristic that has been noted repeatedly by anthropological observers of small-scale political arenas is the "consensus procedure" for making public decisions. Many societies, from American Indian tribes to Indian peasant villages, either do not know about, or they reject, voting and majority rule. Debates and discussions are prolonged and issues are redefined until the decision-makers achieve unanimity.[3] A major change that has been sought by modern governments—in North America and India, as in many other areas—is the "democratization" of politics in small-scale political arenas. When the Canadian government in 1924 installed a "democratically elected" council on the Grand River Iroquois Reserve in Ontario, it initiated a sharp factional conflict which continues to the present (Nicholas, 1965, pp. 46-58). In many parts of rural India, the attempt of the Congress government to have village councils elected

[3] The various meanings of "consensus," and the sociological characteristics of the councils in which consensual decisions are reached, are examined in Bailey (1965).

by universal adult franchise has sharpened already existing factional conflicts and has made some local systems, whose factions were previously
peripheral, into segmentary factional political systems (Nicholas, 1963).

In situations of rapid social change, factions frequently arise—or
become more clearly defined—because factional organization is better
adapted to competition in changing situations than are the political
groups that are characteristic of stable societies. Traditional Iroquois
matrilineages could function only under the rule that government was
by the council of chiefs. Factions, on the other hand, are not necessarily
bound by only one set of rules, either traditional or modern. Thus it is
possible for the Mohawk Worker faction on the Six Nations Reserve to
oppose the tribal council, which is elected under the modern set of rules,
by supporting the reinstallation of government by the chiefs, who are
chosen under the traditional rules of adelphic succession. When universal
adult franchise elections were introduced in rural India, factional organization proved to be the most successful way of bringing in votes, although votes had never before been essential for obtaining political rewards. When the indenture system was ended in Fiji, the settlements of
Indian laborers were set free, and, with virtually no internal authority
systems, they formed themselves into political communities. Factions
arose "automatically," as a way of organizing people in political conflicts
(Mayer, 1961, pp. 122-125).

If factions constitute the dominant mode of political organization,
groups that are not factions are often "induced" to act as if they were.
The Potter caste group in Govindapur village, for example, is a tight-
knit, localized, corporate group; all the men are members of a single
patrilineage. Govindapur politics, however, is primarily organized by factions, and in village politics the Potters act more like a factional group,
fighting against or allying themselves with factions in the dominant caste
—as if they were equals rather than members of a stratified and subordinate caste (Nicholas, 1965, pp. 37-41).

By contrast, in Chandipur, which does not have a segmentary factional political system, the economically rising Carpenter caste group
directs its energies against the dominant caste, unable to exploit a cleavage within that group. On the Six Nations Reserve, in 1957, one of the
four "Longhouse" groups (followers of the traditional Iroquois religion)
broke a strict Longhouse rule and participated in the council election;
it cast a bloc vote, and was thereby almost solely responsible for the
victory of the chief councillor. By acting as a faction—and violating a
cardinal rule of one system to participate in another—this Longhouse
group had quickly and efficiently found a place of strength in a segmentary factional political system.

THE ORGANIZATION OF FACTIONS

I have referred at various points to factions as "leader-follower groups." These groups are composed, initially, by some action of the leadership; no one is "automatically" a faction member, as he might be a member of a lineage. Faction leaders are ordinarily competitors for political power—there is little other incentive for organizing such a group, since holding a faction together is costly in resources that could be used in other ways. The faction leader must have greater control over resources (material, human, or both) than any of his supporters, because they are involved in a transaction in which the leader gives something—a job, land, money, protection, etc.—in return for political support.

Control over resources is much more evenly distributed throughout some political arenas than others. In the villages of Radhanagar and Govindapur, for example, landholding is much less concentrated than in Chandipur (Nicholas, 1963, p. 21). Where control over resources is dispersed, there tend to be more competing centers of power, that is, more factions. A faction leader may get the "edge" in resource control by having a few more kinsmen or a little more agricultural land than another leader. Writing about factionalism in the Mysore village of Namhalli, Beals (1959, pp. 433-434) described the core of each faction as a "clique." Some cliques are made up of a strong family, its affines, and its servants; a small, close-knit caste group, or a group of young men who had been schoolmates, might also compose a clique. This form of factional leadership, which is adapted to overcoming the resource weakness of individual leaders, requires strong consensus in the political objectives of the leading clique.

In factional organization, the content of the transactions from leader to followers is diverse, though the followers all return political support to the leader. In Radhanagar and Govindapur, factions were built up in the following ways: 28 per cent of the families were kinsmen of their faction leaders, and 27 per cent were economic dependents of their leaders; 21 per cent of the supporters were resident in the neighborhood of which their faction leader was head, and 14 per cent gave their support on grounds connected with caste; and 10 per cent were families that took protection from a powerful foe by becoming supporters of one of his opponents (Nicholas and Mukhopadhyay, 1962, p. 32). No single type of support would provide enough strength to make an effective political conflict group; leaders had to use all the varieties of resource at their disposal to obtain a significant number of followers.

The content of the "support" returned by followers to their leader varies from time to time, and between arenas. Prior to the introduction of the universal adult franchise in Radhanagar and Govindapur, the only occasion for which a faction leader might have to mobilize all followers would be an all-out fight with an opponent. I know of no such fights in either village, though faction leaders often spoke as if major riots were imminent. When supporters were required in a meeting of the village council, a few well-placed and articulate followers would ordinarily be enough to show the strength of particular faction leaders. With voting, of course, everyone counts, and faction leaders nowadays must try to mobilize every adult villager.

The contrast between the internal structures of factions and political parties is clearly marked in the transaction that connects followers to leadership. Factional supporters are tied to their leaders by very diverse transactions—a plot of land to sharecrop, a kinship connection, a common enmity, etc. Members of a political party need make only a specified gesture of allegiance (usually to the principles of the party rather than the leadership), sign a list, and pay their dues. The party is a corporate group that continues whether or not a particular follower or a particular leader is present; a faction, by contrast, may disintegrate when the leader dies or ceases to exercise control over the political action of his followers. There is no jural rule of succession to factional leadership positions, though there may be regularities of practice in any arena.

FACTIONAL CONFLICT

The object of organizing a faction is to give the leader an advantage in political conflict. The object of entering into political conflict is to increase one's control over resources, either by adding to them or by subtracting from an opponent's. It is only in conflict that factions become visible. The anthropologist may have only the conflicting claims of rival politicians about the size and composition of their support groups until these claims are put to the test in a political event. Leaders themselves may be uncertain about the side a potential supporter may take; past experience is often a poor guide to present factional affiliation.

The forms that factional conflict may take are unusually varied: the police may be called in to prevent one's opponents from committing a breach of the peace they had never contemplated; an unimportant follower of an opponent may be severely fined for a minor infraction; the unanimous decision needed to accept a new school may be held up by one side because negotiations for the funds were carried out by the opposition. A Govindapur faction leader built a brick arch across a public footpath running through his property so that his chief rival's laborers would have to carry headloads of paddy from the fields to the threshing floor by a mile-long circuitous route.

Segmentary factional political systems are frequently found in arenas where rapid social change is under way, where the rules of political conflict are fluid and ambiguous. These same arenas—peasant villages or tribal societies in contact with the urban, industrial world—are frequently characterized by economic stagnation; resources are fixed. It frequently appears that the dominant mode of political action in such arenas is the attempt to reduce the resources of the opposition. Beals (1959, p. 436) says that relations between the two leading factions in Namhalli village consist of "boycotting each other and of trying to create incidents which would cause some or all members of the other faction to lose money or property." Such tactics undoubtedly prompted Siegel and Beals (1960a, p. 107) to see factionalism as "disruptive," and to refer to it as "a particular type of non-adaptive inter-personal conflict" that arises from a complex "interaction of external stresses and internal strains."

I have tried to show that factions constitute a form of political organization that is particularly well adapted to certain kinds of arenas. In an Indian peasant village, where resources are fixed, or nearly so, the only gain one can make is at the expense of his opponent, and any loss by one's opponent is a relative gain in resources. A village politician may simply want to increase his own resources, whether he reduces his opponent's resources or not. However, under the circumstances created by police, courts, land laws, etc., he may be unable to do more than make his opponent lose resources.

We may see this as an unfortunate situation, in that competitors often force one another to take resources outside the already poverty-stricken villages and spend them in government courts. We may think this kind of conflict is "nonadaptive" from a moral point of view (either the anthropologist's or the villager's), but structural analysis indicates that this is likely to be the most efficient way that is available to the competitors for taking part in politics.

New forms of conflict are of course replacing some of the older ones, in Indian peasant villages and in other factionally organized political arenas. Universal adult franchise elections of village council members, as well as members of state legislative assemblies and the Indian parliament, provide a new focus for conflict between factions. Village politicians now compete for access to development funds and for positions of favor in the eyes of local government administrators. Political parties have found that village factions provide access to village votes, and factions may therefore be an incidental vehicle of political "modernization" in rural India.

REFERENCES

BAILEY, F. G. 1960. Tribe, caste, and nation. Manchester University Press.
———. 1965. Decisions by consensus in councils and committees. *In* M. Banton (ed.), Politics and the distribution of power. London: Tavistock.
BARTH, FREDRIK. 1959. Segmentary opposition and the theory of games: a study of Pathan organization. Journal of the Royal Anthropological Institute, 89, 5-21.
BEALS, ALAN. 1959. Leadership in a Mysore village. *In* R. L. Park and I. Tinker (eds.), Leadership and political institutions in India. Princeton University Press.
EVANS-PRITCHARD, E. E. 1940. The Nuer. Oxford: Clarendon Press.
FENTON, W. N. 1955. Factionalism in American Indian society. Actes du IVe Congrès des Sciences Anthropologiques et Ethnologiques. Vienna (1952); 2, 330-340.
FIRTH, RAYMOND, *et al.* 1957. Factions in Indian and overseas Indian societies: a symposium. British Journal of Sociology, 8, 291-342.
FORTES, MEYER. 1945. The dynamics of clanship among the Tallensi. Oxford University Press.
———. 1949. The web of kinship among the Tallensi. Oxford University Press.
FRENCH, DAVID H. 1962. Ambiguity and irrelevancy in factional conflict. *In* Muzafer Sherif (ed.), Intergroup relations and leadership. New York: Wiley.
MAYER, ADRIAN C. 1961. Peasants in the Pacific. London: Routledge & Kegan Paul.
———. 1965. The problem of the quasi-group. *In* M. Banton (ed.), Anthropological approaches to the study of complex societies. London: Tavistock.
NICHOLAS, RALPH W. 1963. Village factions and political parties in rural West Bengal. Journal of Commonwealth Political Studies, 2, 17-32.
———. 1965. Factions: a comparative analysis. *In* M. Banton (ed.), Politics and the distribution of power. London: Tavistock.
NICHOLAS, RALPH W., and MUKHOPADHYAY, TARASHISH. 1962. Politics and law in two West Bengal villages. Bulletin of the Anthropological Survey of India, 11, 15-40.
REDFIELD, ROBERT. 1955. The little community. University of Chicago Press.
SIEGEL, BERNARD J., and BEALS, ALAN R. 1960a. Conflict and factionalist dispute. Journal of the Royal Anthropological Institute, 90, 107-117.
———. 1960b. Pervasive factionalism. American Anthropologist, 62, 394-417.

IMPOTENCY AND POWER: A CROSS-CULTURAL COMPARISON OF THE EFFECT OF ALIEN RULE [1]

Harriet J. Kupferer, UNIVERSITY OF NORTH CAROLINA AT GREENSBORO

INTRODUCTION

There have been several occasions in which colonial powers or stronger societies have imposed political systems on native peoples where none had existed previously (see Read, 1959; Brown, 1963; Honigmann, 1961; Dunning, 1962). Most frequently, a native leader is appointed by an agent of the dominant society, or the mechanics of balloting are introduced and officers are elected. The introduction of elementary political systems has had varying consequences in specific societies. Such differences are probably functionally related to the cultures and social systems of the colliding societies. One may examine the ramifications of such an introduction on the subordinate peoples, on the agents of the superordinate society, or on the native leaders.

In this paper we will attempt to analyze the various leadership and authority expectations attendant upon the status of "band chief," and their effects upon role performance. Further, by contrasting this case study with one from another culture area, we will suggest that a number of variables may be operative in the role behavior of native officials.

In Rupert's House, which is the sub-Arctic Cree settlement from which these data come, the position of chief is achieved rather than ascribed. Role behavior, growing out of the normative expectations accompanying the status, plus idiosyncratic behavior that results from individual perceptions and definitions of the situation, are not enough to explain the enactment of role in this setting. The particular characteristics of this social system result in a typical or "modal role behavior" [2] that is largely ineffectual.

Rupert's House, founded in 1668, is located on the east coast of James Bay, Quebec, at the mouth of the Rupert River. Approximately five hundred Indians and twenty resident Euro-Canadians make up the

[1] This research was conducted while the writer was supervisor of the University of North Carolina at Chapel Hill Field School in Anthropology. An earlier version of this paper was read at the 63rd Annual Meeting of the American Anthropological Association, in Detroit. My colleague, M. Elaine Burgess, was helpful in its preparation, and Richard Preston also commented on an earlier draft.

[2] For a discussion of distinctions in role behavior, see Goffman (1961, pp. 85-98).

settlement. Significant among them are the Hudson's Bay Company manager, the game warden, a fundamentalist Protestant missionary, an Oblate priest, three school teachers, two nurses, and the widow of a former
Hudson's Bay Company manager. Unlike the Indians on the west coast
of James Bay, Rupert's House people are not treaty Indians and do not
occupy a reservation. All the land that the Indians exploit, exclusive of
that owned by the missions and the Hudson's Bay Company, belongs to
the province.

Originally, the sub-Arctic Cree wandered over a hunting territory in
small, kin-based bands. Honigmann (1956, p. 58) states that there were
few groups larger than the family with which individuals enjoyed any
sense of solidarity. The core culture of all northern Algonkians was described by Spindler (1962, p. 14) as consisting of hunting, fishing, gathering family groups, with an atomistic social structure. There was no
aboriginal source of authority and legitimate power save that of the head
of the family. A kind of informal leadership was recognized, however, in
that a "good man," wise in the ways of the people or skilled in the hunt,
might be sought out for counsel, but he did not have the power to
coerce. There was no mechanism to enforce a headman's decisions or
wishes (Driver, 1961, p. 330).

Just as the phenomena of authority and power were largely unknown
to the Cree, the idea of large permanent settlements or villages was
foreign to them. In fact, there was no word in the Cree vocabulary that
is equivalent to "village" or "band," although a word for the latter term
developed from a growing dependency upon the Hudson's Bay Company and the Indian Affairs Branch of Canada. Those Indians who over
the years returned to summer at the same Hudson's Bay post were eventually designated as bands by the Canadian government for purposes of
administration. Power and authority were also introduced by the practices of the Hudson's Bay Company and the Indian Affairs Branch, and
the branch recently instituted the position of "band chief" in Rupert's
House.

Since the introduction of the position of chief, there have been three
officeholders, each selected by the men and women of the band. The
present incumbent has been chief for ten years. There is one living
ex-chief, now serving on the council, which is an "advisory body" to the
chief.[3] Prior to the institution of the position, the Hudson's Bay Company
manager served as "chief." The extent to which this function of the
manager was made explicit is unknown, but the arrangement had at least
the tacit consent of the Canadian government.

The seasonal cycle of the people is now only semimigratory. During
the winter, most mature men—those who are not otherwise employed—

[3] The advisory council is part of the "democratic apparatus" that was introduced
with the office of the chief.

leave the post for their trapping territories. Some men take their families, but others do not; therefore some older persons, some wives, and many children are left in the settlement. At the close of the trapping season the trappers return to the post to await the spring fishing. When the fish are abundant, spring fishing camps are set up. As the weather grows warmer, fishing decreases, and the campers return to the settlement for the summer—during which time sporadic wage-labor is available, but not enough to provide employment for all. Early fall brings a return of the fish, and later in the fall migratory birds appear. Once more the people move a few miles from the village to establish camps for fishing and fowling. With the return of winter the cycle starts again. Despite this seasonal change in sources of food and money, the post is never totally abandoned by the Indians; there are always—for one reason or another—some who do not leave.

Of the Euro-Canadians, the teachers leave during the summer, and the others have annual holidays at different times during the year. Depending upon the status—nurses or Hudson's Bay Company manager—temporary replacements are sent in; so there is always a nucleus of resident whites.

NORMATIVE ROLE EXPECTATIONS OF THE BAND CHIEF

The differences in expectations of a chief are both cultural and structural, with Indians and Euro-Canadians holding conflicting views. The Indians' perception of the status and role of chief has its roots in the aboriginal concept of leadership; and differences in present expectations are a matter of degree, not of kind. The necessary qualities for chief, as far as the Indians are concerned, can be summed up in the phrase "He must be a good man." [4] One informant, when asked whether he would like to be chief, said: "I am not good enough. A chief has to be a good man—one who doesn't do anything bad." The meaning of "a good man," although difficult to ascertain, implies an ethic of morality not unlike that associated with the traditional type of leader.[5]

In addition to this ethic, the people have developed a clear idea of what they expect the chief to do, or what his normative role is consonant with their contemporary socioeconomic situation. He must look out for

[4] This notion of "good" as a prerequisite for the chief has a wide distribution. At the request of the local Indian agent, the Great Whale River and Richmond Gulf Indians elect a chief. "Ideally, only a 'good man' will be elected chief. . . . He is a moral leader and a person noted for his generosity" (Honigmann, 1962, pp. 60-71).

[5] Honigmann (1957, p. 369) contends that "ambivalence characterizes thinking about leadership. Indians regard firm leadership as desirable. Yet no pleasure comes from exercising power. Too great evidence of power is resented and feared by those whom it affects."

the people, take care of the children, order rations for the poor, send those who are ill to the hospital, and share his own food if need be. It is apparent from these expectations that the ideal role of chief involves not only assistance and counseling, it requires sufficient power and acumen to maneuver in the Euro-Canadian world.

As we have pointed out, the position of chief was imposed through official white action, and although such a status in Western society would normally imply both leadership and legitimate authority for initiating action, local Euro-Canadians do not hold these expectations of the role. Their comments and behavior suggest that they perceive the chief's role as largely that of liaison between Euro-Canadians and Indians. The whites view both authority and leadership as resting largely with themselves. Indeed, Dunning (1962, p. 217) notes that in northern Indian posts the Indian Agent frequently vetoes the nomination of candidates whose names have been proposed in the normal democratic process. These agents delegate little authority; more often, they exert their authority over the Indians through the chief.

On the other hand, the Euro-Canadians reflect some ambivalence in regard to the chief's role. Many of their comments indicate that they think the present chief is a more effective leader than his predecessors, and he was often described as the best chief in the James Bay area. At the same time, he was accused of being too bossy and too demanding. One informant contended that the chief did not like whites and that the band might be better off if it had a "leader" who did. The evidence of an inconsistency in white expectations of the status of chief can be related, in part, to the "democratic ideal" that such a position should carry some power and authority, but, because this would conflict with their own power and authority, they are reluctant to yield their superordinate place in the social structure.

ROLE PERFORMANCE OF THE CHIEF

Ideally, all aspects of Indian life—economic, health, education, and social—are responsibilities of the chief. There are, however, only a few spheres within the life of the settlement over which the chief has legitimate authority—independent of the Euro-Canadian residents. Among these are planning the wedding feasts and other social events, control of the children, and preliminary funeral arrangements. The wedding feasts and dances are excellent vehicles for demonstrating his administrative and leadership ability. He names the women who are to prepare the food; the arrangement of the benches and festive table are made under his supervision; and the guests are seated at his direction. As people enter the hall for the dance, he shouts orders in Cree. (Some of his comments are not flattering: "You, fat lady, sit down.")

He assumes responsibility for children in several ways. He has the bell rung at night, which is a signal for them to return to their homes. He visits the school occasionally to inquire about their behavior, and he once placed a notice in the store notifying the women to keep the children away from the motorized sleds. Such, then, are the kinds of behavior the chief can undertake without Euro-Canadian intervention.

However, the segments of life that are of utmost concern to contemporary Indians are those over which the chief has little or no control: economics, health, and education.

ECONOMICS

Economic matters—employment, beaver quotas and payment, and government assistance—have the highest priority for the Indians, and it is in this aspect of life that the chief is most impotent. The predictable pattern of interaction between Euro-Canadians and the chief in matters of employment can be seen in the following situations.

A government-owned sawmill operates during the spring and summer months, and the Indian Affairs Branch appointed the chief to oversee the mill. This responsibility includes the hiring of men, but *only those whom the Hudson's Bay manager approves*. The manager records the men's time, and provides credit at the store for their work, and the Indian Affairs Branch then recompenses the company.

In other situations it may be other Euro-Canadians whose superordinate position controls the chief's behavior. An engineer came to the post to make a survey for a new floating dock, and to run a survey for a new school. He elected to work through the Oblate priest rather than the Hudson's Bay Company manager. In the presence of the writer and the engineer, the priest sent for the chief, who came to the mission cap in hand. The priest explained in Cree the nature of the work, and told the chief whom to hire. The chief departed, returned in about fifteen minutes, and said that all the men would report at eight the following morning.

A similar situation occurred when the Hudson's Bay Company employed the priest to oversee the building of a new home for the company clerk. The priest, in turn, hired the chief as foreman, and gave him instructions with regard to the hiring of Indian carpeters. This lack of autonomy of the chief in the area of employment elicits such comments from the men of the band as "He always hires the same men" or "He always sees to it that his relatives have work."

Beavers, although declining in numbers, still constitute a source of income for Indians who trap. Individual quotas are established by the government's Fish and Game Commission, and (unlike Ontario, where the pelts go to the open market) Quebec province buys the pelts and sets the price. Frequently, there is a long interval between the delivery of the pelts and receipt of payment. The chief, who has no authority in this area, is nevertheless a target for the discontent engendered by the long wait for payment. We witnessed one such episode when a long-standing member of the community (and a good trapper) went to the chief while intoxicated and angrily demanded his check. This is another example of the way in which people expect that the chief, as a "good man," will take care of his people—an expectation, given the structure of the system, that he is unable to meet.

Money from various assistance programs are an important part of the economy. In addition to regular assistance, emergency rations can be issued to those in acute circumstances. In such cases the procedure is to go to the chief, who is empowered by the Indian Branch to wire or call the Indian agent, who will issue the rations. Because of language and other technical problems, the chief informs the Hudson's Bay manager, who makes the call. However, the manager interferes in the formalized channels of the chief's legitimate authority by exercising his discretion in this matter. If, in the manager's judgment, the family requesting emergency assistance is "undeserving," "lazy," or "improvident," he may neglect to relay the request.

It is difficult to know whether this informal subverting of the chief's power is done with the tacit permission of the Indian agent. There is some evidence, however, that the chief is unaware that interference has occurred with his request for action. The deprived family, after waiting for rations that do not appear, will turn on the chief in anger. Although he has acted according to his own and the Indians' normative role expectations, his responsibilities are abrogated.

HEALTH

Health is second to economics as a focus of the band's concern or anxiety. Births and minor illnesses are ordinarily handled by the nursing station. Periodically, people are dissatisfied with the attention they receive there, or they may, for various reasons, wish to bypass this service and be flown out to the hospital at Moose Factory. They communicate their desires to the chief, who then intercedes for them with the nurse in charge. Only she has the authority to have a patient sent out, and, depending upon the seriousness of the condition, she may or may not act according to the chief's request. Here again he is blocked, for he has neither the knowledge necessary to decide whether or not to ask that the sick person be flown out nor the power to implement these requests when he does make them.

EDUCATION

The school at the settlement has six grades. From the seventh grade on, children are sent away to boarding schools, but it is not possible for all who complete the sixth grade to continue their education. Decisions with regard to continuing are made by the principal of the school, in a courtesy consultation with the chief. At present, all of the chief's younger children are, or have been, in "outside" schools. Parents who have aspirations for their children, and who are refused the principal's permission, accuse the chief of favoritism and capriciousness. In actual fact, he has little or nothing to say about who will be permitted to go on, although he may report the aims of certain families for their children. Decisions are based largely upon scholastic aptitude and performance of the children.

ATTITUDES OF THE CHIEFS TOWARD THEIR STATUS AND ROLE

The consequences of the chief's subordinate status to the superordinate whites in many crucial situations inevitable brings about discontent with his role performance. I was told that when each of the three chiefs was elected, he had the popular support of the people. In time, each had found that, unable to meet certain role expectations, his popularity decreased and in some circumstances open hostility manifested itself. They have been accused of "looking out" for themselves and their families and of failing to take care of the people. Whether the chiefs ever fully recognized the causes for their dilemma, the two still living express disenchantment with the position,

The former chief asserted that he would never run again. His feeling about the conflicting expectations of his role can be seen in the following comments.

The chief works for nothing and they [Indians] think he should give them everything. The first chief we had here, he wasn't too bad; he did his best but the band says he's no good. After him they chose me, then they say I'm not good. Now they say the same thing about Malcomb. You have to be a pretty good man to please these people.

The current chief, Malcomb, also shows discontent with his position. His daughter reported:

He is getting fed up with it. People come over to his house drunk and jump on him, accuse him of telling lies, then the next day when he goes over to see them they swear up and down that they were never there.

Malcomb is frustrated by his inability to provide rations, effect employment, or meet all the Indians' needs. There is evidence that he also resents demands placed upon him by the whites, which he does not have the ability to resist. The simple plan of setting up a fishing camp for himself may be thwarted by pressure from a member of the Euro-Canadian community to remain in the settlement to oversee a construction job. This is an economic loss for him, for—although he is paid—the money is no substitute for a good supply of fresh fish.

COMPLEXITIES OF ROLE ENACTMENT

The role enactment of an individual occurs largely in face-to-face situations with other people, who can be referred to as "role others." Because everyone occupies a position or status with definable behavior constellations, human interaction is a matter of the meeting and interplay of roles. Our data demonstrate that the status of chief at Rupert's House carries more than one set of role expectations. The chief—in his role as chief—has two clusters of "role others" with which he must interact. Each cluster of "role others" has expectations of the chief that are opposite and irreconcilable insofar as his rights and duties are concerned.

The Euro-Canadians comprise one cluster of "role others." Each of them occupies a status—nurse, teacher, priest, manager—and each acts in a more or less typical manner, consistent with his position. But there is another status that is common to all these people, that of the Euro-Canadian in an Indian settlement. This dimension—added to their particular statuses—places them in a superordinate position in the Rupert's House social system. Thus the combination of particular functions, plus the role that is inherent in the status of Euro-Canadian, comprises the power group with which the chief must interact. This segment of the "role others" has implicitly, if not explicitly, defined the role of chief as a liaison between the Euro-Canadians and the Indians, and he acts accordingly.

The other segment of the "role others" with which the chief interacts is the band members, who have normative expectations that the chief tries—with varying success—to meet. As we have demonstrated, his efforts are usually nullified. The Indians recognize that the Euro-Canadians are in power positions. A telling point here is that the Hudson's Bay Company manager is referred to as "the boss." The Indians are aware that he issues directives, and they know that the game warden acts as policeman for the settlement, and that others in the post have legitimate or illegitimate power. What they do not understand, however, is that their expectations of the chief, which do not include the exercise of power over them, include authority and decision-making ability that he simply does not have.

The effect of operating in a social structure that is composed of two different culture groups may be, as in this case, differential role definitions of one status. When one of these groups is dominant, the subordinate expectations are not likely to be met. In the case of the band chief, regardless of the abilities of the specific incumbent, it results in what we have called a "modal role" behavior that is largely ineffectual from the Indians' perspective—and perhaps also from that of Euro-Canadians if it is measured against the gap between their ideal and real norms for the role. The net results are the band's gradual disaffection for the chief and the chief's increasing sense of frustration. Effective role performance can seldom be executed where there are two sets of role expectations, of the same status, in a social structure that is characterized by superordinate-subordinate organizations.

When we compare our findings with a case study in New Guinea, some interesting differences are uncovered. Brown suggests that the imposition of foreign rule does not always restrict the power of aboriginal authority: the opposite can be true—alien rule can lend new power to the indigenous officials it establishes (1963, p. 1).

Her material is drawn from the Chimbu area of New Guinea, where, until the arrival of colonial powers, the societies were stateless. Settlements in New Guinea are small and dispersed; and "leadership is not formalized and political units are not fixed" (ibid, p. 2). Unlike the Cree, whose basic cooperative unit is the nuclear family, clans and subclans are the cooperative units. Authority rests largely with the heads of clans or subclans. Other leaders ("big men") achieve their position through good exchange relationships with other men. They are effective speakers, and possess the personality traits that are necessary to perform the tasks by which wealth is acquired. Few of them remain leaders throughout their adult life, and none of them can be sure their fellows will support their opinions and positions (ibid., pp. 3-7).

After the arrival of colonial powers (Germany initially, followed by Australia), community and district leaders were appointed, many of whom were former headmen. These men remained in office only as long as the Australian agent from the government station regarded them as effective. Ultimately, these officials were replaced by younger men less aware of tradition, and at least partially acculturated. Like the Cree band chief, these leaders had to please two parties; but, unlike the Cree, the frequent result of their behavior was advancement of their self-interests at the expense of others. The consequence of alien rule in New Guinea was the creation of a new power structure. "Tribal leadership changed in a generation from the absence of any fixed authority ('anarchy') to a system giving the officials the opportunity to dominate ('satrapy')" (ibid, p. 3).

It is apparent that the current role of the New Guinea headman is not conflict-inducing, nor does it result in impotence. In addition, the status carries significantly more permanent power than the traditional "big men" possessed.

CONCLUSION

Because of the great differences in the results of the innovations of political leaders in these two societies, we must assume that other factors —in addition to the absence of indigenous political structures—are operative; and we may put this in the form of tentative or working hypotheses.

There is a relationship between the presence of resident aliens and the role of the native official.

There is some congruence between the traditional expectations of a leader and the role of an imposed one.

There is a correspondence between the role enactment of the contemporary leader and the modal overt personality characteristic of the culture.

There is a connection between the behavior of the "chief" and the exploitation of the ecology and attendant social organization.

There is a relationship between the manner in which an official comes into the status—appointed or elected—and his behavior.

It well may be that there is a functional association among some or all of the variables and the predictable behavior of the native power figures.

REFERENCES

BROWN, PAULA. 1963.   From anarchy to satrapy. American Anthropologist, 65, 1-15.

DRIVER, HAROLD. 1961.   Indians of North America. University of Chicago Press.

DUNNING, R. W. 1962.   Some aspects of governmental Indian policy and administration. Anthropologica, 4, 209-231.

GOFFMAN, ERVING. 1961.   Encounters. Indianapolis: Bobbs-Merrill.

HONIGMANN, JOHN J. 1956.   The Attawapiscat swampy Cree: an ethnographic reconstruction. Anthropological Papers of the University of Alaska, 5, 23-79.

————. 1957.   Interpersonal relations and ideology in a northern Canadian community. Social Forces, 35, 365-370.

————. 1959.   World of man. New York: Harper & Row.

————. 1962.   Social networks in Great Whale River: notes on an Eskimo, Montagnais-Naskapi and Euro-Canadian community. Ottawa: National Museum of Canada Bulletin.

KUPFERER, HARRIET J. 1964. Leadership and authority: the man in the middle. A paper presented at the American Anthropological Association Meeting, Detroit.

READ, K. E. 1959. Leadership and consensus in a New Guinea society. American Anthropologist, 61, 425-436.

RUBEL, A. J., and KUPFERER, HARRIET J. 1963. Atomistic societies. A paper presented at the American Anthropological Association Meeting, San Francisco.

SPINDLER, LOUISE S. 1962. Menomini women and culture change. American Anthropological Association Memoir 92.

ANARCHY WITHOUT CHAOS: ALTERNATIVES TO POLITICAL AUTHORITY AMONG THE KUIKURU

Gertrude E. Dole, VASSAR COLLEGE

INTRODUCTION

The Kuikuru are a Carib-speaking tribe in central Brazil consisting of a single settlement of about 145 individuals. This society is very loosely organized and has an extremely permissive culture. The settlement comprises nine multifamily houses. In most of the houses at least some of the families make up extended family residence units of various types, fraternal, sororal, bilateral, patrilocal, or matrilocal. However, individual nuclear families not infrequently change their place of residence, making the extended family organization unstable as well as varied.

Neither households nor extended families have formal leaders, except that older members command the respect and cooperation of their offspring. There are no prescriptive rules of kin group or local exogamy; a person may choose his mate from within the settlement or from another group. Postmarital residence follows no rigid rule. Ideally, a couple resides for a time with the parents of the bride, and later with the family of the groom, but this custom is waived in many instances. The kinship structure is cognatic, and there are no lineal kin groups. Nor are there any age-set organizations, or other sodalities. Finally, most of the ceremonies are primarily secular, exerting very little supernatural control.

A corresponding degree of permissiveness is found in the culture's political sphere. The Kuikuru recognize one of their members as headman; but the present [1] headman is a leader in title only. He exerts no control whatever in political, economic, or ceremonial behavior. As a result, formal leadership and authority are so weak among the Kuikuru as scarcely to exist, and infractions of norms often go unpunished. Adultery, for example, constitutes a delict, but there is no mechanism for punishing it. A jealous bride may fight with her unfaithful husband early in their marriage, but older couples merely tolerate mutual infidelity. Hence an extraordinary amount of extramarital sexual relations occur without causing open hostility.

There is virtually no means of recovering a stolen object or of pun-

---

[1] "Present" refers to 1954, when the data on which this paper is based were obtained.

ishing a thief. In one instance, a man discovered that his steel file, which is a rare and highly valued item among the Kuikuru, had been stolen. He had no way of identifying the thief or of recovering the file, and, being without any kind of redress, this man gave vent to his frustration by weeping.

ALTERNATIVES TO POLITICAL CONTROL

One might expect the pervasive lack of prescribed rules of behavior and the complete absence of effective central authority to result in social chaos, but this does not occur. The Kuikuru have developed alternative mechanisms to ensure peaceful co-existence and a considerable amount of cooperation. Perhaps the most effective of these mechanisms are the measures taken to combat supposed witchcraft. The Kuikuru attribute to witchcraft such misfortunes as deaths, personal ailments, failure of crops, and all disasters resulting from accidents. It is the unfriendly, quarrelsome, stingy, uncooperative persons who are suspected of sorcery. A suspected sorcerer may suffer a mild form of social ostracism. In one instance, the family of a man who was thought to be working witchcraft was left to occupy a multifamily house alone because others feared that their children would die if they were to live with that man.

If a person is suspected of causing several disasters within a short period of time, tension in the community may become very great, and the suspect may be killed. Some years ago, when an unusual number of children died, many persons in the society concurred in suspecting the same individual of causing the deaths. After obtaining the approval of those persons informally, one man took it upon himself to execute the suspect. It is significant that the suspect was somewhat marginal to Kuikuru society, having come to it from another community; moreover, he had no male kin who could avenge his death.

It can be seen that the occasional killing of a supposed sorcerer is a process of social selection through which antisocial individuals are eliminated. To be safe from the suspicion of working witchcraft, therefore, one must cultivate the amiable personality that is so important to the existence of this permissive society. As a matter of fact, hostility is almost never manifested overtly among the Kuikuru. On the contrary, these people are unusually amiable, cordial, generous, and willing to cooperate with one another.

The norm of being amiable deters individuals from accusing one another of delicts; hence, in the absence of effective political or kingroup control, interpersonal relations have become a kind of game, in which almost the only restrictive rule seems to be not to show hostility to one another for fear of being suspected of witchcraft. When a minor delict is committed, the guilty person can maneuver his way out of the difficulty through evasive actions. He may boldly lie about it, and turn the blame on another, knowing that he will not be pressed for the truth. Or he may escape from the uncomfortable situation by leaving the community to visit or live indefinitely with another tribe in which he has relatives, and thus avoid conflict.

It may be noted that, in moving to another community, a person may be suspected of having been ostracized from his own community. This was suggested by the Kuikuru's difficulty in comprehending the ethnographers' desire to live with them: they asked if the fieldworkers had been "kicked out of their society," and whether they would be allowed to return home.

A more formal mechanism for social control is divination. When a man discovered that someone had taken the fruit he had stored for use in a festival, instead of making an accusation he engaged a shaman to divine. After putting himself into a trance with tobacco smoke (see Dole, 1964), the shaman named a teenage boy as the thief. It is perhaps not pure coincidence that the boy was a son of the unfriendly, uncooperative, rather stingy man who was generally disliked in the community, and who was already partially ostracized because some persons thought he practiced witchcraft. The boy was not openly accused, and no punishment was meted out, but his identity became known to the entire community through gossip. Whether or not the boy was guilty, the people believed he was.

Divination is also used to assess guilt in more serious crises. For example, when two of the nine multifamily houses in the Kuikuru settlement burned, a shaman divined, and then revealed that the fires had been caused by a Kuikuru who had left the group some years previously and had never returned. Moreover, the shaman reported that the lightning that had set one of the houses afire was actually sent to kill the shaman himself.

This episode is of considerable interest because it illustrates several principles of Kuikuru social control. The accused had only one close male relative, a very weak and effeminate brother, who was not liked by the Kuikuru and who had also left the community. Thus, as in the execution of the supposed sorcerer, blame was placed on a person who was not well integrated into the society and who had no strong male relatives to support him. In addition, there was resentment against the accused man because he had neither claimed nor released a Kuikuru girl who had been promised to him some years previously (she was still in puberty seclusion, waiting for him to claim her). The situation was aggravated by a shortage of girls: the secluded and betrothed girl was the only one available in the Kuikuru settlement at that time, and several single Kuikuru men were looking for wives.

Finally, one of the single men, who happened to be brother of the shaman, asked for the girl, and her mother agreed to the marriage. On the very next day her house burned. The marriage took place about ten days later, and a few days after that a bolt of lightning in a thunderstorm badly bruised the shaman and burned down the house in which he and his newly married brother had lived. The coincidence of these fires and the marriage of the shaman's brother to the fiancée of another man clearly suggested that the latter was angry and had sent the fires by witchcraft.

During the course of the divining ceremony, the shaman carried on dialogues with various interested members of the community. When he finally disclosed the identity of the culprit, it created considerable anxiety. One after another, several individuals stood apart in the plaza and spoke in long monologues. The most excited of these was the shaman's elderly wife, whose first husband had been killed by lightning. In the heat of the excitement, the shaman's brother left with a few companions to kill the man suspected of witchcraft. Although it was admitted that he should have spoken to the headman before undertaking this mission of revenge, he did not do so because, it was said, "he was too mad to talk to anyone."

This incident indicates that although individuals may not accuse one another, the shaman, with the weight of supernatural authority, can make a public indictment. In this way divination makes it possible to rid the society of a marginal member who causes resentment and anxiety. Again, as in the case of the stolen fruit, it was the shaman and not the headman who acted as adjudicator. However, in the process of divining he sounded out public opinion, and reflected the consensus in his verdict. Therefore, although divination ostensibly puts the onus of the decision on the shaman, the shaman deduces, formulates, and expresses the will of the people.

Paradoxically, witchcraft itself—the only crime for which punishment is meted out—seems never to occur; although all Kuikuru, including the shamans, fear the effects of witchcraft, they apparently never practice it (see Dole, 1964). However, in their function as social controls, there is little difference between the effects of the actual practice of sorcery and the mere belief that it is practiced. The belief alone has a double function. Not only does it explain accidents, illness, and other disasters—by attributing them to the malice of others when the natural causes are not understood—it also seems to deter asocial behavior by repressing aggression and fostering social integration and conformity to the norm of peaceableness.

Aside from divination and homicide, there appears to be no formal mechanism for the control of adult male behavior among the Kuikuru; but a few milder formal sanctions are occasionally applied to women and children. If a woman or a child is lazy, or steals, or displays anger, it is sometimes arranged to have that individual scraped with a row of needle-sharp fish teeth, which is a very painful process. However, the Kuikuru regard this treatment more as a cure or prophylaxis than a punishment—which is true also of two ceremonies in which youngsters are scraped with fish teeth or are ritually struck on the back with a hank of cotton threads.

Another sanction is said to be gang rape, to which any woman who looked at the secret flutes would be subject. No instance of this treatment was observed or reported among the Kuikuru, but there is reason to believe that it might occur if the taboo were broken. Gang rape as a form of punishment has been reported among various societies in the area surrounding the Upper Xingú region of central Brazil, where the Kuikuru settlement is located. It occurred among the Mundurucu if any woman "spied on the sacred trumpets" (Murphy, 1956, p. 427). Among several Cayapo peoples it occurs as a "punishment imposed by the headmen" (Diniz, 1962, p. 28). If an Apinaye girl has relations with her chosen mate before he has completed his initiation into the warriors' age class, she is raped by other men and made a "wanton" (Nimuendajú, 1939, p. 79). When a Sherente girl is raped, her husband and some of her kinsmen punish the offender by raping the offender's wife (Nimuendajú, 1942, p. 37). In a very insightful manuscript (not yet published), Wagley reports the custom of mass rape among the Tapirape, a treatment that was administered to women during epileptic seizures and as punishment for a habitual lack of cooperation, for refusal to submit to scarification, and for refusal to have intercourse with a husband. According to Wagley (in a personal communication), a similar custom also obtains among the Caraja; and, among the Bororo, a woman is "driven to the men's house when she displeases her husband" and is there subjected to intercourse with various men (Cook, 1907).

The other sanctions in Kuikuru society appear to be of a diffuse type, such as complaining and gossip. If, for example, a person refuses to lend or to give his possessions when this is requested, or, on the other hand, if he asks for too much from others, the Kuikuru may complain in a querulous tone, or grumble, or treat the offender with silence or with terse answers. This also applies to persons who refuse to cooperate. Kuikuru do not hesitate to tattle on one another, and they gossip freely about petty theft and lying. Finally, if a young man is lazy, he may find it very difficult to obtain a wife, for a young girl's parents tend to put off such an undesirable suitor with the excuse that their daughter is too young to be married.

MOBILIZATION OF GROUP LABOR

As in the punishment of crime, mobilization of group labor is accomplished among the Kuikuru through channels that are outside the political structure. The nuclear family is largely self-sufficient in economic activities. All exchange, including intertribal trade, is carried out by individuals independently. Every adult male prepares a garden, and his women harvest and process the crops; however, members of several families frequently join in cooperative activities. In the absence of a strong decision-making political agent, plans for these cooperative activities are usually made informally, in conversations among relatives and friends or alternatively, in conversations among men who meet to smoke in the plaza each evening. These men are shamans, and they have no official political status. They are not, necessarily, heads of extended families or of households; they join the circle because smoking is the prerogative of shamans, and because they like to smoke. The present headman is not a shaman, and therefore he does not join the smoking circle. In spite of the informal nature of the shamans' association, they are a potential unit of leadership and they do make plans for group activities.

After plans have been made for a large cooperative undertaking, the necessary labor is recruited by the device of throwing a party for those who will join in the work. Whenever a man needs help in building a house or carrying a newly cut canoe to water, for example, he asks for volunteers. He is referred to as the "owner" of the undertaking, and, together with his wife, he is responsible for providing food for the work group as pay for its help.

This device is used by many peoples, but the Kuikuru have elaborated it into a major cultural complex by attaching it to the entire ceremonial cycle of singing and dancing. Each of some twenty Kuikuru ceremonies is associated with a set of hereditary officials, who are known as "owners," "askers," and "performers." Every ceremony is "owned" by a person (or sometimes more than one), and when the people want to have a ceremony performed, an official asker makes a formal request to its owner; if the owner agrees, official singers and dancers perform the ceremony and the owner pays the performers and the asker with food that is prepared by his wife. (For a more detailed treatment of the owner-asker-performer complex, see Dole, 1956-58.)

Economic projects that require a considerable amount of cooperative labor are sometimes linked with one of the ceremonies. On such occasions, all able-bodied men may join in the work party; the performers sing and dance, and the owner pays not only the workers but also those who provide entertainment in connection with the work.

Thus cooperative work among the Kuikuru is initiated by various individuals, and it is performed primarily for the individual's benefit and at his own expense. This is in contrast to some other Tropical Forest societies, where cooperative labor is organized and directed by the headman or by another official. Like the use of divination to establish guilt, the individual sponsorship of parties to mobilize labor can be viewed as an alternative to formal political leadership. It would be of considerable interest to determine why the Kuikuru lack formal political authority and how substitutes for formal political leadership arise. Definitive answers to these questions would require a thorough historical and cross-cultural investigation (which is beyond the scope of this paper), but a brief discussion of the sociocultural milieu in which substitute mechanisms occur among the Kuikuru may throw some light on the problem.

DISCUSSION

The lack of central political control that characterizes Kuikuru culture has been described by a leading political anthropologist as "democratic to the point of near anarchy" (Hoebel, 1954, p. 294). Hoebel also notes that "primary, informal mechanisms of social control," instead of formal political leadership, are found among the "lower primitive societies"; that is, "simple collecting and hunting societies" (p. 293). This implied correlation of a lack of political structure with the lower levels of culture poses a problem of interpretation, for the Kuikuru are definitely not one of the "lower" or "collecting and hunting" societies; rather, they are full horticulturists, with unusually sophisticated economic practices and an elaborate cycle of ceremonies.

Moreover, it is quite clear that the Kuikuru once had stronger political leadership than they have at present. The position of headman is inherited patrilineally, and the headman is said to have special privileges and responsibilities; for example, he is said to own the tribal land. The tradition of the headman's patrilineal succession and ownership of the land are so strong that some Kuikuru believe the land is now owned by a man who is the son and grandson of an outstanding former headman —but who was removed from the Kuikuru settlement to the city of Cuyaba in 1943 and has not been with the Kuikuru since that time.

It is also the stated responsibility of the headman to decide when to move the settlement and where to relocate it; and former headmen have in fact discharged this responsibility and are remembered as great headmen. Another responsibility of the headman is to receive visitors and to represent the society in dealing with other tribes; and a former headman is reported to have negotiated with a hostile delegation from another group about a death that the group attributed to Kuikuru witchcraft: the Kuikuru headman offered them his sister in order to prevent hostilities.[2]

Within his own community, it is said that one function of a headman is to call out the daily work plans and to harangue his people about preserving tribal customs. In a neighboring and closly related group, the present headman, in fact, arranges for work and ceremonies, and makes long speeches in the plaza every night; he speaks forcefully and his people listen respectfully (Cunha, 1954, p. 39). It is also said that the headman should reprimand wrongdoers, such as petty thieves.

In actual fact, as we have noted, the present headman does *not* perform any of the leadership responsibilities: he does not give counsel to his people or reprimand them for misdemeanors, or represent them in relations with other groups; he makes no decisions on cooperative work; and when a series of fires made it seem dangerous to remain in the current site of occupation, another man made the decision to move the settlement. Because he does not perform his leadership role, some of the Kuikuru refer to the present headman—with disdain—as a "little headman," and a "little-bit owner of the land."

There is other internal evidence of a formerly more effective political structure among the Kuikuru. Besides the headman, the Kuikuru also recognize about a dozen other men as nominal "secondary leaders." These men are referred to as *aneti*, and are said to "help" the headman (the rest of the people are referred to as *kamaga*, and have no leadership status). No specific functions of the *aneti* were stated by informants, but in answer to questions about who would succeed the present headman in the event of his death, most of the names mentioned as likely successors were of those who had been mentioned—independently—as *aneti*. Moreover, most of these individuals played a special role in the exchange of goods within the community.

The Kuikuru have a formal system of exchange, *uluki*, which is conducted as a pleasurable pastime (Dole, 1956-58, p. 129). Exchange is presided over by a trading captain, a *uluki aneti*, and the list of the *uluki aneti* largely coincided with the list of *aneti*—and also with the potential successors to the headman. The *uluki aneti* solicits items in a formalized dialogue, inquiring what will be offered for exchange and what price the trader wants for it, as spectators stand about and consider the items offered (much like a crowd at an auction).

A similar phenomenon among the Trumai has been referred to as a "trading game" (Murphy and Quain, 1955, pp. 42-44), and as "ceremonial trading" among the Bakairi, where it is a form of intertribal exchange that is organized and supervised by the respective tribal headmen (Oberg, 1953, pp. 72-73). Also, in the headwater region where Brazil borders on British Guina, the Waiwai use a ritual dialogue when

2 This offer was "rescinded" when the Kuikuru killed the entire delegation of visitors, out of fear that they were still dissatisfied and would remain hostile.

one of two partners wishes to coerce the other into trading a coveted item (Fock, 1963, p. 217).

Because the headman exerts no leadership among the Kuikuru, and because no specific political functions are attributed to the *aneti*, it might be assumed that their status as political personnel has no significance. Comparative data show, however, that functional systems of primary and secondary leaders are found among other peoples in the tropical forest; for example, headmen and deputies are reported among the Carib-speaking Waiwai—who have many other cultural similarities to the Kuikuru. (The Waiwai headman announces plans for intertribal festivals to his deputy in a formal chant, like the trading dialogue mentioned above, and the deputy passes the information on to an "employe," who is a lesser deputy and who must deliver the message to the community to be invited. The invitation is again passed down through the same system of deputies, and finally to the people themselves [Fock, 1963, pp. 204-208].)

Among another Carib-speaking group—the Camaracoto in Vene-zuela—the headman customarily appointed a deputy leader whenever it became necessary (Simpson, 1940, p. 525). In addition to two district chiefs among the Caribs on the island of Dominica in the seventeenth century, there was a headman in each village, and several canoe cap-tains—one for each war canoe (Breton, 1665; Taylor, 1946, p. 182). On the Vaupes River, whenever a district chief left his territory he delegated authority over his own and other local groups to a deputy; in a public ritual chant, he said to each group in turn: "This lies within thy do-main. This must be guarded and ruled" (McGovern, 1927, p. 206). In the same general area, "when a Siusi chief leaves his village for a long period he delegates his powers to a deputy . . . in a lengthy, monotonous speech" (Fock, 1963, p. 223). Taken together, these data strongly sug-gest that the *aneti* organization is a vestige of a formerly functional system of deputy leaders among the Kuikuru.

If Kuikuru leadership was once stronger and more formal, why has it become weak and diffuse? The apparent simplification of political or-ganization among the Kuikuru can be attributed in part to demographic and social disturbances. In the past few decades, some of the Upper Xingú tribes, including the Kuikuru, have suffered acute depopulation through epidemic diseases of European origin—to which the Indians have no natural immunity. Several tribes that were mentioned by early observers have been reduced below the minimal size at which a tribe can maintain an independent existence; and remnants of these groups have amalgamated with the remaining settlements. In the Kuikuru settlement, for example, there are individuals from at least four defunct tribes, and some of the refugees from the moribund communities were families of former leaders.

Epidemics have had another consequence. Not infrequently, the headman had died before the oldest son and heir was mature, and the absence of a legitimate heir made it necessary for an adult male in another family to assume the responsibility of leadership. Genealogies of Kuikuru leaders over the past century show that some of the men who have thus assumed leadership were descendants of leaders in defunct communities. When this has occurred, their sons also have been considered heirs to the position of headman. Hence depopulation and amalgamation, together with the tradition of patrilineal succession, have distributed leadership among several families and established claims to succession in various patrilines.

Sharing the right of succession inevitably weakens the claim of a candidate and dilutes his authority. Because of uncertainty, lack of agreement, and even competition for leadership status—which result from a distribution of the right of succession among several lines—there undoubtedly is a tendency to neglect leadership training among the youths, and men who are quite unsuited find themselves recognized as headmen, but without the necessary training for providing leadership.

The lack of leadership by the titular headman is in marked contrast not only with Kuikuru concepts of leadership but also with some of the other Tropical Forest societies. Among the various Cayapo groups along the Xingú River, for example, in addition to planning and supervising cooperative planting the headman harangues his people, outlining work plans and exhorting his people to maintain cultural norms (Banner, 1961, p. 18). Banner regards the political organization of these tribes as "totalitarian, although on a small scale," and one that "dominates the Indian from the cradle to the grave. Individual freedom is subordinated to the interest of the group," and an individual or group that breaks with a strong Cayapo leader "can count on being relentlessly pursued" (p. 21).

According to Nimuendajú, the Canella headman also has considerable authority: it is his duty "to maintain customary law," and "when his decision is requested [in settling interpersonal conflicts] it is held binding" (1946, pp. 159-161). Similarly, the Sherente headman settles internal disputes, harangues at length on tribal customs, and "everyone owes him obedience." When one Sherente man repeatedly abandoned his wives, the headman ordered several other men to kill the delinquent, and this was done (Nimuendajú, 1942, pp. 13-15). Among the Apinaye, it was also the headman who ordered the death of a supposed sorcerer (Nimuendajú, 1939, p. 31). And when a Shavante headman judged five men to be dangerous to the welfare of the society (according to a personal communication from Vladimír Kozák) he had them executed. Although the principal role of the headman among the Kraho is that of peacemaker, he is said to have "absolute authority" (Schultz, 1959, p. 351).

The Bororo headman directs ceremonial and intertribal relations, sings out the daily work plans, gives orders for cooperative hunting and fishing, and leads his people in warfare (Frič and Radin, 1906; Colbacchini and Albisetti, 1942, pp. 137-138). When the Cashinahua were observed in the 1920's, the headman orated from his hammock in the morning and then visited each person in turn, giving individual orders for the day's work; and in this society permission for marriage had to be obtained from the headman (Carvalho, 1931, p. 228; Abreu, 1941, p. 119). On the Vaupes River, the headman of each settlement exerted considerable authority in cooperative work, warfare, and festivals; the more important headmen even exercised some control over more than one settlement, and periodically received the headmen of those settlements to discuss tribal policy with them (McGovern, 1927, pp. 162 ff.). Also, among the Maue and Yagua the headmen direct communal activities and exert considerable authority (Leacock, 1964; Fejos, 1943)—as the Tikuna and Mundurucu headmen once did, before Brazilian agents began selecting the leaders as intermediaries between the natives and the Brazilian agencies (Nimuendajú, 1952; Murphy, 1960).

These societies, all cited as having effective political organizations, have in common another feature of social structure: exogamous unilineal kin groups.[3] The apparent correlation of lineal kinship with effective political organization among Tropical Forest tribes of South America suggests that political authority may be functionally related to lineality. This suggestion is supported by the fact that the lineal kinship structure provides stable, well-defined channels through which authority may be exercised. In additional, lineal successors tend to derive increasingly greater prestige and political strength through veneration of former leaders in their line of descent.

Sahlins has noted this effect in Polynesia, where lineal kin groups of various types are found, and where patrilineal succession predominates (Sahlins, 1958). He also notes, in another work, that:

The position of paramount chief is reinforced through deification of his ancestors, themselves former paramount chiefs, and through connection (in belief) of this main line of descent to the important god or gods of the pantheon. The chief is then the direct descendant of the gods. By consequence, a certain degree of sacredness and power, *mana*, is felt to be an inherent aspect of chieftainship (Sahlins, 1953, p. 2 [also see Best, 1924, pp. 95, 100]).

Cognatic reckoning, on the other hand, is diffuse and affords no clear channels of authority. The kin groups overlap, and—as Eggan pointed out for the Sagada of Luzon—each individual is a member of more than one kin group and may therefore be unable to support either side in a dispute because of his conflicting loyalties.

[3] The Yagua and various groups on the Vaupes River have customarily been described as patrilineal with exogamous patrilocal settlements, which are referred to as "clans" or "sibs." That these exogamous unilocal groups are also lineal has not yet been adequately established; nevertheless, the alignment of kin is the same as in the fully lineal societies.

Personal kindreds overlap . . . since every sibling group has a different kinship circle. . . . In cases of conflict they can act effectively [only] to the extent that the opposing individuals have separate kinship circles; where they overlap, the relatives concerned will have divided loyalties and will be concerned with compromise and arbitration (Eggan, 1960, p. 30).

If effective political authority is functionally related to lineality, we should expect to find the political structure weakest among societies that lack lineality. Returning to the Kuikuru, it will be recalled that this society is cognatic and that the position of headman, although in theory it is inherited patrilineally, in fact frequently passes from one family to another. Moreover, several other societies with cognatic kinship structure in the tropical forest of South America lack strong central authority. These include the Waiwai (Fock, 1963), the Barama River Caribs (Gillin, 1936), the Camaracoto (Simpson, 1940), the Makushi (Farabee, 1924), most of the Tenetehara settlements (Wagley and Galvão, 1949), and the Tapirape (Wagley, 1940; Wagley and Galvão, 1948a). In spite of some degree of matrilocal residence among the Tenetehara, Makushi, and Waiwai, there are no lineal kin groups in these societies.[4]

The Tapirape are of special interest because their history over the past seventy years closely parallels that of the Kuikuru. Formerly, five Tapirape settlements were organized into matrilineal, matrilocal extended family houses, each with its own leader; but the population has been drastically reduced by disease, and the remnants of the five former settlements have amalgamated. Today the households are ambilocal; kinship is reckoned bilaterally; and there are several leaders in the single remaining settlement who are members of surviving leadership families. They are all called "capitões," but their authority is limited (Wagley, 1940).

The Tenetehara also are of interest because they are intermediate in type between the lineal, politically strong societies and the cognatic, politically weak societies. Matrilocal extended families predominate among the Tenetehara, but there are no unilineal kin groups, and kinship is reckoned bilaterally. Local group leadership is not now hereditary: the Indian Service appoints a leader of one of the several extended families as headman in each settlement. In most instances the appointed official has little authority over his settlement because all of the extended

---

[4] All Tapirape men belong to one or the other of two patrilineal ceremonial groups. There are also eight "feast groups," in which membership for women is inherited matrilineally and for men patrilineally. However, these groups are not exogamous and are not related either to the basic kinship structure or to the political organization (Wagley and Galvão, 1948a, p. 168). Similarly, although the Waiwai have a generic term for some close matrilineal relatives, this group is not exogamous because marriage with one's sister's daughter is permitted; nor does the group provide a channel for succession to leadership. It is interesting, however, that Fock interprets the terminological recognition of such a group as a vestige of a system of matrisibs (1963, pp. 194 ff.).

family heads also participate in policy decisions with the headman (Wagley and Galvão, 1948b, pp. 140-141). In a few instances, however, "he actually governs the village. He gives orders daily and they are carried out" (*ibid.*, 1949, p. 21).

I will not attempt further analysis of the political systems of the cognatic societies cited above, but it is relevant to note that the headmen lack authority to administer punishment and that behavior is controlled only by alternative mechanisms, such as sorcery, divination of guilt, formal public dialogues of accusation and coercion, and individual retaliation by homicide or magic "blowing."

CONCLUSION

I have suggested that the lack of effective political authority in primitive societies can be traced, at least in part, to the absence of exclusive channels through which leadership may be exercised and through which authority may be transmitted from one generation to the next. Among the Kuikuru and some other Tropical Forest societies, effective leadership is impeded by the absence of lineal groups and by the sharing of authority among several families as a result of depopulation and the amalgamation of remnant groups.

A more extensive investigation might establish a functional relation between cognatic structure and the absence of central political authority. This relation, if established, would help explain some other "anarchical" societies, such as the cognatic Igorot societies of the interior of northern Luzon, which "dispense wholly with constituted authority." In these societies "every man is every man's equal," and their political life consists of "one endless succession of insults, . . . threats, murders, feuds, and reconciliations" (Kroeber, 1943, pp. 141, 144, 160-161). There, as in the cognatic Tropical Forest tribes of South America, social existence depends on the use of alternative devices: oaths, ordeals, duels, wrestling, sorcery, and feuds.

REFERENCES

ABREU, J. CAPISTRANO DE. 1941.   Rã-txa hun-ni-ku-î. A lengua dos Caxinauas. 2d ed.; Rio de Janeiro: Sociedade Capistrano de Abreu.

BANNER, HORACE. 1961.   O Índio Kayapó em seu acampamento. Boletim do Museu Paraense Emílio Goeldi. Antropologia, No. 13.

BEST, ELSDON. 1924.   The Maori as he was. Wellington, New Zealand: R. E. Owen.

BRETON, RAYMOND. 1665.   Dictionnaire Caraïbe-Français, meslé de quantité de remarques pour l'esclaircissement de la langue. Auxerre: facsimile reprint (Leipzig, 1892).

CARVALHO, JOAÕ BRAULINO DE. 1931.   Breve noticia sobre os indigenas que habitam a fronteira do Brasil com o Peru. Boletim do Museu Nacional, 7, 225-256.

COLBACCHINI, ANTONIO, and ALBISETTI, CESAR. 1942.   Os Boróros orientais. Rio de Janeiro: Companhia Editora Nacional.

COOK, W. A. 1907.   The Bororó Indians of Matto Grosso, Brazil. Smithsonian Miscellaneous Collections, 40, 1, 48-62.

CUNHA, AYRES CÂMARA. 1954.   Entre os Indios do Xingu. São Paulo: Edições Melhoramentos.

DINIZ, EDSON SOARES. 1962.   Os Kayapó-Gorotire. Boletim do Museu Paraense Emílio Goeldi. Antropologia, No. 18.

DOLE, GERTRUDE E. 1956-58.   Ownership and exchange among the Kuikuru Indians of Matto Grosso. Revista do Museu Paulista, 10, 125-133. São Paulo.

——. 1964.   Shamanism and political control among the Kuikuru. Völkerkundliche Abhandlungen, 1, 53-62. Hannover.

EGGAN, FRED. 1960.   The Sagada Igorots of Northern Luzon. In George Peter Murdock (ed.), Social structure in Southeast Asia. Viking Fund Publications in Anthropology, 29, 24-50.

FARABEE, WILLIAM CURTIS. 1924.   The central Caribs. Philadelphia: The University Museum.

FEJOS, PAUL. 1943.   Ethnography of the Yagua. Viking Fund Publications in Anothropology, 1.

FOCK, NIELS. 1963.   Waiwai: religion and society of an Amazonian tribe. Nationalmuseets Skrifter Etnografisk Raekke 8. Copenhagen: The National Museum.

FRIČ, VOJTECH, and RADIN, PAUL. 1906.   Contributions to the study of the Bororo Indians. Journal of the Royal Anthropological Institute, 36, 382-406.

GILLIN, JOHN. 1936.   The Barama River Caribs of British Guiana. Papers of the Peabody Museum of American Archaeology and Ethnology, 14(2).

HOEBEL, E. ADAMSON. 1954.   The law of primitive man. Harvard University Press.

KROEBER, A. L. 1943.   Peoples of the Philippines. 2d ed.; New York: American Museum of Natural History.

LEACOCK, SETH. 1964.   Economic life of the Maué Indians. Boletim do Museu Paraense Emílio Goeldi. Antropologia, No. 19, p. 30.

McGOVERN, WILLIAM MONTGOMERY. 1927.   Jungle paths and Inca ruins. New York: Grosset and Dunlap.

MURPHY, ROBERT F. 1956.   Matrilocality and patrilineality in Mundurucú society. American Anthropologist, 58, 414-434.

——. 1960.   Headhunter's heritage: Social and economic change among the Mundurucú Indians. University of California Press.

MURPHY, ROBERT F., and QUAIN, BUELL. 1955.   The Trumaí Indians of central Brazil. Monographs of the American Ethnological Society, 24. Locust Valley, N.Y.: J. J. Augustin.

NIMUENDAJU, CURT. 1939. The Apinayé. Catholic University of America Anthropological Series No. 8. Catholic University of America Press.

——. 1942. The Serente. Publications of the Frederick Webb Hodge

Anniversary Publication Fund, Vol. 4. Los Angeles: The Southwest Museum.

———. 1946. The Eastern Timbira. University of California Publications in American Archaeology and Ethnology, 41.

———. 1952. The Tukuna. University of California Publications in American Archaeology and Ethnology, 45.

OBERG, KALERVO. 1953. Indian tribes of northern Matto Grosso, Brazil. Smithsonian Institution, Institute of Social Anthropology Publication No. 15.

SAHLINS, MARSHALL D. 1953. Polynesian socio-economics. Mimeographed paper for Columbia University Interdisciplinary Project.

———. 1958. Social stratification in Polynesia. University of Washington Press.

SCHULTZ, HARALD. 1959. Children of the sun and moon. National Geographic magazine, 115, 3, 340-363.

SIMPSON, GEORGE GAYLORD. 1940. Los Indios Kamarakotos. Caracas: Servicio de Publicaciones.

STEWARD, JULIAN H. (ed.). 1948. Handbook of South American Indians. Bureau of American Ethnology, Bulletin 143, vol. 3. The Tropical Forest Tribes. Washington: U.S. Government Printing Office.

TAYLOR, DOUGLAS. 1946. Kinship and social structure of the Island Carib. Southwestern Journal of Anthropology, 2, 2, 180-213.

WAGLEY, CHARLES. 1940. Effects of depopulation upon social organization as illustrated by the Tapirapé Indians. Transactions of the New York Academy of Sciences, 3, 1, 12-16.

———. n.d. Antancowí: a Scapegoat. Manuscript chapter in a forthcoming book.

WAGLEY, CHARLES and EDUARDO GALVÃO. 1948a. The Tapirape. *In* Julian H. Steward (ed.), Handbook of South American Indians, pp. 167-178.

———. 1948b. The Tenetehara. *In* Julian H. Steward (ed.), Handbook of South American Indians, pp. 137-148.

———. 1949. The Tenetehara Indians of Brazil. Columbia University Press.

BASES FOR POLITICAL COMPLIANCE IN
BENA VILLAGES

Marc J. Swartz, MICHIGAN STATE UNIVERSITY

In this paper I will examine the question of why the members of a particular society, the Bena of Tanzania,[1] follow the orders of their local political officials even when doing so does not provide them immediate or direct gratification. This question obviously involves psychological issues, but, as I hope to show, it cannot be answered on a psychological basis alone any more than it can be answered on a structural basis alone.

There is no implication here that all Bena individuals follow the orders of all local political officials at all times. During my fifteen months of residence in the Bena village of Palangawanu, I observed several individuals who virtually never did what they had officially been directed to do, and I also encountered other individuals who more or less frequently failed to obey. However, I neither observed nor heard of an occasion on which the vast majority did not comply with the orders of a duly constituted official. In fourteen weeks of survey, which involved brief visits to the other parts of Benaland,[2] all the data obtained indicate that the situation I observed in "my" village was typical, and that, throughout their territory, the Bena follow the orders given them by their headmen and village executive officers. There is occasionally some difficulty about whether an official's claim to his position is genuine,[3] but this

[1] The fieldwork on which this paper is based was made possible by grants from the National Institute of Mental Health, and the African Studies Center, of Michigan State University. I am indebted to my wife, Audrey R. Swartz, for material and spiritual assistance in carrying out the fieldwork, and also for her helpful comments and suggestions concerning this paper. I am also grateful to my colleagues, Charles C. Hughes, Victor Turner, Moreau Maxwell, and Ralph Nicholas, for their helpful suggestions on this paper.

[2] The Bena referred to here are Bantu-speaking agriculturalists who live mainly in the Southern Highlands province of the United Republic of Tanzania. When the first draft of this paper was written, I had not yet had the opportunity to study the so-called "Bena of the Rivers," described by the Culwicks (1937). This paper was first written on the basis of data gathered from the area inhabited by people the Culwicks refer to as the "Bena of the Hills." During the late summer and early fall of 1965 I was enabled to visit the "Bena of the Rivers" by a grant from the African Studies Center of Michigan State University. This brief field trip convinced me that the position taken in this paper applies to both groups, and that division of the Bena into two groups is not justified in most contexts.

[3] The rightful basis of a political official's claim to office was challenged during

issue is always settled quickly, and the accepted official's orders are followed.

It would be possible, of course, to examine the question of why some persons do not follow local officials' orders, but my focus is on the broader phenomenon of compliance. The bases for disobedience will be considered only where they will contribute to the understanding of compliance.

I have singled out obedience in areas that are not immediately or directly gratifying for most people because the orders local political officials issue are rarely concerned with activities that directly gratify a significant number. Political officials at the local level—that is, those with whom villagers have direct, face-to-face contact—engage in four kinds of activities that can be considered political. First, they collect the personal or head tax, which is forwarded to officials who represent the regional and national political structure (this tax is applicable to every adult male and to the few adult females who have a regular cash income). Second, they convene meetings to discuss public affairs, such as national and regional government announcements about agricultural techniques, national elections, the wages to be paid workers hired to help cultivate fields, and matters dealing with health and education. Third, they organize and direct public works, which consist mainly of road and bridge building and the construction and maintenance of such public buildings as community centers, dispensaries, and schools. (The fourth activity is discussed below.)

None of these three types of political activity can be considered directly gratifying. Public works elicit strong, informal complaints, as well as compliance. This is not surprising, since the building of roads and bridges, which constitutes most of this sort of work, is perceived as having little or no direct connection with the lives of those who work on them. A number of villagers suggested that I alone should work on the roads since I was the only one in the village who had a car. The paying of taxes is, if anything, even less gratifying than public works. It is here that most disobedience occurs, and, although most persons pay them, some resist vigorously and turn in their money only after they have been repeatedly warned about nonpayment. Attending meetings is less onerous for many, except for those who have to walk long distances to the meeting place, and some persons report they would have preferred to do other things instead.

Holding court hearings is the fourth political activity carried out by

---

our stay in the Bena village of Palangawanu. The results of this challenge are described in my paper, "Uhuru and Bena Village Politics," now in preparation. For the purposes of the argument to be developed here, the important point of that discussion is that, as the official in question continued in office, and held successful adjudications, he gained legitimacy.

local political officials. These hearings, or *barazas,* are held with considerable frequency, and, unlike the other political activities, they are not at all—or only in a limited way—compulsory. Only the litigants are "required" to attend a *baraza*—that is, they may absent themselves if they wish to—but at least one—and often both—will be present because he believes the *baraza* is likely to advance his interests. The *baraza's* jural status then, as well as its psychological status, is different from the other sorts of political activity.

In attempting to explain the compliant behavior of most Bena individuals, I will first discuss some psychological characteristics that are common to most of them and will try to indicate how these characteristics lead to certain types of motivations. Next, I will briefly examine the structure of Bena society in order to determine where these motivations might find expression. I will then examine the consequences for the political system of these motives, in the perspective of the Bena structure. Finally, I will discuss how motives interact with the social structure in contributing to political compliance.

SOME BENA PSYCHOLOGICAL CHARACTERISTICS

The discussion of Bena psychological characteristics is based on three types of data. Data of the first type were derived from showing pictures that depict, as ambiguously as possible, common Bena social situations. The pictures were shown to thirty Bena men and thirty Bena women, who were asked to make up stories about them, and these stories constitute a sort of projective test.[4]

The second type of data consists of six extensive life histories that were obtained from three Bena men and three Bena women. This information is supplemented by anecdotal material from a large number of other informants.

Important psychological information—the third type of data—was derived from prolonged interviews with a large number of people. The basic purpose of these interviews was often ethnographic, but extremely useful psychological information resulted from volunteered statements and responses to questions dealing with psychological issues.

[4] These data were interpreted with the collaboration of Professor Sidney J. Levy of Northwestern University, who has had extensive experience in interpreting T.A.T. protocols. The characteristics we have found in the Bena are surely not unique to them, and, quite possibly, are present and politically significant in other groups. Among some East and Central African peoples, at least, these characteristics may not only be present but may operate in much the same way as they do in Bena society, as presented here. However, psychological data are currently not available for these other groups, so that the argument presented here is necessarily limited to the Bena. V. W. Turner told me, in a personal communication, that he thinks it likely that psychological configurations I here attribute to the Bena are also common among the Ndembu, Kaonde, Lamba, and other Zambian peoples.

The complete results of the analysis of these data will be presented
in a monograph, being jointly prepared by Sidney J. Levy and myself,
but the work is sufficiently advanced so that it is possible to abstract
three psychological characteristics that are important in understanding
the motives that lead to compliance with the orders of local political officials.[5] These three characteristics are distrust, dependence, and hostility.

DISTRUST

No one who has lived among the Bena can have failed to note the
elaborate precautions they take to assure that obligations will be accepted, recognized, and fulfilled. Everything of consequence in social life
must be done in such a way that it can be proved: gifts, for example,
must be made and accepted before one or more witnesses. The reason
given for this is that if gifts were not given in this way, the recipient
might later be accused of theft. Similarly, debts must be repaid before
witnesses lest the creditor later claim that the obligation was not met.
In a more general way, there is—throughout the Bena culture—an equation of privacy and seclusion with evil, and people who keep to themselves are very likely to be thought sorcerers.

There is, of course, a number of alternative explanations for this
extremely common type of behavior, but there is good reason to believe
that in Bena society it stems from a deep distrust of other people and a
feeling that they cannot be depended upon to do what they ought to do.
This distrust manifested itself in the responses to the pictures that were
shown the sixty informants: there was a constant recurrence of doubt
about the propriety and decency of people's motives. A drawing that depicted a woman half-sitting and half-lying on a mat, and extending her
hand to a man who stood facing her, elicited four main types of response,
all of which indicated a lack of trust.

A common story-response was that the man (most often seen as her
husband, but sometimes as a kinsman) was about to harm the woman,
and she had lifted her hand to ward off his assault. Another type of
story had the woman raising her hand to greet the man (usually not the
husband but a kinsman or neighbor) while the man refused to reciprocate her attempt at a handshake. The third type of story saw the man as
having been lured into the house by the woman, who was asking him
for money or presents, which the man thought she should not have or
did not deserve.

The fourth common story given in response to the picture of the
reclining woman and the standing man was that one of the actors had
told the other something that the hearer believed was untrue. Sometimes
the woman told the man that she was sick and could not work (they
were almost always spouses in this story) and the man wondered

[5] The nature of the relationship between local (i.e., village) political officials
and those above them is discussed in an earlier publication (Swartz, 1964).

whether she really was sick or was just feigning illness to avoid work. Sometimes the man told the woman where he had been or what he was doing or what he wanted, and she was doubtful about the truth of his report.

The theme of distrust was also quite prominent in the stories elicited by the other pictures, but the above examples sufficiently illustrate this characteristic. Naturally, the very limited trust people have in one another can also be observed in everyday interactions, and one of the best examples is the frequent refusal to take a person's unsupported word for something. If A and B, neighbors of long acquaintance, are working in a field some distance from A's house, and if A asks B to go to his house and get a tool that is needed for their work, A's wife—or the children who are at the house—may not give B the tool simply because he *says* A told him to get it. They would require a written note from A or previous notification from him that he intended to send B before they would comply with B's request for the tool.

After inquiring into a considerable number of incidents of this sort, I found that the refusal to give the second party what he asked for was invariably prompted by an unwillingness to accept his unsupported statement about the purpose of getting what he wanted. This lack of trust, it must be stressed, does not occur only among nonrelatives and spouses, but also among kinsmen. The life histories abound with examples of individuals who believe they were betrayed by kinsmen and others, or were saved from betrayal only by their persistent unwillingness to trust others.

Dependence

Distrust is closely related to dependence upon others. It has been noted that one of the main techniques for dealing with other people's untrustworthiness is performance of transactions in the presence of witnesses. It was also pointed out that there is an equation between isolation and evil. These are, in a sense, only surface manifestations of a more profound dependence that is extremely common among the Bena.

Most Bena seem to feel that solitary individuals can accomplish little against the harsh environment and the basically untrustworthy people surrounding them. To gain a living and carry out such essential activities as food preparation, fuel collection, cattle herding, house building, and so on, the cooperation of relatives, neighbors, and friends is needed. But this dependence is not limited to such practical and everyday matters.

In discussing a Bena house that stands in isolation a considerable distance from the nearest neighbors, people invariably mention the misery (*tabu*) its inhabitants are thought to suffer. This misery results, in the discussants' views, from the absence of others to provide help "if it is needed." This help, they speculate, might be necessitated by sickness or attack by wild animals, but the important thing, as the informants see it, is that there be other people around: life without others nearby, and willing to help one, is dangerous and uncertain. This rather diffuse dependence on others is reflected, in the picture-stories, as a constant concern with getting others to do things for and with the central character.

Gaining the help of others is sought through elaborate politeness, amiability, and ingratiating behavior, but the fear that these techniques will not suffice is always present. The idea that one's needs and wishes can be met only through the help of others is as strong as the idea that others' needs and wishes may be in conflict with one's own, and that others may be unwilling to cooperate because they will be fully engaged in the pursuit of their own ends.

Examples of this fear of unmet dependency needs occur throughout the picture-stories. One of the pictures shows a man with the objects that Bena men customarily carry when they travel, and a woman and her children seated in front of a house, possibly watching the man as he passes. The stories told in response to this scene almost always had the man as the woman's husband, leaving on a trip. He was often said to be going to work at some distant place (something Bena men, in fact, very frequently do) from which he would not return for some time. The welfare of the woman during his absence was often in doubt, since he might or might not send her money for the children's clothes and school fees, and his relatives might or might not see to it that the woman was properly provided for. The woman's behavior during the husband's absence was also left in doubt, since she might or might not "remember" him, or see that the children's school fees were paid with the money she might receive.

The underlying point of these stories seems to be not only that the trust the spouses have for each other (to whatever extent they have it) will be called into doubt, but that each is dependent upon the other for important gratifications, even though they are separated, and that this dependence may not be met.

In everyday life in a Bena village, dependence manifests itself in constant requests to friends, neighbors, relatives, and sometimes even strangers, for assistance with work and for food. One of the most frequently recorded characteristics of a "good man" is that he shares things with his neighbors and others, and does not refuse the requests of others.

Dependence—and fear that one will suffer deprivation because of others' untrustworthiness, and also because others try to get all the succor they can—is closely connected to a third psychological characteristic commonly found among the Bena.

HOSTILITY

There is no evidence to indicate that hostile feelings are unusually strong (that is, in cross-cultural perspective) among the Bena, but there is considerable evidence that suggests that the need to control hostility is very great. Prolonged acquaintance with the Bena leaves one with the impression of a gentle and polite people, quick to laughter and slow to anger; but there are insistent indications that this benign and pleasant behavior is achieved at the cost of active effort and constant guardedness.

One indication of the lengths to which the Bena go to prevent the expression of even the mildest hostility is the extreme circumspection with which they speak to and about one another. References to the physical and mental characteristics of another person are most uncommon. For example, Bena believe that offense would be taken if a short man found out that he had been described as short. Also, one rarely hears a Bena say that he is angry: if someone has done something quite grievous to him, he will say he is "sorry" about what the person did, and will deny that he is angry.

This extreme control of hostile expression does not preclude occasional aggression. People are thought to be particularly likely to behave hostilely when they are drinking, and I have seen drunks fight and molest others. I have also seen evidence of privately expressed hostility in the bruised and swollen faces of spouses, and I witnessed a drunk being beaten by four or five sober men who were "teaching him not to be a troublemaker."

Although drinking is not a part of all the instances of overt hostility that I recorded (some fighting between spouses takes place when both are sober), it figures in most of them. Levy's "blind analysis" of the picture-stories [6] captures the indirect and hobbled nature of Bena hostility.

Usually the kinds of aggressive outlets do not seem very forthright or satisfyingly expressive (or require drunkenness as a release and excuse) in comparison to the strong and intense feelings that are apparently involved. They are mainly such things as teasing, being stubborn, quarrelling, grabbing hair, pulling lips—indignities rather than injuries. There is a holding back that seems to reflect an attitude of restraint lest consequences too grave attend the expression of aggression that is really destructive. (Swartz and Levy, n.d.)

The carefully controlled hostility that is present in most Bena finds one of its main expressions in sorcery. We will not go into this complex and involved subject here, but it is worth nothing that sorcery provides an opportunity to express aggression covertly and indirectly. If the sorcery works well, and is not countered in time, not only will the user harm or destroy the object of his hatred and envy (the two reasons always given for sorcery in this society), he will have concealed the fact that he is the source of hostility. Just as being drunk lessens the responsibility for hostile behavior, both on the part of the drunk and on the part of those who chastise him, sorcery serves in the same way by concealing the perpetrator's identity.

[6] Levy's initial interpretation of the picture-stories was made entirely on the basis of the information contained in the stories. This was the first step in his analysis and it is the analysis utilized in this paper. The results of his study are in preparation.

One of the basic factors behind the suppression of hostile acts, and behind the attempt to avoid the consequences of these acts when they are allowed expression, is the fear of retaliation. An indication of the strength of this fear can be seen in a discussion I had with an old man about suicide.

M.S.: I heard some time ago that if one man kills another, the killer sometimes hangs himself. Is that true? What would the killer do that for?

INFORMANT: It is true, and he is afraid of the government.

M.S.: Why?

INFORMANT: He is afraid of both the European government and of the native government before the Europeans came. If a man killed another one, the headman would tie him with rope. The rope would be very tight and it would hurt very much. They would put water on the rope so that it tightened and it was very painful. Because of that pain people were afraid of being tied.

M.S.: So it was a matter of being tied?

INFORMANT: No, they were also afraid of being killed by the *baraza* or being put in prison for as long as two or three years. If you kill your enemy, then you kill yourself, the whole matter is ended and there's no further affair. [*shauri*].

The fear of retaliation is by no means limited to the government. A very strong drive exists to end quarrels between individuals and to forget them. This drive is not limited to the quarrelers, but is shared by those around them. The importance of forgiving a person is as great as his repenting his wrong, and an unforgiving individual will be held in less esteem than a confessed wrongdoer. The explicit reason for this is that if forgiveness is not forthcoming, the trouble will never end and more harm will result. Put in the terms of this discussion, a failure to forswear retaliation is as great (or greater) a cause for concern as the thing that precipitated the desire for retaliation. People who will not forgive and forget show themselves to be threats not only to those with whom they are currently at odds but to everyone else, for it is impossible to know when they might take offense and they have demonstrated that they will not give up their anger.

SOME COMMON BENA MOTIVES

It will be apparent by now that the psychological characteristics discussed are closely related to each other in a number of important ways. Most significantly for the understanding of conformity to local officials' orders, these characteristics converge in the goals they present to many Bena individuals.

The examination of "distrust" and "dependence" shows that a large number of specific goals found in members of this society can be summarized under the general rubric of a search for security. The Bena want other people to help them and to give them succor, both in specific and in diffuse ways, because they feel that they cannot cope with the physical and human environment by themselves. That is, their specific attempts to get others to help them can be looked upon as attempts to enhance and continue their well-being. These attempts, however, are complicated by the perception that other people cannot be trusted; so it is necessary not only to gain the assistance and support of others but to do so in such a way that distrust of these others can be lessened sufficiently to allow a reasonably secure acceptance of their aid. Thus the general goal of getting help and succor is intimately intermeshed with the goal of being secure in relations with others. Needless to say, the two types of goals are distinct and can occur relatively independently. Goals that stem from distrust are quite often present in situations where dependency is not present, or important, but the dependency goals cannot be fully met without the security that comes from gaining the ends that stem from distrust.

Parts of the discussion dealing with hostility showed that Bena fear the aggression of others, and this is perceived as especially dangerous in retaliation for any expression of aggression on their own part. The goals here are concerned with avoiding this retaliatory hostility, or, put another way, with making oneself secure from the harm that others may perpetrate. Obviously, these goals are deeply intermeshed with the general distrust of others, and the avoidance of others' hostility is a part, albeit indistinguishable, of the goals that concern gaining security from others' perfidy.

If we take "motive" to mean the patterned psychological complex that includes a goal, as well as the particular course of action employed in gaining that goal, the motives that arise from the goals we have just discussed fall into a limited range of available sorts of behavior for the Bena. The types of roles that can be played in this society for gaining the aid and succor of others are not very numerous, as is true of roles that will reduce distrust to manageable proportions and minimize the risks of retaliatory hostility.

One of the commonest sorts of behavior for the Bena, as we have noted, is maintaining a mild, amiable, and ingratiating demeanor. This type of behavior can be motivated by any or all of the goals examined here. The winning smile and pleasant word gain assistance and lessen the chances that others will betray one. This bearing also decreases the likelihood that others will perceive one's behavior as hostile and visit retaliation upon him.

Winning ways, however, have their limitations, and, although they are much employed, their usefulness is also limited; and in some situations they are not appropriate. Part of the reason for the less-than-

universal effectiveness of this sort of behavior is that, unaided, it does
not guarantee the reliability of others, nor does it always preclude the
possibility of conflict with the dangers of hostility that it brings. In face-
to-face situations, ingratiation can work wonders; but the affairs of any
particular Bena are not limited to the results of his direct confrontations.
What will happen to one's ally when he is beyond the range of our
smile, and listening to the counsel of our enemies, is not a problem that
can be dealt with by further pleasantness alone. In other words, this
mode of behavior can do little to achieve long-term aid and succor of a
dependable type, and it cannot be depended upon to provide more than
situational assurance of others' trustworthiness and lack of hostility.

Another course of behavior motivated by the goals concerning us
here is limiting important interactions to those with whom there is community of interest. Such people will help one another because in doing so
they help themselves, and can be trusted; for by betraying another they
will also betray themselves. This type of behavior is important in Bena
society, as it is everywhere, but it is restricted in its efficacy by restrictions in commonality of interest. To examine this type of behavior, as
well as the final course of actions to be considered, it is necessary to
discuss the structure of this society.

SOME ASPECTS OF BENA SOCIAL STRUCTURE

Bena kinship is patrilineal and patrilocal, and, although there are no
lineages, there are exogamous clans. These clans are not localized on the
village level but are sufficiently restricted in their dispersion so that most
of the male members of the clan will be found in a dozen or so adjacent
villages, and a few clans will account for all the men in these villages.
The corporate character of these clans is not extensive, and aside from
marriage regulation they serve no function.

A much more important kin group is made up of a man and his sons,
together with their children. This group usually lives close together and
has a great deal of commonality of interest. Some Bena say that the
closest tie in their society is between a father and his son. The tie between brothers, and to a lesser extent between sisters, and between
brothers and sisters, is also said to be highly important. Within this
nuclear family group it would seem that the goals of getting aid and
succor, avoiding distrust, and escaping hostility would be most easily
achieved in a lasting and pervasive way. To a considerable extent this
is so, and most attainments of these ends occur within this group.

However, identity of interest between a father and son is by no
means complete. Although a father and son are said to be able to take
each other's food and pick each other's crops without asking permission,
this freedom does not apply to such possessions as money, clothing, and

cattle, which are conceived as the private possessions of the owner. Should the son (or father) want any of them, he has to ask his father (or son) that he be given them. The norm is that the request be honored, and in practice it usually, but not always, is. The Bena are very much oriented to private ownership, and although they are very often willing to provide economic help to their child or parent, there is no guarantee that they will do so. Further, a man usually has several sons, and, if the sons' community of interest is not complete, that of the sons and the father cannot be complete.

The community of interest of brothers is far more limited than that of fathers and sons. When the brothers marry, their first responsibility (both normatively and in most behavior) is to their own children and wives, and this necessarily decreases the fraternal tie. Brothers are supposed to help one another economically, and they often do, but there is nothing to assure a man that his brother will help him in a given situation.

Outside the economic sphere, fathers and sons often seem to trust one another, but this trust is not without the ever-present possibility of violation. Sorcery between fathers and sons is not unknown (I recorded two cases of this during my fieldwork). It is said to result from envy due to economic or prestige differentials, or from resentment over a lack of respect. This means that despite the closeness of the father-son tie, even if it were possible to limit interaction to that relationship, such a limitation would not alone be a dependable method of achieving the goals that are at issue in this discussion.

This is even more true of the relationship among brothers. Not only is their economic aid more problematic, but this relationship, among all those in Bena society, is thought of as the one most likely to involve withcraft. The limitation of trust in the father is less than the limitation of trust in the brother, and a brother's hostility is far more likely to occur and to find dangerous expression.

The only other relationship in Bena society that involves considerable community of interest is that between spouses. Spouses, in fact, share more common economic interest than any other relationship, and many of the restrictions on the mutual aid between father and son and between brothers do not obtain here. Still, each spouse retains his or her private property; for example, the husband may not kill his wife's children without her permission. Most types of sorcery are said not to be used between spouses, although a wife can use magic to make her husband impotent with all other women. Much of the restriction on common interest in the marital relationship is connected, as would be expected, with the spouses' interest in other members of the opposite sex. A man's taking additional wives is a frequent source of conflict, and adultery by the wife is an additional basis for disjunction.

In all of the common-interest relationships, then, there are important restrictions on the commonality, reasons for less-than-complete trust, and imperfect protection from hostility. Divergences of interests and the optional character of some kinds of mutual aid and support provide the basis for conflict, and this conflict, in turn, raises the possibility of hostile expression. Thus, even in the relationships where there is the greatest community of interest, there is no assurance of consistently or reliably attaining the goals that concern us here.

Since the goals are not always attained through either of the two means we have discussed, it is necessary to see what other behaviors are motivated by the striving for these ends. A third type of behavior in this area is that which seeks "objective" control of the relationships entered into. This control, which also is desired as a means for gaining performance of perceived obligations, redress for betrayal, and a cessation of hostility, stems from the same motives as the other types of behavior we have considered.

ADJUDICATION AS OBJECTIVE CONTROL

Given the distrust and fear of others' hostility, some complications arise with respect to getting acceptable external control. However, this control is desirable for a number of reasons relating to the goals of concern here. If reliable outside assistance were available, it would be possible to satisfy some dependency through the enforcement of obligations entered into with others. Some of these obligations result from the nature of interpersonal relationships of the sort discussed above, but, as we saw, there can be no sure reliance on the fulfillment of these obligations from commonality of interest alone. To make these relationships (father-son, brother-brother, husband-wife) more valuable in meeting the goals of dependency, an external and unbiased agency that could ensure that the parties to the relationships did as they "ought to do" would be extremely valuable. To put this more directly in the framework of the argument being advanced, people are motivated to seek outside assistance in their relations with important kinsmen and spouses by their inability to gain their ends in these relations on the basis of their commonality of interest alone. Furthermore, the consequences of lack of trust are mitigated by external control in that this control provides an alternative source of confidence that expectations will be met.

Nor are motivations for seeking outside control limited to the dependency goals and the lack of trust. The fear of hostility from others can also be reduced by external control. Given an agency that can be relied upon to control the behavior of those with whom one interacts, one's hope of escaping the dire effects of their hostility is promoted. We have seen that many Bena feel that others may interpret their behavior as aggressive and may visit a terrible reprisal upon them for this aggression. External control does not remove the belief that this is likely to happen, but it minimizes the fear of this retaliation by providing a source of control over it. To the extent that external control can bring an aggrieved party to forswear his grievance, it facilitates interaction by stopping the fears of retaliation and counterretaliation within the relationship.

Clearly, what this external control involves is adjudication of the relationships in which there has been a failure to meet the participants' expectations and/or in which the fear of hostility has become intolerable. There is considerable motivation to seek such adjudication, but there are also barriers to its acceptance. The lack of trust, which is an important factor in necessitating adjudication, also militates against its acceptance. If adjudication is to be effective, there must be some confidence in its objectivity; both sides to a controversy must believe that decisions will be based on an assessment of the facts of the matter and not on the adjudicating agency's self-interested bias. But having adjudication carried out by an authority whose impartiality can be trusted, is asking a great deal of people whose lack of trust in others is one of the main bases for the need to have an adjudicating agency. Another requirement of effective adjudication is that there be some basis for believing its resolutions will be effective: that obligations established as genuine will be met, and that hostile activity will be stopped.

In an earlier paper I indicated that adjudication in Bena society proceeds through a number of steps, but almost always depends upon the agreement of both disputants to the decisions reached (1964). If two men quarrel about unmet obligations, infringement of rights, or acts of hostility, they would—ideally—attempt to agree upon both the facts of the matter and the proper course of action to resolve the difficulty. If they can reach such an agreement, and if each is satisfied that the other is behaving in accord with that agreement, no further action is necessary. However, if they cannot agree, or if one or both feel the agreement is not being faithfully discharged, the matter is taken to a senior relative, if the disputants are kinsmen, otherwise to a respected elder in the vicinity. The task of the third party is to get the disputants to agree on the facts of the issue, and, if he is successful in doing this, to bring them to accept a course of action that will reestablish or repair their relations with one another. Should this step fail, the dispute is taken to the lowest-level political official, the headman, who, with respected senior men from his section of the village, will try to perform the role in which the senior relative or the respected elder had failed. If this attempt at adjudication does not succeed, the dispute is sent to the chief political official of the village, the village executive officer, who, in conjunction with the most prestigious men in the village, will try to bring the disputants to agree on what actually happened in the matter at issue and to accept a course of behavior that will end the dispute. Theoretically, the dispute may be taken to political officials above the village level, but this is virtually never done (only three instances of this occurred during my fieldwork).

Many disputes do not go through all the steps normatively indicated, and are first heard by the headman or the village executive officer and their respective colleagues. Where a dispute will be taken is entirely up to the participants. Obviously, the more serious the matter, in either the practical or the emotional sense, the higher the adjudicating agency is likely to be. It is important to note that when the adjudication attempt of the village executive officer and his elders fails, recourse is usually to another hearing by the same agency. The expectation expressed by disputants is that if their controversy can be settled at all, it will be settled with the assistance of this body because there is nothing a higher authority could do that cannot be done on the village level.

Having seen the motivation to participate in adjudication, and having seen the adjudicating agencies available in this society, we must now examine the basis for belief in the objectivity of these agencies and in their ability to gain compliance with their decisions.

In fact, the reasons for belief in the adjudicating agencies' objectivity and for confidence in their decisions are closely related, but before we discuss these reasons we must briefly examine the adjudication procedure. The procedure is the same at all levels (above that of individual, unaided settlement) except that the formality of the proceedings and the prestige of the adjudicators increases as the hierarchy of adjudication is ascended.

Each disputant, without interruption, presents his version of what occurred. After both have been heard, those trying to help end the dispute closely question each disputant on the account he has given. The attempt is to reach agreement on a single story by eliminating conflicting elements in the two accounts. Attention is focused exclusively on the external facts of the matter, and questions of motive and past history are scrupulously avoided.

Until both participants agree on what occurred, no resolution is suggested. Once such agreement is reached, however, the various participants in the adjudication begin to suggest courses of action to repair whatever caused the dispute and to return relations between the disputants to a conflict-free basis. The settlement is not achieved until both parties accept one of the proposed solutions. Once the agreement on facts is achieved, there is usually little difficulty in gaining agreement on a solution, since the solution is the obvious one in terms of what has been agreed upon as having happened.

For example, in a case between co-wives that was brought before the village executive officer and his elders, one woman claimed that the other had been stealing her chickens, but the accused denied any complicity in the disappearance of the fowl. The accused agreed that her co-wife's chickens were disappearing, but said that a cat was taking them. The village executive officer and his elders began to take the accused through an account of the food she had eaten during the period of the chickens' disappearance, and asked her what she was feeding her adult son, who was visiting while on leave from his job on a distant sisal plantation. They scorned her claim of having provided the son with nothing better than the usual diet of cornmeal, greens, and beans, and finally brought her to admit that she had given him meat. A few questions indicating the impossibility of her getting meat either through gift or purchase left her with no other recourse than to admit she had taken the chickens.

The resolution then became, at least in part, obvious. First, she was to replace the chickens she had taken, and she readily agreed to this. The accuser, however, maintained that there should be punishment as well as restitution, but the confessed thief did not agree to this. The hearing of this case was terminated at this point because the disputants could not agree, but a week later the case was heard again. This time, after some suggestion of turning the thief over to the police, the former agreed it would be proper for her to pay a small fine, in addition to replacing the chickens. The accuser then said that she should have something in addition to the birds she had lost, but the court asked her whether she wouldn't be as well off after restitution as she had been before. She agreed that she would be, and tacitly accepted the omission of punitive payment.

It will be noted in this case (as in all cases) that the threat of force was not the direct basis for acceptance of the settlement. The settlement was the result of a mutual acceptance of facts and the participants' agreement to the obvious course of action that followed from these facts. The village executive officer and his elders functioned as an agency to bring mutual agreement to the facts and to the settlement necessitated by the first agreement. They did not impose their own version of what had happened, nor did they impose a settlement of their own devising; they served as an agency for the emergence of objective truth, not as the creators of a solution. The success of the agency comes first from its ability to bring agreement on what happened—and when it cannot bring such agreement it cannot succeed. Having gained agreement on the facts of the case, the adjudicators must then bring the litigants to agree on a course of action. This sometimes involves the threat of force, as in the above example, although usually it does not. In all cases, however, the bases for the proposed action are the facts that have been agreed upon, so that the crucial step is bringing about this agreement— and bringing it about gives the members of the *baraza* the status of an impartial body.

This status for the adjudicating agency removes a good deal of the difficulty arising from the widespread lack of trust. There is little need for the disputants to trust the adjudicators since all have an equal chance to present their version of what happened and to answer questions about that version. Moreover, until they themselves agree to the version proposed by the adjudicators, no settlement can be reached. Similarly, settlements must be agreed upon by the disputants.

This leads, then, to a final question, before we examine how the adjudication process provides important bases for compliance with the orders of political officials: How are disputants brought to accept the common accounts of what happened and the settlements deriving from these accounts? Part of the basis for this acceptance is the ideal progression of disputes up a hierarchy of adjudicators. As ascension of the hierarchy progresses, the prestige of adjudicators increases, and with this increase comes an intensification of social pressure on the disputants.

The success of adjudication depends upon those involved answering questions, and answering them more or less truthfully and fully. Evasion is difficult in proportion to the prestige of those asking the questions and to the number of witnesses to the questioning. Part of the amiability and politeness we noted earlier consists of not being disrespectful to others and not scorning their efforts. Thus, although it is "bad form" to refuse to answer anyone's questions, or to answer them evasively or untruthfully, this is more serious as the number and importance of the people doing the questioning increases. This "bad form," it should be noted, is not merely a matter of simple convention but is motivated by the same goals that bring about the pleasant and ingratiating demeanor that is characteristic of the Bena. As disputes ascend the hierarchy of adjudication, the motivation for cooperative questioning and answering increases both because the people doing the adjucating are more important and because the people attending as witnesses and participants are more numerous.

Thus, in a rather circular fashion, the disputants' motives for agreeable behavior, although not directly effective in gaining all the goals the motives involve, are harnessed in remedying situations that arise out of failure to attain these goals. These motives are particularly active at the political adjudications through the number and importance of the people who might be offended by uncooperativeness and generally disagreeable actions.

The adjudications, then, are successful because they involve a minimal amount of trust; and the disputants are motivated not only to participate in them but to participate in such a way as to increase the likelihood of their success. Successful adjudication does not remove distrust and conflict from within the community, nor does it obviate the fear of others' hostility. However, the adjudication removes these desiderata from being the individual's unaided concern and brings them out where they can be subjected to broad social pressures. When they succeed, the adjudications do not ensure complete harmony, cooperation, or freedom from fear, but they provide a social mechanism that ameliorates the failure of attainment of these goals on a strictly interpersonal basis.

ADJUDICATION AND THE BASES FOR POLITICAL COMPLIANCE

The important personal functions served by the adjudication process in Bena society will be clear by now, and the social functions of allowing interpersonal relationships to proceed despite ruptures consequent upon the failure of individuals to achieve their goals will be readily apparent. The connection between this aspect of adjudication and political compliance remains to be established.

Adjudication provides two very different bases for compliance with the orders of political officials, even when these orders do not involve activities that are directly gratifying. In the first place, adjudication provides political officials with important support through giving them an opportunity to demonstrate their legitimacy. Secondly, adjudication provides a mechanism for dealing directly with failures to comply with political orders in that the officials bring disobedient individuals before the adjudicating agency, where the case is dealt with in the same manner as any other.

If we understand legitimacy to mean behavior in fulfillment of expectations, the roles of the headman and the village executive officer as leaders in the adjudication process give them an opportunity to demonstrate their legitimacy in a vital area of life.

The village political officials do not necessarily participate more actively in adjudication than do the respected men who collaborate with them. That this should be so is necessitated by the nature of adjudication. There can be no single potent figure in any practical sense because the decisions reached are consensual rather than authoritative. However, the adjudication sessions, the *barazas*, are looked upon as being held under the aegis of the official involved and are spoken of as "the headman's *baraza*" or "the village executive officer's *baraza*." People say that they are going to take their dispute to the headman or to the village executive officer for settlement although, in fact, the officials usually do no more in questioning witnesses and proposing resolutions than any of the other important men present.

Partly, the political official's role in adjudication is in acting as the symbol of the process. This, however, is not all. The presence of a large number of people, and of important people, depends upon the ability of the political official to attract them through the respect in which he is held. It has been shown that the success of adjudication depends upon a large number of people and important individuals being present. When the number is small and the prestige of those present is not considerable, the likelihood of a successful settlement is not materially greater than at the subpolitical level. The political *barazas* are depended upon for the settlement of difficult and important cases, of the sort that cannot easily be settled through more informal adjudication. Therefore, the political official's ability to attract the necessary number and kind of spectators and collaborators determines his ability to succeed in attaining a settlement.

By achieving settlements, the political official meets not only the expectation of the disputants that their difficulties will be resolved, he also reinforces the general expectation that he can bring about the resolution of significant disputes. Thus successful *barazas* contribute directly to the legitimacy of the official not only in the eyes of those actually involved in disputes but also in the eyes of those who feel they might become involved in disputes. As we have seen from the analysis of Bena psychological characteristics, this last group is nearly all-inclusive.

Finally, by being able to assemble the number and type of individuals conducive to effective adjudication, the political official demonstrates the validity of his status to anyone who might be inclined to question it. Participating as an adjudicator in a political *baraza* is referred to as "helping the headman" or "helping the village executive officer." An official who can thus publicly command the help of the most important men in the community, and of a sizable number of other people, cannot be easily dismissed.

A political official with a record of successful dispute settlements is in a very strong position for gaining compliance with his orders. He has established himself as a central figure in a process essential to the consistent attainment of goals that are vital to the people whose compliance he seeks. There is, of course, no assurance that his contributions to the community welfare will result in his achieving his own ends, but his role at the center of dispute settlements surely strengthens his position. Having done, and being ready to do, what his "constituents" need of him, he makes it very difficult for them not to reciprocate by doing what he wants of them. They perceive the importance of his contribution to their welfare as very great—great enough that he can ask them to do what they are not directly motivated to do. Put another way, peoples' motivations to settle their differences and gain their ends through adjudication establish a debt that an adjudicator (more accurately, the symbol and central figure in adjudication) can draw upon for fulfillment of the goals he desires even when this desire is not shared by those whose cooperation he needs.

The second way in which adjudication serves to promote compliance with the orders of political officials is more direct. When someone fails to obey an official's orders, the official, as an individual, accuses the disobedient person before a *baraza*. This case is adjudicated in precisely the same way as any other dispute, and the disobedient person, if he loses, is brought to agree that he disobeyed and to accept a settlement, which usually involves both his agreement not to disobey in the future and a restitutive action—such as participating in public works that are not required of the general population. No force is used in bringing disobedient people to the *baraza* for the adjudication of disputes with political officials, nor is force used in carrying out the settlement agreed upon, but the same motivations that bring about participation in other types of adjudication, and that bring compliance with the settlements, are also operative here.

DISCUSSION

Bases for compliance with the orders of political officials in Bena society have been shown to be the result of a rather complex interaction of goals that are the result of common Bena psychological characteristics and the structure of Bena society. The desire for aid and succor from others, the wish to avoid the consequences of other persons' faithlessness, and the fear of others' hostility were shown to lead to polite and agreeable behavior. This behavior, however, was shown to be insufficient for attaining all the goals sought through it.

These goals are particularly important in the key relationships of kinship and marriage, where, however, an incomplete community of interests makes their consistent attainment unlikely. Failure to attain these goals leads to disputes whose seriousness is exacerbated by the fear of hostility, so that disputants are strongly motivated to seek adjudication not only to restore relationships to an acceptable degree of mutual aid and emotional support but also to avoid what are perceived as the dire consequences of continued hostility. Because of the distrust that is central to the Bena character, this adjudication proceeds best through a mechanism that depends upon objective facts rather than upon authoritative pronouncements.

Political officials are the key figures in assembling a company of adjudicators who are able to elicit these facts, and through this role the officials gain "political capital" by having performed a key function —both for the individuals involved in disputes and for the community as a whole. This capital is drawn upon by the officials when they issue orders for activities that are not directly gratifying to those who must carry them out. If the "indebtedness" from these functions is not great enough to bring about compliance with the orders, the adjudicating process itself can be used to bring the disobedient individuals to compliance.[7]

The bases for support, then, derive from an interaction of the psychological characteristics of those who must comply and from the nature of their relationships with those around them. Distrust and hostility are crucial elements in the support for political compliance, as are dependency and the incompleteness of community of interests among even the most closely attached kinsmen and spouses. The adjudication process functions as a focusing element for these diverse supports, and bestows legitimacy upon the political official who represents and organizes this process.

REFERENCES

CULWICK, A. T. and G. M. 1935.   Ubena of the rivers. London: Charles Allen and Unwin.
GLUCKMAN, MAX. 1955.   Judicial process among the Barotse of Northern Rhodesia. Manchester University Press.
————. 1965.   Politics, law and ritual in tribal society. Chicago: Aldine.
SWARTZ, MARC J. 1964.   Continuities in the Bena system. Southwestern Journal of Anthropology, 20, 241-253.
SWARTZ, MARC J., and LEVY, SIDNEY J. n.d.   Bena life and values. In preparation.

[7] The role of the adjudicating process as a support for the authority of political officials is also important in other societies, although the manner in which adjudication provides support for officials—and which sort of officials receives the benefit of this support—may be somewhat different from the Bena case.

Among the Lozi, for example, cases among close kin are not subject to public adjudication (Gluckman, 1965, p. 44). Although virtually all important interpersonal disputes are settled through an adjudicative process that is somewhat similar to the one described in this paper (see Gluckman, 1955), it appears that the superiority of the adjudicating agency over local political officials, and the rules of land tenure, put Lozi adjudication in a different role—vis-à-vis political support—than the one I have tried to show is characteristic of Bena adjudication.

Part II

AUTHORITY AND AUTHORITY CODES

All politics involves the differential possession of power by the members of the group in question. In most societies this differential is regularized by an association that has more than usual political power in particular statuses. Sometimes these statuses are largely and explicitly political in their scope, as in the examples of a national president, a West African king, a Plains Indian warchief, and so on. In other cases the statuses may not be explicitly political and may involve other, nonpolitical functions as highly important components of their roles. Thus the status in question may be like that of "big man"—in Salisbury's description of the Tolai of New Britain—where the occupants of the statuses in question have more control over public goals than do individuals who do not occupy such positions, even though the members of the society may not describe the situation in this way. The Tolai have a highly egalitarian ethic, and all men are formally considered equal, but, despite this ethic, the "big men" have a greater voice in public affairs than do those who are not occupants of this position.

If rights to acquire and use power are regularly assigned to particular statuses, we speak of these rights as "authority" and the system of assignment as the "authority code." In this section the papers concern themselves with the authority codes of a number of different societies. Several papers concern the supports accorded the code in the societies being considered, and one of the papers deals with a struggle of two factions in a group over the establishment of an authority code after a period during which power was not distributed according to any standardized assignment to particular statuses.

In the Tolai case the authority code is supported by what Salisbury calls a "Horatio Alger" ideology. Political offices are most often occupied by "big men," who are "big" because of their success in the accumulation of shell money. Through their participation in clan rituals and funerals, they are able to acquire a much higher return on their invested capital than are the ordinary members of the group, and thus they become wealthy. Because they are wealthy, they command the support and respect of others, and, although all men are considered

109

equal in this society, the ability the "big men" have shown as financial manipulators justifies their positions of power. The authority code among the Tolai assigns power to the rich and the "Horatio Alger" ideology supports this assignment.

Cohen's discussion of the Kanuri shows another aspect of support for authority and authority codes. In this Muslim society, religion provides support for the differential assignment of political power in that Islam teaches a respect for hierarchy. This acceptance of hierarchy, however, does not explain why particular men should be elevated while others have only lowly positions. This Kanuri issue is settled (as in some of the West African societies) by a belief in a quality, *arziyi*, that is found in each man's nature. If a man has a great deal of this quality, he will become politically and financially powerful, lucky at cards, and so on. His success and his possession of power is made inevitable by the amount of *arziyi* he possesses—which, in turn, is manifested by his success. Cohen refers to the beliefs that center around *arziyi* as a "self-validating theory," and, in the terms we are using here, it is clear that this theory—together with the Islamic acceptance of and reverence for hierarchy—provides powerful support not only for the authority code but also for those individuals who occupy the positions that are given power under the code.

Middleton's essay on the Lugbara raises a number of interesting issues, but the central issue concerns the authority assigned to elders among groups of more or less closely related kin. The rules for succession to the position of "elder" are ambiguous; and rivals for the position, or, more accurately, for the authority associated with the position, settle their conflict by appealing to the dead ancestors of the group. These dead forebears are considered the source of all legitimate power among their living kin, and when two men are in conflict for possession of the authority in their group, they show which is the rightful possessor by bringing sickness to the other contestant. The winner in this appeal is viewed as having invoked the dead in the interests of the group's smooth functioning, and this is thought to be a meritorious act.

So far, it would appear that the ancestors serve as a crucial source of support for the authority of the elder, but in fact—although this is so—the situation is more complex. The complexity comes from the fact that invoking the dead and witchcraft differ from each other only in the motivation of the practitioner. Witchcraft is motivated by envy while virtuous invocation springs from concern about the group's welfare. In practice this means that when an elder's motives are brought under suspicion by a rival, the elder's successful invocation of the dead will not necessarily allay the suspicion, and his dependents may become less willing to accept his authority. This, in turn, may lead the elder to invoke the dead more and more, thus further weakening his position by making him appear to be acting on the basis of unworthy motives.

The invocation, then, generally serves as a support for authority among the Lugbara, but, because of its similarity to witchcraft, it also serves as a means for attacking the possession of authority.

Lambert's paper presents yet another aspect of support for authority and the authority code. In Tolai society we have seen that economic activity plays a key role in authority through providing both the standard for entry into powerful statuses and through justifying the occupancy of these statuses by particular individuals. Economic activity is also important to authority in the northern Gilbertese society described by Lambert, but here the importance of this activity is more symbolic than instrumental. In some Oceanic societies the chief's right to collect tribute is a cornerstone of his power and a key element in the system of social stratification, but Lambert shows that among the Gilbertese he studied this is not the case. The tribute brought to the northern Gilbertese chief is a symbolic statement of his special relationship with his people, as well as a statement of the political status of the parts that constitute the society, since only groups that are independent can make presentations. The tribute, as Lambert points out, confirms rather than underlies the authority that is attached to the chief's status.

Miller's paper deals with a situation rather different from that found in the other works in this section. Among the Deer Lake Chippewa he studied, a formal authority code had been in existence for several decades but had never really functioned in the formal manner. This was so partly because of the advanced age and the lack of experience of the chiefs in whom the code vested authority, and partly because of the absence of a tradition of centralized political control in the society, but at least as contributive as either of these reasons was the presence of an educated and able man in a fairly minor position in the group's government. Through his abilities and experience, and especially through his charismatic qualities, he had assumed and retained rights to acquire and use power that went far beyond the formal limits of his status, as defined by the code. When this man died, the factional dispute that arose over the assignment of power was settled only after the political field had been expanded, which involved taking the dispute before agencies and individuals outside the Indian community.

Here then, we have a case in which an authority code had relatively little support in the group's culture and where circumstances (the chiefs' inexperience and the minor official's knowledge and personal qualities) combined to undermine that code. The minor official had no authority in his exercise of power because these rights had not been assigned to his status: they had been assumed by an individual, without regard to the limited rights to the position he held. After his death, factions in the group tried to regularize the assignment of power, each to its own advantage, through the establishment of a new authority code.

The Chippewa case should not be viewed as aberrant. While Miller did his fieldwork during a period of flux; the other papers deal primarily with societies in which the supports for the assignment of power to statuses overcame the opposing forces and the systems were at rest in this regard. However, authority and the codes by which it is assigned are no more guaranteed of stability and permanence than are other aspects of political activity.

POLITICS AND SHELL-MONEY FINANCE IN NEW BRITAIN

Richard F. Salisbury, McGILL UNIVERSITY

Melanesia is an area of multitudinous small-scale societies, all with fiercely egalitarian and individualistic ideologies. A village, or collection of hamlets, comprising 150 to 400 individuals, was—indigenously and in the early stages of colonial administration—the effective political unit. It was independent of most other villages, with which it fought, arranged alliances, married, or traded; it was an independent, sovereign unit. No village would accept the domination of another village, and wars were continually fought to avenge slights to village self-esteem, which usually involved the theft of pigs or the seduction of women.

Equally, within villages, no individual would willingly acquiesce to domination by individuals. This involved a virtual absence of defined political "offices" with occupants who were accepted as having legitimate authority (see Sahlins, 1963). Leadership was accepted, when the situation demanded, from individuals who had proved their abilities; and able leaders, with a sense of "brinkmanship," could continuously produce the appropriate situations and could attain despotic personal power (see Salisbury, 1964).

Melanesia was also a wealthy area, of readily produced food supplies, with elaborate ceremonial systems and with varied systems of trade and the exchange of nonutilitarian "valuables." Malinowski's description of the Massim *kula* system is classic, and many other studies have also shown relationships between the ceremonial exchange systems and the political systems of the area. Early studies, such as those of Oliver (1949) and Hogbin (1939), stressed that individual economic success—particularly success in ceremonial exchanging—was the key to social mobility and acceptance as a (*pro tempore*) leader. More recent analyses (e.g., Salisbury, 1960 and 1962b; Uberoi, 1962) have expanded this insight and applied it to entire political systems. They have shown how the flow of intervillage exchanges of "valuables" parallels the changing pattern of intervillage political rivalries and associations, just as the flow of valuables from "big men" to "rubbish men" parallels the changing lines of interavillage political allegiance. Insofar as these "valuables" are not convertible into consumables, are severely limited in their supply, are handed over in public situations, are storable, and have the form of

113

discrete interchangeable units, they are ideally appropriate as "power tokens" to regulate, measure, and account for the flows of otherwise unallocated political rights (Salisbury, 1960, p. 257).

Critics of these—or similar—analyses have argued that complete inconvertibility is rare, and that the "power token" analysis is invalid where convertibility is present. The existence of inconvertibility is asserted because ethnographers have not looked hard enough; but they have argued that politically powerful "big men" did *not* acquire and give away their shell money or other valuables as part of a political "game," using shells as other gamesters use poker chips or voting blocs. They acquired wealth—critics maintain—as part of a drive for material possessions, acting as economic entrepreneurs in the Horatio Alger tradition, and then, as a by-product of their control over convertible wealth, they acquired political power (see Pospisil, 1963). Without convertibility, it is argued, there is no connection between ceremonial economics and politics, and *with* convertibility a "game theory" approach to the analysis of Melanesian political power is inappropriate.

This paper considers a society[1] in which convertibility is in theory complete, and where material acquisitiveness and entrepreneurship are accepted as part of a true Horatio Alger ethic. It shows that if one goes beyond an easy acceptance of this cultural ideology,[2] and quantitatively analyzes the uses made of ceremonial tokens in this society, a "game theory" analysis is still valid. There are barriers between alternative uses of the tokens; political schemers use them one way, materially acquisitive people use them another way. The political schemers may also acquire consumable wealth, but material acquisitions are not the path to political success. It would be suggested that, in such egalitarian societies, the Horatio Alger ethic may serve as an opiate to compensate the unsuccessful for their lack of power (and wealth), and to justify to them, in terms of "material achievement," the success of persons whose skills are those of the political gamester.

[1] Fieldwork among the Tolai in 1961 was supported by the University of California and the U.S. National Institute of Mental Health, Grant No. MH-04912. I would like to thank Enos Teve; Vin To Baining, M.B.E., M.L.C.; John To Marangrang; and To Lungen for the insights they provided into economic aspects of Tolai politics—and all the people of Vunamami for their hospitality and for their instructions in how to work for economic success.

[2] Reports dated about 1900 stress this ideology. This was a period of rapidly increasing *tabu* stocks (see n. 5), inflation, and boom. Both the German government and missions felt that the use of *tabu* encouraged "waste" and should be eradicated, so that people would be forced into cash-cropping and plantation labor. The bias of these reports, when not weighed against firsthand evidence, detracts from the value of papers that rely exclusively on them, such as Epstein's (1964) life history of a typical Tolai political entrepreneur.

TOLAI SOCIETY AND SHELL MONEY

The Tolai, the 40,000 people who live in the fertile plateau near Rabaul in New Britain, are the most advanced and sophisticated people of New Guinea. They have universal adult literacy; and on their own initiative, in 1963, they amalgamated as a single unit for elective local government. The area is actively involved in cash-cropping copra and cocoa; and wage labor of all kinds—from unskilled road repairers to bank tellers, and school inspectors and under-secretaries in the territorial government—provides almost as much income to yield a per-family income of about $300 per annum. In addition, most families have full-subsistence provided outside the cash sector.

At the same time, the society remains intensely traditional. The religious ceremonials of the *tubuan* are carried out virtually unchanged from the descriptions of 1880—alongside ceremonies of the Methodist and Roman Catholic churches, which are regularly attended by virtually the entire population. Land tenure operates in terms of the traditional, highly flexible matrilineal system, and the matrilineal clans still operate as units for organizing business enterprises, and in the same way as they did in the 1880's. In 1961, participation in clan activities involved the same number of individuals as the activities (described in published sources) involved in 1894.

The Tolai wear a distinctive dress of tailored calf-length waistcloths (*sulu*) and white shirts (copied from Fiji and Samoa), rather than the imitation European dress of shorts and T-shirts worn elsewhere in the Territory. Most important for the present analysis, most transactions between the Tolai use the indigenous shell money, *tabu*, while only Australian currency is used in dealings with Europeans. (Acquisition of shell money by individual entrepreneurial activity, or by hard work, is still an important goal.)

Tabu is produced by processing small nassa shells and threading the resulting buttonlike fragments on lengths of rattan cane. Unit lengths [3] are called by standard terms, the most common of which are the *pidik*, of six to eight inches; the *peapar*, or half fathom; the *pokono*, or fathom; the *rip* or skein of about 10 fathoms; and the *gogo* (*lolo*) or roll, which may contain from 100 to 1,000 fathoms. *Pidiks* are carried around as small change, broken to size, and buy goods for which Europeans pay a shilling. In a Tolai basket-purse, *pidiks* and shillings are both found, together with cigarets, betel for chewing, lime, cigaret

---

[3] As in Haiti (Mintz, 1961), the actual size of units may vary within limits. This makes an apparently rigid and formal system of equivalence into a practically flexible one.

lighters, combs, etc. *Pokonos,* equivalent to 10 shillings (or roughly a dollar), are carried around in small numbers if the owner expects to make a large purchase. Skeins, usually threaded specially for ceremonial payments, are stored hung on hooks in the owner's storeroom, with his rolls. Each roll is ceremonially wrapped in banana leaves, and looks like a car tire as it comes from the factory.

In 1961, according to my estimate, there were about 1,590,000 fathoms [4] of *tabu* among the 40,000 Tolai. Three-fourths of these are stored in rolls (1,260,000 fathoms); one-fifth is held in the more liquid form of skeins (300,000); and one-fiftieth is in the form of fathoms or small change. Shells are fairly readily discoverable in shallow waters near Rabaul, and especially farther west in Nakanai, but the labor cost of processing shells is so great that little new *tabu* is produced each year.[5] Over a thirty-year period, the increase has averaged about 1 per cent per annum, although the population is growing at over 4 per cent per annum. *Tabu* exchange rates in terms of food have less than doubled since 1880—prices cited by Danks (1888, p. 307) vary from 50 to 70 per cent of those for 1961. Australian and German currencies have depreciated about ten times, until a fathom that was worth 2 shillings (or marks) in 1890 is now worth 10 shillings in its purchasing power. There are no direct exchanges of *tabu* for cash, however, and a fiction is preserved that a fathom and 2 shillings are the same. A land purchase for 300 fathoms will still be recorded in official documents as £30.

SMALL-SCALE TRANSACTIONS

Virtually all marketing of foodstuffs among the Tolai—principally such luxuries as taro, lime and betel for chewing, bundles of cooked food and fish, and ochre for "medicines" or ceremonial coloring—is done either by direct barter or by sale for *tabu.* European vegetables, or manufactured goods bought at Tolai retail stores, are sold for cash,

[4] This estimate, and other estimates in this paper, are derived from field data obtained in the areas surrounding Vunamami village and from market surveys in Rabaul, as described in my forthcoming book, *Vunamami: Economic Takeoff within a Traditional Society in New Guinea.* Because of limitations of space, the derivation cannot be presented here. There is probably a margin of error of up to ±25 per cent for all estimates relating to the total Tolai population, although all errors would tend to be in the same direction. Estimates for a single village are probably subject to errors of ±10 per cent.

[5] On the other hand, *tabu* production (like goldmining) is a marginal industry, reacting dramatically to changes in the price of labor or in the exchange value of *tabu.* In the 1870's, around 1900, and between 1947 and 1950, *tabu* stocks may have increased at rates of up to 5 per cent per annum. The annual average of 0.6 per cent increase is based on informant reports for the period 1937-1961. The decline in the price of labor during the depression does not seem to have led to increased *tabu* production. This suggests that a rising exchange value for *tabu* is the more powerful stimulant of production.

however. Foodstuffs are sold in standard units (e.g., the "stalk" of betel nuts or the "bunch" of six taro corns), and each unit is equivalent to one unit of *tabu*. Most are equivalent to *pidik* units, but the bunch of taro is equivalent to the *peapar*, and a ten-pound mackerel is worth a fathom. The woman growing taro or processing coral for lime, and the man catching fish, does so in the expectation of earning *tabu*. At the same time, any coastal person buying taro, or any inlander buying lime or fish, expects to spend *tabu*, and carries change and fathoms with him for the purpose. About 1½ fathoms per adult seems to have been typical from 1880 until 1961.

Tolai ideology stresses that the market men and women are amassing stocks of *tabu* for eventual distribution at their funeral. The belief that such a distribution made possible the entry into the Land of the Dead used to validate this practice, but now the practice continues without the associated beliefs.

In reality, large stocks cannot be accumulated in this way. Total weekly purchases of inland produce by the five hundred inhabitants of the coastal village I studied averaged 12 fathoms' worth in local markets and another fathom's worth in the distant Rabaul market. Market sales by the villagers averaged 1½ fathoms' worth of lime locally, and 2 fathoms in Rabaul. Fish sales take place on the beach or privately within the village; sales to other villages gave an average return of fifteen fathoms a week. The private distribution of fish within the village does not always involve return payments of *tabu*, and the slight reallocation of wealth within the village which it involves will not be considered here.[6] Private arrangements with inland suppliers meant the additional purchase of about 200 fathoms' worth of taro for particular ceremonies during the year. The aggregate figures involve purchases of about 876 fathoms' worth and sales of about 960 fathoms for some two hundred adults. Although considerable individual variation is concealed by these figures, no individual received more than 50 fathoms, nor *could* any individual receive much more, given the aggregate demand. The *net* savings of any individual are considerably less since each seller is also a buyer.[7]

[6] Income from fishing might increase the income for poor families by about 50 per cent above what is shown in Tables 1 and 2, from an average of 8.7 to 13.0. Because approximately two-thirds of the fish would be consumed by poor families, their average expenditures on "other food" would rise from 1.1 to 4.0 fathoms. Rich-family expenditures would rise from 10.0 to 16.7 fathoms. Rich-family incomes would not increase, as most of their sales are to inland villages.

[7] The net movement of *tabu* from inland to the coast, and vice versa, also is small. This conflicts with the impression one gets at different seasons, that all coastals are buying taro and not earning any *tabu*, or that inlanders are buying up all the fish for ceremonials and not selling much taro. If prices were fixed by current supply-demand ratios, they would vary wildly and unpredictably. It is in just such a context that a trade in fixed equivalences is highly desirable, with the "traditional" prices being those that provide an equal balance of trade over the long term.

Considerably larger sums can be obtained by individuals through the provision of specialist services, or through the hiring out of capital assets. Skills in magic, dance or song composition, or carving, and the ownership of canoes or copra driers, exemplify these services. Besides receiving free board, specialists are usually paid with skeins of *tabu*, specially tied to the appropriate length: 20 fathoms for a song or dance composer, 5 for a dancestick carver, down to 1 fathom for each productive use of a five-man canoe. Unskilled helpers also receive their board while working and a gift at the end of the task. Such gifts work out at about half a fathom per day, and this may be taken as the market price of unskilled labor.

The payments to specialists also involve a component of return on a capital investment. A composer invests some 50 fathoms in fees to his teacher, the carver invests ten. The owner of a five-man canoe pays about 100 fathoms, depending on the wood used. If specialists' and hiring fees are considered as the standard labor payment, plus a return to capital, my calculations of the rate of return, based on observations of frequency of usage, indicate that depreciation plus 20 per cent per annum is the standard expectation.

Most single individuals' investments are small, however, and so are their total returns. Within Vunamami village, the greatest return was 60 fathoms to a canoe-owner, who often also crewed, and so in effect paid himself. I knew one highly expert choreographer in another village, whom I encountered at numerous dance ceremonies, who must have been employed full-time for about half the year, and who probably earned about 250 fathoms. This I would take as an absolute extreme, though for short periods skilled canoe carvers from the offshore Duke of York islands were paid at even higher rates. I have no figures on how continuously they were employed, however; the replacement demand for canoes suggests only sporadic employment. All in all, it is conceivable that a skilled artisan could invest and become wealthy, but I neither knew any such individual nor were any semilegendary "Henry Fords" talked about.

Even the relatively large income of skilled workers is subject to certain regular drains, which affect unskilled workers too. At every ceremony, all persons present must contribute by publicly throwing *pidiks* of *tabu* into a central heap. Such contributions are generally called *a nidok*, and should be interpreted both as a payment for witnessing something valuable and as a thank-you gift to the individual (or spirit) involved. At a wedding, for example, where some 120 adults are present, all contribute four times: as gifts to the host, to the groom, to the bride, and to the children of the marriage. These gifts are quite separate from the bride prices, which are private transactions between the families of the bride and groom. For three weddings that I attended, the total contributions averaged 70 fathoms, or .6 fathom per adult.

Similar contributions are involved at preparations for a ceremony in honor of dead clan ancestors (called *a matamatam*), at the entry of masked *tubuan* figures into a village, when "medicine" is eaten to speed dance-learning during practices, and at parties to raise funds to send the village choir to a competition. I estimate that poor families contribute some 10 fathoms annually in this way. Wealthy families, which attend more ceremonies, throw in ostentatiously longer *pidiks* (they let their children contribute too) and may spend 40 or more fathoms.

LARGE-SCALE FINANCE

It is clear that even sums of this order cannot be freely given away by individuals struggling to earn a few fathoms in the marketplace, yet on other occasions relatively immense sums change hands. Bride prices in Vunamami in 1961 were of the order of 100 fathoms for a previously unmarried young bride.[8] Commissioning individual dances costs 50 fathoms and occurs as frequently as marriages, perhaps three times in each village each year.

Most spectacular is the staging of a clan memorial ceremony— *a matamatam*—or the "raising" (*di waturia*) of a *tubuan* spirit. A *matamatam* is performed in each village about every three years and costs its sponsor (or sponsors) some 3,000 fathoms. Each *matamatam* requires that a *tubuan* spirit be "raised" to dance at the ceremony, but several *tubuan* may perform on one occasion, so that *tubuan*-raising is actually more frequent. A *tubuan*-raising costs its sponsor between 200 and 400 fathoms. Nor are the immediate costs the only ones. A *tubuan* raiser must have paid between 15 and 50 fathoms for his initiation into the *tubuan* cult, and about 200 fathoms to purchase the ownership of a particular *tubuan* and its associated ritual. A *matamatam* sponsor must have been initiated and have danced as a masked *tubuan* figure.

These outlays may be seen as business investments, and a ceremony organizer keeps accounts of income and expenditure. At the *tubuan*-raising when I was initiated, the owner's mother's brother had bought the *tubuan* for 200 fathoms thirty years earlier. The current owner spent 205 fathoms to stage a modest *tubuan* dance for a *matamatam*. He received back 250 fathoms in fees from novices who were initiated during

---

[8] This is approximately the same level as in 1884 (Parkinson, 1887, p. 96), when it "varied between 10 and 100 fathoms." There have been changes, however, in the interim. Bride prices in Vunamami were standardized and reduced to 10 fathoms in 1897; they have crept up slowly since then to their present level. Bride prices are higher in other Tolai areas.

the raising cycle, and 50 fathoms in other contributions when the *tubuan* was seen in public. A bigger performance, involving fully masked figures instead of only partially concealed dancers (termed *a tabaran*), could have involved him in larger expenses; he could easily have more energetically canvassed for initiates, paraded more widely, and actively sought out legal cases to adjudicate, all of which would have increased his return. His actual 47.5 per cent annual return on investment could easily have been quadrupled.

The same order of return is expectable from commissioning dances, which are performed several times, and from many other investments that involve large *tabu* investments, such as building ten-man ceremonial canoes, purchasing land, or buying large seine nets. The common feature of all these activities is that the success of the venture depends (after the initial investment) on the enterpreneur's organization of either a large labor force or an uncertain market. It pays to own a dance copyright only if one actively seeks out ceremonies at which to stage the dance and if one can persuade dancers to turn up to practice and to perform. Profitable seine-net fishing demands the availability of a regular labor force to take out the net whenever a school is sighted.

Entrepreneurs acquire a labor force by persuading individuals to subscribe to an association (*kivung*) called by a clan name, and the subscribers work for the association's (and the clan's) success (see Danks, 1888, p. 310). *Kivung* do not usually distribute profits, and thus they provide an avenue for pyramiding accumulations (see Salisbury, 1962b). The entrepreneur administers these, and he is often left in control when other participants leave the *kivung* because of personal animosities. Danks (1888, p. 309) describes similar cases in the 1870's. Two seine-net fishing groups, in Vunamami since 1930, have pyramided capital in this way, and on their break-up have left considerable assets in the hands of the organizers. Some bad feeling has resulted, but it is also true that the organizers used the proceeds philanthropically, to foster both ceremonial and economic development.

In much the same way, the *matamatam* sponsor's outlay of 3,000 fathoms is largely raised by contributions, following his initiative. Let us assume that he proposes to give a ceremony in honor of his dead father. This being a matrilineal society, his father's clan is different from his own. He involves this alien clan in his planning by announcing his intentions three years in advance. With the approval of clan elders (*lualua*), he slaughters a few pigs at a feast to which all clan members are invited. (A feast I attended cost the sponsor the equivalent of 25 fathoms (£12.10.0) for rice and corned beef, although taro and fish would have been more formally correct.) Clan members then contribute small sums to the proposed *matamatam* and "barter" (*kul*) the pork for large sums of *tabu*. Pork that would have sold for £20 (40 fathoms) in the open, European market, earned 693 fathoms for a *matamatam* sponsor in 1961.

The sponsor invites big men of other villages to commission dances and bring teams to the ceremony, for which they gladly lay out their *tabu* in the expectation of collecting fees. *Tubuan* owners, too, are prepared to utilize his ceremony as an occasion for staging their own initiations, etc. The sponsor rebuilds the surroundings of the area planned for the dance, entertains guests during the discussions, commissions one or more dances himself, and (nowadays) purchases the cement for erecting monuments for all the recent clan graves in the local cemetery. His out-of-pocket expenses are more than covered by his pork sales, however.

At the ceremony his biggest outlay is the distribution of lengths of *tabu* to every dancer in every dance group. Fifteen dances, each with sixty dancers, are a typical day's program; most dancers receive about a fathom, though important individuals, such as the wife of the local council president, receive three or more. For each dance, a roll of *tabu* is taken from storage and publicly "carved" (*di poka ia*) before the lengths are thrust in the hands of each dancer. The giving reaches frenzied proportions in the evening as the dances finish. The sponsor then presents *tabar* skeins of *tabu* to several important men, the implication being that they should now give a *matamatam*.

Any important man present seizes the opportunity to *tabar* all and sundry, but especially other important men. He throws a fathom or so at the feet of a friend/rival, and his followers hurl *pidiks* onto the pile for the recipient to gather up. The latter then seeks out another friend/rival to *tabar*, and waits for the next *matamatam*, when he will reciprocate (*bali*) the gift he has received. At a *matamatam*, normal Tolai penny-pinching is in complete abeyance. On the morning-after, the ground is littered with loose shells that have dropped off the dry rattan canes and scavenging small boys are out early.

The other occasion for liberal distributions of *tabu* is at funerals, which have been extensively treated in the ethnographic literature (e.g., Parkinson, 1907, pp. 74-80). At this time the dead man's store of *tabu* rolls is "carved" and distributed to all people present. Attendance is restricted to members of related clans, or about five hundred individuals. A distribution of 1,000 fathoms, or 2 fathoms a head, is a large one, although a few exceptional ones reach 1,500 fathoms. A village with six annual funerals may have one of 1,000 fathoms, and five funerals of less than 100 fathoms, so that villagers, on balance, receive about 1,500 fathoms a year from funerals. With the average of 1,000 received from *matamatam*, this makes a total of 2,500 fathoms received from distributions.

Although these distributions are "made to everyone," larger shares are given to important people. Thus, at a *matamatam*, a *tabu* roll is carved for each dance and is said to be distributed to the dancers, but about half of each roll that I observed went directly to the individual who had commissioned the dance. This is what yielded a profit on his capital outlay. At funerals, I received three times as much as the persons sitting near me. I estimate that although important people are fewer in number, they probably receive half of the total sums given in distributions.

THE FLOW OF TABU

Tables 1 and 2 attempt to summarize the estimates for Vunamami village. The families listed as "wealthy" included all those whose wealth and importance was generally recognized, together with all who appeared to be earning fees or business income on a *regular basis*. In 1961 a poor Vunamami man composed a dance for 20 fathoms, and two poor men were instrumental in collecting funds for transporting the village choir, but I do not feel that these were regular incomes, and I have ignored them in Table 1. The "contributions" received by poor families are largely wedding contributions; the remainder go to wealthy families, either directly or as fees. Most of what wealthy families "invest" also forms fee income for other wealthy families.

From these two tables, contrasting pictures emerge. The poor families balance their tiny current incomes and outgo from produce, counting their *pidiks*, except at ceremonials—when they splurge with contributions or accept largesse with an unconcerned air (deigning to measure exactly how *much* largesse only in privacy at home). They scrimp to save for a death distribution, with a lifetime expectation of saving 300 fathoms. A "big man" drumming up contributions to a clan project may easily "con" twenty "small men" out of their returns from years of work. Half of their savings, in any case, will go to rich men at their death.

The rich men spend about eight times as much *tabu*. Yet, although they spend over four times as much on luxury foods, this item is an insignificant part of their budgets, and is more than covered by their direct earnings. The major part of their financial activity involves the receipt of contributions from rich and poor, and the use of these sums to finance ceremonials, to invest in large capital equipment and in knowledge, and to accumulate for future *matamatam*. At death (if he gave no *matamatam* in his lifetime), the average rich man could expect to own 800 fathoms' worth of material assets and 4,000 fathoms of *tabu*.

These two average pictures seem distinct; in reality, the distinction is probably even sharper. There is a small range of income distribution among the poor, and most people fit well in the picture sketched. There is a wide range among the wealthy, so that—if one or two individuals were excluded—instead of being classed as wealthy because they had

TABLE 1
YEARLY TABU INCOME AND EXPENDITURE—69 POOR VUNAMAMI FAMILIES.

Expenditure			Income		
Taro	275	(4.0)	Lime	152	(2.2)
Other food	75	(1.1)	Fish	600	(8.7)
Contributions	690	(10.0)	Contributions	60	(0.9)
			Distributions by living men	500	(7.2)
			Distributions at deaths	750	(10.9)
	1,040	(15.1)		2,060	(29.9)
Savings (possible)	1,020	(14.8)			

All figures are estimates, stated in fathoms of *tabu*. Figures in parentheses are averages per family. Most savings are hoarded for eventual death distributions.

TABLE 2
YEARLY TABU INCOME AND EXPENDITURE— 15 WEALTHY VUNAMAMI FAMILIES.

Expenditure			Income		
Taro	175	(11.7)	Lime	33	(2.2)
Other food	150	(10.0)	Fish (12 men @ 25)	300	(20.0)
			Fees, businesses	375	(25.0)
Contributions	300	(20.0)	Contributions	855	(57.0)
Investments	300	(20.0)	Distributions by living men	500	(33.3)
Distributions	1,000	(66.7)	Distributions at deaths	750	(50.0)
	1,925	(128.4)		2,813	(187.5)
Savings (possible)	888	(59.1)			

All figures are estimates, stated in fathoms of *tabu*. Figures in parentheses are averages per family. Most savings are hoarded for eventual death distributions.

some income from fees, the general average would rise considerably. The rich become richer and the poor remain poor.

Richness is not merely in property ownership, for all individuals own productive property. The return on investment that poor people receive is enough to keep them from getting any poorer—ranging up to 20 per

cent, but it is not enough to exceed outgo. People who are not satisfied
with such a return but who expect, by the expenditure of some time in
organizational activity, to obtain 50 per cent on their investment accumulate rapidly. One group strives hard, and saves to live up to
the standard; the other group apparently squanders money, but the
squandering is a "social investment" that pays off.

SHELL-MONEY AND POLITICS

So far, the analysis has been made in economic terms, but it is
equally possible to make a political analysis of the activities of the
wealthy. "Wealthy" is perhaps a misleading word. A man, as has been
shown, need not have great riches in order to "behave wealthy," provided he can persuade others to contribute to his enterprise. If he
organizes the contributors so that the enterprise is successful, he gets
prestige and is supported in the future. He may reinforce his political
position by purchasing rights to particular ceremonies, which will justify
his organizing future activities. The more dances he sponsors, the more
he speeds the flow of *tabu* into the pockets of his supporters, and the
more supporters he wins. Squandering and a 50 per cent return on
investment are the marks of political investment; penny-pinching and a
20 per cent return characterize investment in materially productive
goods.

The simplest demonstration of this is provided by the identity
between the politically important men and the "wealthy" men. Thus
in four villages near Vunamami, my records show that 26 *matamatam*
were performed between 1937 and 1962. Nine of these were in Vunamami itself, for which my records are certainly complete—though there
may be a few omissions for other villages before 1945. The highest
political office of the area before 1950 was that of Paramount Luluai, and
after 1950 it was the presidency of the local government council. Nine
of the *matamatam* were given by three individuals who occupied the
highest political office during this period. The individual who was appointed in 1937, and retired in 1952, gave seven *matamatam*, including
several while in retirement.

The next most important position before 1950 was that of the govern-
ment-appointed village headman, or luluai, and, after 1950, that of the
elected village councillor. Eight *matamatam* were given by five individuals at this political level. The remaining nine *matamatam* were given
by individuals who were, or had subsequently become, heads (*lualua*)
of the nonlocalized matrilineal clans that make up Tolai society at
large, one of whom had also been an important Methodist missionary.

A few of the Administration's nominees for political office had not given *matamatam,* and several village councillors had been younger men, so that not every politician was a *matamatam* sponsor; but the giving of a *matamatam* had set the seal on those who were successful. This is clearly shown in the career of the outstanding post-war politician, who had been educated at mission boarding schools, and therefore had not been initiated in the *tubuan* religion. After his first election, he quickly went through the entire cycle of initiation, and gave a *matamatam.* His success thereafter was rapid.

Tubuan owners were also politicians, though not equally active. Two of the three top-level political figures had owned (or otherwise controlled) *tubuans.* The other *tubuan* owners in 1961 were older men, for they remain owners for life if they so desire. Half of them had been village officials before 1951. The remainder, without exception, were either clan heads or acknowledged legal experts. All attended an area conference of Tolai land law, convened by the Native Lands Commissioner in 1961, with the delegates nominated by the Vunamami Local Government council (Smith and Salisbury, 1961).

DISCUSSION

Despite the convertibility of *tabu,* it is possible to differentiate the portion of the flow of *tabu* involved in the political maneuverings of the society from the flow that relates to the distribution of subsistence or luxury goods and services. In more familiar terms, everybody is taxed and pays in the same currency that is used for personal purchases; the tax revenues then finance large-scale enterprises and social services. The annual *tabu* tax revenue of a Tolai village is about 1,740 fathoms, made up of 690 fathoms from the poor, 300 fathoms from the rich, and the 750 fathoms of death distributions that go into the hands of the wealthy.

Perhaps 250 fathoms of the 1,740 support a higher standard of living for the wealthy, and 300 are used for major capital investments. The rest is returned to the poor, either immediately as distributions, or more indirectly after a period of storage. The accumulations of tax funds enable an apparently hand-to-mouth economy of the poor to cope with the periodic, immense expenses of the large-scale ceremonials and building projects that make Tolai society an exciting one to live in. The flow of *tabu* funds through taxation accounts for about 35 per cent of the *tabu* income flow of the society. It is a myth that public administration is cheap and can do without taxation in small-scale societies.

It is true that there are other income flows among the Tolai. Vunamami has an annual cash income of over £A8000, two-thirds from copra and cocoa, and one-third from salaries, and it is virtually self-sufficient in vegetable staples. But about 25 per cent of the cash income goes in direct and indirect taxation to the church, to the local government council of the area, and to the Territorial treasury. Cash is little used in interpersonal exchanges within the village, being reserved for extra-village purchases. Cash tax funds support supravillage services, while *tabu* taxes support intravillage services. Within the village, the ceremonials and building projects also involve taxation of subsistence incomes. Everyone contributes food, and everyone works on an unpaid basis for about one day each week in construction, planning, or organizational activities. Administration in all spheres thus involves about 20-35 per cent of the aggregate income.

Polanyi and others (1957) have used a concept of "redistributive patterns of integration" to describe the organization of such societies as the Tolai, where many small amounts of wealth in the hands of poor people flow into the hands of the wealthy. The wealthy then use these accumulations to provide social services, and by this means they redistribute the wealth to the poor.

At first sight, the concept appears useful for characterizing Tolai society, but, if one investigates more closely, it loses its value. Some form of taxation finances all public services in all societies. The Tolai do not have a single pool into which all taxes flow, nor is there any regulation of the volume of taxation in terms of the services to be provided in the future. People pay for services *after* they have been provided by political enterpreneurs; personal acquisitiveness and impersonal market mechanisms of supply and demand regulate the amounts of *tabu* acquired from crop production and from the organization of *tubuan* ceremonies; the competitive reciprocity of local politicians regulates the volumes of distributions, and it is the feeling of reciprocal keeping up with the Joneses that sanctions the making of contributions to local ceremonies by the ordinary Tolai. The proportion of tax funds that is diverted into raising living standards for an elite—as compared with the amount that returns as benefits for all [9]—is regulated by the size of that elite and by the degree of social mobility into it. The formal

[9] This ratio is, I suggest, the measure of how far a political administration is extortionate. Government and mission reports of the Tolai often used the evidence of *nidok* contributions to say that the *tubuan* leaders are extortionate robbers. Other writers (e.g., Parkinson, 1907) and informants stress the governmental and legal functions of the *tubuan*: "The *tubuan* is the people's government" (*A tubuan ra matanitu kai ra tarai*)—mediating disputes and punishing crime for a fee. The most extortionate aspect of the *tubuan* is probably not the exploitation of the poor by the rich, it is the way that *tubuan* ceremonies, with their seclusion in the bush, often finance drinking bouts, rowdy singing, and hostile behavior directed at women and noninitiates by the poorest, unskilled, roughneck males. Such mobs, mobilized by a clear-sighted leader, who allows them to prey on the peaceful populace, could be a major force in political life, as has been proved in many developing countries.

economic analysis of how flows are regulated shows how deceptive the simplistic use of labels, such as "redistribution," [10] can be.

"Redistribution" is a concept that is foreign to the Tolai. An individual may distribute (*i tibe*); he may present freely (*i tabar*), or make reciprocal presentations (*i bali*); he may barter directly for an equivalent (*i kul*)—but no one would concede that any individual can act as the recipient of funds for redistribution on behalf of other people. This would set that individual up as superior to others, in defiance of a fierce democratic ideology. The individual who collects for a *matamatam* does so by bartering pork for *tabu;* the contributions received by a *tubuan* owner at an initiation, which enrich him, are given not to him but to the masked supernatural figure; the death distribution of a rich man is not only his way of "buying" his way into the Land of the Dead but is talked about as though he is distributing the earnings of a lifetime of scrimping and saving.

People ignore the fact that a rich man's wealth is really the accumulation of contributions from the poor, and everyone asserts the ideology of saving and of producing wealth by one's own efforts. No one will accept a political authority as legitimate, but the "Horatio Alger" ethic is the mechanism that induces the politically weak to accept the power of the politically strong, who are powerful because they earned it.

REFERENCES

DANKS, REVEREND B. 1888. On the shell money of New Britain. Journal of the Anthropological Institute, 17, 305-317.

EPSTEIN, T. S. 1964. Personal capital formation among the Tolai of New Britain. *In* Capital saving and credit in peasant societies. R. W. Firth and B. S. Yamey (eds.). London: Allen & Unwin, pp. 53-68.

HOGBIN, H. I. 1939. Experiments in civilization. London: Routledge and Kegan Paul.

MINTZ, S. 1961. Standards of value and units of measure in the Fond-des-Nègres market place, Haiti. Journal of the Royal Anthropological Institute, 91, 23-35.

OLIVER, D. L. 1949. Human relations and language in a Papuan-speaking tribe of Southern Bougainville. Peabody Museum Papers, Vol. 29, No. 2.

PARKINSON, R. 1887. Im Bismarck-Archipel. Leipzig: F. A. Brockhaus.

[10] But formal economic analysis can be undertaken only when numerical data are available, and the channels of flow of goods and services have been described. Polanyi *et al.* (1957) are inaccurate in suggesting that a formal analysis is impossible. Such analyses were not possible with the data they had; but their work has helped others give the basic institutional descriptions that are the prerequisite for formal analyses.

———— 1907.   Dreissig Jahre in der Südsee Stuttgart: Strecker u. Schröder.
POSPISIL, L. 1963.   The Kapauku Papuans of West New Guinea. New York:
      Holt, Rinehart & Winston.
SAHLINS, M. D. 1963.   Poor man, rich man, big man, chief. *In* Comparative
      studies in society and history, 5, 285-303.
SALISBURY, R. F. 1960.   Ceremonial exchange and political equilibrium. Sixth
      International Congress of Anthropological and Ethnological Sciences
      Proceedings (Paris), 2, 255-259.
————. 1962a.   From stone to steel. Melbourne and Cambridge: The Uni-
      versity Presses.
————. 1962b.   Matriliny and economic development in New Britain. Paper
      delivered at the American Anthropological Association Meetings, No-
      vember, 1962 (to be published).
————. 1964. Despotism and Australian administration in the New Guinea
      Highlands. American Anthropologist, New Guinea Highlands issue,
      66, 225-239.
SMITH, S., and SALISBURY, R. F. 1961.   Tolai land law and custom. Port
      Moresby: Native Lands Commission.
UBEROI, J. P. S. 1962.   Politics of the Kula ring: an analysis of the findings
      of Bronislaw Malinowski. New York: Humanities Press.

POWER, AUTHORITY AND PERSONAL SUCCESS IN ISLAM AND BORNU [1]

Ronald Cohen, NORTHWESTERN UNIVERSITY

INTRODUCTION

Many scholars have commented on the possible origins of the concepts of statecraft that were carried across the Sahara Desert along with the Muslim religion. The fact that these kingdoms have been Islamic for centuries, maintaining their contacts with older Islamic areas as well as the stress they place on being Muslims, has given credence to the view that their political system and its philosophical basis is simply a diffused extension from the greater centers of Islamic culture. This position has also gained force in the well-known feature of Islam's nonseparation of religion and government, so that the political community is viewed as the community of Allah. Any attempt to form a government, either in a new place or by a new faction in the same place, has always been regarded as an attempt to establish or reestablish a better or a purer system—from the religious point of view (Adu Boahen, 1964).

At first glance, the Muslim states on both sides of the Sahara seem very similar. There is a centralized ruler, viewed by the people as a commander of the faithful. There are religious personnel who adjudicate in semiseparate courts, according to the rules of Islamic jurisprudence. Indeed, throughout history the monarchs of these states have taken the long arduous journey to Mecca in order to fulfill their religious obligations, and—from early times onwards—most of the Sudanese kingdoms have been regarded as integral parts of the greater Islamic world by scholars in and beyond the perimeter of Islam.

On the other hand, it seems obvious—although little has been done in this vein—to ask if any differences can be observed in the sub-Saharan emirates when these are compared to similar polities to the north of the desert. It seems senseless to assume that all theological and political functions are either exactly the same, or are similar in their origins. The purpose of this paper follows from this latter point, and presents material on the central concepts of government and world view as they have developed in the cultural tradition of Islam and in

[1] I wish to thank Professor John Middleton for the many helpful criticisms he made of a previous draft of this paper.

129

Bornu, one of the Sudanic states whose contact with Islam is of considerable antiquity.

Power and authority are central, inherent ideas in any political system; they reflect in themselves and in the nature of their connotations, the basic viewpoint the members of a culture have with regard to their governmental system. I have chosen to discuss personal success because it is closely related to Kanuri concepts of power and authority; yet it may not be attributed in any easily perceived way to the Islamic tradition. In what is to follow, I will compare the usage of these terms in Bornu to those in wider Islamic literature, and then attempt to explain the similarities and differences that have been isolated in the analysis.

POWER AND AUTHORITY IN BORNU AND ISLAM

In Bornu, legitimate authority and the responsibility for obedience to it have always been major themes in the culture. In the sixteenth century, a Bornu scribe in the court of the monarch Idris Alooma wrote:

The crown of leadership is purity and justice. Thus every people relies on imitation of its leaders; the leader goes before and the people follow him . . . so every man knows his rights and obligations to others. Most excellent is the fame of just deeds, and justice on the part of a king for one day is equal to service of God for sixty years . . . a place where there is an evil Sultan is better than a place which has none. (Ibn Fartua, 1926, pp. 9-10)

Exactly the same emphasis on the necessity of leadership and on the hierarchical relationship of authority positions was given to me by Koranic scholars, thoughtful peasants, and leaders four hundred years later during my fieldwork in Bornu. Informants felt that society was divided into sets of political roles and that without the increasing scale of authority inherent in such positions, Muslim life i.e., a morally proper existence, would be impossible. Not to have a ruler and his subchiefs was, and is, considered to be a pagan and an evil idea. In terms of the relationship of authority to religion, informants often told me that whether or not a man was a good Muslim, or whether he could be considered a better Muslim than the rivals with whom he was competing for a political position, was an important criterion in the selection for succession to office.

Authority, then, is essentially hierarchical and is essential to a proper, religiously sanctioned social existence. It starts with God and the law, as given by the Prophet, and it is manifested in the hierarchical set of political roles within the state. The most highly valued and most important behavior known to the Kanuri of Bornu is obedience to authority. It is emphasized over and over again in child training, in the household, in daily behavior, and in metaphor; when a person reaches adulthood, it is the most important judgment made of him, which he must also make of others. To have "no shame"—no proper sense of obedience to authority—is considered the worst character defect in Bornu.

In traditional Islamic thought, people are conceived of as being in need of the hierarchical ordering of authority roles, because without rulers men would not cooperate within a society. A century before Imam Ahmed, the early Bornu scribe wrote the passage we quote above and Ibn Khaldun, the Arabic historian, claimed that:

People cannot persist in a state of anarchy without a ruler who keeps them apart. Therefore they need a person to restrain them. He is their ruler, as is required by human nature; he must be a forceful ruler, one who exercises his authority. (Ibn Khaldun, 1958, p. 381)

In another place, the same author said: "Listen and obey even should an Abyssinian slave with a head as black as a raisin be your governor" (p. 397).

Generally, then, in both Kanuri and wider Islamic thought, authority and obedience to authority was and is considered a major facet of the political philosophy inherent in the culture. Religion emphasized this central precept by giving the rulers "another power" (Ibn Khaldun, 1958, p. 320), in addition to that achieved by having many supporters, since it emphasized the desirability of respect for hierarchy itself. Thus Islam helps to stabilize hierarchical authority, and has been used in this way for both sub-Saharan Africa and in the rest of the Islamic world.

A good example of the interlocking of religion and political authority can be seen in the Kanuri custom of the *daiilu*. On the Prophet's birthday, a special ram is sacrificed by the shehu of Bornu (the monarch).

This ram, the *daiilu*, must be especially colored and raised for this specific purpose, and it is killed early in the morning of the feast day. The blood is thought to have medicinal power and people struggle to touch it. After the ceremony, some of the blood is sent to the palace to inform the women there that they may begin cooking the day's feast. In the kingdom at large, especially in the capital city, no ram must be killed before that of the monarch. His sacrifice signals the inception of the feast day, and only when his ceremony is complete may others do the same. Thus the king's temporal authority is enhanced and dramatized by his primacy in the religious sphere.

The *daiilu* ceremony also illustrates another Muslim concept that enhances the power and authority of legitimate rulers. The Kanuri, like all Muslims peoples, have a concept of mystical or supernatural power that resides in religious leaders and sacred objects, and in persons who have contacted sacred persons or things. Thus the blood of the *daiilu* ram is a sacred substance that can bring blessings upon its holder. Anyone who smears himself with it is blessed. Lepers can be seen daubing an afflicted hand with it, and some of it is given to blind people, who immediately apply it to their eyes so that their sight may possibly be

restored. This sacred power, *baraka* (Arabic) or *barka* (Kanuri), blesses
its holder and allows him to bless others and succeed in life through
supernatural or miraculous means.

The first ruler of the second Bornu dynasty, Shehu Laminu (el
Kanemi), is said to have used his supernatural power as a religious
leader to save Bornu from the expansion of the Fulani empire at the
beginning of the nineteenth century. North of the desert, this power is
mentioned by Evans-Pritchard in his discussion of the founders of the
Senusi emirate of Cyrenaica (Evans-Pritchard, 1949). To some extent,
barka can be obtained by anyone who goes on a pilgrimage to Mecca,
especially if he presses himself against the *multazam* (Von Grunebaum,
1951, p. 23), a wall in Mecca whose special sanctity can impregnate the
pilgrims with *barka,* or mystical power.

The main point here, however, is that Islam gives specific powers to a
political leader if he can convince his followers that he is a religious
personage of some note, or if he can obtain the loyal services of holy
men. Throughout the history of Bornu, both of these usages have been
tried. Often, a particular monarch is referred to in the traditions as a
religiously oriented ruler who became enamored of the Koran and studied
Islam. Others are referred to as having had great and powerful religious
leaders in their courts. Whether they tried to obtain *barka* by themselves, or had in their service men with much *barka,* the effect was the
same—that of enhancing successful political authority by adding to it
supernatural powers beyond the reach of ordinary men.

Power, or the ability to influence the behavior of others and obtain
control over valued resources, is something for which all men in Bornu
strive, and for which they always have striven in the past. The way to
achieve power in Bornu has always been through wealth and rank.
These qualities are inextricably linked, and linked as well to a person's
dependents and supporters. A man who is wealthy gives his wealth to
his supporters and achieves rank. A man who has rank can use the supporters associated with his position to obtain wealth for redistribution
and to obtain more supporters.

Succession to authority is never certain in Bornu. Generally, positions
of authority are thought of as passing down agnatic lines on the basis
of personal abilities within the set of agnates. Competition for power
among agnates for leadership positions is a hallmark of Kanuri social
and political life, and is extended even further by the fact that monarchs
and leaders may redistribute positions under their control or functions
and prerogatives attached to positions—and/or these may be usurped
by other persons in the continual competition for power, which runs
up and down the entire social and political structure.[2]

[2] Elsewhere (in "Empire to Colony," n.d.) I have commented on the contribution such competition for power and authority has made to the maintenance of
Bornu government over the centuries.

In many places in his writings, Ibn Khaldun's characterization of the Islamic concept of power is similar to that of Bornu. There is the same claim that power comes from supporters, and the same emphasis on competition, among nobles and others, throughout the society (Ibn Khaldun, 1958, p. 379). He even tells of specific cases (e.g., during the Umayyad rule in Spain) in which noble families competed for power, then each adopted royal names and tried to take over the power of the throne. This intense competition, he claims, resulted in a weakening of the existing monarchy. Power in the political life of the state, like authority, is therefore almost identical in traditional Islamic thought and in Bornu.

PERSONAL SUCCESS

From another point of view, power can be viewed as a much wider concept than authority, for it can also involve culturally defined beliefs about volition, as opposed to determinism. How much power is available to a man in his ordinary life, given the fact that an all-powerful God exists, whose control over all things is supreme? This can also be said for any kind of supernatural power that controls man's ability to choose among alternatives and act in terms of this choice. In this sense, power enters the realm of fate, or destiny, in its relationship to man's behavior.

In Islamic thought the question of fate, as opposed to human volition, has always been troublesome, and there have been several phases through which the idea has passed. At first in the doctrine of *qadar,* it was felt that God was all-powerful, that everything was predetermined, and that therefore man could not be held responsible for his actions (Watt, 1948, p. 165). Later this was changed, and man was conceived of as having power and volition to control his own life because he could reason, and therefore choose. Later still, this rather humanistic position was compromised, so that reason was viewed as a means by which man came to know God's will; i.e., what was already predestined for him (Watt, 1946, p. 165).

In his book on this subject, Watt claims that there are two contradictory strands in Islamic thought, which have never been satisfactorily integrated into a consistent theory of human action. The first is the concept of human responsibility, involving man's power to choose, and secondly there is the conception of divine omnipotence, which reduces freedom of choice to zero (Watt, 1948, p. 29). If God is in fact all-powerful and all-knowing, he has therefore already created what is to come about in the future.

The same author also introduces a pre-Islamic idea, that of *dhar,* or personified time-destiny, which is not often mentioned in discussions of Islamic theology or philosophy. In this concept, time was evidently thought of in the pre-Islamic period as the cause of good and bad fortune, and of death. It was considered impossible to escape it; it was ever present, and it was external to man. Thus Islamic thought grew from a fatalistic past toward a conception of human freedom, but it never completely solved the problem of volition and its relationship to fate and predestination.

In the work of Ibn Khaldun, personal success is considered to be the result of understandable and naturalistic forces that result from a person's own skill and the qualities of his character (Ibn Khaldun, 1958, II, 332-334). Success and happiness result from profit (i.e., achieving a gain for oneself), and profit comes from two sources: labor, which can produce only small amounts of profit, and rank, power, or authority over others, which produces much profit and success. This latter and most desirable state of affairs is achieved not by God or fate but by obsequiousness to superiors, by flattery of them and their families—which Khaldun feels is the most advisable way of achieving the greatest amount of success in society.

For the Kanuri, as for many other West African peoples (Fortes, 1959), the problem of human volition, or of freedom to choose in an already determined universe, is solved for them by their culture. They have a conception of human personality that explains volition in terms of itself, so that it can always be understood to have been predetermined, even though exactly the opposite is true in actual or empirical terms.

After rational, empirical causes are considered—and they usually enter into an explanation in some way—the success or failure of any individual in Kanuri society can be attributed to his *arziyi*. This quality is an essential and variable aspect of human nature; it is essential for success, and variable from person to person, and within the same person, through time. If an individual moves up the political scale, amasses wealth, harvests a good crop, is lucky in gambling, wins judicial decisions, obtains power and authority over others (or makes what power he has work well for him), avoids illness, poverty and derision—or does anything that can be measured in terms of achievement—the degree of his success is the measure of the *arziyi* he has in his *hal* (nature, being, or essence). Like Calvinistic predetermination, *arziyi* is hoped for before the fact, and is indicated and substantiated after the fact—of success.

In answering questions about *arziyi*, informants of all classes and ranks generally agree that no matter how much success a peasant has with his farm, his wife, at cards, or in his craft work, he can never come close to having as much *arziyi* as even a bad district head or village area head. When *finer* discriminations are asked for, disagreements will sometimes arise. Thus when questioned as to who has more *arziyi*, a trader in the city who recently bought a big truck and has a large compound of wives and followers, or a somewhat effete district head, informants answered according to how they ranked wealth alone as compared to political power. Since both of these dimensions of status are usually congruent, but ranked high, the discrimination is often difficult. Nevertheless, there is always—at any level in the society—a large measure of agreement about the amount of *arziyi* contained in the various social roles.

Persons from different levels of the society give a somewhat different picture of the distribution of *arziyi* throughout the society. This results from their different vantage points and therefore differing opportunities for perceiving the social structure. Thus, although many lower-class persons find it difficult to decide whether or not an effete district head has more *arziyi* than the rich city trader, those close to the chief, including himself, feel that the rich trader has more.

This brings up an interesting observation. The judgment of any individual about the distribution of *arziyi* in society at any one time is his particular notion about the arrangement of social roles in the social and political structure. Furthermore, his estimation and distribution of *arziyi* at any one level of the hierarchy—e.g., comparing the behavior of one district head with another—is his judgment of the success the occupants of similar roles are enjoying relative to one another.

Arziyi seems to be used in two related ways in Kanuri culture. First, in an enormously heterogeneous society, it gives a satisfactory answer to individual variations along one of the most affective dimensions of behavior: success in achieving immediate and long-range goals. Second, it is used as an explanation for the nature of the social structure, i.e., of its stratification. Those persons who have higher status, along any dimension of stratification, have more *arziyi*, which accounts for their ability to maintain such a role in the social organization. These two ways of using *arziyi* as an explanation for differentiation are related, so that the result is a Kanuri theory of society that at once validates its structure and that explains the changes in personnel that accompany a system in which personal fortunes may rise and fall rapidly. Thus a high status position in the structure indicates that a person has a comparable amount of *arziyi*. If his performance of the role is shown to have even more *arziyi*, he will outstrip others who occupy the same position and seek the same goals. On the other hand, he may do badly, which will indicate a loss of *arziyi* and a loss of status. *Arziyi* is both a theory of society and a theory of causation that integrates social and individual differentiation under one universalistic, though variable, quality of human personality, personal good fortune, which is continually validated since its presence is manifested after the fact of its operation and behavior.

It should be noted that although there are similarities in effects between the Muslim concept of *baraka* or *barka* and the Kanuri concept
of *ariziyi*, they are very different qualities when they are analyzed in
their cultural context. *Arziyi* is present in all human beings (and only
in human beings), and explains their particular fates; *baraka* is found
in some but not in all human beings, and it can also reside in objects.
Thus Kanuri, like Muslims everywhere, use charms to ward off evil;
the charms are blessed by men with great religious power and are
believed to be efficacious for that reason. Personal success can be enhanced or modified by religious power, and this idea is widespread in
Islam, but, in the long run, the Kanuri see success or failure as the
operation of *arziyi*.

CONCLUSIONS

(1) Kanuri concepts of political authority and power are essentially
identical to those in the wider Islamic society.

(2) There are no ideas in Islam comparable to the Kanuri concept
of *arziyi* or personal success.

(3) Islamic theology and philosophy are not logically consistent
about whether human beings have the power to decide their fates or
whether all of man's experience is predetermined by forces beyond his
control.

DISCUSSION AND INTERPRETATION

That conceptions of power and authority are very similar when
they pertain to offices in the political system in Islamic society and in
Bornu is not surprising. There is a limited number of ways to run these
feudal monarchies, and all require very similar kinds of social relational
systems (Cohen, 1966). When methods vary, it is in the mode of succession to office and in the degree of centralization in the political
system. In neither respect was Bornu different from any of the other
principalities in the Islamic world. Structural similarities are therefore
reflected in the basic similarity between the Islamic philosophy of government and that of Bornu.

On the other hand, *arziyi* or personal success is a very different
sort of concept; it deals not only with government but with the nature
of society and with the causes of human success and failure, given the
fact that man may choose alternative ends and means. At this level of
conceptualization, Kanuri philosophy had answers to questions that
were unresolved in Islamic theology, and questions that are basic in

human experience. Because Islam had only contradictory and material-
istic explanations of why there are differences in society, of why some
persons succeed and others fail, etc., the people of Bornu—and many
other peoples of West Africa who have notions similar to that of *arziyi*
—kept these pre-Islamic ideas after their conversion to Islam.

A more crucial question is raised by this discussion, and it has
meaning for our understanding of human society. Professor Fortes, in
his very interesting *Oedipus and Job in West African Religions* (1959),
commented on the wide distribution or *arziyi*-like concepts for explaining personal success and failure, and on the ultimate relationship these
concepts have to the social structure of the persons who utilize them
to understand life and experience. *Arziyi* is somewhat different from the
concept of fate found among the Tallensi, and, although it is closer to
the concept of the Yoruba, it is again somewhat different. These differences, as Fortes suggests, are due to the differences in the social structures of the peoples who utilize the concept. Tale society is acephalous;
the Yoruba have traditionally had city-states; the Kanuri have always
had the concept of a centralized monarchy, with imperial expansion as
a state goal.

It therefore seems unreasonable to say that only social structure is
reflected here—since so many different kinds of social structures are
represented by the people who use the concept. Furthermore, as we
have seen in our concepts of power and authority, the Bornu political
structure, which serves as a framework for the society, is conceived as
normatively and structurally identical with that of the other societies
in the Islamic world—closer, certainly, than it is to the acephalous
societies of Northern Ghana. Why, then, should *arziyi* simply reflect the
social structure when it appears in so many different kinds of society in
West Africa?

What we are dealing with here is in a sense much more fundamental
than social structure because it deals with timeless questions concerning
man's life, no matter what kind of society he lives in. Why should A
succeed and B fail when both, seemingly, are doing the same thing?
I submit as a basic assumption that the problem of success and failure,
and man's freedom to act in furthering his goals, are related subjects
in every kind of society and culture. Limitations upon freedom are
universally recognized, whether they stem from natural or supernatural
forces, inside or outside the individual. In all probability, all of these
theoretically possible sources of causality are recognized in all cultural
traditions, but greater emphasis on one or another sector of limitation
and causality produces a very different conception of the human
situation.

Some societies stress witchcraft beliefs in explaining malevolence
and failure. Individuals who are "too successful" are often suspected of

having obtained their success by supernatural means, at the expense of neighbors. In West Africa, another idea has been emphasized and developed, which explains success and failure in terms of a quality inherent in the individual (Fortes, 1959; Horton, 1961). Limitations on human action, and even the structure of society and social mobility within it, can be explained by such a theory. In this sense, such concepts of personal success as *arziyi* and witchcraft are polar opposites, for one theory (*arziyi*) explains experience on the basis of something inside the person and the other (witchcraft) explains experience by a theory that supernatural forces have been directed at the individual from the outside.

Since both theories operate from different causal directions—using *ex post facto* reasoning to explain the same thing—we can hypothesize that societies with a concept of personal success that explains success or failure will have a lower incidence of witchcraft than those in which differences in success or failure are explained by the inherent qualities of individuals. Furthermore, witchcraft accusations are characterized by excessive social mobility, upwards or downwards, while concepts such as *arziyi* explain this same mobility as something to be expected. Thus we would also expect societies with *arziyi*-like concepts to be prone, more often than not, to higher stratification than those that explain causality by witchcraft beliefs (although diffusion would carry it across systems, as has happened in West Africa).

Sorcery, as distinguished from witchcraft (Middleton and Winter [1963]), involves techniques that are actually practiced by individuals to produce effects on others, but witchcraft does not require such operations by the witch, who may not know he (or she) "is" one until he stands accused. In this sense, we would expect to find sorcery in societies that have both *arziyi* and witchcraft, since it involves volition by the person from inside himself (*arziyi*) and supernatural action directed at individuals from the outside (witchcraft). In this sense, too, sorcery is like the Muslim idea of *baraka* since it involves the conscious use of supernatural power. It is interesting, therefore, to note that in Bornu persons with religious power are believed able to counter and to practice sorcery. I therefore would suggest that whereas Islam cannot do much to replace such concepts as *arziyi* or witchcraft, because they deal with basic orientations toward ultimate sources of causality, Islam can merge its theology with non-Islamic practices of sorcery because it has very similar traditional ideas.

Finally, it is important to realize that in Islam, and indeed in the tradition of Western civilization, another approach to causality has been stressed that has led to a lack of completeness when men attempt to explain why things happen as they do. Man's actions and his success and failure were deemed as determined partly by God and partly by his own ability to reason—as well as by naturalistic forces in the society around him. By not having satisfactory answers to some basic questions about the roles of these various forces, the traditions of Islam and Christianity left the way open—indeed, partly led the way—to a weighing of causal forces and naturalistic inquiry. The fact that Islam (and much of the philosophical and theological speculation of the West) could not resolve the problems of free will and determination maintained a tension in their intellectual tradition so that thinkers attempted to postulate where freedom began and determination (supernatural or natural) left off.

Ibn Khaldun always looked for naturalistic causes of events, even though he ended his discourses with a phrase such as "God can change everything if he wishes." On the other hand, some societies—as many of those in sub-Saharan Africa—solved the problem of cause and effect, of why human events occur as they do; and in doing this they did not inquire into the nature of experience beyond the bounds of their self-validating theories.

REFERENCES

ADU BOAHEN, C. F. A. 1964. Britain, the Sahara and the western Sudan, 1788-1861. Oxford: Clarendon Press.

COHEN, RONALD. 1966. The dynamics of feudalism in Bornu. *In* Boston University Publications in African History, Vol. II.

———. n.d. Empire to colony. *In* The impact of colonialism. V. Turner (ed.) Stanford: The Hoover Institute. In preparation.

EVANS-PRITCHARD, E. E. 1949. The Senusi of Cyrenaica. Oxford University Press.

FORTES, MEYER. 1959. Oedipus and Job in West African religions. Cambridge University Press.

HORTON, ROBIN. 1961. Destiny and the unconscious in West Africa. *In* Africa, 31, 2, 110-116.

IBN FARTUA, IMAM AHMED. 1926. History of the first twelve years of the reign of Mai Idris Alooma of Bornu [1571-1583]. Lagos: Translated from Arabic by H. R. Palmer, the government printer.

IBN KHALDUN. 1958. The Muqaddimah, an introduction to history [3 vols.]. Translated from the Arabic by Franz Rosenthal. New York: Bollingen Series 43, Pantheon.

MIDDLETON, JOHN, and WINTER, E. H. 1963. Witchcraft and sorcery in East Africa. New York: Praeger.

VON GRUNEBAUM, G. E. 1951. Muhammadan festivals. New York: Schuman.

WATT, W. M. 1948. Free will and predestination in early Islam Lazac.

THE RESOLUTION OF CONFLICT AMONG THE
LUGBARA OF UGANDA [1]

John Middleton, NEW YORK UNIVERSITY

I

In this paper I discuss some of the ways by which conflicts are controlled between members of small local kinship and neighborhood groups among the Lugbara, a society that lacks elaborate or formal traditional political authority. Some of these conflicts may be called political and others may not, although all are—in some way or another, and to some extent or other—concerned with the exercise and acceptance of authority and power. The conflicts are inherent in a segmentary system of this kind, and are expressions of the tensions that arise between persons whose interrelationships are continually changing as they move from one status to another, in terms of descent and generation. In other words, they are part of a continual cycle and development of local groups. Other conflicts are those between the groups that compose a segmentary system of social units, in this case lineages and the territorial sections that are formed around them. Perhaps, following Evans-Pritchard, only these latter conflicts should properly be called political (Evans-Pritchard, 1940). But in the case of the Lugbara, resolution of both types or levels of conflict may conveniently be analyzed together, since they and their resolution form a single system. Conflicts and tensions at one level merge into those at the other, and the means employed for their resolution can best be undersood as alternatives or as processes that should be seen as lying along a single continuum—certainly Lugbara see them so. Conflicts, at both levels, take different forms in different parts of the country, with variations in the composition of local territorial groups.

These conflicts are of two main kinds: those within small local groups

[1] This is a revised version of a paper read at a meeting of the American Anthropological Association at Detroit in November, 1964. I should like to thank Professor Ronald Cohen for many helpful comments, and also Professor Hilda Kuper, who acted as discussant for the session at which the paper was presented. I studied the Lugbara between 1949 and 1952 with aid from the Worshipful Company of Goldsmiths and the Colonial Social Science Research Council, London. The initial writing up of the field data was done with assistance from the Wenner-Gren Foundation for Anthropological Research, New York.

and those between them. The resolution of the former, which are ostensibly over the exercise of personal power and authority, and usually over the allocation of land and livestock, is, in Lugbara thought, controlled by various mystical or religious processes. The resolution of the latter, which are usually over rights in women, was traditionally by feud and warfare; today these have been prohibited, and conflicts formerly settled by fighting are settled in law courts.

The Lugbara are peasant farmers of northwestern Uganda and northeastern Republic of the Congo (Léopoldville), and number about a quarter of a million. The density of the population is as high as 250 persons to the square mile in some parts of their country, so that there is always considerable competition for land.

Traditionally the Lugbara had neither kings nor chiefs, but under the colonial administrations of Great Britain and Belgium chiefs were appointed, and these officials are powerful men. In general, however, they do not intrude very much into the everyday life of small local communities.

The Lugbara have means of maintaining ideally peaceful relations within these communities, of preventing conflict from being expressed too openly (i.e., by violence or serious quarreling), and of ending open conflict if it starts. The main point of this paper is to show how this is done in a society that has no overall political authority, that has very small fields of everyday social relations, that has strong beliefs in the ideals and norms of kinship and in the patrilineal lineage as basic principles of organization, and that has a high density of population, so that open violence is extremely disruptive of ordinary social life. Control of conflict, threats of conflict, and accusations of having caused conflict are factors that are manipulated by people seeking power and authority, who in doing this make use of the changing opportunities presented to them at different stages in the cyclical development of local and descent groups.

The basic residential and local unit, in economic, political, and ritual situations, is a cluster of elementary and joint families that I call a family cluster. It varies from a dozen to as many as 150 people, and is based upon a patrilineal lineage of from three to five generations; it has a single territory; and it has its own head, whom I call an "elder," a functionary chosen by virtue of his senior genealogical position in the lineage. The elder should have virtually complete authority over the members of his family cluster, including members of the lineage, their wives, and various attached kin and clients. The most important persons are the male members of the lineage, and disputes between them tend to disrupt the family cluster; other disputes are generally minor or domestic.

The core lineage of the family cluster is the smallest lineage in a segmentary lineage system. The largest local group, the jural community of Lugbara society (Middleton and Tait, 1958), is the subtribe, based upon a subclan (clans are dispersed units, without political functions). A subclan is defined by reference to its founder, one of the sixty or so sons of the two Hero-ancestors of the Lugbara. It is typically segmented into three levels of lineage, which I refer to as major, minor, and minimal lineages, the last being the core of the family cluster. Many subclans have four or even five levels of lineage, and the number of generations in a subclan genealogy varies from eight to fourteen. The genealogically senior heads of minor and major lineages have the duty of representing the segments at sacrifices, but they have no internal authority over these units. The highest level of an internal lineage authority holder is at the minimal lineage.

There are also rainmakers, one in each subclan, who traditionally had rudimentary political powers in that they could curse the leaders of groups that were fighting each other, so that they were obliged to cease hostilities. And there are a few wealthy and influential men, known as *'ba rukuza* ("men whose names are known"), who could sometimes stop fighting by their powers of persuasion.

Further details of this structure need not be given here as I have described it elsewhere (Middleton, 1958).

II

I shall first discuss conflicts and their resolution within the family cluster, and wider conflicts in a later section.

Lugbara society is of course not static. The family cluster changes its internal organization over time, in a cycle of development whose main stages are fairly clearly distinguishable. The underlying structure remains constant, but the size and composition of the clusters vary, and the pattern of internal dissensions and strains also changes over time. The cluster is segmented into joint families, each consisting of men related by lineage, and their wives and children. There may be two or up to ten joint families, depending on whether the family cluster has reached an early or late stage in its cycle of development. This cycle begins and ends with segmentation into two or more new family clusters, each new group beginning a cycle of growth that continues until it also eventually segments (of course, a cluster may die out, or be absorbed by another if it decreases in population, but this is a secondary pattern).

A joint family may consist of only a couple of brothers and their wives and children, or it may include half a dozen or more men—of three or even four generations—with their wives and children. The men of the family cluster are thus divided by descent, by ancestry, within the lineage around which the cluster is formed. They are also divided by what I call status grades, which are determined by age or by generation or by position of authority within a joint family. Formally, this is by generation, but—as in all Lugbara institutions—the degree of formality is not very high. This "horizontal" division is into five grades: the elder; the "men behind," who are heads of joint families; the "big youths," who are younger married men with children; the "youths" who are unmarried or recently married men without children; and boys. Conflict within the family cluster is conducted in terms of competition against one's fellow lineage members for a higher position, both in descent and status-grade terms.

Lugbara are very conscious that theirs is a near-anarchic society, lacking kings and traditionally, chiefs; nor do they possess an age-set system. They say that the basic principle of orderly social life is "respect": a junior respects a senior, a wife her husband, a sister her brother, a child an adult, and so on. When the patterns of respect (and consequently of authority) are agreed upon by all members of a family cluster, all goes smoothly, under the overall guidance and authority of the elder. But, of course, this orderly pattern never lasts for very long. Although the relationships between members in terms of descent may not change, the relationships between them in status-grade terms do change—and the consequent incongruence between these organizational principles is expressed in quarreling, tension, and conflict.

As members of the grades of "youth" and "big youth" grow older, marry, and have children, they usually need more land (and other resources) and greater freedom from the everyday authority of their formal seniors. The latter wish to maintain their authority; and the "men behind," of course, aspire to become elders on their own, which would involve the segmentation of an entire group—with themselves as the elders of the newly independent family clusters.

These men are all close kinsmen, so that open violence is not permitted among them; instead, mystical sanctions are brought into play. The major sanction is ghost invocation. The Lugbara believe that if a man whose father is dead (usually a senior man) is offended by an act committed by a dependent, he may cause the dead to send sickness to the offender, or to one of his family, to show him he has committed a "sin" (here defined as an offence against the norms of lineage kinship, which typically involves disobedience to proper lineage authority). The invoker has merely to think about the offence while sitting near the ancestral shrines, and the dead know his thoughts and send sickness.

I need not go into further detail, but the main points are (1) A man falls sick, of an indeterminate sickness, thought to be sent by the dead. (2) Oracles are consulted on the reasons for the sickness by the sick man's ritual guardian, who is typically his elder; that is, the guardian-elder is usually the man who invokes the ghosts. (3) A beast is promised for sacrifice if the sick person recovers. (4) After the man's recovery, the beast is sacrificed to the dead and the meat is consumed by the living lineage kin, sitting as a formal congregation.[2]

Certain points in this process are significant here. One is that a dependent is disciplined by the appeal to the dead, who are regarded as benevolent and impartial guardians of lineage well-being. In theory, the behavior of the dead cannot be questioned: whomever they support among the living (by accepting his invocation) is thereby shown to have behaved in a manner befitting a holder of lineage authority; his status, and the way in which he exercises its authority, are in this way validated in the eyes of his dependents.

Conflicts within a family cluster are essentially over the exercise of authority within that group. Any member—at least any adult male—can try to exercise power, but to be accepted as legitimate authority it must be validated by reference to the senior men of the lineage. The elder is the senior living man, but above him in seniority are the dead, and it is they who validate the status of their living descendants, both the elder and his juniors.

The point of this is that a man who wishes to acquire higher status —which usually means raising his position in the system of status grades —must have his ambition validated by the dead. Once the dead show that they accept his new status, they thereby show that opposition to his status is unfounded, and indeed contrary to lineage well-being. The problem, therefore, is how to obtain ancestral validation.

The validation is obtained by oracular statements. The dead communicate with the living in various ways: by appearing as specters, by sending omens, by sending dreams, and (most commonly) through oracles. This last means is thought to be the most reliable, the most important reason being that the oracle operator makes verbal statements to the client consulting him.

The oracles are of several types. First resort is always to the rubbing-stick oracle, which is merely a piece of stick manipulated by an operator: the way in which the stick twists in his hands gives him answers to questions, which he repeats to his client. The other oracles are all mechanical, and are used only to confirm the statements of the rubbing-stick oracle. The questions put to the oracle operator include the source or nature of the sickness (i.e., from the dead or from witchcraft or sorcery), the identity of the person who has invoked the dead, the identity of the ghost who has sent the sickness, the nature of the original deed that caused the process to be set in motion, and the nature of the sacrifice needed to remove the sin and sickness. For a man to be

---

[2] I have described this procession in detail in Middleton, 1960a. Much of the material in the following pages is summarized from that book, and I need not give further references to it here.

shown as an invoker implies that the dead consider his action in invoking proper, and that they consider he has acted properly and responsibly in doing so. This is, therefore, a validation that the dead approve his status.

Situations in which this kind of validation is significant are those of conflict within a family cluster. Although many oracular consultations are straightforward—in the sense that the offense that started the process has no structural importance—a high proportion, perhaps the majority, is concerned with conflict that arises from ambition in terms of descent and status grade. This is seen particularly when the invoker and the sick sinner belong to different segments within a family cluster, the heads of which are competing for authority. In this case, if X, the elder, who is also the head of segment X, can show that he has successfully invoked against a dependent of Y, the head of segment Y, he has shown that the head of segment Y is junior to him in lineage authority and so below him in status. In other words, rather than have Y discipline his own dependents the ghosts prefer that the head of segment X (who is also the elder of the total group) discipline him. If, on the other hand—despite the displeasure of the elder over the sinner's behavior—the ghosts show that sickness has been sent as a consequence of the invocation of the head of segment Y, Y's authority is validated; and if the elder has been so unwise as to make or imply threats against the offender, he is shown to have lost the confidence of the dead.

The principle is simple, but permutations of this pattern are of course numerous, depending on the specific internal organization of a family cluster. The incumbent elder always has an advantage in that if both he and his rival consult oracle operators, and other things are equal, the elder's verdict is usually regarded as the more valid; and much also depends on the fame of a particular operator. After a verdict has been given, a promise is made to make the sacrifice called for by the oracle if the patient recovers—if the patient does not recover, the oracle had been mistaken, because of the action of Divine Spirit or of witches, or because of the inefficiency of its operator. Although an operator can be allowed a certain number of false statements, if they become too frequent he is known as unreliable. There is also another reason for the reputation of a good operator: a good operator (always a member of a family cluster different from that of his client) understands the significance of the conflicts laid before him and gives replies that will resolve them.

I come now to what might be called the second line of attack between rivals for senior authority within a family cluster: accusations of witchcraft.[3] Lugbara believe that witches are men, and, although the exact nature of their power is not understood, it is regarded as a

---

[3] I have published accounts of Lugbara witchcraft in Middleton, 1955, 1960a, and 1963a.

perversion of the legitimate power they exercise in everyday kinship relations. Witches do not transmit their powers to their sons; any man can be a witch; and, although it is assumed that sometimes a man's witchcraft may act without his fully knowing it, it is generally assumed that a man who practices witchcraft knows that he is doing so.

The term for "to bewitch" is the same as "to invoke the dead": *ole rozu.*[4] Witchcraft is evil, ghost invocation is good; but the same term applies to both. The difference lies in the motivation. *Ole* in the context of ghost invocation, means indignation at a sin; in the context of witchcraft it means envy or annoyance at not having one's own way. In either case a man feels annoyance, but in the former case it is annoyance at an act that weakens his authority as a senior man in his lineage and family cluster; in the latter case it is annoyance that people will not let a man gain his personal ambitions irrespective of the well-being of the family cluster. One is meritorious, and a part of a senior man's duty; the other is selfish, and a perversion of the mystical power of kinship authority. Any oracular consultation may show that sickness is the consequence of witchcraft; but oracles cannot name a witch. For this, consultation must be made of diviners, who are women thought to have been possessed by the immanent, or "evil" aspect of Divine Spirit.

A man who invokes the dead against dependents to maintain his position, rather than to look after the well-being of the family cluster, (although the line between them is a very thin one) is liable to be thought a witch. Suspicions of this fall into two main patterns. (1) A young man who is said to be sick as a consequence of ghost invocation may say the invoker is a witch; but no one takes much notice of this. (2) If two men of equal status (in status grade) compete for authority, and if one succeeds in getting favorable oracular statements on several consecutive occasions, his rival will usually suggest that he is a witch— by saying his opponent is "strong" or "too big," or some such euphemism. If others agree, he has cast doubts on his opponent's fitness for authority; if no one agrees, he can let the matter drop and bide his time. There may be a slow build-up of public suspicion about the opponent's motives; sooner or later the rival will become aware of this, as his dependents show themselves unwilling to accept his authority. He usually then finds himself in the position of having to invoke more and more to maintain his authority, and this, of course, means that he runs

[4] I realize that using two English phrases in place of the single Lugbara term may be awkward, but it seems the only satisfactory way of discussing the mystical processes that are called by the same term in Lugbara—and the Lugbara themselves are fully aware that two distinct processes are denoted here. For them, the similarity lies in the common mystical nature of the processes (*ro*) and their motives (*ole*), rather than in the agents concerned, which for analysis are the more significant factors. Also, the very mystical nature and the ambiguity of the situation is crucial for the Lugbora, where as it is necessary to avoid this ambiguity in analysis.

the risk more and more of being thought a witch; he is caught in the system. Finally, unless he dies or virtually abdicates his exercise of lineage authority, he may openly be accused of being a witch. This means he has denied the obligations of lineage kinship, so that others need no longer obey him as head of the family cluster or of one of its segments. The group may then segment; members of component segments (other than the alleged witch's) may move away—perhaps not spatially but merely morally. By this removal the witch is cast out from the everyday system of authority and tension is eased by the removal of its supposed cause.

Accusations of witchcraft should not be considered disruptive, for tension within a group already exists, and gossip and accusations work to resolve the tension. For a short time, of course, accusations exaggerate the tension—until the stage when the matter can be brought more or less into the open and resolved; but the belief in witches within a family cluster is usually a means of resolving conflicts without recourse to open violence. Another way of saying this is that ghost invocation and witchcraft suspicion validate changes that occur in the patterns of relationships between members of the family cluster.

III

I come now to conflicts that occur between members of different minimal lineages and family clusters. The main point in this regard is that ghost invocation and, usually, witchcraft are believed to be ineffective beyond the limits of the family cluster, and so other means must be employed to settle conflicts. Lugbara are not always certain, when discussing the theory of ghost invocation and witchcraft, of their ranges of effectiveness. It is thought that a senior man should be able to invoke the dead against his junior lineage kin who may have moved elsewhere, but this is rarely if ever done. For one thing, it would be an insult to the elder of the particular family cluster in which the junior now lives. And witchcraft, although said to be able to attack kin living elsewhere, is not very effective at a distance. It is the "witchcraft of the hut"—within the family cluster and especially within a small family segment of the cluster—that is the most feared.

Conflicts between members of different family clusters are settled in various ways. If the matter is purely personal, the antagonists may simply fight with sticks, clubs, or knives (spears and arrows are not used); we may call this dueling. The Lugbara would appear (as a personal impression) to be an aggressive and quarrelsome people, and personal duels are frequent. If they lead to death or serious injury, as indeed they frequently do, the respective lineages will become involved, but usually the more responsible kin exert restraint and the matter then is either regarded as closed or is taken up formally by lineage elders.

Besides dueling, which occurs mainly between men who are neighbors but of different lineages (i.e., of host and attached lineages in the same territorial section), conflicts may be expressed in accusations of sorcery (Middleton, 1963a).

Sorcery, as distinguished from witchcraft in Lugbara thought, uses material objects ("medicines") rather than the mystical means of witchcraft. Sorcery between men is practised either by neighbors who are unrelated or by young men who feel resentment of the world at large and scatter poisons and other medicines indiscriminately. That is, the former kind is practised between close neighbors, who do not wish to bring open violence into the situation, but who are unrelated and so cannot use the ghosts to help them; the latter kind is not concerned with personal quarrels but is indiscriminate, and is used by Lugbara as a means of comprehending the general breakdown of lineage authority that has affected Lugbara society in recent years as a consequence of increased social mobility. Sorcery of both kinds is found therefore in areas of great intermingling of small lineage groups, so that men are surrounded by unrelated neighbors rather than by kin, and/or where there is much social mobility.

The more formal ways of settling disputes include, in the traditional system, feuds and warfare, and court actions. Accusations of sorcery may also be made, but this is rare between persons living at any great distance from one another. Feuding and warfare were prohibited by the British and Belgian colonial governments, and the last large-scale fighting was in the late 1920's. But intergroup fights still break out, which are soon stopped by the intervention of government chiefs; and Lugbara still discuss intergroup relations largely in terms of organized force.

Lugbara use the term *a'di* to refer to organized fighting, but it is more convenient for us to use "feud" and "warfare," depending upon the lineage distance between the groups concerned. Within what may be called the "inner section" and the "inner lineage," the sanctions of close lineage kinship prevent prolonged fighting, but beyond it prolonged feuds and warfare were traditionally frequent. The inner lineage may be either the minor or major lineage. It is defined by the recognition of certain obligations that are not recognized beyond it. The most important are that personal kinship terms are used between its members; homicide is regarded as fratricide; and adultery and incest are sinful. Beyond this range these offenses are no longer sins but merely "bad deeds." Within the inner lineage almost all disputes are settled by elders, either alone or in consultation with one another, and open violence (except for dueling) is rare; but beyond it elders regard themselves as too remotely related, and the close lineage ties that inhibit open force are lacking. Fighting within a subtribe was stopped if the elders met and cursed the fighters, or if they called in a rainmaker or a "man whose name is known" to do this. Fighting between subtribes was not stopped in this way; it merely continued until both groups grew tired of the inconvenience of fighting and losing their men in battle—although "men whose names are known" are said sometimes to have persuaded such groups to cease fighting (Middleton, 1958 and 1965).

Conflicts beyond the inner lineage were, and are, usually over women. The subclan is in theory the exogamous group. Marriage occurs freely within a subtribe provided it is between host and attached lineages; and of course it occurs between subtribes and subclans. Also in many subtribes the exogamous group is in fact the inner lineage. Groups whose members intermarry are either unrelated by clanship, or, if they are distantly related, the relationship is considered irrelevant in marital and in political situations. Conflicts between the groups may be resolved only by the threat or by the use of organized force. The same applies to disputes over seduction or impregnation of unmarried girls, over land and other rights, and so on.

The colonial administrations introduced chiefs into Lugbara, but we have not the space to consider the chiefly system at any length.[5] Among the Uganda Lugbara—and the Congo system is similar—there are five county chiefs, each of whom has about five subcounty chiefs under him; subcounty chiefs control a number of parish chiefs, each of whom has several headmen. Headmen usually represent minor or major lineage segments; parish chiefs represent major segments or subtribes; subcounty chiefs represent the larger subtribes or clusters of small subtribes; and county chiefs represent clusters of subtribes. Headmen and parish chiefs are usually uneducated men from the groups they represent, and chiefs and subchiefs are educated men who today rarely, if ever, have authority over the groups to which they belong in lineage terms.

In the judicial system, cases taken to headmen and parish chiefs are those between units that are under their authority, and the headmen try to settle these cases by informal arbitration. I call their informal meetings "moots." If they cannot be settled, they are taken to subcounty chiefs. If, however, cases are between men of different headmen and parish chiefs, the cases are taken straight to subcounty courts, but the headmen of the respective parties first consider the case and then appear with the parties as sponsors. (I am talking here of civil cases; criminal cases —tax evasion and the like—go direct to subcounty chiefs.)

The point I wish to make here is a simple one: the civil cases that go to subcounty courts are those that traditionally would have been settled by feuds or warfare. The structurally impartial position of the subcounty chief enables him to adjudicate between the parties. Lugbara say

[5] I have discussed modern chiefs in Middleton, 1956 and 1960b.

explicitly that the courts have taken the place of feuds and warfare, and the nature of the civil cases tried by subcounty chiefs (and by county chiefs in cases of appeal) bears this out. From figures I collected from a number of subcounty court records for 1953, about 40 per cent were concerned with seductions of unmarried girls; next were criminal cases that were brought by the chiefs themselves; and about 15 per cent were concerned with assault. In the civil cases where I knew the lineage affiliations of the parties, about two thirds were between members of the same subtribe and one-third were between members of different subtribes; in all, about two-thirds were between members of different major sections, including those between different subtribes.

IV

A point that needs mention in this present paper concerns the sanctions used by persons who exercise political authority or the power either to inhibit or to resolve conflicts of various kinds. These persons are several: elders of family clusters; elders who also have the role of representatives of wider lineages at sacrifices and other ritual occasions; oracle operators and diviners; rainmakers and "men whose names are known"; and chiefs, headmen, and other officials of the modern administrative system. The obvious point of difference between them is in the sanctions for their power and authority. The sanctions of elders, oracle operators, diviners, and rainmakers are primarily religious, and chiefs and headmen have the sanction of the superior force of the central government behind them. All, to some extent, depend upon personal powers of persuasion and restraint; but "men whose names are known" must rely solely upon their personal powers.

It is clear that in traditional Lugbara society the persons whose authority included that which might be called "political" had mainly religious sanctions. Their authority was primarily religious: in the case of elders it was thought to come from the power of the dead; in the other cases, it was thought to come directly from Divine Spirit. The ancestors controlled the small-scale relations within the minimal lineage and family cluster, and, to a less extent, the inner lineage and the territorial segment associated with it. These are the lineages classed as *ori'ba* "ghost people"; wider segments are known as *surs*, a term that lacks the religious connotation of the other (see Middleton, 1960a and 1965).

A problem that has faced chiefs and headmen has been that their authority has lacked religious sanction: it has been regarded as part of the alien world of the colonial administrator, whether European or Ugandan.[6] Until fairly recently, however, chiefs and headmen (particularly chiefs) typically gained some of their power from divine powers.

[6] I have published a detailed account of this cult in Middleton, 1963b.

The first chiefs appointed by the Belgian administrators, in 1900—and later reappointed by the British, in 1914—were leaders in the prophetic cult of Yakan (see Middleton, 1960b). They were known as *opi*, a word that also applied to rainmakers and "men whose names are known," and later to chiefs. The main aim of the Yukan cult was to remove European power and certain epidemics, which, since all appeared at about the same time (the end of the last century) were assumed by Lugbara to be interrelated. The cult leaders seemed the obvious people to be put forward as chiefs because they had the necessary spiritual powers to be able to cope with Europeans. All of these men and their successors—including all the famous Lugbara chiefs up to about 1950, when the last of them was retired—were known as much for their religious as for their administrative powers; subcounty chiefs, who usually lacked these powers, were those who bore the brunt of Lugbara opposition to the alien government. This was due partly, of course, to their structurally intermediary and ambivalent position in the administrative hierarchy, but it was largely due to their lack of proper religious authority.

There are, then, five ways in which conflict between and within small local groups, including territorial groups based upon patrilineal descent and those in loosely defined neighborhoods, may be resolved among the Lugbara: (1) open violence between individuals, or dueling, which involves only a few persons and is very informally structured; (2) ghostly sickness, thought to be caused by invocation by a senior man who is offended by the sinful behavior of a dependent; (3) accusations of witchcraft (between kinsmen); (4) accusations of sorcery (between unrelated men of the same neighborhood); and (5) feuds and warfare, which today have been replaced by court actions. The means that are used in a specific situation depend upon (*a*) the relationship of those in conflict with one another and (*b*) the stages reached in the cycle of development of the family cluster and also of lineage groups of a higher segmentary order.

LUGBARA METHODS OF CONFLICT RESOLUTION

Members of a family cluster	Members of the same inner lineage	Unrelated neighbors	Members of different inner segments but of the same subtribe	Members of different subtribes
——— Ghost invocation ———				
——— Accusations of witchcraft ———			——— Accusations of sorcery ———	
	——— Agreement by respective elders ———			
——————— D u e l i n g ———————				
			Feud	Warfare
		——————— Modern courts ———————		

It may be somewhat inaccurate to write of the "resolution of political conflict" in societies of this kind, if we accept Evans-Pritchard's definition of "political," to which I referred earlier. Feud and warfare may resolve particular disputes between particular lineage groups on particular occasions, but it is inherent, in segmentary lineage systems of this type (Middleton and Tait, 1953 pp. 12 ff.), that conflict is not only a jural mechanism but also an inherent quality. This has, of course, been mentioned elsewhere (Middleton and Tait, 1958, p. 21):

One of the crucial features of the feud is that mentioned by Radcliffe-Brown. . . The relationships between the feuding parties is such that hostility between them, although permanent, must be inhibited in those situations in which they become allies in military, economic, ritual or other collaboration. If it were not at least temporarily inhibited, mutual alliance would be an impossibility. It is thus typically found with a segmentary lineage, the feuding parties at one level being coordinate and politically equal segments that may unite at a higher level against more distant groups. The fact that a segment acts as a feud unit marks its separate identity as against other segments in one situation, and its joint unity with coordinate segments in others. As a permanent condition feud is one aspect of the continuity over time of a series of segmentary groups—it is, as it were, genealogical differentiation translated into action.

Within the family cluster and the inner segment the situation is different: conflicts are resolved, even though they are bound to break out again at a later stage of the cluster's cycle of development. But, because the cluster segments in time, the units between which there is conflict will not be the same. At a wider range, that of feuds and warfare, the units—in Lugbara theory at any rate—are always the same: a state of conflict between them is normal. In Lugbara, in short, the limits of the jural community, of the field of everyday political relations, are defined by the presence of permanent feud, warfare, and also of sorcery (see Middleton, 1954, 1960a, 1965). It is only within this field that conflicts should or need be resolved, and, paradoxically, that social relations might well not deserve the label "political."

REFERENCES

Evans-Pritchard, E. E. 1940.   The Nuer. Oxford: Clarendon Press.

Middleton, J. 1954.   Some social aspects of Lugbara myth. Africa, 24, 3, 189-199.

———. 1955.   The concept of "bewitching" in Lugbara. Africa, 25, 3, 252-260.

———. 1956.   The role of chiefs and headmen in Lugbara. Journal of African Administration 8, 1, 32-38.

———. 1958.   The political system of the Lugbara of the Nile-Congo divide. *In* J. Middleton and D. Tait (eds.), Tribes without rulers. London: Routledge & Kegan Paul, pp. 203-229.

————. 1960a.   Lugbara religion: ritual and authority among an East African people. London: Oxford University Press.

————. 1960b.   The Lugbara. *In* A. Richards (ed.), East African chiefs. London: Faber.

————. 1963a.   Witchcraft and sorcery in Lugbara. *In* J. Middleton and E. Winter (eds.), Witchcraft and sorcery in East Africa. London: Routledge & Kegan Paul, pp. 257-275.

————. 1963b.   The Yakan or Allah Water cult among the Lugbara. Journal of the Royal Anthropological Institute, 93, 1, 80-108.

————. 1965.   The Lugbara of Uganda. New York: Holt, Rinehart & Winston.

MIDDLETON, J., and TAIT, D. 1958.   Tribes without rulers: studies in African segmentary systems. London: Routledge & Kegan Paul.

THE ECONOMIC ACTIVITIES OF A
GILBERTESE CHIEF [1]

Berndt Lambert, CORNELL UNIVERSITY

Studies of Oceanic economic and political organization have emphasized the chiefs' status as foci of redistributive activities. Redistribution is an economic process in which certain goods produced by a group are collected or appropriated by a central authority and subsequently allocated to other members, perhaps after a period of storage. It is probably part of all economic systems, but it is more prominent in the absence of self-regulating markets. Redistribution occurs in groups as small as extended families, which generally pool the produce of their estates under the control of their heads. More complex forms of the process are based on the collection of goods by holders of political power, such as chiefs, feudal aristocracies, or bureaucracies. The rulers often retain a portion of their income to support themselves, their kinsmen, and their servants and followers. They may store the remainder against a time of scarcity or may make it available to the inhabitants of regions that do not produce goods of that kind (Polanyi, 1944, pp. 49-55, and 1957, pp. 250-256).

In Polynesia and Micronesia, the goods collected and distributed by the chief were primarily foodstuffs, especially one or more of the important crops grown by the society. Sahlins (1958, pp. 3-5) has argued that because presentations made to a Polynesian chief represented a surplus over the subsistence requirements of his people, redistributions increased in scope and frequency with the growth of productivity. As larger populations and greater quantities of goods were drawn into the redistributive network, a status level of artistocrats, intermediate between chief and commoners, came into being to help administer the flow of contributions. The chief was not only exempted from cultivation, but also had sufficient food at his disposal to support retainers and to subsidize craftsmen. He was able to feed the workers on large communal projects. The increased political power that grew out of his control of resources enabled the chief to supervise production, even by householders, and to employ

[1] This article is a revised and expanded version of a paper entitled "The Functions of Redistribution in the Northern Gilbert Islands," which was presented at the 1964 annual meeting of the American Anthropological Association at Detroit. Field work on Makin Island from 1959 to 1961 was sponsored by the Tri-Institutional Pacific Program under a grant from the Carnegie Corporation.

155

physical punishments to enforce his will in these and other matters. Hence Sahlins holds that the degree of social stratification in particular Polynesian societies is ultimately correlated with their levels of productivity.

In some of the smaller Oceanic societies, however, this "tribute" in food is apparently a confirmation of the chief's authority, rather than a foundation for it, because the amount collected is relatively small and the recipient must dispose of it almost immediately in a culturally prescribed manner. The chief increases his resources by the cultivation of his own estate and by contributions from his kinsmen, whose obligations toward him may be of the same order as those they would have toward an ordinary relative. In Polanyi's terms, the chief combines redistribution with householding and a kind of reciprocity, and the former process may not be economically the most important of the three (Polanyi, 1944, pp. 46-50, 53, and 1957, pp. 250-253).

On the Polynesian island of Tikopia, for example, a chief and his household produce most of the food they eat. Periodic gifts of food and of special types of raw material constitute a steady stream of additions to the chief's wealth, but the small surplus that remains after reciprocal gifts have been made to the donors is soon consumed by his family, relatives, and neighbors. The chief is more than a simple redistributor of tribute, since his own orchards can be drawn on by the people (Firth, 1950, p. 191). On Micronesian Truk, a chief receives gifts of food from the lineages of his district at periodic feasts in his honor. All of these contributions are immediately redistributed, after the chief has selected the largest bowl for himself and his lineage (Goodenough, 1951, p. 142). In societies of this kind, descent groups probably expend only a small fraction of their production on gifts to the chief. Nor do they benefit by his redistributions. The storage of food is often unnecessary or unknown, and the area covered by the redistributive network is too small for local variations in crops or resources to exist. The principal function of redistribution here may lie in the ritual rather than in the economic sphere.

In the case of Truk, Schneider (1961, p. 221) concludes that gifts of food symbolize the relation of a chief to the lineages established in his district. They publicly acknowledge the chief's residual rights to their lands in this way. Coult (1964, p. 38) has suggested that Polynesian redistribution activities may serve primarily to demonstrate the current affiliations of ambilineal descent groups.

It could not be maintained, of course, that redistributions are always economically unimportant, or that productivity is unrelated to social stratification. If production increases or if new forms of wealth are made available, the chief may employ an existing network of collection and distribution to obtain valued goods, to increase the number of his followers, or to support large communal tasks. He can also improve his economic position by extending the network, as after a war of conquest. Moreover, a society that produces only a small or uncertain surplus is not likely to have the sort of status differences that are symbolized by redistributive activities. It is necessary, however, to take into account all of a chief's sources of income and paths of expenditure in order to evaluate his economic role and the possibilities for change inherent in it. Redistribution in a particular society can then be interpreted in the context of other economic activities and of the total social structure.

The chiefs whose economic role will be described in this paper reigned over the atoll of Butaritari and the reef island of Makin,[2] the northernmost of the Gilbert Islands. The two islands have constituted a single society since time immemorial. The distinction between chiefs, aristocrats, and commoners was drawn more sharply there than in most of the southern Gilberts, and resembles the condition in the Marshall Islands. The three status levels traditionally possessed different, but overlapping, rights to most estates. The territorial organization of the villages cut across the bonds of relationship between aristocratic and commoner descent groups. Each of the eight villages on Butaritari and the two on Makin were autonomous entities under a headman and council of elders. Almost all the lands in each district were controlled by descent groups localized in the community. The combined population of Makin and Butaritari was around 2,000 in the nineteenth century (J. T. Gulick, n.d.; Stevenson, 1901 [2], p. 56). The number of inhabitants was only 1,945 at the time of the 1905 census, but it has since increased to over 3,000.

The native culture has been strongly influenced by Europeans for more than a century. The first trader in coconut oil arrived in 1846 (A. Gulick, 1932, p. 58), and there were eleven in residence by 1889 (Stevenson, *ibid.*, p. 76). An American Congregationalist mission station was founded in 1865 (Bingham, 1867), French Catholics began their work with a visit by a priest in 1891-92 (Sabatier, 1939, pp. 161-166), and three-fourths of the population now adhere to this faith.

The most important social changes were instituted by the British administration after the establishment of a protectorate over the Gilbert and Ellice Islands in 1892. During the next two decades the people were compelled to abandon their houses scattered through the forests, and to move into the villages, where their descent groups were formally localized. The extended family was dissolved when the traditional large dwelling was replaced by a smaller house with a raised floor. In 1922

[2] American maps incorrectly call Butaritari "Makin" and Makin "Little Makin" or "Makin Meang." The name of the principal village on each island is 'Butaritari" and "Makin," respectively, which will be referred to as "Butaritari Town" and "Makin Town."

the first British lands commissioner altered the old rules of tenure by granting many additional persons full rights to collect coconuts on the estates of descent groups. He destroyed the basis of the system of social stratification by assigning the high chief and his siblings a quarter of almost every plot of land and by giving the aristocratic and commoner co-owners equal rights to the remainder.[3]

Sources for the period from about 1860 to 1922 contain abundant material on the operation of the economic system. The high chief's right to collect coconuts and his claims to contributions of money and taro from his subjects were recorded by Robert Louis Stevenson (1901), who spent two months on Butaritari in 1889, and by the ethnographer Augustin Krämer (1906), who visited the island in 1899. Older informants remember bringing taro or fish to a chief who was staying in their village, and attending the life-crisis feasts of chiefs on Butaritari. The histories of descent groups and their estates provide additional data. Finally, some remnant of the high chief's economic role survived until the abolition of this office in 1963, and his activities previous to the land reform can thus be described with some assurance. An outline of the social structure of the two islands at that time will be presented as a preliminary step.

The lands of each village district were apportioned among estates that belonged to ambilineal descent groups or ramages (Firth, 1957, pp. 5-6). Each ramage was associated with at least one house site in the village, from which it took its name, even if most of its members lived away from the settlement. It usually owned several forest plots, which were larger than the house sites and were planted principally to coconuts (rather than breadfruit). A ramage also owned a garden for the cultivation of the atoll taro (*Cyrtosperma chamissonis*), or a share in the common garden of the village. These gardens were excavated to a depth of about eight feet, since *Cyrtosperma* roots must be in contact with water. Rows of stones divided the ramage garden into beds that belonged to sibling sets or to paired brothers and sisters. The membership of the ramage consisted of descendants of the founding ancestor or sibling set who had inherited a share in the taro garden. The intermediate ancestors might be of either sex.

Many varieties of *Cyrtosperma* are grown, but they can conveniently be assigned to two classes. The small varieties need no cultivation after the tops have been planted, and readily multiply by suckers, so that they are usually seen growing in clumps. The large kinds have few or no suckers, and require fertilization with leaves and humus placed around

---

[3] The administrative changes in native land tenure are described in the reports of various lands commissioners. These records were made available to me through the kindness of the Commissioner of the Gilbert and Ellice Islands District, Mr. R. G. Roberts.

the plant in a ring of dried coconut or pandanus leaves. Corms of the larger varieties, particularly those that have attained an enormous size after years of careful cultivation, are formally presented to kinsmen at life-crisis ceremonies and to the high chief. Each plant requires at least four square feet of growing space. Since beds usually have regular outlines, it is possible to estimate their capacity by counting the plants along each side.

The ramage gardens of Kiebu, the smaller of the two villages on Makin island, were easily measured because they are joined in a single large excavation, rather than scattered over the interior of the islet, as is frequently the case. The relatively small gardens of the ramages Rikoia and Te Ai Kaina had a capacity of 1,700 and 2,200 large taro plants, respectively. One of the largest gardens, that of the Tabweaang estate, which was once the joint property of the village headman's ramage and its associated commoners, had space for about 11,000 plants. Perhaps two-thirds of a garden's area is devoted to the larger varieties of taro, the remainder being planted to the smaller varieties or left uncultivated. Some expansion of the Kiebu gardens is continually under way; the boundaries of the main taro-growing area are pushed out, hills within the garden are gradually removed, and small gardens are excavated south of the village. This expansion is limited, however: taro will not grow near the shore and hard work is required to prepare a new bed, even when iron spades are used to move the soil and crowbars to break up the rocky platform above the water level. The area of the gardens of the adjacent Tabweaang and Te Buutia estates has been increased by only about 3 per cent in the last generation. It is possible to estimate the amount of taro grown in the late nineteenth and early twentieth centuries, and thus the effect of redistribution on the economy.

A married couple usually resided on a site where the husband's parents or grandparents had lived previously. A ramage was thus localized around some of its members, mostly men, who were related to one another either through men or women. Until about two generations ago, the nuclear families occupying a plot of village land constituted a single, large household, with up to twenty-five members. The oldest man in residence was usually head of the household and manager of the ramage estate. The household controlled all the forestland that belonged to the ramage; and other members of the descent group could collect coconuts there only with the elder's consent. The absent members retained the right to cultivate the beds they had inherited in the ramage taro garden, but those who lived in other villages often left their beds in the care of the elder or of other resident kinsmen.

A ramage that owned a large estate often sent some of its members to one of its unoccupied house sites and assigned them nearby forestlands to cultivate. After several generations, only one branch of the ramage would have the right of settling on the site. By then, the subsidiary household would be well on its way to becoming the nucleus of a new ramage, whose autonomy was publicly recognized when its elder was permitted to represent it on the village council—and when its members brought taro to the high chief as a separate group. Around 1910, Kiebu village, with a population under 200, contained twenty or twenty-one households, seventeen of which were the headquarters of independent ramages. The household is now based on a single nuclear family, although it usually includes other kinsmen as well.

The great majority of estates was owned simultaneously by two ramages, one commoner and other aristocratic. The commoner ramages traced their descent from immigrants, from natives whose more remote ancestry had been forgotten, and from ex-aristocrats who had been deprived of their rank after being defeated in a struggle over the chieftainship. These ramages were not segments of larger descent groups, since, among commoners, the descendants of siblings did not maintain a special relationship after their mutual independence had been recognized by the community. There were two series of aristocratic ramages: the Butaritari aristocrats, descendants of a high chief, and the Makin aristocrats, descendants of a headman of Makin Town.[4]

Succession to these two titles normally followed a rule of patrilineal primogeniture, although the high chief's hereditary right was regularly challenged by one or more of his father's full brothers' sons. The heir's younger brothers and sisters were assigned estates and founded new aristocratic ramages. The headman's ramage, in all of the villages except Makin Town, had been founded by a collateral kinsman of the high chief. His duties were to transmit messages from the ruler and to act as executive officer for the local council of ramage elders. The Butaritari and Makin aristocracies constituted descent groups of a higher order, or maximal ramages, of which the landowning aristocratic ramages were segments. The Butaritari aristocracy was especially cohesive; its elders met in council to install a new high chief and to make important decisions that affected him, such as the identity of his principal wife.

A commoner ramage was bound to the total society by virtue of an association with a particular aristocratic ramage. The nature of the relationship depended on the maximal range of the aristocrats and on whether or not the two groups occupied the same house site. Commoners who shared a communal dwelling with the descendants of a high chief were compelled to cultivate taro for their superiors' benefit and had no voice in village affairs. Others avoided the burdens of co-resi-

---

[4] The designations "Butaritari aristocrats" and "Makin aristocrats" are my own. In the local dialect, the high chief, his siblings, and his children are called *uea*, and the other aristocrats *toka*. The commoners are described as "workers" (*taani m'akuri*), "helpers" (*tabonibai*), or "young men" (*rorobuaka*).

dence by linking themselves to aristocrats residing elsewhere, usually in the high chief's village of Butaritari Town. Linked ramages owed one another hospitality and attendance at life-crisis feasts, but the commoners did not have to provide the aristocrats with food on other occasions, and they were represented on the village council by their own elders. The Makin aristocrats also lived with commoners, but typically cultivated their own share of a taro garden. Associated ramages acted as a single corporate group in some situations, especially those concerned with the ownership or transfer of land. For example, if a member of either group committed murder or adultery, the other had to acquiesce in the alienation of part of the jointly owned property as compensation in order to avoid involvement in a feud.

The economic role of the high chief can now be considered. His traditional sources of income fell into three categories, which will be described separately: (1) the everyday procurement of food from the estates where he resided or that were reservd for him, and from his affinal kinsman; (2) the contributions made to his life-crisis feasts; and (3) the formal deliveries of food that acknowledged his ultimate rights to the resources of his islands. No hard and fast correlation can be made between particular kinds of income and particular methods of consumption. Broadly speaking, however, food in the first category supported the chief's family, dependents, and workers, and food in the second category —and in part the third—was redistributed to the people in general. It is noteworthy that although the chief was entitled to gifts from all the villages and from most of the estates of the society, he had little control over the timing or amount of these presentations. Under certain circumstances they could even be diverted to a rival. The high chief's authority in noneconomic matters was also quite limited; he seldom punished offenses, except those committed against himself and his kinsmen, and only occasionally mediated family quarrels and interramage disputes.

The high chief resided on a Butaritari Town estate over which he exercised rights like those of aristocratic landowners. A ruler of the early nineteenth century, Nan Te-atuu-ma-te-ataata,[5] seized it from the sons of Nam Mannarara, his father's brother, after defeating their attempt to usurp the chieftainship. Some of the descendants of Nan Te-atuu-ma-te-ataata's elder sister were permitted to share the high chief's house site and estate as a gesture of respect. The co-resident subordinates were descended from children or grandchildren of Nam Mannarara who had been reduced to commoner status by Nan Te-atuu-ma-te-ataata.

The high chief also possessed superior rights to several other estates on Butaritari and Makin that did not belong to the aristocrats. The

---

[5] In the Butaritari-Makin dialect, the names of males are preceded by *Na, Nam, Nan,* or *Nang;* the corresponding female prefix is *Nei.* The letters *b', bw, m',* and *mw* represent velarized consonants.

Makin lands had been the property of Nam Mannarara's wife's brother, who was killed by the headman of Makin Town after the main fight over the succession to the chieftainship. It is said that Nan Te-atuu-ma-te-ataata's principal wife, who was a daughter of Nam Mannarara, insisted that these estates be set aside to produce food for her children. Nan Te-atuu-ma-te-ataata and his successors also had rights, to the exclusion of aristocrats, to an isolated district on Butaritari atoll where he had lived with his foster-grandfather. Two ramages of Butaritari Town acted as the high chief's stewards, with the duty of collecting provisions from the commoners on his outlying estates and of cooking the food at his feasts.

The high chief's official residence, in villages other than Butaritari Town, was the home of the local headman. He also spent periods of varying length in the households of maternal and foster relations. The visiting chief and his companions were supplied with food and other goods from the estates on which he stayed, supplemented by gifts from the other ramages of the villages.

The high chief's wives and children frequently received contributions of food from his brothers-in-law. Ordinarily, a man did not take food to his married sisters because they or their children could exercise their claims to their hereditary lands at any time. The high chief's wives passed neither ramage affiliations nor land rights to their children, so that their brothers had a permanent usufruct to the property that would otherwise have fallen to the sisters' share. The sisters' children often became linked aristocrats to their maternal ramages later on. Stevenson (1901 [2], pp. 59-62) described marriages to "heiresses" as a principal means of buttressing the throne.

The high chief Nan Teitei impoverished himself by giving up all but one of his seventeen wives upon his conversion (around 1880). The chief's brothers-in-law were under special compulsion to bring taro when he or his wives fell ill. The history of one ramage relates that, when the high chief Nan Teauoki lay on his deathbed, three brothers of one of his wives not only withheld food but resented a fourth brother's generosity so much that they killed him by pressing a coconut log on his neck as he slept. In revenge, the Makin Town headman had the murderers buried alive in Nan Teauoki's grave. On the other hand, brothers-in-law who displayed particular generosity might be given use-rights to plots of land. In the avunculocal Trobriand islands, too, deliveries of food by the subclans of the chief's wives were a principal means of support for his house (Malinowski, 1929, pp. 110-113). However, there they were an expanded version of an obligation binding on the brothers-in-law of commoners as well, rather than a practice carried on only for the chief's benefit.

The private income of the high chief was sufficient to fill the needs of his household, even though it was the largest residential group in the society. The high chief, his children, and probably his adult siblings were exempt from productive labor. They pursued tasks that interested them, however. A recent high chief, Na Koriri, and his children expanded, planted, and cultivated a taro garden that his predecessor had purchased. Na Koriri also excelled as a midwife (a specialty usually reserved for women) and was an expert canoe builder. The last ruler, Na Uraura, was good at making eel traps and at catching eels and octopi on the reef, but he neither tapped toddy nor cultivated taro regularly.

Formerly, chiefs symbolized their status as recipients rather than producers of food by their extreme corpulence (Krämer, 1906, p. 319; Wilkes, 1845, p. 74). The high chief's children were beaten when they did not finish the rich foods served to them, and were carried around at mealtimes so that they would eat more. "Disgusting," the name given to a piece of land near an old residence of the high chief, was explained by an informant as referring to the quantities of surplus food that were thrown away there to rot.

The high chief was responsible for supporting persons who were temporarily excluded from the ordinary subsistence economy. Informants agreed that one of his principal duties was to care for strangers. Perhaps the importance of this function is connected with the fact that Butaritari-Makin society has always recruited a significant portion of its members by immigration. In the past, the high chief provided strangers with food and might secure land rights for them. Even at the time of the field study, a native of another island who was unable or unwilling to live with relatives was encouraged to stay at the high chief's house, and was often given money for his passage home. Local people sometimes fled to the protection of the chief's household because they feared vengeance or the wrath of kinsmen.

Some of the high chief's income was expended for the maintenance of craftsmen and laborers. According to Wilkes (1845, p. 94), some of the house and canoe builders in the Gilberts were dependent on chiefs and received no special reward for their work, while free specialists were paid mostly in foodstuffs. Even in this century, a high chief had a carpenter living with him for a time, probably while his European-style house at Makin Town was being built. It was more usual for the recent high chiefs to arrange for the construction of their houses and canoes on the same basis as other people, however. The director of the project generally received three meals a day, food for his family, and a gift when his task was completed. Ordinary workers were served at least one big meal each day.

The man who directed the construction of a canoe for the high chief, Na Kaiea II, received a quarter-plot of land for his services. His assistants belonged to the ramage on whose land the chief was staying at the time. Members of this ramage also provided food for the builders. Na Kaiea's successor, Na Koriri, himself supervised the construction of the 40-foot-long *Taoba,* one of the largest canoes in the Gilbert Islands. He was assisted by only four men, whose food he supplied himself. In 1961 the *Taoba* was in the hands of the Kuuma villagers, who used it to transport their copra to Butaritari Town. They agreed to keep the big canoe in repair and to take the high chief to Makin whenever he wished.

In pre-contact times, when each plank had to be laboriously adzed out of a coconut trunk, the construction of a large canoe took a long time and required many workers, and this must have strained even a high chief's resources. In constructing his canoes, as in caring for strangers, the high chief used his ample resources to accomplish tasks that were beyond the capacity of ordinary households, sometimes employing a large number of people on a major undertaking. The workers received no payment except their meals. Na Kaiea II once had the young men of Makin island reinforce the wall of his taro garden with stones, and later he asked the people of Makin Town to enlarge the garden by removing a mound and its projecting ridge. The last independent high chief, Na Bure-i-moa, had his subjects construct a long stone wharf on the lagoon shore of Butaritari Town; he then charged trading ships a fee of three dollars for each day they anchored there (Krämer, 1906, p. 320).

The entire population of Butaritari and Makin formerly contributed to the great feasts celebrating the installation of a new high chief and the life-crises of the ruler and his children. On such occasions the elders of the Butaritari aristocracy decided on the amounts to be delivered by their own Butaritari Town ramages and by the other nine villages. The village headmen and councils then determined the size of each household's contributions.

The people at large took the part of the high chief's kindred at his life-crisis ceremonies. The first marriage of Na Kaiea II, which probably occurred before World War I, was the last time that a high chief's wedding was celebrated according to the traditional pattern. Na Kaiea's bride was the paternal granddaughter of a headman of Kiebu village. The first feast was served by her father's ramage to the people who had come to Kiebu in a fleet of canoes to escort her to her wedding. After the church ceremony, a much larger feast was held at Butaritari Town. Every household on the two islands, except those of the bride's kinsmen, brought food, and the high chief had ropes stretched across the road to detain passersby so that everyone would attend the celebration.

Redistribution on a smaller scale occurred at the life-crisis feasts of the petty chiefs, who were initially the full brothers of the high chief, and who succeeded him in turn if he died without issue. Early in the nineteenth century, the three younger full brothers of Nan Te-iti-ma-raroa became petty chiefs and were invested with a degree of superiority over the other aristocrats. The estates controlled by the latter constituted the petty chief's domain (*te mwii,* literally "inheritance"). None of the three domains was localized since each included lands in several villages. It is possible that petty chiefs escorted visitors from their domains into the high chief's presence. Each petty chief was also assigned an estate of his own and founded an aristocratic ramage.

The status of petty chief was hereditary until the domains were reassigned to the full siblings of a new high chief. The sons of the old petty chiefs often sought to avoid an inevitable reduction in their own rank by seizing the paramount position. Their attempts were usually foiled, partly because the people believed that only the eldest son of a chief possessed the full supernatural powers of chieftainship. Sterility in the chiefly house permitted Nan Te-iti-ma-raroa's full brothers' descendants to retain their rank for about two generations, but soon after the turn of the century domains were assigned to the three children of Nan Taabu's first wife, including the next high chief, Na Kaiea II. Later these siblings agreed to transfer a relatively small number of estates to the joint control of a son and daughter of the high chief's second wife. A petty chief was referred to as *te teei* ("child"—in the sense of "young person" rather than "offspring") by the ramages of his domain, probably because he had lived with some of them in his early years. When he visited a village as an adult, these ramages again invited him to stay on their lands.

Attendance at the life-crisis feasts of petty chiefs was augmented by the ramages of their domains. All of these descent groups brought gifts to Butaritari Town for the celebration. There the person being honored made the round of the local households belonging to his domain, accompanied by the visitors. At the end of the celebration, the people from the other villages received a share of the durable gifts, such as mats, that had been presented by the kinfolk of the petty chief's spouse. Their "canoes were filled," as the phrase went, with taro from the gardens of the Butaritari Town ramages they had visited.

The high chief had ultimate or supreme rights to almost every estate on Makin and Butaritari. (A few were exempt because they belonged to aristocratic ramages that had rendered outstanding services to a high chief in time of peril.) On rare occasions the chief exercised his rights to confiscate land as a fine, or to allot it to an immigrant. His claims received regular recognition, however, when ramages and villages brought him a share of the produce. The most frequent and important gift was taro, but coconuts, fish, and porpoises were also presented. The bulk of this revenue could not be stored for long, and so was redistributed almost immediately, the chief thereby sustaining his reputation for generosity. There is no evidence that the Gilbertese followed the Polynesian custom of associating supreme land rights with the power of placing a taboo on the harvesting of vegetable food.

When the high chief visited a village, he received taro from its estates, gifts which were called *to uaroko*. If the associated aristocratic and commoner ramages shared a dwelling, the time and the size of the presentation were normally determined by the aristocratic elder, after consultation with his dependents. The elder took the lead in the joint presentation and sat near the high chief during the feast that followed, while persons of lower rank ate apart. Linked aristocrats organized a delivery of taro to the high chief only if they resided on another house site in the commoners' village; they could not summon their nominal subordinates to bring taro to Butaritari Town. Commoner ramages that did not have superiors in their home village made gifts to the high chief on their own initiative.

The average gift comprised twenty or thirty large taro corms, a quantity that probably never exceeded 3 per cent of the plants of the larger varieties growing in the garden. The cultivators—who were generally commoners in any event—were assessed contributions of taro in accordance with the shares they held in the ramage garden. The partition of the garden, in turn, reflected the genealogically determined divisions of the ramage. The smallest unit of assessment was the bed or two that had been inherited jointly by a group or pair of siblings. Since deliveries were made by landowning groups, a sibling set was sooner or later called on to participate in the presentations of all of its ramages. The frequency of ramage contributions in the traditional society is unknown.

The high chief preserved some of the taro by burying it until it was needed to feed the next group making a presentation. The remainder was turned over to his household, to those of his stewards, to the ramage he was visiting, or to strangers. One chief is said to have exchanged the showy but tasteless corms presented to him for the smaller kinds he preferred.

A petty chief also received formal gifts of food, and eventually money, from ramages of his domain that were localized in the village where he was staying. After the conversion of the people to Christianity, Christmas and New Year's were regarded as particularly appropriate occasions for such presentations. Na Kaiea II (reigned 1910-1954), unlike previous high chiefs, did not receive gifts from estates outside his personal domain. His main economic advantage over his siblings lay in his annual "day" (which will be described below). Na Uraura (reigned 1959-1963) received only a trickle of *uaroko* gifts from the ramages once allotted to his father, Na Koriri (reigned 1954-1959), Na Kaiea's half brother. His siblings and his father's sisters' children received none at all, and so had to provide for their families' needs entirely from the produce of their own lands.

Occasionally village headmen would assemble the council of elders to prepare a communal gift for the high chief. The council assigned each household a contribution of taro (usually one large corm), toddy molasses, fish, and money. The present was taken to Butaritari Town by the elders or their representatives. The high chief shared his gifts with the aristocratic ramages of Butaritari Town, who in turn were obliged to "fill the canoes" of the visitors with taro and other food. A fish called *te ikarikiriki* (*Gymnosarda*), which was abundant about Butaritari, was a particularly prized countergift. An occasion for a general collection and distribution of food may have been the great annual feast (presumably a religious ceremony) held on Butaritari about midwinter in honor of Nan Teauoki, the ancestor of the high chiefly line (Wilkes, 1845, p. 100).

After the middle of the nineteenth century, the high chief Na Kaiea I (reigned *ca.* 1850-1879) became interested in purchasing European trade goods, which at first consisted principally of firearms and distilled spirits. He obtained the necessary money by taking advantage of his supreme land rights to monopolize (for a time) the trade in coconut oil or copra. He thereby imposed new burdens on his people, but he also distributed some of the income among them—in his own fashion.

Alone in his islands, it was he who dealt and profited; he was the planter and the merchant; and his subjects toiled for his behoof in servitude. When they wrought long and well their taskmaster declared a holiday, and supplied and shared a general debauch. The scale of his providing was at times magnificent; six hundred dollars' worth of gin and brandy was set forth at once; the narrow land resounded with the noise of revelry; and it was a common thing to see the subjects (staggering themselves) parade their drunken sovereign on the forehatch of a wrecked vessel, king and commons howling and singing as they went. At a word from Nakaiea's mouth the revel ended; Makin became once more an island of slaves and teetotalers; and on the morrow all the population must be on the roads or in the taro-patches toiling under his bloodshot eye. (Stevenson, 1901 [2], pp. 56-57)

The high chiefs retained the right to take all the coconuts on Butaritari and Makin until the partition of the lands in 1922, but the successors of Na Kaiea I exercised their prerogative only at long intervals. An old man remembered only two occasions on which the high chief had come to Makin for that purpose: once in the reign of Na Bure-i-moa, when my informant was a child, and once in that of Na Kaiea II. The high chief arrived from Butaritari accompanied by young men and girls, who helped the natives collect coconuts and make copra during the day, and then joined them in dances every night. When the coconuts of the smaller village, Kiebu, were exhausted, its people followed the high chief's party to Makin Town to assist in the work there. The high chief fed the coconut collectors from his own resources, from the gardens in his domain, and with food purchased with the copra receipts. The owners of exempted estates, who delivered no taro to the chief, usually permitted him to pick coconuts from their palms.

The high chief's traditional claim to the produce of his islands included rights over the ponds where *baneawa* (*Chanos chanos*) fish were raised. The largest ponds in Makin Town and Kiebu belonged to the headmen's ramages, with whom the high chief stayed on his visits to their villages. The high chief was considered to be the owner of the ponds as long as he lived in a headman's house. His hosts provided *Chanos* from time to time to feast the ramages that brought him taro. One informant stated that all the fish in the Makin Town ponds were removed periodically for the high chief's benefit. A few *Chanos* were probably eaten on the spot by the fishermen, but most of the catch, which might fill as many as ten large coconut-leaf baskets, was turned over to the chief. He did not redistribute the fish immediately but had a large quantity preserved by baking in an earth oven, followed by drying in the sun.

Stranded porpoises were a windfall for a people whose craving for fat was seldom satisfied. Certain villages had ramages of porpoise-callers who possessed magic formulas for bringing these mammals onto the reef. I learned of the disposal of a large school in the 1920's from a contemporary account in a mission newspaper. The porpoises came ashore below the village of Kuuma; the inhabitants retained enough meat for their own feast, and sent the rest to the high chief Na Kaeia II in Butaritari Town, who distributed the meat among the households of the villages round about. The particularly fatty back portion of a porpoise was reserved for the high chief himself.

The custom of presenting captured turtles to the chief for distribution has been reported in the Marshall Islands (Erdland, 1914, pp. 41-44), the Gilbertese-speaking population of Ocean island (Maude and Maude, 1932, pp. 285-287), and the island of Abemama in the central Gilberts (Stevenson, 1901 [2], p. 161). It was probably once practiced on Butaritari, too, although my informants had no recollection of it.

The high chief was theoretically entitled to a portion of any large fish, such as a tuna, caught by a man of the village in which the chief lived, but in fact only men on friendly terms with the chief appear to have shared their large catches with him regularly. The chief usually received a big fish he saw being hauled in or brought ashore, however; the fisherman would have been ashamed to act otherwise, and he received a good meal as a reward.

The high chief Na Bure-i-moa (reigned 1888-1910), who had surrendered his elder brother's monopoly of the copra trade, had two main sources of cash income. Eleven foreign traders each paid him a patent of a hundred dollars, and his subjects paid a head tax at the rate of a dollar for a man, half a dollar for a woman, and a shilling for a child.

According to Krämer, who expressed distaste for the entire chiefly house, Na Bure-i-moa "issues numerous invitations to banquets and then charges each guest two marks for some salted fish and taro." The money was used for the purchase of uniforms and arms for the chief's guards— and for the enlargement of the chief's brother's photograph, among other things. (Stevenson, 1901 [2], p. 68; Krämer, 1906, p. 320 [I have translated the quotation from Krämer.])

The British administration stopped the high chief from collecting fees from traders, but it permitted the payment of the head tax, nominally on a voluntary basis. This levy gradually replaced the presentation of taro and other foodstuffs by villages, although the traditional *uaroko* gifts by ramages continued. It became customary to turn the money over to the high chief on the anniversary of his installation, which was known as his "day," and which Butaritari and Makin usually held in alternate years. The elders of the island assessed each household about five shillings for this purpose in the twentieth century. At the formal presentation of the money, the high chief provided a feast for the assembled elders with food purchased at the store and taro from his own beds. After Na Kaiea II had received a large sum of government money for replanting coconut trees on land that had been used by the American forces during World War II, he gave £100 to the elders to buy food for a feast. A dance in the evening always concluded the high chief's "day."

Makin failed to hold a day in 1960-61, probably the first time in living memory. Some people explained this departure from custom by the fact that the island had been engaged in preparations for the Colony Conference that met there in August, 1960. A more fundamental reason, however, was that one of the co-headmen of Makin Town felt that the high chief Na Uraura had rejected the authority of the elders in a land dispute. The headman refused to participate in the council's discussions concerning the high chief, and several other men followed his lead. But the annual day was held on Butaritari in 1961.

Failure to contribute to the high chief's day or to his installation ceremony was treated as an offense against the village, which the elders punished as they did other refusals to participate in communal undertakings: the delinquent was usually haled before the council and shamed by a public lecture. The penalty of ostracism was imposed in some aggravated cases, and the offender who had been "sent to Coventry" was prohibited from entering the forest or visiting his neighbors, and from receiving help in any task, until he begged the council's pardon and made restitution. I do not know whether the same penalties were inflicted in the pre-colonial era.

In summary, the gifts made to the high and petty chiefs originally had little economic significance, either for the donors or for the recipi-

ents. The presentations of food were only a very small proportion of a
ramage's large taro plants, and even less of its other crops. Breadfruit,
the staple for half the year, and such everyday foods as coconuts, pandanus, and the smaller varieties of taro were omitted, or included only
incidentally. It is not surprising, therefore, that the virtual abandonment
of presentations to the chief did not result in any shortage or malappor-
tionment of food. Only the special redistributions of stranded porpoises
and the pond fish assured each household of a fair share of a valued
resource.

Nor did the high chief need his subjects' contributions, most of which
he soon gave away. His private sources of income appear to have sufficed
for his expenditures, which were generally of the same kind, although
much heavier, than those of other households. The public deliveries of
goods to the chief were potentially of economic importance, however,
since they could be used to transmit wealth other than perishable foodstuffs. Recent high chiefs obtained substantial amounts of cash through
traditional channels.

The redistribution of gifts of food on Butaritari and Makin can be
interpreted as a demonstration of a relationship between a chief and his
subjects. People brought huge taro corms to weddings, births, homecom-
ings, sickbeds, and funerals in order to claim ramage membership or
the future assistance of kinsmen. They indicated their dependence on
the chiefs by acting as their kinsmen at life-crisis ceremonies. (The pro-
hibition against using kin terms to refer to a chief was another symbol
of his peculiar status.) They also acknowledged the chief as the ultimate
source of their land rights, and as a privileged mediator of their disputes,
by presenting taro to him at other times—a recognition that was to some
degree voluntary. It was the village councils or the ramage elders, not
the high chief himself, that determined the amounts the chief would
receive. Sometimes the people even exercised a limited choice of recipients for their contributions. The traditional history of the society gives
two instances of food being diverted from an heir apparent to his half
brother or father's brother's son. The legitimate heir was then compelled
to fight for his title against the pretender.

Once established in power, the chief might kill any of his kinsmen
who intercepted deliveries of food from commoners or aristocrats, and
seek to gain popularity by the generosity of his own gifts. There is
a tradition that a high chief, Nan Tetab'akea, wished to make his
brother's son, Nan Teauoki, his successor in preference to his own sons.
He advised Nan Teauoki always to give the best part of his catch of fish
to the largest ramages on Butaritari. These groups then became Nan
Teauoki's allies in the war for the chieftainship. Chiefs in the era of
the copra trade were admired for spending large sums of money on
feasts.

The procedure of collecting and redistributing taro also made manifest other kinds of social relationships. A newly created ramage showed its independence by making its own presentation to the high chief. Aristocrats and commoners who lived in the same village indicated that they were co-owners of an estate by making a joint presentation. The relationship displayed in this way afterwards served as a reason for giving and receiving substantial help. A village, too, demonstrated its corporate identity when it brought taro to the high chief. As Stevenson observed, intervillage rivalry was great enough to cause brawls among the young men when several communities were assembled at Butaritari Town.

REFERENCES

BINGHAM, HIRAM. 1867.   Letter in The Friend, 18, No. 8, (August 1, 1867), 72.

COULT, ALLAN D. 1964.   Role allocation, position structuring, and ambilineal descent. American Anthropologist, 66, 29-41.

ERDLAND, A. 1941.   Die Marshall-Insulaner. Leben und Sitte, Sinn und Religion eines Südsee-volkes. Anthropos Ethnologische Bibliothek, Vol. 2, No. 1. Münster: Aschendorffsche.

FIRTH, RAYMOND. 1950.   Primitive Polynesian economy. New York: Humanities Press.

————. 1957.   A note on descent groups in Polynesia. Man, 57, 4-8 (article 2).

GOODENOUGH, WARD H. 1951.   Property, kin, and community on Truk. Yale University Publications in Anthropology, 46. Yale University Press.

GULICK, ADDISON. 1932.   Evolutionist and missionary, John Thomas Gulick. University of Chicago Press.

GULICK, JOHN T. n.d.   Journey of the missionary schooner Caroline on her first voyage to Micronesia, 1852.

KRAMER, AUGUSTIN. 1906.   Hawaii, Ostmikronesien, Samoa. Stuttgart: Strecker u. Schröder.

MALINOWSKI, BRONISLAW. 1929.   The sexual life of savages in northwestern Melanesia. Ethnographic account of courtship, marriage, and family life among the natives of the Trobriand islands, British New Guinea. London: Routledge & Kegan Paul.

MAUDE, HARRY E., and MAUDE, HONOR C. 1932.   The social organization of Banaba. Journal of the Polynesian Society, 41, 262-301.

POLANYI, KARL. 1944.   The great transformation. New York: Farrar & Rinehart (1957. Boston: Beacon Press).

————. 1957.   The economy as instituted process. In Trade and market in the early empires, Economies in history and theory, Karl Pollanyi, Conrad M. Arensberg, and Harry W. Pearson (eds.). New York: Free Press of Glencoe.

SABATIER, ERNEST. 1939.   Sous l'Équateur du Pacifique. Paris. Éditions Dillen.

SAHLINS, MARSHALL D. 1958.   Social stratification in Polynesia. American Ethnological Society. University of Washington Press.

SCHNEIDER, DAVID M. 1961.   Truk. *In* David M. Schneider and Kathleen
    Gough (eds.), Matrilineal kinship. University of California Press, pp.
    202-234.
STEVENSON, ROBERT LOUIS. 1901.   In the South Seas (2 vols.). Collection of
    British authors. Leipzig: Bernhard Tauchnitz.
WILKES, CHARLES. 1845.   Narrative of the United States exploring expedition
    (Vol. 5). Philadelphia: Lea & Blanchard.

PROBLEMS OF SUCCESSION IN A
CHIPPEWA COUNCIL [1]

Frank C. Miller, UNIVERSITY OF MINNESOTA

For almost half a century the affairs of the Deer Lake tribe [2] of Chippewa [3] Indians in Minnesota have been conducted by a tribal council operating under a written constitution. Although this modern form of government stands in marked contrast to aboriginal Chippewa political organization, it nevertheless furnishes some interesting case materials for the analysis of succession to office and of some of the general problems inherent in the process. I shall consider briefly some aspects of political organization during the early phases of contact, the establishment of the modern council, and the patterns of succession to office. Then I shall analyze in detail a recent dispute over succession that led to a sweeping reorganization of tribal government.

The nature of Chippewa political organization before the coming of the Europeans has been the subject of considerable controversy. The view that had been accepted until recently is exemplified by Barnouw's concept of "Chippewa atomism":

. . . there was no economic cooperation outside of the family unit. There was no communal hunting . . . no camp circle, no organized council of chiefs, no policing system, no regularly constituted military societies, and no symbols of group integration. Every man was for himself or for his own family; and there were few activities which linked the isolated families together. (Barnouw, 1950, p. 16)

James (1954, pp. 283-284) criticizes this point of view and suggests that among the southern Chippewa there was considerable concentration of population, warfare involving rather large war parties, and incipient centralization of political authority. In a series of recent ethnohistorical works by Hickerson (1956, 1960, 1962, 1963), there is a concerted attempt to demonstrate that the ecology of both hunting and warfare, in the areas that became Minnesota and Wisconsin, furnished a basis for a

---

[1] The investigation on which this paper is based was supported by Public Health Service Research Grants No. MH 04982 and MH 10683, from the National Institute of Mental Health, and by National Service Foundation Research Grant No. G 13020.
[2] Names of people and places are pseudonyms.
[3] Although "Ojibwa" is the most satisfactory term for the cultural category as a whole, it is preferable to use "Chippewa" for those who live in the United States because that is what they call themselves.

more elaborate sociopolitical organization than is indicated by Barnouw's formulation. Although Hickerson's interpretations seem to be overly enthusiastic in some ways, he has demonstrated the importance of village life and some communal activities for the southern or southwestern Chippewa before the imposition of the reservation system in the latter part of the nineteenth century.

Hickerson denies the view of Barnouw (1950) and Friedl (1956) that Chippewa chiefs lacked authority, but he admits that the subject of chieftainship is complex and in need of further study. Some of the kinds of chiefs among the nineteenth century Chippewa were:

. . . hereditary chiefs, chiefs made by agents, and nonhereditary war chiefs. There were "pipe lighters," or "speakers," who acted as spokesmen for civil or village chiefs, and also Mide leaders. Warren wrote of chiefs who were recognized heads of gentes, and these, it so happens, appear in most instances to have been prominent village chiefs. (Hickerson, 1962, p. 47)

Questions of the degree of authority and of the relationships between different varieties of leaders need not concern us here; the point of interest for this paper is that the pattern of village chieftainship was well established in the nineteenth century.

In the literature there is scant discussion of practices and norms relating to succession. In one of the early classics of Chippewa studies, Warren (1957, pp. 316-319 [originally published in 1885]) briefly describes some particular lines of succession. It is clear that hereditary chieftainships are transmitted patrilineally, usually to the eldest son. It is equally clear that such a rule is not followed if a chief has not effectively carried out the duties of his office, or if the firstborn son is considered unfit to assume the responsibilities.

During the nineteenth century the major feature of political organization at Deer Lake was the system of seven bands, each with a chieftainship inherited patrilineally; but much ethnohistorical research needs to be done before we can judge the relevance of Hickerson's view (1962, pp. 49-50) that the "band, when all things are considered, was the most vital economic unit." And whether the Deer Lake villages served the important political and military functions that Hickerson describes for Leech Lake—(here I follow his practice of using real names)—is another question that needs to be investigated. We know that the chiefs, together with the adult males of the reservation, conducted negotiations with the United States government, and the names of the men were listed under their chiefs' on the government roll for annuities and commodities. The bands were localized, the members living in the general area of the chiefs' residences. Two or more bands might be found in the same large community, or a band might reside many miles from its nearest neighbors.

During the latter part of the nineteenth century, basic economic and cultural changes led to the disappearance of the bands as social units, but this did not undermine the importance of the chiefs. Most of the original area of the reservation was ceded to the federal government, to be made available to homesteaders and lumbermen. The most direct result of the loss of land was the reduction of the subsistence base, so that the population could no longer support itself by hunting and gathering, which became subsidiary to small-scale agriculture. The shifts of population that accompanied the economic change destroyed the territorial basis of band organization, but—again—the chief did not disappear; important aspects of their role persisted and were the basis for the emergence of the tribe's first centralized government. Chiefs had always had an important role in negotiations with the United States, although treaties were also signed by the adult members of the tribe.

After 1905, treaties and land cessions ceased, but there were still important issues that concerned the future of Deer Lake and the use of its resources. The overriding question was whether the tribe should follow the traditional practice of holding land in common or should allot it to individuals under the provisions of the General Allotment Act, enacted by Congress in 1887 and designed to promote the individualistic standards of land tenure favored by the national society. Despite many external pressures for allotment, and a faction of relatively acculturated mixed bloods that favored it, Deer Lake remained a closed reservation that was held in common by the members of the tribe. Other issues were the use of extensive stands of timber and the claims of other Chippewa groups in Minnesota to a share in the land and resources of Deer Lake. Having seen their vast patrimony of forest and prairie reduced by land cessions, the chiefs and their people faced continuing threats to the integrity of their remaining homeland. The changes brought by the encroaching pioneers produced responses in Chippewa social organization and intensified the need for centralized leadership.

The major political response to new circumstances was the creation of a tribal council that came to be called the Chiefs' Council because it was based on the principle of hereditary chieftainship. It consisted of the seven chiefs, five representatives selected by each chief, and two officers selected by the entire council: chairman and secretary-treasurer. The major initiative in organizing this council came from a member of the tribe whom I shall call Paul Barnett. Born at Deer Lake, of a white father and an Indian mother, and educated at business colleges in the midwest and the east, he returned to the reservation to serve in various government posts. When the council was organized, in 1918, he became secretary-treasurer, and held this post until his death thirty-nine years later.

A literate and intelligent man, and a dynamic leader, Barnett began to exercise more and more influence in the council, and finally came to assume virtually complete control over the major decisions. The means by which he acquired control were not particularly complicated. Because there was no tradition of centralized authority, a leadership vacuum prevailed. A new form of government had been created, and Deer Lake lacked both the cultural equipment and the personnel to operate it effectively. The chiefs, some of whom were old and infirm, were bewildered by the need to face a world they had not made; they felt they had been tricked in treaty negotiations with the United States government, and they saw a need for protection against the manipulations of the Indian Bureau. Barnett, with his experience in government service, his ability to deal with representatives of the dominant society, and his repeated demonstrations of his genuine interest in the welfare of Deer Lake, enhanced his power by virtue of the need for the kind of services he could perform. The awe and respect with which he was viewed by his supporters suggests that the authority he exercised may be considered "charismatic," in Weber's sense (1947, pp. 358-363). His authority as an individual far exceeded the limited scope of the formal office he held.

Now that the nature and the background of the council have been delineated, we can consider the question of succession in some detail. Radcliffe-Brown (1952, p. 32), conceiving of succession in some detail. terms, defined it as the "transmission of rights in general." When Firth (1964, p. 145) said that it is a "process of replacement, with public recognition, whereby titles, offices, authority, roles and other indicators of status are transferred from one person to another," he made Radcliffe-Brown's definition more denotative.

We may distinguish three types of succession to political office: hereditary, appointive, and elective. These are analytical categories; in an actual political system, two—or even three—types may be found. It is widely assumed that hereditary succession is automatic, that only the other two types involve any decision or allow any choice. Firth rejects this point of view; he asserts that, although a well-defined system of patrilineal or matrilineal succession

gives genealogical persistence . . . it does not account for the actual succession of individual to individual in genealogical relation. Granted, say, that patrilineality in a particular society is invariable, selection is required from among patrilineal kin and secondary principles are needed as a guide. Some societies adopt election from a general body of male kin; others allow emergence by contest. (Firth, 1964, p. 69)

He further maintains that even systems that designate an individual— for example, male primogeniture—may have ways of preventing a witless or irresponsible person from taking office.

The Deer Lake council combined, in a single body, two types of succession: chieftainship was inherited patrilineally, and other members and officers were appointed. The brief constitution that established the council contained no provisions about the transfer of office. The understanding was that chiefly succession would proceed as it always had, according to the custom of the tribe. Custom specified that a chief designate his successor from among his sons, or, if none was considered fit, from among close patrilineal kin; hence there was a certain amount of choice, even in hereditary offices.

The councilmen who were appointed by individual chiefs had no specified term; they served indefinitely, at the pleasure of the chief, and could be replaced if the chief wanted to appoint someone in their stead. Similarly, the terms of the officers were not stated in the constitution; it was assumed that officers served until the council appointed replacements. There was no explicit limitation on the choice: the council was not required to select officers from among its members.

Succession to the three sets of offices proceeded smoothly for almost forty years. Because the constitution contained no provisions regulating the succession of chiefs, the council proceeded to name a new chief whenever an incumbent died. During the forty-year period, each chieftainship was vacated at least once, and some were vacated several times; there were fourteen occasions on which a new chief was selected. Table I shows that although sons were named only five times, in most other cases close patrilineal kin were chosen.

TABLE 1

RELATION OF SUCCESSOR TO FORMER CHIEF

Relation to chief	Frequency
Son	5
Son's son	1
Brother	2
Brother's son	1
Father's brother's son	2
Other patrilineal relationship	1
Unrelated	2
Total	14

I have not been able to discover evidence, either in documents or by interviewing elderly informants in the field, of serious disputes about succession before 1957, even though opposition to the influence and policies of Paul Barnett developed in the 1930's. Some of the opposition was represented on the council, and there were occasional objections to councilmen appointed by new chiefs, but the minority was not strong enough to affect significantly the composition of the governing body. The opposition served as a limitation on the power of the dominant faction, but it operated within the bounds of the established system and was not able to gain power in Paul Barnett's lifetime.

Although the system of succession operated rather placidly for many years, nevertheless there was a potential strain in the fact that the true influence of Paul Barnett was greater than the significance of his office. To state the issue in Weberian terms, the charismatic authority of the officeholder exceeded the bureaucratic authority of the office. In such a situation the problem of succession is likely to be acute, since the full import of charisma cannot be transferred to a successor.

The death of Paul Barnett (March 14, 1957) precipitated a crisis of succession that forced a reexamination of the nature of the chiefs' council. The many issues that were raised were not to be resolved for almost two years; and the Deer Lake Indians were to experience an inquiry by the federal government, and to write and adopt a new tribal constitution. A close examination of the events and disputes of these years will reveal the reverberating effects of a conflict that began as a crisis of succession.

The great significance of Barnett's death is indicated by the fact that James Barnett, his son and the chairman of the council, called a tribal meeting on March 27 to discuss filling the vacancy in the office of secretary-treasurer. Nothing in the tribal constitution required that a general meeting be held; in fact, selection of officers was the responsibility of the council alone. The meeting was attended by 125 to 150 adults and was conducted principally in the Chippewa language. Most of the discussion was carried on by ten individuals. There were no votes, but it seemed to be the general consensus that James Barnett and Robert Martineau, the leader of the opposing faction, should be considered for the position of secretary-treasurer. The next day, at a meeting of the council, the two were formally nominated as secretary-treasurer, but the vote was challenged because it exceeded the possible total of 42. In the resulting confusion the meeting was adjourned without a decision having been made.

On April 2 another meeting was held, and maneuvering to adjust the roster of chiefs began. A vacancy existed because a legitimate heir, Roger Finley, had declined to fill a position when his father died in 1953. The council moved quickly to fill this vacancy with Walter Green, who had no conceivable hereditary right to the chieftainship. One of its next actions was to silence the opposition of Head Chief Arthur Brown by adopting a resolution that deposed him, even though there was no constitutional authority for such an action. Walter Page, who was Brown's cousin, and who supported the Barnett family, was appointed to replace the deposed chief. James Barnett was reappointed chairman of the council; and Ruth Barnett, his sister, was selected as secretary-treasurer. After the meeting, three of the remaining chiefs—Joshua Feather, John Lightning, and Walter Stewart—withdrew from the council and canceled their appointments of councilmen in protest against the action taken by Arthur Brown. Because one chief was incapacitated, there was now only one chief who was an active supporter of the officers, plus the man named to replace Brown.

Robert Martineau seized the opportunity presented by the deposition of one chief and the defection of three others. Under his leadership, the chiefs called a meeting to organize what they considered to be a legitimate council. They met on April 27, presented their rosters of councilmen, and accepted the claims of James Clark and Roger Finley to chieftainship.

The newly constituted council passed a resolution reaffirming the right of Andrew Brown to be head chief, and it appointed Douglas Eagle as chairman and Roger Martineau as secretary-treasurer. In this action they unwittingly followed what might be called the "Barnett principle" of organization: the real leader was made secretary-treasurer, the post that required the greatest facility with the English language and through which communication with external authorities was channeled. (I shall call this council the Martineau council, since Martineau organized it and was the dynamic force behind it.) There was considerable discussion of James Barnett's claim that his council (which I shall call the Barnett council) was still the legitimate representative of the tribe. The four chiefs on the Martineau council asserted their right, as a majority of the hereditary chiefs, to organize the sole governing body of the tribe, and they repudiated the actions of the Barnett group. The minutes were forwarded to the agency superintendent as support of a claim for recognition as the governing body of the Deer Lake Chippewa Indians.

The Barnett council had been meeting at the same time, and took action similar to that of the other council: it passed a resolution that stated it was the only governing body on the reservation and that repudiated the claims of all other individuals. The councilmen filled the vacant chieftainship left by the incapacitated Booth Matthews by electing James Barnett chief; then they designated him head chief. By authorizing Barnett to appoint temporary councilmen in the absence of chiefs, they gave him considerable power to modify the composition of the council; after all, most of the chiefs were absent by virtue of their association with the rival council. These maneuvers by the Barnett faction, because they ignored the principle of hereditary chieftainship and gave the chairman power not provided in the constitution, were to furnish ammunition to the opposition as the dispute progressed.

TABLE 2

COMPARISON OF ROSTERS OF CHIEFS

Chiefs' council April 1, 1957	Barnett council April 28, 1957	Martineau council April 28, 1957
Arthur Brown (head chief)	Walter Page	Arthur Brown (head chief)
Claude Beaumont	Claude Beaumont	(no claim to a
Joshua Feather	Joshua Feather (resigned)	rightful chief)
John Lightning	John Lightning (resigned)	Joshua Feather
		John Lightning
Walter Stewart	Walter Stewart (resigned)	Walter Stewart
Booth Matthews (incapacitated)	James Barnett (head chief)	James Clark
Position not filled	Walter Green	Roger Finley

The rosters of chiefs of the competing councils are summarized in Table 2. To evaluate their respective claims, we must remember that only five chiefs were active at the beginning of the dispute, and all had a clear hereditary right to the position. Since the deposition of the head chief was obviously unconstitutional, and despite the fact that the defecting chieftains were still listed by the Barnett council, the Martineau council contained four of the five who had clear titles. The other two positions were questionable because of the circumstances in which they were filled. The Martineau council had the advantage in that the men they selected were in the direct line of patrilineal succession, whereas those of the other council had no claim of chiefly ancestry.

The succeeding months saw a persistent effort by the Martineau council to gain recognition from the Bureau of Indian Affairs, which continued to deal with the Barnett council. As far as I have been able to determine, the initial position of the bureau was that the Barnett council represented continuity in tribal administration in that it occupied the offices and possessed the records and official seal of the tribe, and that the bureau would not recognize another body until there were compelling reasons to do so. Robert Martineau returned to his regular employment in Minneapolis and coordinated the faction's efforts from there. I propose to examine these efforts to illustrate how Indians attempt to obtain a hearing for their causes, and, in particular, to reveal the role of congressmen in the process of communication.

In 1957 the congressional representative of the district in which the reservation is located was a Democrat; one of the senators was also a Democrat, and the other was a Republican. Martineau wrote to all of them, presenting his case and enclosing copies of the minutes of the April 27 meeting. It is instructive to compare the reactions of the representative, a relative novice in politics, and the Democratic senator, an experienced and highly regarded politician—both of whom received a communication from Martineau dated May 19. The representative responded on May 23, and maintained that James and Ruth Barnett were the recognized officers of the council. I do not have any firsthand information about the representative's reasons for taking this position, but I think it is highly likely that she relied on the advice of local whites who were active in Democratic politics. The Barnett family was traditionally affiliated with the Democratic party, and Paul Barnett had been well acquainted with local officials and party workers. Regardless of the reasoning behind the representative's decision, it proved to be politically unwise; strong opposition in some of the Deer Lake communities helped defeat her in the next congressional election.

Not having been directly involved in county politics, the Democratic senator was able to see the issues in a broader perspective. He acknowledged Martineau's letter and transmitted it to the Commissioner of Indian Affairs with a request for information about the bureau's position. On the basis of the information he received, the senator urged that the B.I.A. make a fair and just decision and that the matter be determined at an early date. The Republican senator took essentially the same stand.

During May and June, various leaders in the Martineau faction wrote to congressmen, to the Secretary of the Interior, and to the Association on American Indian Affairs to request support of their campaign for recognition of their council. The immediate outcome was that the Bureau of Indian Affairs referred the question to the solicitor of the Department of the Interior for a legal opinion. The resulting opinion, issued on November 22, 1957, carefully analyzed the issues in the dispute and concluded that the council of chiefs must be considered the legitimate governing body of the Deer Lake tribe.

But the solicitor did not specify whether the Barnett or the Martineau council was to be considered the legitimate council, and both claimed to be the council of chiefs. The Barnett council was attended by one hereditary chief, James Barnett had been appointed chief to replace one who was incapacitated, and the other chiefs were considered to be on the roster but absent. The Martineau council was created by a majority of the hereditary chiefs, who then added two more whom they considered had legitimate claims to chieftainship.

Perhaps the essential legal question raised by the action of the Martineau faction was not posed by the bureau or considered by the solicitor: Do the chiefs, or a majority thereof, have the authority to withdraw their rosters of councilmen and create a new council with new rosters?

The relevant article of the constitution states only that each chief shall have power to appoint five members. If the power to appoint implies the power to dismiss, and if a majority of chiefs can form a council, the Martineau council would have to be considered legitimate. But the office of the solicitor was not explicit on these essential points.

The members of the Martineau council were pleased with the result; according to their reading of the solicitor's opinion, it agreed with their position. On November 28, there was also a significant development in the other council: James Barnett died; and his son, Bruce, was appointed to succeed him as head chief and as chairman of the council.

In spite of the solicitor's legal opinion, the dispute now seemed more confused than ever: The Martineau council thought the solicitor supported its position; the Barnett council proceeded as if it were the legitimate governing body; the superintendent continued to do business with the latter, but had sufficient doubts about its legality to ask the advice of the area director. The area solicitor, in turn, asked the Department of the Interior's field solicitor in Denver for an interpretation of the November 22 decision, and the field solicitor consistently construed the opinion as legitimizing the Barnett council.

The process of legal review had followed its painstaking course, and an unambiguous (although not unarguable) determination of the council dispute had finally been made. The chiefs of the Martineau council found that victory had eluded them after being within their grasp. On the prompting of Martineau, they realized they were not prepared to deal with the legal complexities and sought the advice of an attorney in a town near the reservation. He conducted a close study of the issues, and on January 11, 1958, sent a long letter to the Democratic senator that presented the chiefs' position in detail and requested a reconsideration of the case.

While the Martineau council was enlisting professional legal assistance, the Barnett council attempted to consolidate its position by replacing—on its roster—the chiefs who had resigned. These changes were made during January and early February of 1958, but they did not modify the constitutional situation of the council: only one chief had an hereditary right to chieftainship.

The appeal to the senator proved effective; and the Bureau of Indian Affairs decided to hold a full-scale inquiry on the reservation. Before we consider the final outcome, perhaps it is appropriate to examine the forces affecting the dispute in order to make better sense of the confusing events that have been chronicled in this section.

First, there was the situation created by the personality and leadership of Paul Barnett and by the inclinations of the council he served. In a very real sense, the chiefs were responsible for the confusion that faced the tribe when Paul Barnett died, for they had permitted a gradual usurpation of power as the secretary-treasurer gained their trust by demonstrating his concern for the welfare of the Indians and his ability to deal with government officials and other representatives of the larger society. He became the dominant figure on the reservation because his qualities of mind and temperament prepared him for the role—and because, in the early years of the council, there were very few men with experience in administration or in white society.

Just as Barnett had many of the virtues of strong leaders, he had some of the defects that are often associated with those virtues. He did not realize the importance of training others for leadership and preparing them to continue his policies after his death. Douglas Eagle, however, had attempted to do something about this problem.

Before Paul died I used to get up at the Tribal Affairs Association and ask, "Why don't we ask old Paul to quit? He is old now, he can't go on and on, and besides we got to be trained. We need young men to carry on. After he dies what are we going to do? Are we going to go to wherever his grave is and ask him what to do?"

The efforts of Eagle were futile, and the death of Paul Barnett plunged the tribe into the most serious crisis in the history of the council.

It soon became apparent that the charisma of the leader could not be transferred to his followers, and the chiefs were unwilling to grant potential successors the same degree of power that Barnett had exercised. In an attempt to consolidate a weakening position, the Barnett faction took two actions that further weakened its position. To silence the opposition of the head chief, they had him deposed by a majority vote of the council. A few weeks later, as the defecting chiefs were organizing another council, James Barnett was appointed head chief— in clear violation of the principle of hereditary chieftainship. Although the Barnett faction retained the loyalty of a majority of the appointed councilman, it completely alienated all but one chief and lost the support of many persons to whom the traditions of chieftainship were emotionally potent symbols.

The other essential ingredient in the conflict was the long-standing existence of an organized opposition. The death of Barnett presented the first real opportunity to gain control of tribal government. Martineau recognized that the chiefs, for all their detachment from everyday administration, were central in both the system of tribal authority and the loyalty of the Deer Lake Indians. The confusion that followed the death of Paul Barnett, and the mistakes of his followers, gave Martineau the opportunity to mobilize the chiefs on the issue of legitimacy. This issue gave his faction a positive policy that favored a council based on hereditary chiefs, and grounds for attacking the opposition for its attempt to perpetuate "Barnett family rule," as it came to be called.

For many years the Tribal Affairs Association had criticized the politics of the council and the tendency toward one-man rule; it had acted as a restraint on the Council, but had been unable to control the direction of reservation policy. After the death of Barnett, the leaders of the Tribal Affairs Association moved vigorously to enlist the support of the chiefs and to organize a council, and it asserted it was the legitimate governing body of the tribe.

Despite the fact that local and area offices of governmental agencies seemed eager to have the Barnett council recognized, the persistence of the defecting chiefs induced the bureau to hold an investigation on the reservation. Although the chiefs were not able to gain recognition, they succeeded in challenging the authority of the controlling faction. The investigation was conducted during February, 1958, by three senior officials of the Department of the Interior; they collected documentary evidence from the offices of the B.I.A. and the council, and heard testimony both in Sandy Point and Ogemah. Their purpose was to determine as exactly as possible the tribal customs pertaining to chieftainship, and, on this basis to resolve the council dispute in a just manner.

The committee of inquiry documented the assumption that hereditary chieftainship was an accepted part of tribal custom, and many individuals confirmed that the hereditary principle had not been written into the constitution simply because it was universally understood at the time the document was drafted. Records showed that chiefs had remained in office until death, or until they were unable to serve for physical or mental reasons. It was customary for the eldest of the family group to suggest a successor and for the council to confirm the designation, or to settle disputes between rival claimants.

Having established that the hereditary principle was fundamental, the investigators measured the claims of the rival councils against this standard. They found that most of the dissatisfaction at Deer Lake resulted from the fact that the Barnett council had gained control of the tribe's resources and activities, thus affecting the daily lives of the people. In addition, they criticized the council for its actions in deposing and electing chiefs, pointing out that the constitution did not empower the council to elect chiefs or to remove them from office.

Nor did the officials from the Department of the Interior uphold the claims of the Martineau council. They pointed out that the council had not exercised governmental authority but had merely held organizational meetings, and that it did not include all the hereditary chiefs. They also recognized although the conflict between the councils was conducted in terms of a dispute between rival sets of chiefs—that the significant struggle, beneath the surface, was between individuals who were ambitious for council offices.

The committee of inquiry recommended that neither council be recognized, and that the tribe adopt a new constitution that would establish a more adequate and less ambiguous form of government. The final outcome was that the new constitution provided representative government for the first time in the history of Deer Lake, with councilmen elected from districts on the reservation and with officers elected at large. In January, 1959, Robert Martineau was elected chairman, and his supporters won the other offices and most of the council seats.

In this paper I have attempted to demonstrate that a dispute about succession led to a breakdown in government because of two factors. (1) The influence of a leader was based, in part, on charismatic authority, which exceeded the bureaucratic authority of the leader's office, and therefore could not be transmitted to would-be successors. (2) An opposition faction then used a succession dispute to further its attempts to gain control of a tribal government.

The problems of succession were never resolved; instead, the tribe abandoned its traditional system and adopted a new form of government that provided for elective succession.

REFERENCES

BARNOUW, VICTOR. 1950.   Acculturation and personality among the Wisconsin Chippewa. American Anthropological Association, Memoir No. 72.

FIRTH, RAYMOND. 1964.   Essays on social organization and values. London School of Economics, Monographs on Social Anthropology, No. 28.

FRIEDL, ERNESTINE. 1956.   Persistence in Chippewa culture and personality. American Anthropologist, 58, 814-825.

HICKERSON, HAROLD. 1956.   The genesis of a trading post band, Ethnohistory, 3, 289-345.

———. 1960.   The feast of the dead among the seventeenth century Algonkians of the Upper Great Lakes. American Anthropologist, 62, 81-107.

———. 1962.   The southwestern Chippewa. American Anthropological Association, Memoir No. 92.

———. 1963.   The sociohistorical significance of two Chippewa ceremonials. American Anthropologist, 65, 67-86.

JAMES, BERNARD. 1954.   Some critical observations concerning analyses of Chippewa atomism and Chippewa personality. American Anthropologist, 56, 283-286.

RADCLIFFE-BROWN, A. R. 1952.   Structure and function in primitive society. London: Cohen & West.

WARREN, WILLIAM W. 1957.   History of the Ojibway nation. Minneapolis: Ross & Haines (originally published in 1885).

WEBER, MAX. 1957.   The theory of economic and social organization. New York: The Free Press of Glencoe.

Part III

In this section a variety of relationships between political and ritual entities, processes, mechanisms, and structures is considered, in contexts both of repetitive and radical social changes. The connection between religious action and the maintenance of legitimacy is evident in all four articles. Friedrich shows how, in the pre-revolutionary past, the annual fiesta round at Naranja in Mexico—a round that embraced in its arrangements a system of five neighboring villages—brought into close positive connection with religious symbols, which designated the axiomatic values of this peasant and Catholic culture, the focal political community and political field, the political regime, the government, the structure of political statuses, and the political officials of the community. In other words, the ritual cycle vouched for, and in a sense periodically regenerated, the legitimacy of the political system.

In the Naranja setting, too, ritual may be seen to have an intimate relationship with political disputes and conflicts. Unlike many of the African examples, where ritual tends to be performed contingently, in response to specific occasions of misfortune, public ritual in the Naranja area was principally articulated by the liturgical calendar of the Catholic church. Nevertheless, even in these more generalized circumstances, certain rituals clearly (among other functions) redressed, in omnibus fashion, conflicts that had accumulated between components of the political community. Thus Friedrich writes:

Holy Week, with its pageantry, shared expenses, and reciprocal visiting, served to focus the ritualistic religion of the Naranjeños and to strength cultural bonds, probably of preconquest origin, that meant so much to the five communities. For Naranja and Tiríndaro, the Easter cycle provided a peaceful outlet for a deeply felt rivalry that occasionally found expression in slingshot battles between groups of youths.

Professor Colson discusses the difference between the legitimate stranger, the witchfinder who is "a stranger to the people but not to their society [and] who is committed to the same standards of judgment," and the stranger who lacks legitimacy, the "Europeans who may be known to the people but who remain strangers to their standards

[and] may seek to manipulate them to their *private ends*" (our emphasis). It is because of his legitimacy, as an impartial catalyst of "a situation in which local people are too closely involved for a decision to be reached," that the alien diviner, who operates in accordance with the system of religious beliefs, can be invoked as a "redressive mechanism" in a "phase development" to use the terms presented in the introduction to this volume. The outcome of his seances, in effect, gives or withholds mystical support with regard to aspects of the "situation in which he is called upon to operate"; i.e., it grants or denies them legitimacy. Of course, it is not only a diviner's "alienness" that supports his legitimacy: he must also acquire the reputation of making valid or workable decisions.

Power is a coin: the "heads" side is often political power, with emphasis on the initiation of action, on command; and the "tails" side might be called compliance and obedience. In an older English vocabulary, the difference would have been expressed by "action" and "passion." It is easier to understand why persons seek mastery and command than why they obey and comply. Yet command is impotent without obedience; power is powerless without compliance. These issues were discussed in the Introduction, in connection with the concept of legitimacy, and here they again emerge importantly as we consider the relationship between political and religious actions. Clearly, an important emphasis of religious action is upon creating and restoring in members of a political community the capacity to obey officials, commands, and judgments that it simultaneously declares to be legitimate.

If specialized political offices possess the "power of the strong," specialized ritual offices possess the "power of the weak"; and the latter is really power since its withdrawal incapacitates the bearers of political power per se. This complementary—and sometimes antithetical—dyad appears in many cultural dimensions. In the classical anthropological literature we see it in the distinction between the Namoos and Tales among the Tallensi (Fortes, *The Dynamics of Clanship among the Tallensi* [Oxford University Press, 1945]). The chief of the Namoos, collectively descended from politically better-organized invaders, appears at the great Golib festival at the "husband" of the Great Tendaana (or high priest) of the autochthonous Talis. The Talis have greater ritual powers over the earth and its fertility than the Namoos, who have closer links with the ancestral cult, which has high political value in this segmentary lineage system. At another level of relationship, we find among the Nuer of the Nilotic Sudan, who are patrilineal, that the mother's brother's power to curse is feared more deeply than the father's jural authority, though this may be harsh. The mother's side has "the power of the weak" (Evans-Pritchard, *Nuer Religion* [Oxford University Press, 1956], p. 166).

Instances could be multiplied from the literature. Indeed, in this book the Tonga diviner, an alien outside the structure of the political or parapolitical issues he is asked to analyze, would represent one example. Just as striking is the distinction made by the Kinga of Tanzania (described by Park) between warriors—who represent the "power of the strong," who have "duels of honor and trials of strength," and raid neighboring Kinga princedoms—and the priests, who do not take part in physical aggression. Yet it is medicine supplied by priests that "gives strength to a man's knees" and turns the legs of a raiding party to water if it "crosses the invisible line of another medicine." In these and other ways, notably the "priestly pilgrimage," the priestly "power of the weak" restrained conflict between Kinga princedoms and enforced general compliance with cultural standards that transected the separate Kinga political communities.

In an important aspect, politics may be defined, in Banfield's terms, as the processes of human action by which conflict between the common good and the interests of groups is carried on or settled, always involving the use of or struggle for power (or, as we would put it, power to command). Religion in the societies studied by our authors seems to be pragmatically connected with the maintenance of values, norms, and sentiments in which the common good is expressed (whose precise articulation with components of the political order constitutes legitimacy in the given society) and with the prevention of the undue exercise of power. The "powers" of blessing, cursing, or divining are often allocated to exostructural personalities, or groups, or categories of persons. Even when priesthoods become "built-in" to a political structure and acquire power to command, as well as the role of representing all members of the community in the aspect of being commanded, many of the symbols by which the priestly office is defined—such as plain or ragged garments and habits, and humble modes of behavior—are drawn from the cultural repertoire of the politico-jurally inferior: slaves, servants, women, or juniors. These inferiors represent the quintessence of compliance, just as war chiefs, princes, nobles, and headmen represent the quintessence of command.

Because most of the societies considered in this section are relatively unspecialized, their relationships are multiplex, and their groups are multifunctional, many offices combine political and religious roles. The Kinga prince is a case in point. "His youth is spent in the manner of an active leader among men . . . but when he is placed upon the throne by his priests he is withdrawn from the people and dedicated to a kind of rule whose mood is not secular but . . . sacred." Thus struggles for ritual roles often have a political character—as is exemplified in this book by Middleton's analysis of the Lugbara elders' struggle to attribute the illness of a junior to their successful invocation of ancestral ghosts.

An elder who can substantiate his claim to have "invoked" a ghostly sickness on another has ipso facto legitimated his claim to political authority over his rival. Another example of this is Turner's account of the competition between Ndembu elders and their village and inter-village followings for key ritual roles in boys' circumcision rites.

Friedrich's and Turner's articles illustrate the complex situations that may arise in periods of rapid social change when rival standards of legitimacy co-exist. The intrusion of the modern industrial economic system into the traditional agricultural order of Naranja, accompanied by capitalist and socialist ideologies, has produced uneven changes in the several dimensions of its social organization. New roles have come into being, new forms of stratification have replaced the old, as new ways have been introduced of organizing production, distribution, and consumption.

"Local and regional politicos, who owe their position to agrarian socialism" now seek "religious" or quasi-religious reinforcement of their positions in a new fiesta, that of Primo Tapia, a "martyred" anticlerical leader, and this has brought the state bureaucracy into the heart of the local community in the symbolic form of "visiting bureaucrats and politicians" who deliver "lengthy orations" at a "lavish banquet of turkey." In a sense, however, the new legitimating fiesta has been grafted to the older religious type, for Primo Tapia has assumed (since his death) many of the attributes of a patron saint. How satisfactory ideological ritual will prove as a substitute for religious ritual in what is still a small-scale agrarian community is unknown, since the latter's symbolism more faithfully reflects the "nonlogical" components of experience, biological and cultural, that elicit major gratifications in human collective life.

Turner's paper tells us of a skirmish in a long war between the forces of Ndembu traditional religion and the secularizing trends of socioeconomic change—here represented not so much in a positive ideological form as in a straining toward independence from traditional constraints of a political and jural character. The temporary success of the *ancien régime* may in this instance have been partly due to its rival's lack of an ideological stance, which had no world-view that was in any way consistent with the empirical situation, or that would provide evaluative yardsticks; the latter could only struggle for prestigious roles within a traditional religious ceremony. This proved to be their undoing, since they thus committed themselves to accepting a system of values in which they occupied positions of lower status than the elders they sought to oust. In terms of the traditional standards of legitimacy, their rivalrous activities were weakly supported, and they could appeal to no new and authoritative criteria. It is probable, in the course of a long series of such petty crises, that changing communities become increasingly receptive to the messages of prophetic movements or political ideologies.

REVOLUTIONARY POLITICS AND COMMUNAL RITUAL

"Revolution . . . brings on the speaking of a new,
unheard-of language . . . another logic . . . a revalu-
ation of all values. . . ." E. ROSENSTOCK-HUESSY

Paul Friedrich, UNIVERSITY OF CHICAGO

INTRODUCTION

Of the various human institutions, the legal and jural order and the formal patterns of government have been competently studied by many anthropologists. But—until the recent work by Barth and others—there had been comparatively few analyses of politics; that is, of the relatively informal patterns and processes for controlling the decisions of a community. In small communities politics—if taken in this sense—largely resolves itself into the techniques and workings of kinship networks and local factions. This interplay between political actors is always significantly tied to the psychology of the leaders and to the economy, particularly to the use of the soil and other productive resources; yet as centrally political as factional leadership or the control of production, is ideology. By ideology I do not mean a quasi-religion with the structure of a lie (Mannheim, 1953, p. 238), although these properties are often apparent; rather, I mean an organized and intelligible set of ideas and beliefs that are related to action, to defending or changing an existing economic, social, and religious order (C. Friedrich, 1963, p. 89). A particularly interesting problem is posed by the politics of revolution, which is devoted to the sudden and complete transformation of the moral and religious basis of a community. What follows will explicate the effect—on the communal ritual of a Tarascan pueblo—of an outstanding revolutionary, of revolutionary behavior, and of a distinctive revolutionary ideology.[1]

Let us turn to the second variable: ritual. Since the last quarter of the nineteenth century, analysis of ritual has ranged (with not infrequent brilliance) from Durkheim's theories (1925) to Gough's (1959) *tour de force* on Nayar cults of the dead. The term itself has been variously

[1] My fieldwork was conducted in 1955-56 over a period of eighteen months, fifteen of them spent in Naranja and Tiríndaro. As in my 1963 article, actual persons and place names have been used. I am grateful to Margaret Hardin, Robert Laughlin, Melford Spiro, Carl Friedrich, and Richard Tubesing for their valuable comments; to Richard Blaisdell for his helpful information; to Donald Danker for his valuable archival assistance; and to Sidney Mintz for advice during and after the field trip.

employed: in one generic and extremist usage, ritual is "any expression of cultural form" (Leach, 1954, p. 4); another definition would limit its ways of performing religious acts (Beals and Hoijer, 1956, p. 496); some psychoanalytically oriented individuals tend to use it for repetitive, involuntary sequences stemming from compulsion; but perhaps most anthropologists would think of ritual as any prescribed, formal behavior that is not essential to technical or practical affairs. Malinowski, Redfield, and others have demonstrated that an individual often experiences an intimate emotional and conceptual interpenetration of the ritual and nonritual.

In this article I have taken ritual to mean sets of repetitive and culturally specific ceremonies or performances relating to the supernatural or to some similar body of authoritative or abstract persons and ideas (such as "progress"). I also assume that ritual is analytically detachable, to a relatively great degree, from the practical problems of plowing a field, governing a pueblo and the like. This detachability varies enormously. For example, the rites of passage, such as a wedding, are interwoven with the physiological and psychological growth of the individual. At the other extreme, the annual cycle of Catholic fiestas in a Tarascan village constitutes a relatively free-floating design, linked in a relatively arbitrary and contingent way to the economy and social structure. For the same reason, annual cycles may respond sensitively to political change. In other words, communal rites and politics, especially political ideology, are interdependent, and change in either may influence or precipitate change in the other.

Ritual and political ideology are parts or dimensions of culture, and may be thought of as the expression or articulation of the deeper-lying values, attitudes, ideas, and sentiments of the individuals in a community. The classic theoretical formulation of this notion of "the collective representation" was given by Durkheim, although I hasten to add that it would be unwise to follow his sharp dichotomization between the "sacred" and the "profane"—at least in the case of Tarascan communal fiestas and agrarian ideology. The notion of collective representations is explicit or implicit in many ethnographic accounts: Evans-Pritchard, for instance (1953), has shown how the rituals of naming, extolling, raising, and sacrificing cattle reflect many of the deeper Nuer values; and Spiro (1964) has demonstrated a somewhat similar function for an explicit ideology that he calls "the moral postulates of kibbutz culture." But just as valuable as either a deductive, logical account, such as Durkheim's, or a synchronic, structural analysis, such as that by Evans-Pritchard, would be historical test cases that show how changes in the governing ideas have directly or indirectly impinged on ritual behavior or symbolism. In other words, I think there is need for more empirical demonstrations, from more cultures, of interdependence or cohesiveness between ritual and political ideology. Just as Geertz (1957) used Javanese data to show how change in the social system led to change in the ritual components of culture, so in what follows have I attempted to demonstrate how and why change in politics, especially political ideology, was faithfully and rapidly reflected by changes in the form and symbolism of ritual. More concretely, I have sought to demonstrate that the form and content of an annual fiesta cycle changed in response to an anticlerical ideology and the activities of anticlerical leaders.

The two major axes of this article are ethnological reconstruction and political history, adumbrated or illuminated by anthropological ideas about ritual and social structure. I will begin with a brief socio-cultural sketch of a Tarascan pueblo, with particular attention to the politico-religious system; this is the background or context. Then comes a review of the annual fiesta cycle as it has been reconstructed for the turn of the century by a combination of historical and comparative techniques, published field reports, special visits to culturally conservative towns (except Pichátaro), participant observation of the entire fiesta cycle during 1955-56, and by lengthy interviews, especially with old women in their sixties and seventies.[2] The following section details the historical events and trends that contributed to or constituted the anticlericalism of Naranja and her neighbors. The next part outlines the drastic transformations in the annual fiestas that followed, more or less directly, from agrarian politics. I conclude with a summary of alternative hypotheses and a reaffirmation of my basic theme.

THE COMMUNITY IN 1885

The pueblo of Naranja lies, fairly accessible, high in the cool, green mountains of Michoacán in southwestern Mexico. During the 1880's its population of about eight hundred largely monolingual Indians depended primarily on a great swampy lake for fish, mussels, and aquatic birds, and for the rushes that were woven into mats and baskets for export. About thirty families manufactured sombreros, and another thirty raised wheat, maize, and beans in the foothills and sierra to the south. Marshlands and sierra were owned and used communally, and even elsewhere the community participated in many ways in the managing of individual holdings. Naranja traded heavily with other Tarascan pueblos, and relations were particularly close and many-sided with Tiríndaro, only half a

---

[2] These pages purport to be a needed addition to our limited knowledge of the annual fiestas in Tarasco. It has become fashionable to asseverate that Mexican fiestas are well described and understood, and this is true of Cherán among the Tarascan-speaking pueblos. But it is generally not the case—as anyone learns to his chagrin when trying to do comparative work.

mile away to the east. In sum, adaptation to a specialized ecological niche was combined with a diversified and open economy.[3]

Naranja was laid out compactly in a grid, with the stores, townhall, parish house, church, and religious fraternity all facing inwards toward the cemetery in the central plaza. The villagers lived in one- and two-room houses of timber or adobe, or in huts of stone and thatch. Such dwellings might be occupied by immediate families, but more frequent were expansions that included two or more brothers, or a father and one or more married sons, or some similar group.

Marriage was largely within the community, and involved a combination of mutual affection and parental arrangement and sponsorship. The protracted and expensive wedding was the major rite of passage in the life cycle. The baptismal ceremony, however, created the crucial *compadre* bond between parents and godparents. Above such dyads of natural and fictive kin were two political factions, several name groups organized in terms of bilateral descent, and several religious societies concerned with the fiestas and other communal activities.

There were no clear-cut social classes, although people were internally differentiated on the basis of wealth, personal character, and their participation in religious ritual. Prestigious older men (*los principales*) represented families and name groups, and governed public affairs through informal deliberation (however, I lack evidence for a tightly structured civil-religious "ladder" of the sort analyzed by Carrasco, 1961, and Wolf, 1957). Toward the close of the century, a particular family, the Cruzes, was dominant, and the principal Cruz was the informal political chief.

The organization of religion took two main forms. The esteemed priest, in the first place, exercised a decisive control through his sermons in Tarascan, his role as confessor, his part in baptisms, weddings and communal fiestas, his informal judicial function in morals cases, and his personal contacts with wealthy mestizos and with other clerics—there were three in just the county seat of Zacapu. This priest was central in the local economy because of the large fees he collected for the performance of mass and the sacraments. The many Catholic ecclesiastics in the region were probably "fanatical," as is alleged, in that they maximized their ritual functions; but apparently they were not corrupt, exorbitant, or promiscuous, as was true in some parts of Mexico at the time.

The second form of religious organization was divided among several classes of local officials, who were selected from among two or three candidates for each position by the corps of elders who had sponsored the annual round. The officials were of three kinds. The new sponsor, or

---

[3] I have elsewhere (1963) sought to demonstrate that Naranja, while decidedly corporate, is and apparently has been just as decidedly "open" (at least for many generations).

prioste, was charged with the organization and much of the expense of the fiestas. This often forced a man to sell valuable property, but did not threaten his subsistence, and was more than compensated by the acquired prestige. Together with the *prioste,* five to ten "captains" were selected to help with the financial load, and to dance as "Moors" on several occasions. The third group of selected officials were the seven to eleven attendant virgins, devoted to the cult of the Virgin of the Assumption and of the Rosary. These attendants, or *huananchas,* together with their families, assisted the sponsor at every step, and several times a month adorned the church with candles and various kinds of flowers. In 1900, as today, the office of *huanancha* functioned as a coming-out for the socially prominent adolescent girls. Throughout the year, other minor officials were named for jobs or contributions connected with particular fiestas, and financial help was given by many relatives of the *prioste.* All in all, hundreds of persons took active part. Fiesta life was complex, socially integrating, emotionally rewarding, and ebullient.[4]

The cycle of annual fiestas, aside from its organization, reflected some basic properties of the semantics of ritual. The behavior and belief of a fiesta involved two distinct networks of symbol and meaning. On the one hand was the Catholic network, related to the national ecclesiastical and theological system, and symbolized by the priest, by the rites of the sacraments, and by the pictures and icons of a fairly populous pantheon of saints, such as John the Baptist, and of aspects of members of the Holy Family, such as Our Virgin of the Assumption, of the Rosary, and so on. Naranja's wooden image of Our Father Jesus portrayed a tortured man, streaming with blood and staggering forward beneath a cross. Every individual and community stood in a propitiatory or supplicatory relation to one of these supernatural figures, who could be appealed to for the alleviation of sickness or help with the harvest. The Catholic symbols were tied, by and large, to a simple theological tissue of comparatively expurgated ideas (Foster, 1960, p. 15). With the exception of the minor St. John ceremony, all of the fiestas to be depicted below involved only two biblical protagonists: Mary and Jesus. This dogmatic simplicity, this theologically "pure" focus, is another confirmation of the universal claim that pre-agrarian Naranja was "very religious, very fanatical."

Matching the Catholic network was a far more complex one of ritually ordered symbols that included alcoholic beverages, grain and meat dishes, and a plethora of masks, costumes, dances, and mummery and mimicking. Most elements of this second network were sensuous and

---

[4] León (1906, p. 426), reporting on nineteenth-century Pichataro, lists thirteen categories of fiesta officials, including two kinds of principal sponsors and the eight captains of San Francisco.

concrete; many referred to a wide range of fauna and flora; some were orectic in that they involved or implied the physical appetites. These symbols reflected a largely implicit system of local superstition, moral notions, and remnants of a preconquest, pagan ideology—notably in the references to moon worship. However, the logical dichotomy between Catholic and folk symbolism and belief should not be confused with the culture history of the various components: many folk ingredients were of Spanish or Mexican national origin—as when the "Moors" danced on Assumption day—and many ingredients of the Catholic symbolism were patently local—as when *tacári* grass was used to symbolize the Virgin great with child. Symbols from either network could be tied to the economy or to politics: digging sticks were employed to plant the sacred seed on Corpus Christi.[5] In more general terms, the component symbols of the annual fiesta mediated between all parts of the Catholic and folk networks, as well as between many other subsystems in the village culture. This mediating and presumably integrative role was instanced by the dance of "the little old men": on the one hand, their brick-red masks, their fox-like barks, and their spry, agile steps provided a compelling sensual image; on the other hand, their number was twelve (after the apostles), and they danced only at religious, communal fiestas—as opposed to rites of passage and secular occasions—and their withered senescence and intermittently simulated decreptitude ironically linked them to the governing elders, the "principal ones" or "old ones" of the civil-religious hierarchy.[6]

The empirical reality of the two networks, of the symbolic and ideational dualism, was brought out with singular clarity in the course of revolutionary politics. As will be shown, the early anti-clericals tried to do away with the network of clerical behavior and Catholic theology while preserving, and even revitalizing, the material and sensuously pleasing aspects of the folk symbolism. Later leaders sought to sweep away everything. Recent times have witnessed a revival of both networks, although in enervated, debilitated form.

THE ANNUAL FIESTA CYCLE

All of the fiestas to be described were given every year, and were initiated during the first week of December by the selection of the new officials. The cycle began on the day of the Immaculate Conception,

---

[5] Such symbolic interpenetration constitutes, I think, a serious qualification of Carrasco's generalization (1952, p. 23) that "technological rites are almost nonexistent."

[6] Beals (1964, pp. 149-154) and Barragan (in *Mendieta y Nuñez*, 1940, pp. 172-173) describe different varieties of this dance, so diagnostic of the Tarascans.

December 8, when the new *prioste* and the *huananchas* received crowns of rough leather and took part in a lengthy procession around the cemetery in the central plaza, the priest chanting in Latin and the girls bearing sacred images on their shoulders. A large meal was contributed by the in-coming *prioste,* who had a cow slaughtered for the feast, and by the *huananchas,* who brought tamales. This feast, the first of many, may have integrated for the guests politically, since their participation was often more or less obligatory.[7]

On December 15 came the *Tacári Fiesta*, so named because a donkey had to be brought down from the sierra laden with the long *tacári* grass, full of medicinal properties and presumably a symbol of Mary great with child. The drowsy burro would be met by almost the entire population, crowded around a long file of about twenty marriageable girls who danced in figure eights, swinging their blue shawls. Having joined with the burro at the outskirts of town, the *huananchas* and the *prioste*—the latter often quite drunk—would dance a special jig while the female relatives of the former distributed pieces of sugar cane to the spectators and festooned the principal actors and guests with strings of tamales made of wheat flour. The whole group then wound slowly into town in a long, straggling procession and made a complete circuit of all the streets. They were led by the donkey and the jigging *prioste*, who here as at many other fiestas personified the delight in food and drink. The dancing girls were constantly assailed by young men, often their clandestine suitors, who stabbed at them with cow horns and tried to snatch away the shawls and embroidered handkerchiefs with which the girls made bullfighter's passes.[8] Finally arriving at the church, a night's lodging was requested for the doll image of the Christ Child, which, practically unnoticed, had been riding atop the burro during the entire trip.

The following week served to bring large segments of the town together in cooperative tasks and pleasures, and to set the atmosphere for Christmas. For eight successive evenings the family of each *huanancha* would provide a small domestic fiesta for friends, relatives, and other *huanancha* families. They supped on maize gruel and huge wheaten fritters soaked in brown-sugar syrup, while watching the "little old men" dance in the back yard. Then groups from ' the *huanancha* homes strolled over to the house of the annual sponsor each accompanied by a band of four or five instruments. The rest of the evening would be spent

---

[7] The otherwise valuable accounts by Beals and Foster do not give adequate data on the ritually appropriate foods, a matter of great concern to the Tarascan participant.

[8] Curiously, the female was identified with the bullfighter in these rites of courtship, whereas she was likened to a fallen calf during the feast at the second stage of marriage. The Virgin of Guadalupe was not specially celebrated, apparently because December 12 conflicted with the Christmas cycle, but many villagers made pilgrimages to other towns.

in talking, and drinking orange-leaf tea laced with brandy.[9] The request of lodging for the Christ Child, although technically the purpose of these fiestas, was usually omitted in practice. After the last evening, entirely sponsored by the *prioste,* most of the people walked through the festooned and lantern-hung streets to a midnight mass in the church, illuminated by hundreds of candles and hangings of white paper.

The important fiesta of the New Year was highlighted by a vast consumption of tamales, cocoa, beef, and fritters; first at an evening banquet for several hundred persons, then at a breakfast after midnight mass, at a second breakfast on New Year's morning, and at a concluding meal served in the center of town during the afternoon. Only about a third of the population partook of these repasts at any one time, and one may assume that acceptance of hospitality was determined by complicated questions of status and by the individual's personal feelings toward the *prioste.* The entire scene was enlivened by a number of dancing groups: the weird "little old men"; the *huananchas,* costumed as shepherdesses in flouncing, ample skirts and broadbrimmed sombreros hung with gaudy ribbons; some twenty-five "negritos" or "black-reds" (*turicharotse*), wearing black masks and white shirts, pranced and somersaulted in a series of carefully rehearsed figures; finally, much mirth was anticipated from the dozen or so *maringuías* (men dressed as women) in dark-blue skirts and shawls, and masks of white silk.[10]

The fiesta of Epiphany or the Three Kings, on January 6, included a high mass, and a dance by twelve "Moors" mounted on horseback and masked with black or white scarfs. Three "captains" usually went about disguised as the Magi.

On February 2, or Candlemass, a special mass was said, and candles were blessed that would be burned when someone was dying. Masses were also held on other important days, such as Ascension Thursday (forty days after Easter), St. Isidore (May 15), Sts. Peter and Paul (June 29), St. Francis (October 4), and Holy Innocents (December 28).

The annual day of the patron saint, Our Father Jesus, one of several "movable" fiestas, fell around the end of February or the beginning of March. The comparatively secular officials administered the general and commercial phases, whereas the sacristan, the *cabildes,* and the sodality were charged with gathering funds to meet the religious expenses— notably the gigantic fees demanded by the two to four participating priests. The fiesta integrated Naranja socially in that dues were levied against all citizens and many persons performed assigned tasks and

[9] In 1956 the climax of these evenings came when long poles were used to break a huge clay doll, or similar object, filled with sweets and suspended high in the air. I am in considerable doubt whether the custom of these *piñatas* was observed in Naranja in 1900, and I failed to make inquiries while in the field.

[10] The *maringías* have been revived in Tiríndaro, and they dance in Tacari Kuntan and one other occasion.

served on committees. Commercial and religious links were reaffirmed with almost all of the other Tarascan towns.

During the afternoon of the day preceding the fiesta, three bands would start tooting and strumming, surrounded by impassive Naranjeños in their white cottons. Pilgrims from some one hundred Tarascan and mestizo communities would then collect outside the town and stage "the entry," accompanied by musicians, each group bearing as its "crown" a beribboned icon set in a wooden box. Many of the lined, careworn faces were strangely twisted as the pilgrims chanted, often out of tune but utterly serious. The processions eventually passed into the church for the mass, which sounded a fervently religious tone for the fiesta and emphasized the miraculous powers of the bloody image of Christ. That night a mystery play, featuring Lucifer, was enacted outside the church by the light of candles and lanterns.

On the main day the plaza would be packed with hundreds of merchants from more than eighty Tarascan communities and mestizo centers. Strolling about, the casual participant could purchase a complete range of colorful and useful goods to last throughout the year. Meanwhile, confessions, masses, and almsgiving lasted throughout the day in the crowded, tenebrous church. In and around the central graveyard, dances were carried out by a dozen or more swaying and bobbing groups: plumed "Apaches," the decrepit-looking but energetically stamping "little old men," and by sundry relicts from the Spain of Philip II—maidens in snow-white gowns and boys in light pink garb, dancing sedately around a Maypole. (These dances were performed only at religious fiestas and were essentially religious in function.) As the day advanced, formal religiosity was supplanted by drinking and uninhibited conviviality that lasted throughout the night. Sometimes the concluding, thunderous fireworks were not ignited until the misty dawn had swirled into the green valley, and peasants hurrying to their fields in Tiríndaro would know that the fiesta to Our Father Jesus had finally terminated.

The religiosity, commercialism, and hubbub of the Father Jesus fiesta was followed shortly by *Carnaval*, which lasted six days. Each of the five to ten captains was called upon to provide a pig, three chickens, fifteen pesos, and about 150 pounds of a ritually specified tamale made of wheat dough. The hard-pressed *prioste* contributed a steer, and great quantities of *atole* gruel, and arranged and paid for two musical bands. Eating and wassail culminated on the last day, when all the religious officers and hundreds of their followers successively visited the home of each captain. Here the *huananchas* would perform a bullfighting dance, armed with horns with which to stab at their sarape-wielding boyfriends. Oranges and sharp-edged sections of sugar cane were hurled by appointed women at the crowd; everyone ducked his head, and the children scrambled for the harvest. One could hardly see through the crisscross of flying produce, mixed with clouds of cornmeal tossed in great fistfuls.

The sensuous expressions of carnival were followed by the silence of Lent, which begins on Ash Wednesday. The diet was limited to fish and foods made from maize.

Holy Week was an elaborate regional ceremony, staged alternately and cooperatively in five-year cycles by Naranja and four neighbors (including Tiríndaro and Tarejero, the other lacustrine pueblos that later joined in the agrarian revolt). Holy Week began with Palm Sunday, but it was announced on the following Tuesday evening by eerie blasts from the belfry, and a procession of "Hebrew soldiers" dressed in vermilion and holding pikes. Most conspicuous were the "Judases," boys and young men attired in black shirts and white masks who raced tirelessly through the town shaking "bags of silver" and relentlessly lashing out at any young males unfortunate enough to come within reach of their cracking bullwhips. Other mysterious shapes began to roam the streets, among them "Death," totally white but for black skeletal stripes, who carried a huge ax across his shoulder and howled balefully. Some of the arriving pilgrims were penitents, moving on their knees for hundreds of yards, or even several miles, as they approached Naranja, and often genuflecting before or inside the church for excruciatingly long periods.

The four-hour pageant during the evening of Good Friday entailed the memorization of lengthy speeches from a Spanish text, copied out by hand in the state capital and often enunciated with effect by local talent. The highlights of the Passion play, attended by over a thousand spectators, were the Last Supper, the ablution of Christ's feet (often thickly encrusted with dirt), the apprehension of Christ, and his lengthy trial in the so-called Sanhedrin—especially constructed that afternoon of boards and timbers. (Similar platforms were used the morning and afternoon of the following "Saturday of Glory" for staging the judgments of Pilate and Herod.) The pageant concluded with the Stations of the Cross—singularly, one of the stations was a wooden statue of the Three Marys, dressed in blue and white.

Easter Day was the time of a climactic religious procession of over five hundred villagers and pilgrims; they formed a wide column and, each holding a large candle, slowly circumambulated the pueblo. On Sunday night, "Judas" was publicly burned in effigy, amid dazzling fireworks, a doom that fittingly impressed the wide-eyed children who had been terrified by his whip during the preceding week. Holy Week, with its pageantry, shared expenses, and reciprocal visiting, served to focus the ritualistic religion of the Naranjeños and to strengthen cultural bonds, probably of preconquest origin, that meant so much to the five communities. For Naranja and Tiríndaro, the Easter cycle provided a peaceful outlet for a deeply felt rivalry that occasionally found expression in slingshot battles between groups of youths. Individual skill in acting brought prestige and served to mark out potential leaders and public speakers.

Like Holy Week, the annual fiesta of Corpus Christi also reinforced ties among several culturally affiliated pueblos of the region. A few days before the end of May, or in early June, the Naranjeños would start to stage small dances; the *huananchas* were dressed in blue, some "cowgirls" wore dresses of new, brown flannel, and the wives of the captains wore flannel skirts and embroidered blouses. Five groups of pilgrims would then sally forth from Naranja to all the other villages. Each group included some *huananchas* and captains, and carried an image of the Virgin; they were preceded by a squad of horsemen, dressed in the suits of rough hide that characterize the Michoacán cowhand. Similar processions from the five neighboring villages—the same as those represented during Holy Week, plus Comanja—would begin to arrive at about the same time. On approaching the outskirts of Naranja, the visitors were met by a large column of horsemen, and a mock battle ensued, the men pairing off and "playing with machetes" to the great excitement of all onlookers. Each of the five visiting groups also brought a mule that was laden with two sheaves of wheat, and measures of maize, squash, bean, and broadbean seeds; the mules, with the sacred seed on their back, were raced, pushed and lashed around the edge of town by shouting mule skinners in brilliantly colored sarapes. Young men competed at climbing a greased pole.[11] By this time the air reverberated with music from five or six bands.

During the entire week of Corpus, the pilgrims remained in Naranja and the Naranja pilgrims remained in the other five villages, each close to its "chapel," and fed by the local *prioste*. In a merely quantitative sense, this meant that one to two hundred Naranjeños spent a week or more in contiguous villages and that Naranja played host to about the same number of visitors. Such patterns, since they involved the *huananchas,* probably increased the frequency of intermarriage among the inhabitants of the six communities.

On Corpus Christi day, teams of horses were hitched up and open spaces in the cemetery were plowed and sown with the sacred seeds. The vernal rite of rebirth, through planting the first seed, was thus mixed symbolically with reverence to the hallowed ground of the dead in the center of the village. The *huananchas,* and many elderly women who had borne candles into the church the previous night, would then start to dance through the streets and into the yard before the church. At the

---

[11] I have no evidence of professional role-switching, of men making tortillas or women sewing—as in Tzintzuntzan. I also lack evidence for the Spanish-style *tarasca,* a longnecked, dragon-like "creature" that is rolled on wheels and manipulated with cords by men inside.

same time many mummers, of both sexes, emerged for "The Dance of the Professions" (which Naranjeños still enjoy enumerating): peasant, fisherman, weaver, seeder, potter, shinglemaker, woodcutter, tanner, hatmaker, baker, carpenter, muleskinner, beekeeper, and thief. There was mock barter and stylized joking and buffoonery among the dancers. Each would mimic the gestures of his trade, the fishermen raising and lowering their nets, the peasants hoeing and shovelling, and the thieves struggling desperately with the muleskinners. Some trades, such as tanning, were limited locally to one or two practitioners; others concerned only one village, such as Azajo—with its professional thieves. Yet other trades such as pottery making were the results of diffusion or the survivals of very ancient patterns.

On Corpus Christi evening the mules were driven for a final turn around the town, the thieves hiding in ambush and springing forth with club and pistol to rob the maize. (This bit of symbolic conflict was discontinued before the agrarian period because of the near-fatal wounding of a participant.) Because of its size and expense, a successful Corpus fiesta required the cooperation of all the religions officials: *prioste, cabildes,* captains, and the *huanancha* families. Corpus, more or less coinciding with the onset of the rains, was the only fiesta that marked a change of season.

A minor fiesta on June 24, the Day of St. John, was climaxed by an attractive equestrian show, which can still be witnessed. Pairs of fast horses coursed down a long road outside Naranja; a ribbon-bound pigeon was passed rapidly from behind the head of one rider into the hand of his partner, who took it from the front, but also returned it from behind. The race often ended in a thunder of hoofs and a cloud of choking dust, while the pigeon—if with luck it broke loose—flew desperately to a nearby roof.[12]

So important and so religious were the masked personages of the annual cycle that fiestas were often named after a dance group rather than a saint. So it was with "Moors," on August 15, formally dedicated to Our Virgin of the Assumption. The religious sodality was charged with the event, but it was the captains and the League of Women who took up collections throughout the year to pay for the daily masses during the first half of the month. On Assumption Day seven or eight "Moors" would appear in colored ribbons and white masks, with spurs and swords. Dismounting, they would dance before the church, and then in other parts of the town throughout the day. Eight captains, mounted and dressed in Spanish baroque costumes, would stage a "Dance of the

---

[12] I have no evidence that St. John's was "a sort of agricultural groundhog day" (Foster, 1948, p. 218), which may reflect the relative lack of importance of rain and agriculture in the Naranja of 1885. A similar ceremony involving riding and the catching of pigeons obtains in Cherán today (Beals, 1964, p. 129).

Soldiers." The series of masses, the religious dances, and the hundreds of pilgrims from other Tarascan towns all combined to make Assumption the major fiesta of a purely religious nature; commercialism, in the form of booths and peddlers, was absent, and the day closed with a massive procession of Naranjeños and visitors, all holding candles.

The Tarascans have "a culture of masks" (Gómez Robleda, 1941, p. 223), and this was most evident during the pagan gaiety of Tiger Day, around the beginning of October. Although formally devoted to the Virgin of the Rosary, the activities and emotions of the villagers centered on a key animal in their symbolic world: the motley, horned "tigers." The fiesta started in the evening, when the *huananchas* danced through the town, mimicking a bullfighter with their shawls. (In preconquest times these maidens had been devoted to a lunar cult.) They were followed by musicians who blew monotonously on native flutes and beat on diminutive drums. The parade always ended inside the flower-bedecked church.

The next morning some sixty men and boys would don gray-and-white tiger costumes and deer-face masks with the antlers intact. They assembled on "Calvary Hill," which was probably the site of a former temple to the moon, and which commanded a magnificent vista of the Zacapu valley, black and green, stretching away to the north. Under the clear, azure sky of October, the frolicking "tigers," in twos and threes, would dance repeatedly to the rhythm of special "tiger tunes" played by the local band. The dances called for much mutual butting, followed by wild kicking and gyrating, then rough-and-tumble wrestling, and finally a slow hop across the grass. Toward the close of this terpsichorean play, a procession of chanting women would arrive, bearing an image of the Virgin. Then the "Three Kings" would do a brief step, wearing masks that made them look like flaccid ogres. Shortly afterwards everyone descended—some rolling drunkenly—down the slope to Naranja for a mammoth banquet of beef, pork cooked in *pozole*, and great quantities of maize and chili combined in prescribed recipes. The crushing expenses of the Tiger Fiesta, though paid mainly by the *prioste*, were shared by the *huananchas* through a complicated system of economic obligations.

The yearly cycle of community fiestas was brought to a close by a three-day celebration: the Day of the Angels, the Day of All Saints, and the Day of the Dead. On three preceding Fridays the *prioste* would have distributed anywhere from a quarter to a whole cheese to scores of individuals, at great expense to himself; but the costs were largely made good when the recipients of the cheeses reciprocated, according to their relation to the *prioste* and their economic and social status. On the afternoon of October 31, the *prioste* would give a fiesta of wheat tamales and beef guts in red chili sauce for his personal friends, for the political leaders, and for all the *huananchas* and their immediate families.

Late in the afternoon all of the guests, followed by the village band, would walk to the outskirts of town, where the *prioste* would jig to tiger tunes, surrounded by a large crowd and by the *huananchas* garlanded with flowers. As he shuffled about, the female relatives of the *huananchas* would arrive with huge baskets of wheat tamales, which they draped in long strings on the *prioste* and musicians and distributed among the assembled people. The entire company would then dance back through the town to the church, headed by the drunken *prioste*, who, sweating under his load of tamales, was enjoying the chance to play his focal, costly role. During the evening the families and relatives of the infants and children who had died within the past three to five years (the "little angels": *los angelitos*) would conduct private ceremonies in their homes, pronouncing a few prayers before the religious images, laying out bread to nourish the child's soul, and finally hanging small bunches of purple flowers before the door.

During the following Day of the Dead, the same persons would repair to the cemetery in small family groups and decorate the graves with orange flowers (sometimes orange and purple flowers) and with baked bread in the forms of horses for deceased boys and of dolls for deceased girls. All such offerings were heavily adorned with tropical fruit. After two hours of sitting by the grave and chatting quietly, the bereaved would file home and consume the funerary gifts. The expenses for the day were met by the deceased child's godparents, and were later balanced out by the parents through a return gift of tortillas and spicy beef broth. In the concluding ceremony of November 2, all appropriate relatives would go to the centrally located burial grounds to enact a similar vigil, adorning each grave with candles, assorted floral displays, and large arcs of white and purple flowers. Only this Day of the Dead, and St. John's, lacked masks and dancing.

ANTICLERICALISM: BACKGROUND

The pageantry and demanding organization of the religious cycle were undermined by a long series of historical events and processes. First, the environment and the entire economy of Naranja, like those of many other villages, were profoundly transformed by the policies of the dictatorship of Porfirio Díaz (1878-1910), particularly the so-called "rape of the pueblos" by Spanish entrepreneurs in collusion with local mestizos and government officials. Between 1885 and 1900, the swamp-like lake of Zacapu was surveyed, drained, and converted into an enormously productive maize bowl, divided into several plantations. This ecological revolution, although not directly affecting the fiestas, did deprive the Naranjeños of their main resource, and forced most of them into local peonage, or migrant labor on the sugar plantations of the Pacific coast. Between 1900 and 1910, several new lines of transportation to the outside world were opened by the landlords to facilitate the marketing of their maize. Local leaders began to agitate, and soon organized a series of committees for agrarian reform. In sum, an ecological revolution motivated basic changes in economic institutions that were to eventuate in the political cataclysm of the 1920's.

The next decade was one of national political tumult and pervasive social disorganization. The Mexican Revolution, erupting in 1910, brought the intermittent intrusion into local life of sundry army detachments, and bands of Villistas, Zapatistas, and other insurgents; and many Naranjeños sallied forth to fight. New notions of agrarian reform and social justice came to be rhetorically and psychologically fused with radical anticlericalism, which was signaled by a series of turning points along the road to agrarian revolt: in 1911 the fiesta of the patron saint, Our Father Jesus, was discontinued; in 1912 several drunken mestizos from the plantation were attacked and killed by a Naranja mob; in 1918 the village priest precipitously left because of political unrest, and thereafter many children went unbaptized and couples unwedded; in 1919 the regional leader for agrarian reform, a son of the Naranja village chief of the 1880's, was assassinated near the Pacific coast by agents of the landlords.

During the same decade (1910-20) the heads of the two mestizo families in Naranja consolidated their position as leaders of an authoritarian pro-clerical, pro-landlord *cacicazgo* that was contrary to the will of most villagers. The Zacapu region came to be controlled by a combination of immigrant Spanish and mestizo landlords, strongly supported by the clergy and local mestizos, or "fanatical Catholics." By the same token, many of the landless Indians in Naranja, Tiríndaro, and Tarejero were economically and ideologically ready for rapid changes in politics and religion.

PRIMO TAPIA, "THE ANTICHRIST"

Political change is often determined by men with the ability to lead and to envisage a different way of life for their followers. One such decisive individual was the brilliant, indigenous revolutionary, Primo Tapia, a nephew of the assassinated agrarian agitator. Like many revolutionaries, Tapia acquired an excellent education from a Catholic lay seminary, although he was expelled in his senior year because of a scandalous liaison with an older mestizo woman. He then spent fourteen yars in the United States, first as a migrant manual laborer, then in a brief association with a group of influential Mexican anarchists in exile in Los Angeles. Tapia later claimed that he had slept in the anarchists' house, and collected dues at their political meetings, and that they had paid for his study of English at a night school. Certain it is that he acquired an essentially anarchist ideology that stemmed from Bakunin and Kropotkin, as reworked by the Spanish anarcho-syndicalists of the turn of the century (Brenan, 1944) and by the Los Angeles circle, especially its leader, Ricardo Flores Magón, "the ideological precursor of the Mexican Revolution" (Barrera Fuentes, 1955, pp. 302-303).[13]

The positive points of this anarchist ideology were material improvements, especially land reform, and a socioeconomic organization based on the voluntary association of village communes, labor unions, and other small groups. On the negative side was an extreme hostility toward institutionalized, large-scale authority, especially the state and the church. Tapia learned to articulate a vitriolic hatred for the clergy and an utter cynicism for supernatural power, whether religious or magical. On the other hand, none of his recorded or remembered statements have the utopian ring of Bakunin and Flores Magón.

After the arrest of his mentors, Tapia left Los Angeles, and for the next nine years he worked in various western states, and was active in organizing Mexican migrants for the Industrial Workers of the World (the "Wobblies"). He absorbed much of the tactics and ethos of anarcho-socialism, and acquired an irreverence that was later reflected in songs and phrases in Tarascan and Spanish about sending "abbots and capitalists to join the Brothers in Space," etc. In 1919 he and three cousins allegedly got into trouble and were apprehended (but escaped) during labor agitation in the wheat and sugar-beet farms around Bayard and Scotts Bluff, Nebraska.[14] Tapia returned to Naranja a politically sophisticated, trilingual revolutionary. His striking appearance is conveyed by the words of his biographer (Martínez Mugica):

Prominent in the crowd was a man of robust build, medium height, swarthy face, and black eyes and moustache. He was dressed in a light woollen suit of dark shades that contrasted with the peasant manta of his companions. He wore a black felt hat. . . .

During 1921, he was able to unify the inchoate agrarian committees into a powerful league of the Tarascan pueblos in the Zacapu valley. Like Ricardo Flores Magón, though on a lesser scale, his words had a

[13] Ethel Duffy Turner, a participant and expert in anarchist activities during these years, writes that Ricardo lived secretly in Los Angeles after his release from prison in 1910. The offices on Fourth Street, where he subsequently published *Regeneración*, had several bedrooms, and "Tapia might have slept there" (letter of March 30, 1964). However, this is just an informed guess. No other Naranjeños were with him, and I have never been able to find any direct, incontrovertible evidence of Tapia's Los Angeles sojourn. Tapia's claim to have been "a student of the Flores Magón" has not yet been validated.

[14] According to Pedro López, Tapia was the main organizer of an unsuccessful strike. The October, 1919, issues of *The Farmer's Exchange* of Bayard and the Scotts Bluff *Star Herald*, report the arrest of small groups of "hard-boiled Wobblies," and their trial under the syndicalism laws.

"terrible persuasive force." His success as an orator before peasants, acknowledged by all, is best expressed in his own words:

I myself didn't know that I had been born into this briny world with the gift that people would hear me, that my rude, rough phrase could dominate not only men but also the female comrades, whom I have in my control in certain towns in this land of the immortal Ocampo, and the cradle of so many rascals.

To dozens of young, illiterate, and landless peasants his message of anticlericalism, agrarian reform, and "progress" produced a sense of conversion, as is clear from the words of a follower:

Primo used to explain everything to us, that such-and-such ideas were wrong, and that such-and-such ideas were right, and that it was a pure lie that we would be sent to hell for taking part in agrarianism. . . . Ever since I joined him I have never gone to church. (Friedrich, 1965, p. 123)

Tapia was in a position of strength because his agrarian revolt was an enforcement of the national law: passage of the crucial measures of 1915, 1917, and 1922, had guaranteed for each Naranjeño carefully defined (if theoretical) rights in the lands of the plantations. By 1924-25, as a result of political influence and adroit, well-financed litigation, the plantations were expropriated, and redistributed on a massive scale to the four major towns of the Zacapu valley. Naranja, for example, received 1,432 acres of superb black soil. Primo's sense of a mission accomplished is transparent in the religious idiom of a letter of December 19, 1925.

"Our *ejidos* almost swamp Cantabria. We are masters of the land. As far as this point is concerned, my ambition is achieved, and I ask nothing more of the world. . . . all the world is agrarian, even the dogs, and those who do not want to take communion with my ideas are done in, defeated."

Local governments were organized under powerful executive committees, staffed by agrarian leaders and fighters, and the entire agricultural cycle in the new *ejidos* was carried out by brigades on a communalistic basis. In line with his anarcho-socialistic ideology, Tapia also organized, and led, a state-wide League of Agrarian Communities, which was linked in principle to world socialism and was devoted to attacking the "priests and abbots."

Agrarian reform was inextricably connected with acts against the Catholic priests and church. A symbolic episode in 1921 was the planting of the central plaza to flowers and bushes, and moving the cemetery to a plot outside the village, "for purposes of hygiene." Later that year many of the "fanatically Catholic"—and illiterate—villagers were hoodwinked into signing what they were told was simply a petition for a new priest, but which was later affixed to a petition for land reclamation.

Primo Tapia was concerned with organizing peasant women because "as long as they are under the influence of the priest he will wrest the

last secrete from them" (letter of 1923). Subsequently he could report
that

One can already talk to them with complete confidence, as to any partisan.
They no longer let themselves be duped by the men with the cassocks. I have
even demonstrated to them the evidence that the priest is our enemy, and not
with sophisms (*sofismos*), but with the Bible in my hand.

The local peasants, indeed, often viewed Tapia as "the Antichrist,"
or as a preacher, apostle, or miracle-worker. By 1924, large Feminine
Leagues, of seventy to one hundred or more members, were active in all
of the pueblos, were holding their meetings in the church, and were running cooperative stores, poultry farms, and similar enterprises.

Through his persuasiveness and organizational abilities—and the use
of violence—Tapia created an unusual degree of ideological homogeneity among those who remained in Naranja, and to a lesser extent, among
the inhabitants of Tiríndaro and Tarejero. A somewhat idealized version
of his political role is communicated in a letter of February 7, 1925, from
the then president of the National Agrarian Commission.

. . . Primo is a son of the people . . . who can count on the attachment,
the affection, and the respect of all the native Indians of the region; the
peasants who see in him their chief who has never deceived them, who has
never exploited them, and who is always with them in danger. You know very
well . . . what the natural leaders are for our people. The people follow them
without asking where they are going, and even when these chiefs manage to
make a mistake . . . it increases the confidence they enjoy if they correct their
mistake in time.

Generally speaking, Tapia was a charismatic leader, in part because he
operated in a context of beliefs in a supernatural order, and in part because he could inspire and galvanize an emotional loyalty, both to himself, and to the new, secular order. Through his astuteness, courage, and
"serenity," he exemplified one local ideal of the leader.

Tapia's ideology, although far-reaching, was not apocalyptic; this was
illustrated by his compromise on communal fiestas, which was not recorded in letters or other documents but is unambiguously implicit in
many logically connected acts. It appears to have been made for two
reasons. First, as several Naranjeños pointed out, he saw the annual
fiestas as an enormous source of revenue, once the sponsors and clergy
had been replaced by civic officials. Second, he recognized and apparently agreed with the sharp but implicit dichotomy (outlined above)
between the official, national Catholicism with its sacraments, masses,
and sermons administered by the clergy and the largely or potentially
folk religion with its dances and pageantry. He sought to attach or re-
ticulate the sensuous, folk stimuli of the fiestas to the new moral and
political order of agrarianism.

The resulting concatenation had an almost medieval quality, as if

"God and the devil . . . divine spirit and gargoyle, had been in intimate communication with each other" (Wolf, 1964, p. 148). For example, Tapia performed enthusiastically as Christ's defending advocate in the "Sanhedrin" during the theatrical mysteries of Easter Week, and it was only after his death that the major fiestas of the Three Kings, *Carnaval*, Corpus Christi, and the Assumption went into decline. He also revived the moribund fiestas of the patron saint, Our Father Jesus; and in 1925, he personally organized its most sumptuous performance, animated by dozens of masked dancers, including several groups of "little old men." In the mystery play, Tapia acted the part of Lucifer, thus epitomizing his intuitive sense of leadership in a culture full of mummery, masks, and other forms of personification. On the other hand, the one thousand-odd pesos in taxes on market space collected during the fiesta were used later for agrarian litigation. And Tapia announced that the fee for masses would be reduced from three hundred to nine pesos, "the minimum wage for workers who toil in the broiling sun." This outraged the three priests who had been persuaded to officiate. Believers, including his own mother, vilified Tapia as "an antichrist."

Despite his acting in religious fiestas, and his humorous "Wobbly" songs, Tapia could be "severe" and "hard"; in the words of a regional poet, "his career had a dark background." One of his nephews said that "Primo was of a violent character, although at heart he was good. He had the small fault of being in agreement with bad things, including revenge and killing, and because of this he surrounded himself with ambitious persons." Violence was combined with contempt for the eschatology of his clerical opponents. Tapia's own words convey this attitude with typical condensation and verve.

. . . the anathemas of the clergy . . . from the pulpits and the confessionals invoke the eternal fire for agrarians "who want another man's property." "Honorable people cannot be agrarians because the lands already belong to their legitimate owners," says the irate voice of the Levites, at times creating ruptures within families and between friends.

At first, agrarian violence was largely in response to frequent (and well-documented) raids, beatings, kidnapings, and imprisonments by the local allies and militias of the landlords. Primo himself is not known ever to have killed anyone; but by 1922 his "fighters" were retaliating with force, and soon took the initiative in ambushes, nocturnal house raids, and street shootings against "believers" and "reactionaries." In 1923, during the turmoil of the Delahuertista movement, Primo and several cousins, including Pedro López, led a posse of about one hundred mounted agrarians around the Lake Pátzcuaro region, and were later accused of murdering some conservative leaders, and of "other atrocities." A few days later they attacked Tiríndaro, and captured and slaughtered nine of the foremost "Catholics." Shortly thereafter, the priest fled by night, and the agrarians confiscated the gold, silver, and linens in the church. A similar fate awaited the specialists in the other form of belief in the supernatural. In 1925 a group of young agrarians, led by Primo, broke into the house of the main witch, ran her out of town, and intimidated her rivals. To this day belief in witchcraft is comparatively insignificant among Naranja men. Local violence reached a crescendo during 1924-25, when, after a provisional grant of land from the plantation, over one hundred families were simply driven from Naranja. Some returned after signing an "agrarian census," and supported the petition for the final grant, but the majority settled permanently in the country seat or in distant pueblos. During the same months, many individuals were killed or wounded.

Anticlericalism in the pueblo was supported by legal decrees and informal political influence emanating from the state and national capitals; for example, all alien priests were ordered deported, many parochial schools and seminaries were closed, and many clerical practices, such as the public wearing of vestments, were curtailed. In retaliation the church staged a general strike, and between 1926-29 no masses were said.

At the national level, anticlerical programs and ideology during the Calles presidency (1924-28) were accompanied by a relentless weakening or assassination of "local chieftains"; in 1926 soldiers and disguised agents of the national president kidnapped Primo Tapia, who had been branded a "bandit" and "Communist." After being led along barefoot most of the day, with a noose around his neck, he was lynched in the sierra. On the same afternoon four women leaders set off by foot "to help Primo." Passing a cemetery near Lake Pátzcuaro, one of them thought she heard three trumpet blasts. "That was for Primo," they said to each other, and hurried on, reaching the state capital the next day with their feet bloody and swollen. Later, the horribly mutilated body— a grisly analogue to the bloodied statue of Naranja's patron saint—was brought back and buried in the graveyard overlooking the new *ejidos*. The words with which several villagers reported the sadistic lynching imply the victim's future status: "He was not killed, he was martyred."

During the spring of the "martyrdom," disease and sickness carried off thirty infants and children. It was soon widely believed among the women that "the Virgin needed thirty *angelitos* for the two choirs that would sing for Primo as he entered heaven." Such new myths were congruous with the structural transformation by which Tapia later became the town's "other patron," replacing the principal casualty of the anticlericalism of the thirties: Our Virgin of the Assumption.

ANTICLERICALISM AND FACTIONAL POLITICS

After Tapia's death, politics changed rapidly; regional and local unity decreased; the next nine years witnessed pervasive and sanguinary factional strife between Tapia's "Bolshevik" followers, which included most of his relatives, as against a larger and relatively moderate faction. The latter favored, and achieved, two successive subdivisions of the communalistic *ejido* lands into plots inalienably attached to individual families; after 1928 the land was sown and tilled by families, while the work brigades were limited to harvesting and canal drainage. Yet despite these fracturing processes, the "agrarians" of the entire valley had enough in common to form an army of more than four hundred to hunt down groups of "Christians" (*cristeros*) in Jalisco and southern Michoacán. All over the Zacapu valley, "Christians" lived under precarious circumstances; in 1929 about twenty were killed during a street fight in the county seat (Anguiano Equihua, 1951). Continuous harassment of the clergy was not precluded or even inhibited by the dominance between 1932-34 of the so-called "conservative agrarians." Partly because of ideological fervor, Naranja and Tiríndaro secured their reputation as bastions of the left-wing politics of Lázaro Cárdenas.

Anticlericalism in many Mexican villages had been closely connected with national policy. In 1934, Cárdenas of Michoacán campaigned for the national presidency, with strong planks against "religious fanaticism." Idols, processions, and many aspects of ritual were to be forbidden, and parochial schools were to be persecuted even more than under his predecessors. Violent anticlericalism began to sputter in Michoacán as groups of armed Red Shirts clashed with "believers." Cárdenas' formal election, and subsequent seizure of *de facto power* from Calles in 1935, soon had local repercussions. The agrarian leader of Tiríndaro, released from a district jail, returned to his village, and with a posse of three hundred Cardenistas captured and lynched the leaders of the Christian agrarian party in the village. Radical agrarianism was converted into anticlerical fanaticism as activities that even smacked of Catholicism were ruthlessly suppressed. Many alleged believers were driven from town, or abducted from their houses by night and murdered with knife and pistol; an entire family was butchered with machetes in the sierra. There were no religious fiestas at all until 1940. Tiríndaro's anticlericalism was related to the distribution of land: in a population of about two and a half thousand the *ejido* was monopolized by 105 families of *agraristas*. During the factionalism of the thirties, as in the reform of the twenties, the violence of anticlericalism seems to have covaried with the severity of pressure on land.

Meanwhile, several Naranja leaders had achieved strong connections or positions in the state machine of Cárdenas. Particularly militant in his anticlericalism was Pedro López, who from 1932-35 had served as secretary general of the "glorious" (and extremely powerful and statewide) Confederación Michoacana de Trabajo. From 1935-39, Naranja flowered as a center for agrarian reform, political control, and active anticlericalism over a wide territory in and around the Zacapu valley. Her leaders demonstrated their character as "revolutionaries without stain" by burning icons, by confiscating gold and silver paraphernalia, and by institutional and direct armed attacks on the clergy and "Catholic conservatives" in other pueblos. Within the village itself, the most sacred of the fiestas, Our Virgin of the Assumption, was completely stopped, and the others were curtailed—except Tiger Day and All Saints-Day of the Dead. The *caciques* forbade taking the sacraments, and parents caught baptizing their children were denounced in full assembly, and often threatened with expropriation. This caused terrible conflicts of value, especially in the women.

The latent struggle for control of the rich *ejido* lands, and for the symbols of power over the community, led in 1937 to a second tragic schism as the faction that had triumphed over the "conservative agrarians" only two years earlier divided again under the leadership of two cousins of Tapia. Local shootings rapidly multiplied: from 1937-39, twenty-one Naranjeños died in skirmishes and ambushes; but, despite such casualties, both of the new factions competed in advocating the historical descendant of Tapia's new ideology: Cardenismo. By this time, ritual was determining politics in the sense that the loss of the fiestas— with their commensality and other social life—probably contributed to a sort of political anomie while increasing the functions of kinship-based groups and of rival factions seeking to justify their acts in terms of a new ideological legitimacy.

The presidential election of 1940-41 brought a mollification of the anticlerical hard line and the inception of a new era of working compromises between organized Catholicism and revolutionary socialism. In Tiríndaro, the megalomaniacal *cacique* was overthrown, and by the mid-1950's most of the fiesta cycle had been fully restored, largely because of the enthusiastic support of immigrant mestizo laborers who had not experienced the reform and the conservative and still landless majority that had survived it. By 1956, the fiesta to Tiríndaro's patron saint, Our Virgin of the Redeemer, was attended by over three thousand pilgrims, and it terminated with an imposing procession. A resourceful young priest occupied a large house on the plaza, and Tiríndaro itself had been elevated from a parish to a diocese.

Naranja also witnessed a rapid retrenchment after 1940. The leaders began to allow loyal members of the old religious sodality and the League of Women to reinstitute some of the fiesta cycle; Our Virgin of the Assumption was celebrated in 1943. During the mid-1950's, a "third party" (led by a nephew of Tapia) emerged with a curious combination of objectives: "material improvements in the spirit of Primo Tapia," and many concessions to those who wanted to restore the former system— particularly public religious processions and a priest in Naranja's still vacant parish house. But at the crucial town meeting, attended by the diocesan priest from Tiríndaro, several leaders and "fighters" (all nephews of Tapia) appeared without notice and dispersed the women and "conservatives" with pistol shots. Shortly thereafter, the organizer of the third party was ambushed, together with his son, and both fled to Mexico City.

By 1956, a sort of balance had been achieved between the "revolutionaries," tied to the state political machine, and the "Catholics," who were indirectly in touch with the ecclesiastical hierarchy. But the priest and the extreme anticlericals have both become relatively weak. The priest has no hand in the fiestas, is allowed to enter the pueblo only one afternoon a month (with no tolling of the bells), and does not administer the sacraments within Naranja [15]; his near nullification has of course been integrally related to the restructuring of power relations within the pueblo. Tapia's anticlerical ideology still lives; as one Naranjeño put it: "I like to read the Bible because it says there what the clergy are, and that if Christ returned they would want to kill him again." However, only a half dozen leaders have such strong opinions, and still refuse the sacraments or participation in a fiesta. Most villagers have reaccepted a modicum of religious life.

The local organization of fiestas and its relation to politics has changed in several ways; in general, the resuscitation has been gradual and incomplete. The eight *huananchas* still dance, but the extent of their parents' obligations has greatly contracted. Captains are no longer selected; and the religious sodality has not been revived. Most of the *priostes*, now called *cargueros*, have been old and relatively apolitical *ejidatarios*, weakly playing half-forgotten roles. There has been an interesting synthesis of old and new between aging *agraristas* and young "revolutionaries." For example, the most lavish annual series was financed in 1953 by the outstanding female agrarian, a first cousin of Tapia, with funds her son was earning in the United States. However, although one's personal and political past may be made more "respectable" or legitimate by financing fiestas, I have no evidence that political authority depends to any significant degree on having served as a *carguero*.

Finally, Naranja no longer has a council of elders, or ex-*cargueros*. As in most of the Tarascan area, there has been "no blooming of the traditional *cabildos*" (Carrasco, 1952, p. 32); even the words *cabilde* and

---

[15] The exclusion of the priest from communal functions seems to set off the Zacapu region from many other Tarascan towns (Carrasco, 1957, p. 34); even in highly conservative Azajo, a priest was not allowed to participate in the construction of a new church in the early 1950's.

cabildo are rarely used. "The principal ones," formerly supported by the civil-religious system, have been replaced by "the princes," many of them Cruzes, and all of them agrarians. Through violence, conversion, and land reforms, Naranja has become a *comunidad agraria* in a fuller sense than most pueblos.

TRANSFORMATIONS IN THE FIESTA CYCLE

The acts and ideas of anticlericalism have had both generic and specific repercussions. In the generic class belong those that affect substantial portions of the pueblo's social organization, such as the sharp reduction in the participation of the men, the debilitation of the old *carguero* system, the institutional separation of religion and politics, near autonomy in the organization of ritual, and finally, a drastic weakening of the religious ties with other communities. On the other hand, anticlericalism has been reflected specifically but systematically in various parts of the annual fiesta cycle. In addition to their political implications, these transformations illustrate much about the dynamics of ritual symbolism. They are reviewed below, not chronologically, but by types of process.

Two fiestas are still given a full performance, and today contribute a fusion of the folk, agrarian, and Catholic systems. Most widely appreciated of all the year are the fiestas of the Christmas season; no villagers abstain on ideological grounds, and all but three of the leaders watch. In part, this cultural persistence is socially motivated: Tacári, since it includes the major rite of courtship, is a time for all marriageable girls to dance in the streets and encourage suitors; and the house-to-house visiting of the *posadas* gives their fathers, many of them agrarian leaders, a chance to display hospitality. But the hilarity of Tacári, and the singular ebullience of the Christmas rejoicing, also stem from the fact that it is normally during the second week of December that the peasants go into the *ejido* to begin harvesting the maize, that is, the annual first fruits from the land won under Primo Tapia. The Christmas season thus illustrates a fundamental feature of ritual: symbolic ambiguity—or discrepancy between meanings (Turner, 1964, p. 39).

The second fiesta to survive is that of the patron saint, Our Father Jesus. But although its size, duration, and number of participants equals or exceeds that of 1900, many constituent meanings and functions have altered. Thus, though the *carguero* and the women's league arrange and pay for clerical services, the organization itself falls largely in the hands of the civic officials, who pocket most of the intake (between 1,000 and 2,000 pesos). There are, at most, five dance groups, and no "little old men." The business aspect has become more prominent; in 1956 the groups of Tarascan pilgrims were small, and many visitors complained of the change in spirit and the decline of Tarascan speech. Finally—and analogous to the Christmas season—the date of the fiesta coincides with the end of maize picking in the agrarian *ejido:* Our Father Jesus has turned into a commercialized harvest festival. This illustrates the process of ritual change whereby constancy in dimensions may be combined with drastic shifts in their makeup and purpose.

Three important fiestas endure in somewhat reduced circumstances. A minority in the town still takes part in the feast of St. John, but, at the main equestrian ceremony of dove-snatching, the young leaders sit around drinking beer—with money from *ejido* taxes—watching other leaders and athletes career down the racetrack. This secular situation may reflect the fact that during the thirties the agrarians used their new income to acquire fine mounts, and, with the coaching of locally stationed cavalry officers, became renowned for their skills.

A somewhat similar background may account for the survival of Tiger Day. A large minority still relishes the role of the "tiger," but many are unaware of Our Virgin of the Rosary. This may be because in the thirties and forties the fiesta was not only divested of its hagiographic associations but was transmogrified into an occasion for manly display by the "most valiant," most of whom were young, anticlerical leaders and "fighters." Thus, both the riders of St. John and the wrestlers of the Rosary illustrate a fundamental process: the transference of affective, aggressive qualities to the elements of a sacred (or formerly sacred) ritual.

The third somewhat contracted fiesta is the unit of two autumn days devoted to honoring the dead. By 1956, the long preparatory period, the feast on Halloween, and the tamale symbolism were not staged by the *carguero,* and no priest was invited to say mass. Otherwise, All Souls and the Day of the Dead do not seem to have been affected by the agrarian reform. In part, this may have been because both events were strongly felt to be "indigenous," and distinct in crucial particulars from the "Catholic" ceremonies in neighboring mestizo pueblos. In part, the vitality of these funerary days may stem from the death-consciousness connected with the incredible record of assault and homicide that have earned for the Zacapu valley the sobriquet of "The Slaughterhouse of Michoacán." This concatenation of death and agrarian politics was particularly clear in the case of Primo Tapia, who had been obsessed by dreams and premonitions of a violent end. The memory of his "martyrdom" still lives, and his statue and tomb now dominate the central plaza, just as the cemetery used to in former times. During the 1950's, the female relatives of Tapia began buying candles and having masses said for the repose of his soul. On the Day of the Dead in 1956, about twenty adolescent girls with burning candles held a long prayer before his monument; as one said afterwards, "Primo was against the priests, but he fought so that we could eat!" In more abstract terms, Primo Tapia, through his relation to death, has developed into what Sapir called a condensation symbol that "strikes deeper and deeper roots in the unconscious, and diffuses its emotional quality to types of behavior and situations apparently far removed from the original meaning."

Three fiestas, enormously popular in the 1920's and fondly depicted by old-timers, have shrunken to caricatures of their former selves. New Year's lacks the three communal banquets and the dance groups, and is limited to a small minority of the devout. The same is true of the Three Kings; even the several masked "Moors" who perform before the church at high noon are ad hoc volunteers, not elected *capitanes*, the primary symbols of the former civil-religious authority. Carnival is still exciting, but mainly for the seventy-odd women and children who assemble for the throwing of tropical fruits. These three fiestas illustrate the formal pattern of abridgement: With a weakening of its total significance, the components of a ritual may be gradually eliminated until, at the last, only one diagnostic event remains to mark the day.

More extreme developments have affected three focal ceremonies; all required clerical cooperation in the form of numerous masses, and all were systematically attacked by anticlericals during the 1930's. In 1956, Corpus Christi went unobserved, and no one walked over to watch Tiríndaro's skeletal reconstruction of The Dance of the Professions. Corpus, together with Easter, constituted the two regional fiestas that linked Naranja to four other communities; and the fate of Corpus is part of the recent history of intercommunal politics that first split off Azajo and Zipiajo, the two neighbors with little available land, and correspondingly little agrarian sentiment. Tarejero, though sharing in the reform of the 1920's, broke with "those of Naranja" during the local and state factionalism of the following decade. Today, very few persons from either town ever attend fiestas in the other. Yet the persistence of some ancient ties is reflected by the attendance of three to four hundrd Naranjeño visitors at the full revivals of Easter Week in Tiríndaro: the "revolutionary sincerity" of the agrarian politicians in one town has been complemented by the renewed religious fervor of "reactionaries" and "Catholics" in the other. These changes illustrate the functional relation between communal ritual and intercommunal politics.[16]

Easter used to vie with Assumption in the dominance of purely religious elements. More specifically, Assumption was the fiesta most integrally linked with the network of clerical symbols—attendant priests, masses, hagiographic explicitness—and with the civil-religious politico-

---

[16] Between ten and thirty-five Naranja pilgrims still attend eleven outside fiestas every year, inclusive of those in the county seat, and eighty or more attend the "very important fiesta" of El Señor del Rescate in distant Tzintzuntzan (Friedrich, 1963, p. 368).

governmental system of *priostes, cabildes,* captains, the League of Women, and the religious fraternity. On the other hand, Assumption was nearly, or at least relatively, devoid of the two non-Christian networks: the commercialism of the fiesta markets, and the material and orectic symbols—the gargantuan portions of highly spiced foods, the masks of animal faces, and so forth. With reference to these four specific networks, Assumption was "the most religious" of all the fiestas—and consequently the most ruthlessly attacked by the anticlericals. Today the only happening on August 15 is a pilgrimage to the state capital by a half-dozen elderly women. Assumption illustrates not only the formal process of total loss but also, because of its links to Primo Tapia, the antithetical polarization of dominant rituals. From another point of view, a major ritual that stresses the importance of a single principle of social organization does so only by blocking the expression of other important principles (Turner, 1964, p. 44). Because of its "purely religious" character, Assumption proved the least viable during rapid political change.

Finally, two secular fiestas have entered the annual cycle and become major events. In 1900, Independence Day was announced as a national holiday, but was otherwise unobserved; by 1956 it included the recitation of patriotic speeches by children and the town officials, the parade of a band and about fifty village men, a theatrical enactment of the Proclamation of Independence by Hidalgo in 1811, and the explosion of firecrackers attached to a "pyrotechnical mule."

April 26, the day Primo Tapia was assassinated, is now celebrated by large groups of children from neighboring pueblos who march into Naranja with bands and deliver sentimental poems and eulogies on a platform amid swirling clouds of dust. During the afternoon a lavish banquet of turkey with *mole* sauce is served for all the leaders, followed by the lengthy orations of visiting bureaucrats and politicians, and these are often men prominent in state and national politics, as in 1956, when Naranja was visited by the national secretary of the *Campesina.* The memorial does not call forth as many people or as much enthusiasm as the great religious fiestas of yesteryear, but it is strongly supported by the local and regional politicos, who owe their position to agrarian socialism.

The status of the Primo Tapia fiesta within the annual cycle is ambiguous. The villagers clearly and explicitly dichotomize between civil and religious fiestas, and, because of the conflicts of faction and opinion over the years, most villagers still have a realistic view of Tapia's faults and defects: he is not a saint in any pantheon. At the same time, the fiestas are thought of as great occasions that mark the year, irrespective of their greater or lesser religiosity. Local leaders, Tapia's relatives, and the (usually left-wing) school teachers, have all joined with the passage of years to create a myth in Pareto's limited sense of a historical fact with fictional appendages (1935, p. 350). Just as Tapia's impetuous and violent personality knit the community together during the 1920's, so now his memory, fused with its mythical penumbra, has come to play a more vital role in local culture than any saint or complex of Catholic dogma.

In terms of a more general theory, Naranja has witnessed an unusual synthesis of what Nock (1933) called "the two opposing poles in man's spiritual history. One is the system of religious observances of a small unit with elementary needs and interests"; that is, the local round of Catholic fiestas. "The other is the religion of a prophetic movement"; that is, Primo Tapia and his anarchism-socialism, which, taken together, have become a partial substitute for religious myth and dogma.

GENERAL CONCLUSIONS

The preceding analysis has by no means assumed or postulated that changes in a communal ritual can be determined only by politics; on the contrary, the data under consideration have suggested explanation in terms of alternative hypotheses. Thus, the village has passed through several economic conditions: from original abundance to impoverishment to precarious affluence; and the economic system itself has changed: from local industries to plantation peonage to a completely communalistic *ejido* to an *ejido* divided into inalienable family plots. But these changes in wealth and economic structure have not co-varied directly with ritual change.

Second, there has been little change in most dimensions of the social organization: the nuclear family, the *compadre* system, and bilateral kindred and descent; the absence of social change cannot explain ritual change. The few major exceptions, such as the shift to marriage by elopement or capture, are related to ritual change only in the indirect sense that they were produced by the same or connected causes.

Finally, the profound assimilation to the national, mestizo culture— signaled since the 1930's by increased bilingualism, a new highway, and many altered customs—does not appear to be correlated with the loss and attrition in religious ritual. On the contrary, many mestizo villages that escaped anticlericalism have today the sort of vitality in ritual that marked Indian Naranja in 1900.

The main alternative hypotheses may well explain ritual change in many other villages, and may have had certain indirect or secondary consequences in Naranja, but it would appear that the primary determinant of the rapid and drastic change in the communal ritual in Naranja has been its change in politics: in political behavior, in leadership, and, above all, in ideology.

REFERENCES

ANGUIANO EQUIHUA, VICTORIANO. 1951. Lázaro Cárdenas, su fendo y la política nacional. Mexico.

BARRERA FUENTES, FLORENCIO. 1955. Historia de la revolución Mexicana: la etapa precursora. Mexico.

BARTH, FREDRIK. 1959. Political leadership among the Swat Pathans. London: Athlone Press.

BEALS, RALPH. 1946. Cherán: a sierra Tarascan village. Washington: Smithsonian Institution, Institute of Social Anthropology, Publication 2.

BEALS, RALPH, and HOIJER, HARRY. 1956. An introduction to anthropology. New York: Macmillan.

BRENAN, GERALD. 1944. The Spanish labyrinth. An account of the social and political background of the Civil War. New York: Macmillan.

CARRASCO, PEDRO. 1952. Tarascan folk religion: an analysis of economic, social and religious institutions. Middle American Research Institute, Publication 17. Tulane University, pp. 1-64.

———. 1961. The civil-religious hierarchy in mesoamerican communities: pre-Spanish background and colonial development. American Anthropologist, 63, 3, 483-497.

DURKHEIM, EMILE. 1925. Les formes elémentaires de la vie religieuse (2d ed.). Paris.

EVANS-PRITCHARD, E. E. 1953. The sacrificial role of cattle among the Nuer. *In* S. and P. Ottenberg (eds.), Cultures and societies of Africa. New York: Random House, pp. 388-405.

FOSTER, GEORGE M. 1948. Empire's children. The people of Tzintzuntzan. Washington: Smithsonian Institution, Institute of Social Anthropology, Publication 6.

———. 1960. Culture and conquest: America's Spanish heritage. New York: Wenner-Grenn Foundation.

FRIEDRICH, CARL J. 1963. Man and his government. New York: McGraw-Hill.

FRIEDRICH, PAUL. 1963. Naranja y el mundo exterior. Revista Interamericana de Ciencias Sociales, 2, 3, 346-375.

———. 1965. An agrarian "fighter." *In* Melford Spiro (ed.), Context and meaning in cultural anthropology. New York: Free Press of Glencoe.

GEERTZ, CLIFFORD. 1957. Ritual and social change: a Javanese example. American Anthropologist, 59, 32-54.

GOMEZ ROBLEDA, J. 1941. Pescadores y campesinos Tarascos. Mexico.

GOUGH, KATHLEEN. 1959. Cults of the dead among the Nayars. *In* Traditional India: structure and change. Milton B. Singer (ed.), Philadelphia: Publications of the American Folklore Society, Bibliographical Series, 10, 240-272.

LEACH, EDMUND R. 1954. Political systems of highland Burma. Harvard University Press.

LEON, NICOLAS. 1906. Los Tarascos. Noticias históricas, étnicas y antropológicas. Tercera parte. Etnografía postcortesiana y actual. Anales del Museo

Nacional de México. Segunda Epoca, 3, 298-479. Mexico City: Imprenta del Museo Nacional.

MANNHEIM, KARL. 1953. Ideology and utopia. New York: Harcourt, Brace & World.

MARTINEZ MUGICA, APOLINAR. n.d. Primo Tapia, semblanza de un revolucionario michoacano.

MENDIETO Y NUNEZ, LUCIO (ed.). 1940. Los Tarascos. Mexico City: Imprenta Universitaria.

NOCK, ARTHUR D. 1933. Conversion; the old and the new in religion from Alexander the great to Augustine of Hippo. Oxford: Clarendon Press.

PARETO, VILFREDO. 1935. The mind and society (4 vols.). Andrew Bongiorno and Arthur Livingston (trans.). New York: Harcourt, Brace & World.

SPIRO, MELFORD. 1964. Kibbutz: venture in utopia. New York: Schocken.

TURNER, V. W. 1964. Symbols in Ndembu ritual. In Max Gluckman (ed.), Closed systems and open minds: the limits of naivety in social anthropology. Chicago: Aldine.

WOLF, ERIC. 1957. Closed corporate peasant communities in Mesoamerica and central Java. Southwestern Journal of Anthropology, 13, 1-18.

———. 1964. Santa Claus: notes on a collective representation. In Robert A. Manners (ed.). Process and pattern in culture. Essays in honor of Julian H. Steward. Chicago: Aldine.

THE ALIEN DIVINER AND LOCAL POLITICS AMONG THE TONGA OF ZAMBIA [1]

Elizabeth Colson, UNIVERSITY OF CALIFORNIA, BERKELEY

Anthropologists have recently begun to pay new attention to the importance of the stranger or alien as an agent used by competing groups within a community. His presence permits them to maneuver for position without committing themselves irretrievably to a stand that might force a major confrontation and the breakdown of all ongoing relationships. In practice, of course, there are degrees of strangeness and different categories of alienness. A community is likely to choose as its agents those aliens or strangers who are most suitable to its purposes in particular situations.

In this paper I shall be concerned with the use the Tonga of Zambia make of one particular type of stranger: the impartial stranger, of the same social universe, who shares a common set of values with the Tonga. The alien diviner or witchfinder is precisely this, an alien whose behavior is predictable because it is based on standards accepted by the patron community, and whose findings are therefore intelligible and acceptable. An alien diviner, however, is useful only in internal difficulties. If other aliens, with radically differing values and interpretations are also

[1] Material for this paper was collected between 1946 and 1963 in the course of five periods of research among the Tonga of the Southern Province of Zambia. In all, I have spent something like five years with the Tonga of the Plateau and the Gwembe Valley. All research was sponsored by the Rhodes-Livingstone Institute, Lusaka.

The evidence for the analysis here presented is not as firm as I would like. I have talked with Tonga about witchfinders, but have never seen one at work nor talked with one at any length. Both plateau and Gwembe neighborhoods are said to have summoned witchfinders in recent years, and they have also worked on European-owned farms in the railway belt. Informants remember similar occasions in the past, and I have no evidence that belief in the efficacy of the witchfinder is greater now than when I first visited the Tonga.

It is possible that I am misinformed about the lack of involvement of Tonga chiefs with witchfinding sessions. I am better satisfied with my information on the role of diviners. I have known, talked with, and watched many diviners at work, and have collected information on hundreds of divinations, most of which attribute misfortune to the anger of the shades of the dead.

I thank my colleague, Dr. Thayer Scudder, for access to his field notes on the Gwembe Tonga, which corroborate my findings on the lack of involvement of the Middle River Tonga in witchfinding movements. I also thank Dr. Ronald Cohen, of Northwestern University, for his comments on the original draft of this paper.

involved as protagonists and judges of the action, the stranger status of the diviner or witchfinder becomes irrelevant.

DIVINERS AND WITCHFINDERS

The Tonga of Zambia consult diviners on numerous occasions: in emergencies involving illness, accident, death, or other misfortunes; and to find explanations for untoward events of one kind or another. They also seek from them prognostications on various planned courses of action. The one who consults the diviner may be concerned only with his own private concerns, or he may appear as the representative of a kin group. He may consult either local or strange diviners, who may use a variety of divination techniques. Any diviner visiting a new area, whether he be a Tonga or a complete alien, is likely to find local clients who say that a man from a distance, knowing nothing of local affairs, is more likely to give a true divination than a local man who knows all about the one who seeks enlightenment. Tonga will also travel considerable distances to consult diviners of reputation.

For minor matters, people are usually content with the services of local diviners who are part of their community. The only rule they follow is that a man or woman should seek a neutral tool; no man may divine his own matter. It may be enough that the diviner is outside the immediate household group: this removes him sufficiently from the situation so that he counts as a neutral intermediary between the inquirer and the divining power. Important matters, including death divinations and the divinations of misfortune to men of importance, are usually submitted to a number of diviners, one of whom is sought at a distance. The pronouncement of the stranger is then likely to be preferred and remembered as the correct diagnosis—because it has come from someone outside the community and because it has cost a good deal more in effort and money than any local divination.

The famous diviners who attract customers from distant areas have impressive foreign techniques, usually learned in areas whose people are reputed to have powerful medicines. They charge high fees for their services. Where the local diviner may have to be satisfied with a fee of a 6d and a small basket of grain, the famous diviners can expect to receive fees of several pounds, and even more in difficult cases.

But the local man with a small reputation and the foreign diviner known throughout the countryside have the same role, and one can be substituted for the other. A man may consult one or the other, or both, though he may feel that one gives the better divination.

Consultations with such diviners are a private matter, or at most the affair of a kinship group—even where matters of sorcery may be suspected. Men consult them to confirm suspicions against kinsmen and neighbors. A man may also consult a stranger in a distant neighborhood to test the validity of accusations that he himself is the sorcerer who has killed. But the one who consults a diviner in such matters is under no obligation to circulate what he has been told once he returns home; at most, he is under obligation only to share the findings with his kinsmen —who may or may not give the findings credence. No publicized action follows. The action taken is either secret or is cloaked in an explanation that saves the face of the sorcerer, lest he be provoked to further malevolence.

It is a different matter when the Tonga consult a witchfinder. Here the client is a community, not an individual or a kin group. The Tonga habitually use the same term for both witchfinder and diviner, and indeed the witchfinder may also be a practicing diviner. (I am using separate terms for clarity in writing, and have adopted the common English term of witchfinder, which fits well enough with Tonga ideas on the subject.) They stress that the witchfinder's primary task is the discovery of the sorcerers who are killing the people and making life miserable for all.[2]

In fact, the witchfinder is a proclaimer of sorcerers rather than a discoverer. The people have long since decided who are their local sorcerers; private divinations have named them, and the gossip has been whispered through village and neighborhood. The Tonga summon the witchfinder not to discover their sorcerers but to proclaim them publicly in a manner that permits people to cope with them. Occasionally it may happen that the witchfinder clears a suspected sorcerer—and probably all suspects hope that this will happen. Among those he accuses there may be one or two about whom suspicion has not previously hovered, but a complete reversal of general expectations would hardly be tolerable.

The witchfinder is therefore the mouthpiece of suspicion through whom the community proclaims its knowledge and the medium through which it comes to terms with its known sorcerers.

Sorcery is most effective at close quarters, and it is most likely to be used by those who have personal enmities or ambitions. In individual instances of divination, it is upon kinsmen and neighbors that the accusa-

---

[2] The Tonga do not believe that people have an inherent power for evil that can be inherited. I am therefore translating the term *mulozi* as "sorcerer" rather than "witch," the verb *ku-lowa* as "using sorcery," and the form *bulozi* as "sorcery."

Diviners and witchfinders may be called *usondo*, "he who divines," or *munchapi*. This latter term apparently came in with one of the great witchfinding movements of the 1920's. In the 1940's, I noted that *munchapi* usually referred to diviners whose technique included the use of mirrors, into which they gazed to find their answers. More recently, at least in some areas, it has become a general term for many diviners. *Munganga* includes both herbalists and diviners; I am not certain that it would also be used of the witchfinders.

tions usually fall. The witchfinder sought to cleanse a village, when sorcerery is believed to be rife, must therefore of necessity be an alien, a stranger. This ensures his neutrality, for as an unknown man from a distance he cannot have been involved in the local misfortunes that are the pretext of his summoning. He is not a kinsman who would seek to shield the guilty. Even if he is a sorcerer, and his clients assume that he is, his sole interest in this matter is his business contract with the village and the earning of his fee. Sorcerers do not have a society that links them together against nonsorcerers, and a sorcerer ordinarily has no reason for protecting another.

The witchfinder's client is the village, not an individual; and his report is to the village. He is empowered to discover all the sorcerers who are causing trouble for the people, and he is expected to test everyone living in the village or in the neighborhood. For this reason he enters villages or neighborhoods only at the invitation of the headman, who acts after consultation with other senior men and women.

Those disclosed as sorcerers are publicly accused. For the first time they can be brought to account openly. They are given a choice: they may repent, surrender their charms and medicines, and drink the medicine that will destroy them and their kin if they revert to evil ways; or they may remain proclaimed sorcerers, the inevitable butt of all accusations when things go wrong. Accused but recalcitrant headmen would find their villages melting away; heads of homesteads might be abandoned by their followings; household heads might be deserted by spouses and children. The accused sorcerer who accepts the verdict has the opportunity to reform, which allies him again with his fellows—though at the cost of the influence that his medicines had gained for him.

Despite the fact that the witchfinder is a stranger with no local interest in the community in which he works, he affects the balance of power within the community. The Tonga, like many others, suspect those who have wealth, power, and influence of using sorcery to bring themselves forward—though they also suspect those who lack power and advantage of turning to sorcery through envy and malice, or in an attempt to best those who have been successful.

Leaders of the factions within a neighborhood are usually suspected sorcerers; they are commonly said to be in a relationship known as *basikulowanyina*, which can be translated as "those who are bewitching one another." They are certain to have powerful medicines. A man would be a fool, the Tonga think, if he sought to acquire prominence before he had acquired the medicines to protect himself against all those who would feel envy at his rise. But the line between having powerful medicines for protection and using these medicines against others is believed to be exceedingly thin, and a man of prominence is therefore treated as being potentially dangerous.

Tonga society has few institutionalized positions of leadership. Ambitious men acquire influence over others, but this influence depends—at least to some extent—upon the belief in the efficacy of medicine. The sorcerer is one who has become irresponsible in his use of medicine and magic, and therefore a general danger. His reform, because it involves the loss of his medicines, also undercuts the basis of his influence.

The invitation to the witchfinder implies that leading men and women —as well as the lame, the halt, and the blind—may stand accused. The public confrontation and discrediting of one or more such men is likely to be the outcome of the invitation.

CHIEFS AND HEADMEN

Given the possibilities in the situation, it seems strange that the witchfinders are patronized by villages and neighborhoods, the smallest local units, rather than by the chieftaincy, the larger political entity. Certainly, those most likely to be suspected of sorcery live close at hand, but this does not explain why witchfinders are not used by chiefs and their rivals, for these too are very firmly immersed in the local setting, and most of their quarrels are comparable to those found within a village or neighborhood.

Until recently, politics among the Tonga has been of the "village pump" variety. Tribal organization and chieftaincies were imposed from above in the early days of colonial administration, and only in the past few years has the tribal organization of the "native authority" (or "local government") became meaningful to more than a small handful of chiefs and educated men. Chieftaincies had a much closer impact upon the people through the chief's court and its officials and through the direct association of the chief with his people. Nevertheless, most Tonga think of chieftaincy as an alien institution; and they view their own chief as a village headman who has received special powers from the administration.

Although a chief is involved in local life as a private individual, this fact tends to remove the office from the local situation. The office has been defined by aliens, in this case Europeans, and the authority of the office and of the incumbent chief himself exist because a chief is the agent of the administration and has its power behind him. Until very recently, the chief *as* chief was controlled by those outside the scope of any political maneuverings that could be carried on in terms of a people's common set of values, and to which chief and opponents could appeal for justification.

The chief was subject to local pressures; and local interests were involved in filling the post. Short-term groupings sometimes emerged to support one or another candidate for the chieftaincy, but on the whole the system served to protect the chiefs from immediate responsibility to their people. Indeed, the chiefs first became responsible to public demands with the rise of national political parties. Because extralocal power had created the chiefs in the first place, it is not surprising that parties based on more than local interests were required to make them concerned about popular support.

Until the appearance of the parties, the Tonga attitude toward chief and district messenger was much the same. It was worthwhile to intrigue for or against either one, or indeed with him, but there were limits to this intrigue inasmuch as a chief or district messenger could be deposed only from above; the intrigue had to be phrased in terms acceptable to the administration.

It is for this reason, I suggest, that Tonga chiefs did not become involved, in their chiefly capacity, with witchfinding—although a chief consulted diviners, as did his subjects, in his private capacity (some chiefs were even diviners of some fame). Private consultations might accuse the chief of sorcery against the people of his village or chieftaincy as the chief might accuse his rivals as the source of his own misfortune, but open accusation of a chief through the witchfinder did not take place.

After all, a formal charge of sorcery against a chief would have little effect; nothing could force him to accept a judgment and abandon his sorcery: the administration did not regard a witchfinder's pronouncements as evidence nor recognize the sins a witchfinder denounced. The witchfinder's impartiality, based on his alien character, was therefore irrelevant.

Effective action against a chief in his official capacity meant presenting him as nepotic, corrupt, inefficient, biased, arbitrary, or treasonous. These were the sins recognized by the administration, though not of course by the Tonga—who expected men to favor their kin, to know a good thing when they saw it, to procrastinate before interfering with others, and to evade (if not oppose) the demands of the administration. Killing by sorcery or the use of medicine to produce drought or plague were not crimes against which the administration could act; but it might punish the *accusers*.

The techniques of the witchfinder could therefore not be used—either to depose the chief or to threaten him with deposition if he refused to reform. Public discovery and conviction of his sorcery would leave his people still at his mercy. They could not leave him, as they could a recalcitrant headman, because a mass movement of defiance of the chieftaincy would undoubtedly lead to an inquiry in which the crime of witchfinding would be compounded with the crime of encouraging treasonable action against authority. The people had to stay under the jurisdiction of the chief, where they continued to be answerable before his court.

Thus the chief was not vulnerable, as was the headman, who could be pressured into retiring, or reforming, by a threat that he would be abandoned. The headman was far enough removed from the alien sphere of authority that an official investigation was unlikely to follow the "disappearance" of his village. He had no court before which his villagers must appear. The headman was vulnerable; the chief was not.

On the other hand, the witchfinder could not be used as a sure and effective ally against a chief's enemies; the latter could not produce a witchfinder's evidence before the administration in justification of an action he had taken against his rivals. The people could also ignore the findings, for the chief—himself a sorcerer—could be held to have corrupted the medicine of the witchfinder and forced it to indict the innocent. Opposing factions could argue that there had not been a fair test, and that the real cause of trouble remained undetected. The opposition was also well aware of the laws of witchcraft and sorcery. In a contest between a chief and his opponents, the chief's attempt to submit his case to the rulings of a witchfinder would have supplied opponents with ammunition that "counted" with the administration.

In other parts of Zambia and elsewhere in Africa, chiefs have used witchfinders and have controlled the oracles that have accused men of sorcery, even in the days of colonial rule. The Tonga chiefs' abstention is therefore due to more than a simple appreciation of the attitude of the administration. I suggest that it rested upon the chiefs' realization that they were not regarded by their people as holding legitimate offices that should be upheld at all costs. No chief, therefore, could argue that he had the right to use medicines to protect chieftaincy and the nation against the forces of evil. The people did not accept chieftaincy as a necessary institution; they trusted to their own medicines to protect themselves and the members of their homesteads.

Tonga chiefs, as chiefs, therefore did not involve themselves in witchfinding, although they shared the beliefs of their people in the prevalence of sorcery and in the efficacy of the witchfinder in controlling sorcery. If a witchfinder operated in a chief's territory to free his people from the evil of sorcery, this was a good thing so long as the man did not attack the chief. The fact that headmen, the holders of the lowest office in the official hierarchy, might fall under attack from the witchfinder did not affect the chief's tolerance. He took no responsibility for his headmen, who were neither his appointees nor his men. An attack upon a headman was not an attack upon a chief.

In a chief's eyes, his people behaved in a reasonable fashion if they rid themselves of a sorcerer headman; if necessary, he would even help them to disguise the facts of the case behind a tale that would be more palatable to the administration.

THE ALIEN WITCHFINDER

The witchfinder is acceptable to Tonga clients because, as an uncommitted stranger, he can catalyze a situation in which local people are too closely involved for a solution to be reached. But he is a stranger only in the sense that (1) he is uncommitted to any group of contestants, and (2) he has no reason to shield the guilty or accuse the innocent. He is not a stranger to the system of beliefs, or standards, that controls the situation in which he is called upon to operate. He can therefore be used as a neutral implement in forcing evil men to come to terms with the rest of their fellows.

The witchfinder is called upon to perform a specific task, set for him by his clients, and his behavior is predictable. He will not suddenly redefine the situation in his own terms and demand that his clients accept his dictation. He can be used because those who consult him are prepared to carry out the decisions he helps them reach. Thus he is effective on the village and neighborhood levels, but not on the chieftaincy level —where others than his clients would be implicated in carrying out a decision that arose from his work. At the chieftaincy level, where the standards of those involved differ radically, the impartiality of the uncommitted stranger is irrelevant.

The Tonga (as communities) do not consult other aliens whom they know, though they seek to manipulate them to their private ends. These are Europeans who may be known to the people but who are strangers to their standards. Because Europeans are not committed to the same ends, they do not accept limitations on their actions that those Tonga who might consult them would think desirable. In other words, the alien witchfinder is usable for community purposes because the result is predictable; the alien administrator official, or missionary is not usable in the same way because no one can predict the outcome if he is consulted.

REFERENCES

COLSON, ELIZABETH. 1958. Marriage and the Family among the Plateau Tonga of Northern Rhodesia. Manchester University Press, for the Rhodes-Livingstone Institute.
———. 1960. Social organization of the Gwembe Tonga. Manchester University Press for the Rhodes-Livingstone Institute.
———. 1962. The Plateau Tonga. Manchester University Press, for the Rhodes-Livingstone Institute.
SCUDDER, THAYER. 1962. The Human Ecology of the Gwembe Tonga. Manchester University Press, for the Rhodes-Livingstone Institute.

KINGA PRIESTS: THE POLITICS OF PESTILENCE [1]

George K. Park, PITZER COLLEGE, CLARMONT, CALIFORNIA

It may be helpful to begin with a brief sketch of the political organization of the Kinga, and this may be conveniently done by comparing them
rather broadly with the Nyakusa, their better-known neighbors, with
whom the Kinga have certain ties. Kingaland is high in the Livingstone
Mountains, looking south and southwestward upon Lake Nyasa (when
Kinga priests go down to sacrifice in Nyakusaland their vertical descent
is more than a mile). An important measure of isolation is afforded by
such a position; indeed, the rough terrain divides the Kinga into four
fairly autonomous subsocieties, each governed—like the Nyakusa tribe-
lets—by a chief or prince, and each comprising several thousand widely
scattered homesteads, all centered upon a royal court and a sacred
grove. It is said that, many generations ago, one of the four rulers,
the high prince, sent three lesser princes—his younger brothers—to rule
their separate lands.

A series of remarkably detailed reports describes the Nyakusa as an
expanding people whose segmentary—or ultrasegmentary—political organization was nicely geared to producing maximum ferment within an
orderly but always burgeoning framework of personal authority and
ritual-ceremonial practice (Wilson, 1951, 1957, 1959). The Kinga had
also been a politically expanding people, before European contact, but
their expansion was on a smaller and probably much less ebullient scale.
Numbers make a difference, and so perhaps do mountains, for the latter
seem to have set Ukinga apart for a life harder than that on the Nyakusa
plains, a life more suited to goats than cattle—and certainly without
banana groves. Whatever the demographic and ecological factors that
set special conditions for the development of the Kinga polity, I shall be
concerned in this paper to describe a balance between priest and prince,
religion and politics, rather different from that which has been described
for the Nyakusa.

On the level of mythos, the distinction can be made quite simply because Kinga and Nyakusa chiefs, so far as they have religious responsibilities on behalf of their people, direct their major acts of sacrifice to

[1] Fieldwork was carried out between 1961 and 1963 while the author was Senior
Research Fellow at the East African Institute of Social Research, Kampala, Uganda.

the same shrine. The shrine is ascribed to Lwembe, whom I shall call a god, and the Nyakusa chiefs claim descent from him—at least in the sense that they are known as "sons of Lwembe." In 1936 there were over one hundred such descendants of the god Lwembe, each of whom could claim an autonomous chiefdom (Wilson, 1959, p. 19).

The Kinga have a more symmetrical segmentary structure, despite the fact that several of their lesser rulers claim no kinship with rulers of the princely line. Among the Nyakusa, offerings to Lwembe express the unity of the land in the sense of a common dependency of all the chiefs upon their founding ancestor. But the Kinga offerings show a good deal more, for they reveal (as the Nyakusa could not) a unitary structure. It is conceivable that the Nyakusa might have developed a unitary state on the basis of a pyramidal royal-genealogical charter; but that charter, in a society of one hundred co-equal chiefdoms, characterized by very limited local ritual cooperation, is lacking. The scattered alliances for local cooperation are centered upon the shrines of recent common ancestors; Monica Wilson states that somewhat distant ties are easily broken, and she doubts that a comprehensive system of progressively inclusive cooperative alliances ever culminated at the shrines of a supposed original generation of "sons of Lwembe" (1959, pp. 70-71).

The Kinga, on the other hand, express precisely, in their offerings to Lwembe, the pattern of ritual dependence by which they are bound symmetrically into segments of increasing inclusiveness. It is a structure of a frankly political kind—expressive of subordination and dependency rather than co-equal alliance—up to the level of the princedoms; but there is, throughout, a balancing emphasis upon local autonomy. If authority within the prince's local village-domain had the character that Max Weber (1949, p. 347) labels "patrimonialism," we would still need another name (such as the much-mooted "feudalism") for the polity represented in a single princedom taken as a whole.

The Kinga princedom consisted of a central village-domain, belonging to and providing the main support of a prince, together with a series of peripheral domains, of varying importance, whose internal structure tended—so far as wealth and numbers of the citizenry allowed—to replicate the royal domain. The four princedoms, although genealogically articulated in a manner that expresses a particular rank-order, should be regarded as co-equal on the plane of politics: centralization of the Kinga polity was hieratic and mystical, not chiefly and practical. It is preeminently (although not, as among the Nyakusa, exclusively) in connection with offerings to Lwembe that the unity of the people is demonstrated. Goods must be brought from each village-domain, through channels, to the high prince, and then they are taken by a priestly assemblage to the god Lwembe.

The Kinga mythos has not elevated Lwembe to the status of a chiefly apical ancestor; indeed, it *could* not, for the Kinga royal line by tradition came out of the east. The relationship is instead modeled on that of the prince to his younger brother, or "establishment" to "young rebel"— Lwembe is supposed to have been banished by the high prince of the Kinga because he showed something of the character of the Trickster. Lwembe could make things sprout and grow wondrously; on his way to Nyakusaland he urinated many times, and at each place there is found an ever flowing spring; in short, Lwembe was a marvel, and when he died his powers were turned to working vengeance upon the establishment that had banished him: he is now the source of all the major tribulations that beset the Kinga in their mountainous land. All the people of those mountains—Kinga and not-quite Kinga—are taught that they must pay tribute to Lwembe, through the prince who banished him, if they would hope to survive.

I think it would be very hard to understand this teaching except as the doctrine of the priests. It is not, surely, a doctrine that in an unambiguous way exalts the living prince and his line. Pestilence comes from the royal family—so the doctrine seems to say—and is visited upon all alike, throughout the land, because of a wrongful act once done by the high prince. But if it were really as simple as this, how could such a myth be the "charter" of a strong and expanding monarchy?

The matter is not, after all, that simple; the Lwembe myth presents a sort of paradox, but it is a paradox of the sort well suited to religion— in context it had better be called (in the theologian's sense) a mystery. Lwembe's full character is that of a god, as quick to shower good upon man as to rain destruction. His people, says the myth, are only the Kinga people (with their descendants now in Nyakusaland); it is from them he demands his due, in the manner the dead will always have it: a share in the produce of the land that was once, or should have been, his.

My capsule summary does not do full justice to its subject, but I would argue that it puts the right light upon the working relations between prince and priest in Kingaland. The tribute of the land, and its tribulations, belong preeminently and mystically to the prince. He is the vessel of the land's fertility and virtue: tribute fills his kraal, feasting fills his court, his houses are filled with his progeny and his favorites, his games and the drums of war fill the air with the sounds of his fierceness.

But the prince is also—chiefly in the case of the high prince—the vessel of fear and dismay. Paradoxically, he is not himself a warrior; in battle he transfers his crown to another. He cannot join the feasting, but must stay hidden. He cannot judge a case in court, but gives his mantle to another; he must deal with the conflicts of men through chosen intermediaries. When he emerges from the fastness of the royal stockade, within the royal grove, he is hidden in a litter, surrounded by his servants. As for the sacred grove, where the ritual work of the kingdom is done and the medicines of war are kept, the prince dare not enter it for he is always ritually impure through contact with his wives. Maintaining fertility in that sense is his preeminent religious duty.

In the institutionalized role of high prince lurks something of the paradox of wondrous power and frustrated impotence told in the myth of Lwembe. It is the role, not the personality, of the prince with which we have to deal: until he sits upon the leopardskin, and is charged by his priests with the duties and the dangers of the throne, he should be the boldest of all the youths, royal and commoner, gathered about the court. As a boy, he sleeps with his peers, flesh against flesh; as a youth he enters the lists in all the games of war. He travels about the land with a band of armed youths, judging, drinking, and confiscating the royal share of every bridewealth. When he marries, his activity is expanded, not curtailed. So, at least, the elders of today insist things used to be.

Somewhat in the manner of the generalized role of the Nyakusa chief, then, the youth of the Kinga prince is spent in the manner of an active leader among men. But when he is placed upon the throne by his priests, he is withdrawn from the people and dedicated to a rule whose mood is perhaps sacred—and not secular. The throne is beset by dangers on every hand. This is why its incumbent must be insulated from the daily, secular life of his princedom; why he must deal through commoner intermediaries (priests, judges, warriors, eunuchs, messengers); why he must have a royal taster to save him from poison; and why his mannerisms are stylized in a mode we would call paranoid. The throne works a change in the man. He becomes a vessel of its danger, and—paradoxically—his seclusion is proof of its power. So it is that the executive authority in war, judging, and ritual fell upon a ruling set that acted in the name of the throne and perpetuated the throne's mystique, simultaneously one of danger and abundance.

It is at this point that I should emphasize the role of priest within the governing set; and again it is useful to compare Kinga with Nyakusa usage. The Nyakusa chief, with minor exceptions, is his own ritual practitioner; the professional priesthood of that land is concentrated in the comparatively small establishment that Monica Wilson identifies with the "divine kingship" of the living successor to Lwembe's chiefdom—today a chiefdom in name but with no sufficient secular following. There are also priestly roles in some of the best-established Nyakusa chiefdoms, for a chief may sometimes place his rain stones in the charge of a younger brother, thus founding a hereditary line of local rain priests (Wilson, 1959, pp. 73, 114). But hereditary priestly lines appear to have little genealogical depth, and usually it is the chief who possesses the stones and calls down the local rain; the important control of rain and weather over the whole land lies with the external shrines of the god Lwembe (and, for some chiefdoms, his supposed brother Kyala).

Local efforts are, in fact, organized by the local chiefs in response to a broad range of tribulation and pestilence. The form of the ritual is exoteric: public demands for action, public meetings for discussion and prayer, a public decision upon the proper ritual remedy; but the mediator and principal executor throughout all this is the chief (Wilson, 1959, pp. 102-113). The performance of ancestral sacrifice on behalf of a chief, to be sure, is private, and often devolves upon a junior relative; these simple ritual tasks may be delegated in a number of ways, or they will customarily devolve upon a person of special status. Otherwise, the ritual specialists of a chiefdom are normally and properly designated by the ethnographer as "doctors" and "diviners." "Priest," designating one who sacrifices on behalf of a superior, is perhaps just as proper, but the word tends to suggest a higher degree of ritual specialization than is usually found in Nyakusa. It is worth noting that in the only "secret and fearsome" fertility rituals reported for the Nyakusa, Kinga priests play a major role (Wilson, 1959, p. 121).

In contrast to the Nyakusa chief, the Kinga prince or princeling relies for all ritual services upon a professional class of priests resident within his proper domain. Although I cannot here attempt a general account of the position and varied functions of such a priest, I can suggest something of the special nature of his role vis-à-vis the secular organization of power. A way to begin the analysis is to insist that—although in a real sense the several Kinga princedoms were secularly divided but ritually united—the influence of the priest was such (even in the control of warfare) that secular division could be said to have been subject to ritual constraints.

There is also a small paradox here. Kinga informants insist upon the boldness with which their warriors entered the lists in the royal games— their tales of duels of honor and trials of strength are like those in a Viking saga or a Spartan children's tale—yet their accounts of war abound in descriptions of panicked flight. Their explanation for this departs from their firm premise that victory and defeat in war hinge only upon the relative powers of priestly medicines on either side. A war party never sets out directly from what we might call the powwow—a priest intervenes. Protective medicine—the same that is incessantly required to protect the prince from sorcery and poison—was required to give strength to men's knees, for it was known that an enemy priest would have drawn an invisible line of another medicine that, when one crossed it, would suddenly turn his legs to water. Each warrior therefore knew that if (in our terms) a moment of panic should possess him after he crossed into alien territory, the numbness in his legs meant he should flee as best he could, for the mystical power of the enemy priest was greater than the power he had himself received.

Of course, lines were drawn on each side; after a fleeing warrior was safely back behind his own line he could take courage again, for the enemy could not know where the line had been drawn, and was open to sudden, fierce, and invincible ambush as soon as he had crossed it. Because each man had only a good shield and a handful of spears, which could be replenished only behind one's own lines, it was not the kind of warfare that maximizes duration of contact or depth and permanence of penetration. Its practical goals were the snatching of a few cattle, or women, or revenge by wounding or killing a single enemy fighter. It was difficult, even with both sides' accounts of the same battle, to tell which side had won.

One sort of war, of course, was not subject to such mutual, ritually sanctioned understandings; but both the Bena and the Hehe invasions of Ukinga seem on the whole to have failed, though both were gruesome. Another war—that of the Maji-Maji rebellion, which aligned three Kinga chiefdoms and a powerful German force against the easternmost Kinga chiefdom, had very different sanctions—and was so ruthlessly destructive that the eastern realm of Ukinga has not truly recovered from it after more than fifty years. The evidence suggests that the Kinga could be sufficiently warlike, and that it was the priestly involvement that had kept their internecine wars within certain bounds.

It is difficult, of course, to judge such matters. In principle, we know that consensual definition of a situation, powerfully sanctioned, may be the most effective of all instruments of social control. It is difficult, at the distance we now must work, to ascertain the morally suasive powers of priestly ritual in an African society whose autonomous structure of authority had never been challenged; but I am certain that the position from which the priesthood spoke to the people of ancient Ukinga was unique and supreme. More than any other members of the court, the priests were the spokesmen of the prince; they were constantly about his (supposed) errands. The warrior band that judged the country, found witches, and seized the bridewealth tribute was directed, and accompanied, by a priest. Bridewealth tribute was the economic foundation of the royal court and its centralizing redistributive system. A priest was the intermediary who kept the royal gate; and a commoner approached it hunched to the ground and whining an honorific greeting in a woman's voice. Above all, only the priests understood and handled the hugely dangerous medicines, which made the throne what it was; and only the priest passed regularly, immune from harm (except in actual battle), from one princely court to another.

Another point. Except for the priestly office, the only truly corporate office within the ruling set, no rule of succession governed the group's important commoner roles; but every princely throne had three senior priests, with their junior apprentices. Usually, the apprentices were the priests' sons or grandsons, and, because all worked together, the office could not be interrupted by death—and no one outside the group had a voice in choosing the successors. In theory, this was also true of the princeship; the succession, as commoners understood it, was only by primogeniture, but such a rule is seriously qualified when priests make so much of the danger to a prince's life from a stronger-willed brother. Normally, in fact, the priests had much to say about the retirement of an aging or impotent prince, about its timing and the appropriateness of the recognized heir; and, when a prince died on the throne, the death was concealed for at least a month, and was revealed by the priests only in a sudden announcement (at dawn) of the enthronement of the successor. Whoever the chosen heir, after the priestly drums had rolled it was certain he ruled from that moment onward; and there were Kinga rulers, on various levels, whose succession was irregular: the result of a ritual *fait accompli*.

Within each chiefdom was a central, princely domain, and a series of peripheral domains, headed by princelings, each with his complement of priests. The princeling was an active judge and warrior, but, like the prince, he supervised and did not perform ritual acts of an official nature. A princeling normally did not visit his overlord but sent a nominal yearly tribute by his priests, expressing his allegiance. The princeling's tribute was derived from the tax he levied upon bridewealths in his domain and had no pronounced ritual value. But also, an offering was gathered by the princeling from the village heads of his domain and was sent on to his prince, which was called for yearly by the high priests in connection with the uncertain onset of the rains on an account of pestilence, drought or inundation, epidemic disease, or blight.

For convenience, we will refer to the latter offering by its central element, an iron hoe-blade, made especially for—and sacred to—Lwembe. Sacred hoes were always to be found in a princeling's sacred grove. A hoe had to remain there a year, ministered to by the priests, before it could pass—after another year in the grove of the high prince—inward to the central priestly-and-princely domain. After this, it could be carried in the grand-priestly procession that followed the supposed path Lwembe took in fleeing to the place of his death in Nyakusaland.

Secular tribute, one might say, followed the same process as the sacred offerings as far as the court of the high prince, and it established the lines of fealty; but the amount of secular tribute diminished greatly with each step above the smallest political segment. No substantial wealth passed out of a princedom except at the time of the yearly offering to Lwembe, when many "gift hoes" were sent, in addition to the sacred hoes, not to stop with the high prince but to pass on to the Nyakusa chiefs. The overall unity of the Kinga was thus affirmed more by a ritual transaction—mystical redistribution, if you will—than by material sanctions.

I conjecture that the comparative symmetry and peacefulness of the

Kinga polity, compared with the Nyakusa, would not have emerged and persisted had it not been for the professional stature and ambient citizenship of the priesthood. And I would argue that the education of the priest, which made him what he was, must from the beginning have been at the school of Lwembe or one of his kind. Every year, and with every exceptional crisis in Kingaland, a ferment of activity begins in the local domains with a concern for the local welfare; the local ritualistic resources are soon exhausted, having produced no results; and priests pass from one area to another—until the ferment amounts to a call from the people upon the high priest. The sense of urgency grows among those gathered near the capital; then, in the high priest's name—and on behalf of his prince and of a nation in peril—the priests call for movement of the oblatory hoes. Finally, there is an assembly of the priestly collegium at the most sacred grove of the Kinga people, and a long and hazardous series of ritual acts in concert, each step of which must somehow come out to the satisfaction of all.

We cannot recount the details of the priestly pilgrimage here. At its height, the first rituals of Kinga priests at the grove of Lwembe in Nyakusaland began in July, and could not end until October. Sacred hoes, and many gift hoes and food offerings, had to be collected from each part of the land and properly accounted for; the movement of all such goods had to be engendered by a sense of need; and the movement must properly express the precise mystical order that united all of the Kinga polity. At each step of the way there must be sacrifice and the gaining of propitious signs. The progress was often harassed, and harassment always meant that a critical step in the ritual series had been omitted or was unsuccessful—one must send back to repair the error.

Mood—especially at the culminating encampment in Nyakusaland—was dominated by the character and the temper of Lwembe. Day after day the hoes and the gifts of food and beer must be solemnly placed; night after night the offerings were heaved and dashed about by a manic, invisible hand: the signs were bad; error must be repaired and the offerings restored.

By the time Lwembe had relented, and on the morning that the sacred double hoe of the Kinga high prince at last stood erect in the gateway to Lwembe's mysterious dwelling, I imagine that the pilgrimage had also been a practical success. The visiting priests had been feasted sufficiently by their Nyakusa hosts to recompense them for their troubles, for their long discussions, and for the great load of gift hoes they had presented to their hosts. At the end, to be sure, the priestly collegium dispersed to the four separate and secularly opposed chiefdoms; but there was often common business to discuss, or there might be medicine to secure from Ukisi, on the lakeshore, or beyond.

The Kinga priesthood was of separate lineage from the princely rulers. Most of the priests claim to have been *in situ* before the ruling group, which brought the name Kinga, arrived. Their medicines and their methods, in rainmaking, witchfinding, or king making, seem to have found a proper niche in the politics of pestilence.

REFERENCES

WEBER, MAX. 1947. Theory of social and economic organization. A. M. Henderson and Talcott Parsons (trans.). New York: Oxford University Press.

WILSON, MONICA. 1951. Good company: a study of Nyakyusa age-villages. Oxford University Press, for the International African Institute.

———. 1957. Rituals of kinship among the Nyakyusa. Oxford University Press, for the International African Institute.

———. 1959. Communal rituals of the Nyakyusa. Oxford University Press, for the International African Institute.

RITUAL ASPECTS OF CONFLICT CONTROL IN AFRICAN MICROPOLITICS

Victor W. Turner, CORNELL UNIVERSITY

Extended case histories of disputes in African villages, neighborhoods, and chiefdoms reveal that each dispute tends to have a life cycle with distinct phases.[1] Since relationships in these small face-to-face communities tend to be multiplex, with total personality involvement in activities of all types, whether these may be defined as primarily domestic, jural, economic, political or religious, the consequences of interaction in one type tend to affect the premises of interaction in the immediately succeeding activities of another.[2] This tendency can best be described, and later analyzed, if we adopt Dorothy Emmet's view, the result of a cogent but complex argument in her book *Function, Purpose and Powers* (1958), that a society is "a *process* with some systematic characteristics, rather than a closely integrated system, like an organism or a machine" (p. 293).

A dispute, then, has a life cycle that is systematized by routines, procedures, and symbols that establish the character of its successive phases or "situations" as primarily "political," "ritual," "economic," and so on. Some of these situations may be prescribed and predetermined by custom; for example, religious performances that occur at fixed points in the annual cycle, or regularly reformed initiations into age-sets. Other situations have a contingent, ad hoc character, sometimes developing out of the dispute itself, sometimes representing a response or adjustment to events originating outside the community.

A dispute runs its course through a series of situations of different types, but two kinds of sequences are involved. The first is purely chronological: situations, of whatever type, are temporally juxtaposed. The second is typological: situations of the same type follow one another,

---

[1] Examples of these may be found in Clyde Mitchell's *Yao Village*, J. Middleton's *Lugbara Religion*, J. Van Velsen's *The Politics of Kinship*, and V. W. Turner's *Schism and Continuity in an African Society* (see References at the end of this article).

[2] See Max Gluckman's discussion in *The Judicial Process among the Barotse of Northern Rhodesia* of multiplex relationships as those that "serve many interests," and his argument that "multiple membership of diverse groups and in diverse relationships is an important source of quarrels and conflict; but it is equally the basis of internal cohesion in any society" (pp. 19-20).

but at a remove. Between one political situation and the next a number of different types of situations is interposed: perhaps a ceremony, perhaps a collective hunt, perhaps a fiesta. Chronological sequences are continuous; typological sequences are discontinuous; at least this is the case in on-going interactions, regardless of their qualities.

But there is another sense in which chronological sequences are discontinuous and typological sequences are continuous, for certain kinds of issues are thought to be appropriately confined to certain types of situations. It is widely held, for example, that in legal and political situations conflicts of interest, opinion, and purpose may be ventilated, discussed, underscored, or resolved. On the other hand, many kinds of ritual situations are concerned with social unity and solidarity, and with the suppression of overt expression of disputatious actions and sentiments. Thus, when a ritual situation immediately succeeds a political situation, the contentious issues raised in the former are kept in abeyance in the latter; but, at a later phase in the social process, the dispute may again attain public status in a new political situation.

The point I wish to make here is that the intervening situations will have left their imprint on the subsequent patterns of behavior. The second political situation will have been influenced by the ritual and economic situations that separate it from the first, because one and the same set of persons moves, in ever changing patterns of relations, through all of them. For example, a dispute between two village factions may threaten, in the first political situation, to become violent. At that point the obligation of all members to participate in ancestor worship or in a life-crisis ceremony may supervene; and their enjoined cooperation in ritual may then have a curbing effect on their political rivalry, so that— when next their roles are politically defined—their differences may be composed peacefully and rationally instead of disrupting community life. On the other hand, political rivalries may carry over into ritual situations and markedly affect their behavioral patterns.

It must not be thought that a community's social life is entirely constructed out of "situations." A social situation is a critical point or complication in the history of a group, and most groups are subdivided into parts that possess varying degrees of autonomy; and a considerable proportion of an individual's social participation is in the purposive activities of these subgroups, such as the nuclear family, the ward, the lineage segment, the age-set and so on, rather than in those of the wider group, such as the village or the chiefdom.

Situations that involve groups of large span and great range and scope are relatively few. When they occur, however, the roles, interactions, and behavioral styles that constitute them tend to be more formalized than those of subgroup behavior. The gradient of formality may extend from the mere display of etiquette and propriety, through ceremonial action, to the full-blown ritualization of behavior. Even when situations develop spontaneously, out of quarrels or celebrations, they rapidly acquire a formalized or structural character. Most anthropólogists have observed that, in the course of village quarrels, the contend-ing factions draw apart, consolidate their ranks, and develop spokesmen who present their cases in terms of a rhetoric that is culturally standard-ized. Situations, too, have rather clearly defined termini: the investigator can observe when they begin and end.

Thus a society is a process that is punctuated by situations, but with intervals between them. Much behavior that is intersituational from the perspective of the widest effective group may, however, be situational from the perspective of its subgroups. Thus a nuclear family may have its own situational series, its family councils, its acts of worship devoted to its "Lares atque Penates," its gardening bees, and so on, and these may have little to do with the functioning of the total community. Yet, especially in regard to its disputes, the family may not be able to control divergencies from its inbuilt behavioral norms by its traditional machin-ery and these become a matter for the community. They may then pre-cipitate community-wide social situations.

Doing fieldwork among the Ndembu of Zambia, I collected a fair amount of data in the form of extended case histories, and thus was able to follow the vicissitudes of a social group over time. In several publi-cations I have, in a preliminary way, indicated how I think such dia-chronic studies should be made in the context of village organization; but here I would like to recount a series of situations I observed, over a short period of time, that involved the social group I have called a "vicinage."

An Ndembu vicinage is a cluster of villages with matrilineal cores; it has a changeable territorial span, and is fluid and unstable in its social composition. It has no recognized internal organization that endures be-yond the changes in the identity of its villages making it up; but it is not just a neighborhood around *any* village. The vicinage becomes visi-ble as a discrete social entity in certain types of situations, and a particu-lar headman within it usually exercises moral and ritual leadership.

Villages in a vicinage do not move as a compact bloc; each moves in its own time and to its own chosen site—either within the same, or to another, vicinage. The frequency with which Ndembu villages change their sites—as a result of shifting cultivation, of quarrels with neighbors, or in search of economic advantage—means that the composition of vicinages is constantly changing: new villages move in from other areas and old villages move out. It also means that each vicinage is sociologi-cally heterogeneous; few of its component villages have mutual ties of matrilineal descent, or even originate in the same chiefdom.

What, then, are the types of situations in which the vicinage emerges
as a significant social group? These situations are dominantly ritual, but
they have political implications.

The vicinage I want to consider here contained in 1953 eleven villages within an area of twelve square miles, and I shall code them alpha-
betically and numerically in this exposition. Village A1 was founded by
the sister of the senior chief about 1880. Village A2 split away from A1
(a few years before my investigation) and built a new village a quarter
of a mile away. One mile from A1 was B, which came in the nineteenth
century from another Lunda chiefdom in the Congo. Two miles from
A1 was village C, inhabited by the autochthonous Kawiku people who
inhabited the area before the Ndembu arrived (more than two centuries
ago); C broke away from a larger Kawiku village in another vicinage
twenty-five years earlier. A mile and half on the other side of A was D,
which arrived from another Ndembu chief's area fifty years earlier; its
headman was related to that chief (the senior chief's institutionalized
successor) and of the same matrilineal dynasty.

Four miles from A, in yet another direction, was E1, whose headman
was descended from a son of the first Ndembu senior chief, and who considered himself the "owner of the land" (though the British authorities
had abolished his chieftainship while retaining its title, Mwinilunga, as
the name of their administrative district). Near C, the autochthonous village, were villages F1 and F2, which came thiry-five years before from
an Ndembu chief's area in Angola; the matrilineal core of F2 consisted
of descendants of the former slaves of F1. Near them was village G,
founded by a woman who split away from the village of the senior headman of all the Kawiku autochthones in yet another vicinage.

In addition to these villages were three small, modern, residential
units—called "farms" by the Ndembu—that were based on the nuclear
family and were not recognized by the British administration as tax-
registered villages: farm A2, originally from A but located near B, and
farms E2 and E3, within a short distance of E1.

The series of situations I want to describe embraced the membership
of all these residential units and was concerned with the decision to
hold, and the successive stages of, a boys' circumcision ceremony (mukanda). These rites are held approximately every ten years, boys between six and sixteen years are circumcised, and the social group from
which initiands is drawn is the vicinage (with a few exceptions that
need not concern us here). The ceremony is complex in character, rich
in symbolism, lasts throughout much of the dry season (from May to
August or September), and involves several of the vicinage's senior men
as officiants.

To act as an officiant is an index of status. The process of selecting
ritual officiants is, in the sense employed by such scholars as Levy

(1952), Easton (1959), and Fallers (1965) "political," for it is concerned with "making and carrying out decisions regarding public policy, by . . . institutional means." The public recognition of status thus acquired has further political implications in that these officiants may later be called by the territorial chief—whose area is a multiple of vicinages—to act as counselors and assessors in his court.

The four major ritual functionaries are: (1) the "sponsor," the headman of the village near which the camp of initiands' parents and close kin is built; (2) the "setter-up of circumcision," the male member of the village that contributes most sons (and other junior male kin) to the group of initiands; (3) the "senior circumciser," the leader of a group of circumcisers, who undertakes the task of circumcising the senior initiand (usually the oldest son of the "setter-up of circumcision"); (4) the "lodge instructor," who is responsible for the teaching and discipline of the initiands during the long period of bush seclusion in a ritual lodge. (There are several other important ritual roles, but these four are the major objects of competitive importance.)

In the vicinage I am speaking about, the decision to hold *mukanda* began with a decision of the people of E1, E2, and E3 to call a meeting of all the villages to discuss the desirability of committing the vicinage to this exacting task. In their private council they planned that the headman of E1 should be sponsor, that the head of farm E2 should be the setter-up, and that the headman of D should be the senior circumciser. Their case was to rest on the fact that E1 was traditionally "owner of the land," that the E2 headman's sister's son had four uncircumcised sons to be initiated, and that D was the most efficient circumciser in the vicinage. At the vicinage council, however, A1 strongly opposed this "slate" when its composition was hinted at; fear of A1's prestige and sorcery restrained the E bloc from advancing it openly.

A1's prestige was the product of several factors. First, the headman was a close relative of the senior chief and lived in that chief's realm. He was, moreover, in the line of direct matrilineal descent from several former senior chiefs, one of whom founded his village. He was a councilor in the senior chief's court and could be regarded as his representative in the vicinage, although he had no institutionalized political authority over its members. Second, he had already acted as sponsor of two previous *mukanda* ceremonies in the village. Third, he had acted as senior circumciser, as well as sponsor, in these and in other performances of *mukanda* in various Ndembu vicinages.

With such a formidable area of qualifications for senior ritual roles, why was it that E1 and his coterie ventured to aspire to usurp A1's position? These "young Turks" had several points in their favor. I have said that where relationships are multiplex the consequences of one set of interactions influence the premises of the next; and there had been many

signs that A1's prestige was in decline. A2, for example, had split away
from his village, taking more than half of its original population with
him. Gossip about A1's sorcery had helped to precipitate this schism; A1
had been rigidly opposed to modern changes of all types, and was regarded as a master of traditional expertise, including malevolent magic.
He had, moreover, insisted on being paid the deference due to a chief.
In short, he represented the *ancien régime*.

Many others in the vicinage no longed adhered to its norms and
values, and some of them—including E1, E2, E3, and A2—had worked
as labor migrants in the towns of the then Northern Rhodesian copper-
belt. A2 had left A1's village partly to emancipate himself from the
latter's traditionalism, and others saw this successful breakaway as a sign
that the old man had become a "has-been." Furthermore, the E cluster
had always resented the deposition of their headman from the position
of "government chief," holding that he was the first Ndembu chief to be
so installed and that his fall was due to the machinations of the senior
chief and his close matrikin, including A1.

Thus a mixture of modern and traditional considerations impelled
them to use the occasion of *mukanda* as a bid to restructure the vicinage
prestige system. Also, they opposed A1's claim to be senior circumciser
on the grounds that old age had made his hands unsteady and he might
harm the initiands. This was another aspect of the attitude that he was
"over the hill."

In situation 1 (sponsorship), which had a political character, A1 managed to obtain the support of A2 with the argument that the rites should
be sponsored by senior members of the royal matrilineage and by proposing that A2 should be the setter-up, since he had three sons ready to
be initiated. The village cleavage between A1 and A2 was thus put in
abeyance by the need to unite against the E faction.

Villages A1, A2, B, C, and G, moreover, constituted a connubium
with a relatively dense network of affinal interconnections. A1 and A2,
between them, managed to secure the support of the heads of B, C, and
G. It was therefore decided that A1 should sponsor the rites, and A2
should be the setter-up.

During the interval between this meeting and the day appointed for
the beginning of the rites, the E faction began a series of intrigues to bar
A1 from acting as a circumciser. They spread much gossip to the effect
that not only was A1 too old to operate properly but that he would use
his ritual power and medicines to bewitch the boys.

On the opening day of the rites, after many intervening events (in
which both sides tried to enlist my support as an influential stranger),
the role of senior circumciser was still unfilled. E faction still supported
D, and it imported another autochthonous headman from the next vicinage, with whose village they were linked by marriage, to circumcise
beside D. In addition, they had played so hard on the fears of A2 for

the safety of his three sons, the eldest of whom would be circumcised by A1, that he secretly supported D against his mother's brother.

The afternoon and night before circumcision (which occurs some hours after dawn) constitute an important ritual situation for Ndembu. The circumcisers set up a shrine and display their lodge medicine baskets; the initiands' parents' camp is ceremonially erected; and a night-long dance with traditional songs and drum rhythms is held. Traditional symbolisms and rites, with the observance of traditional food and sex prohibitions, dominate the scene; for a time, the old Lunda culture is paramount.

In this situational context (situation 2), headman A1 made an impassioned speech in which he stressed the danger to the initiands of mystical powers that might become active if people were to cherish grudges in their hearts against one another, if taboos were broken, and especially if open quarreling were to break out. He emphasized that the ritual officiants must cooperate with one another if "our children" were to pass safely through the mystical dangers of *mukanda*.

I heard much grumbling against A1 around the beer pots of the E faction during the night, and expressions of fears of his sorcery if they should offend him; it seemed he was getting the upper hand. The dramatic moment came next morning (situation 3), when the boys were ritually snatched by a lodge officiant from their mothers, taken beneath a symbolic gateway out of the domestic realm of their childhood, and borne crying to the secret site of circumcision in the bush.

Litters of leaves had been prepared for the boys, each litter attended by a circumciser and two assistants. The senior initiand was borne to the site, and quick as thought, A1 rushed to the *mudyi* tree beneath which this initiand was to be circumcised, inaugurating the rite. He beckoned with his hand and croaked: *Kud'ami* ("Take him to me"). (Actually his work was neat and effective, and the boys he operated on all recovered well.)

This terminated the situation in A1's favor. Sociologically, he had succeeded in reasserting his status, and not only his status but the "Ndembu way of life," in face of the opposition of the "modernists." He had also vindicated the claim of the royal matrilineage to moral authority over the vicinage. The fact that no one challenged his claim to act as senior circumciser indicated that traditional Ndembu values, at least in this type of situation, were collective representations that still had considerable power to compel assent. Furthermore, only three circumcisers operated: A1, D, and yet another member of the senior chief's matrilineage, who resided in another chiefdom. The defeat of E faction was complete.

Only a brief analysis is needed to put this case in its theoretical perspective. The dispute between A1 and E may best be understood not in

terms of synchronic structure but in terms of the dynamic properties of
the vicinage social field and in terms of the situational series.

When the situation was defined politically, it seemed that E faction
might succeed in at least nominating the senior circumciser, since they
were numerically superior and better organized and could appeal to
those elements most sensitive to modern changes. But when the situation
was defined ritually, and when several ritual situations followed one another immediately, traditional values became paramount, and A1 played
on the relative conservatism of Ndembu to maintain and even enhance
a status that had political implications.

The outcome of this particular dispute process was also an index of
the degree to which Ndembu were still committed to pre-European
values. This conservative bias is still with the Ndembu, for, until very
recently in Central African national politics, most of the Ndembu supported Nkumbula's African National Congress rather than the more
radical United National Independence Party of Kaunda; and they were
staunch partisans of the policies of their fellow Lunda, Moise Tshombe
in the Congo.

Finally, we may venture, as a tentative proposition, that if a person
occupies political and religious positions of some importance, his *political* power is reinforced at those points in the seasonal cycle or group's
developmental cycle when his *ritual* office gives him enhanced authority.

REFERENCES

EASTON, D. 1959.   Political anthropology, *In* B. Siegel (ed.), Biennial Review
     of Anthropology. Stanford University Press.
EMMET, D. 1958.   Function, purpose and powers. London: Macmillan.
FALLERS, LLOYD. 1965.   Political anthropology in Africa. *In* New directions
     in anthropology. London: Tavistock.
GLUCKMAN, MAX. 1955.   The judicial process among the Barotse of Northern
     Rhodesia. Manchester University Press.
LEVY, M. J. 1952.   The structure of society. Princeton University Press.
MIDDLETON, JOHN. 1960.   Lugbara religion. Oxford University Press.
MITCHELL, J. CLYDE. 1955.   The Yao village. Manchester University Press.
TURNER, V. W. 1957.   Schism and continuity in an African society. Man-
     chester University Press.
VAN VELSON, J. 1964.   The politics of kinship. Manchester University Press.

Part IV

POLITICAL
FIELDS AND THEIR BOUNDARIES

The emphasis placed on the importance of processes in the study of politics should not be taken to mean that structural variables are without importance. On the contrary, great significance is attached to understanding the structures of the groups involved in political activity and the structural positions of key actors. The point has been made that political activity cannot be assumed to take place within predetermined boundaries. To limit investigation of political processes in a specific case to, say, a lineage or a village assumes a wholeness, isolation, and completeness of the activities that take place within the lineage and village that is simply not borne out by the facts.

What happens in a hypothetical lineage may be crucially affected, for example, by what happens, or what has happened, in another lineage, in the national government of the lineage's country, or at a nearby mission station. At the other end of the spectrum, the entire lineage or village may not be involved in the activities in question, and an understanding of what occurs will depend upon a correct delimitation of effective and interested units over time. Political processes do not observe group boundaries in any lasting and constant way; so our examination of these processes must be made with the recognition of their spatial, social, and temporal mobility firmly in mind.

In keeping with this recognition, we have used the "political field" concept to refer to the space-time area in which political activities occur. The inclusiveness or scope of a political field will expand and contract over time in that groups and individuals who are not currently involved in the processes may become active in them tomorrow, next year, or a decade hence, and presently active units may temporarily or permanently withdraw from the field.

As new groups and individuals become involved and interested in the processes under consideration, and as similar units withdraw, the structure of the field changes; there is a realignment of support and opposition among the field's constituent parts. Nor is this the only way in which the field is restructured. Even without a change in membership, the field can change its structure through the emergence of new organizations

247

among the already present constituents or the disappearance of old
organizations.

Hughes' paper provides examples of changes in the political field
from both sources. The politics of the St. Lawrence Island Eskimos were
deeply affected both by a reorganization among the units that had been
involved in their affairs for a considerable period of time and by the
addition of new elements.

Among these Eskimos, in the nineteenth century, the main constituents of the political field had been the patrilineal clans and their informal representatives, the clan elders. Political activity in this period was
occupied with interclan rivalries and disputes, which were sometimes
settled by informal meetings of clan elders. At the end of the nineteenth
century, this field was expanded by the involvement of foreigners in the
settlement of disputes. These cultural outsiders (missionaries, school
teachers, and captains of coast guard cutters) possessed considerable
power for settling disputes, and thus changed the structure of the field
as concerned those processes with which they were involved.

A further change, this time by reorganization rather than by expansion, occurred some thirty years later, when the Eskimos decided to have
an elected, permanent council. This new organization was the first locus
of centralized decision-making, and, although it was organized along the
same lines as the former informal group of clan elders and concerned
with much the same issues, it also restructured the field. This restructuring was in the form of a new organization within the field, which necessarily brought about an alteration in the relationships of the other parts
of the field. However, because the new organization was so similar in its
composition and concerns to the defunct clan elders' group, its impact
was not great. It was able to draw to itself much the same support the
elder had, and, because it had few basically new responsibilities, this
support sufficed for its operation.

After the Second World War there was yet another change in this
political field. First, the composition of the council changed so much that
it was no longer similar to the old elders' group, and it was unable to
maintain the support the earlier group had enjoyed. Second, the political
field expanded with entry into island affairs of such powerful factors as
the national government, the military, the national educational system,
and tourists.

All of these units became involved in the decisions and settlements
that formed the core of the islanders' field, and the council was the only
organization in a position to deal with these new elements and the issues
they raised. The council as now constituted, however, did not have the
support, experience, and skills for meeting the new problems effectively.
The new composition of the council, and the enlargement of its area of
operation, which Hughes refers to as an increase in the "behavioral

arena," are shown to be crucial factors in the council's decreased effectiveness.

Gallin's paper provides another example of the alteration of a political field both by a change in scope and by internal reorganization. In the Taiwanese village he studied, many disputes had formerly been settled through the efforts of local notables, lineage heads and landlords, and the villagers were extremely reluctant to involve the national government's representatives because of their presumed harshness—and because of the financial cost. In other words, the field in which these settlements took place effectively excluded elements from outside the local community. Morover, the villagers were closely tied to their land by (among other things) the absence of alternative economic opportunities, so that the composition of the field remained constant through a check on contraction as well as through the restriction on expansion.

This doubly restricted field was organized according to a hierarchical system of relationships that applied both to kin and to non-kin. The high position of the notables in this hierarchy, and the respect in which they were held by those whose disputes they mediated, were the key factors in the willingness of the disputants to accept their mediation. Or, to put it differently, the organization of the field was an extremely important factor in understanding the processes under consideration (settlement).

In the last fifteen to twenty years, both the scope and the organization of the field have changed. Perhaps the most important basis for the earlier political field, affecting both size and organization, was the land tenure system, and this was changed in several respects by the national government. These changes reduced the economic control of the landlords and lineage heads and made less crucial the strict observance of the hierarchical rules for respect and deference.

The land reform that altered the organization of the field was accompanied by increased opportunities for employment in the city and by increased population pressure, so that ties to the land became less compelling. The ability of participants to leave the field, together with a change in the field's organization, very much weakened the effectiveness of the mediation of local notables. A final undercutting of this effectiveness resulted from the lessening of the obstacles to increasing the field by involving national government representatives in mediation. That is, the increased contact with the national government, which resulted from working in the city and from a rise in educational attainment, brought about a change in attitude toward the government and a greater willingness to allow its representatives to deal with disputes.

It is worth noting that, in the Taiwanese village, the scope and organization of the political field were deeply affected by the direct intervention of an agency (the national government) that had originally been outside the field; in the Eskimo case, however, actions within the original field (the decision to elect a council and then the change in its composition) were highly important in eventually altering that field. Therefore, we can say that alteration in the scope and organization of a political field can be affected either from outside that field, as it was originally constituted, or by decisions and processes entirely within the original field.

Tuden's paper takes up an issue rather different from the ones already mentioned. His work is not concerned with the expansion and contraction of political fields, or even their reorganization. Instead he directs attention to the fact that processes of quite different types can go on within the same field, and that leading roles in these dissimilar processes may well be awarded to different statuses within the field, rather than there being one status or set of statuses predominant in all political activities regardless of their character. In both of the cases he analyzes he finds that, for certain important kinds of political processes, statuses extremely peripheral to the political field play vital roles.

Among the Ila, Tuden found two distinct sets of processes in the political field. First, there are the economic and ordinary, small-scale disputes that involve the members of the patrilineal kin group, which is the primary social and political unit. Second, there are matters that concern the fertility and health of the people of the several primary units that occupy the same territory, and wide-scale or extremely serious disputes. The first type of process takes place under the leadership of the heads of the local descent groups. This status derives its support from the kinship connections between its occupant and its public, and from the occupant's personal qualities, such as generosity, ability to mediate disputes, and lack of jealousy.

The second kind of process is under the control of mediums. Each territory has its territorial spirit or god that is responsible for the welfare of the people in the kin groups that occupy the territory. This god always takes possession of a particular person, and it is through this individual that the god makes clear his decisions concerning the welfare of his people and the disputes among them. Unlike the local descent group leader, the medium is not connected to his "constituents" through bonds of kinship; in most cases he is either a descendant of slaves or a stranger, and he is never a member of any of the kin groups in his territory. The only qualification for this office, in addition to the marginal political position, is a "good heart."

Among the Swat Pathans, Tuden again finds two different processes in the political field and different types of statuses in controlling positions for each. First, there is conflict for land and supporters, carried out under the leadership of khans who gain their positions by intrigue, force, and lavish entertainment of followers. Second, there is compromise of differences and mediation of the endless disputes among the khans and their followers. These compromises take place under the control of the mullahs, holy men who hold their positions by renouncing all the things (power, wealth, and physical pleasure) that are the objects of conflict among the khans and their followers, and by their reputations for piety and morality.

In both of his cases Tuden finds that leadership in the daily affairs of economic allocation and conflict between groups is carried out under the leadership of individuals who occupy statuses at the center of the political field. They are firmly enmeshed in the bonds that tie the political groups together, and they are clearly identified with the interests of one or more (but not all) of the units in the political field.

Tuden, in addition to these central political statuses, finds others that have some of the qualities of leadership but that are only peripherally involved in the main activities of their societies. He argues that their importance derives from their distance from the main interests that divide the groups that constitute the political field. These "detached" statuses function as mediators and promoters of overall group solidarity and are accepted in this role because of their structurally insured objectivity. In other words, the ability of the occupants of such statuses as mullah and spirit medium derives from the fact that their political positions are near the boundaries of their fields. Further support for this position can be seen in Colson's discussion (in Part III) of the "alien diviner" among the Tonga.

Fried's analysis of the political aspects of clanship in Taipei provides further insight into the significance of the internal organization and the boundaries of political fields. His discussion is concerned with the place of the clan in wider political activities. He shows how the clan, as a more or less stable and tightly organized group, functions in such processes as the enhancement of the prestige of society-wide political leaders, the implementation of the directives of the central government, the involvement of outsiders in the support of the political community, and the functioning of the electoral process. In most of these activities the clan members—especially its leaders—use the clan's organization and resources as a basis for gaining advantages in dealing with the wider political community; but in some respects the community and the government use the clan to further their ends.

It is important for our understanding of the "political field" concept that we examine the status of Fried's clans. Should they be considered as constituting units within the field of society-wide, or perhaps city-wide, political activities, or should they be viewed as separate political fields intersecting the broader field? This issue will have occurred to the reader with respect to other papers in this volume, and Fried's paper provides an excellent opportunity to deal with it.

It will be obvious that two or more political fields can exist at the same time, with the activities of the fields involving some—or conceivably all—of the same participants. The boundaries of a field are established by the "interest and involvement" of participants in the processes going on in the field. This means that, in some sense, we can speak of a political field composed of all human beings (or at least of all who are interested or involved in processes that have anything to do with war and peace, relations between East and West, the United Nations, etc.), the "participants" being very large and inclusive units, such as nations, blocs of power, and so on. It also means that we can speak of political fields that are limited to villages, wards, clans, or neighborhoods. The deciding factors in determining the boundaries are whether involvement and interest are direct and active and, more important, what our perspective is.

In Fried's paper we see, for example, that officials who attempt to gain city or national office sometimes stress their connections with a clan in order to provide themselves with the support of the members of that group. These officials assume that if they are successful in achieving identification with the clan, they will win the votes of its members. Looked at from the viewpoint of such an official, the clan is seen as only one unit among many in a field composed of all who can support or oppose him in an election. However, if we look at the same problem (whom the clan will support) from the point of view of the internal dynamics of the clan, the fact that many candidates seek support, and that other units also give or withhold his support, are "givens" and the clan is seen as a separate field that is composed of the factions and elements within its membership. The "givens" in a political field are significant, sometimes even crucial, but they affect the field by being manipulated by the actors in the processes under observation rather than by actively influencing the processes by their own dynamics.

How a clan ritual is planned, who directs the work, and so on are events that may have the utmost importance in understanding the processes that go on within the clan—viewed as a separate political field. These processes, however, are not materially important when we consider (as Fried does) how political officials use the clan rituals to enhance their prestige. From this perspective, the ritual is a "given" in officials' gaining support, and its importance for understanding the officials' behavior and the processes involving them derives not from its internal dynamics but from how the officials use it.

Because Fried does not consider the internal processes of the clans in his paper, but rather the part the results of these processes play in the political activities of the city and nation, the political field he deals with is broader than the clan; and the clan is a unit within that field. At the same time, it is possible to deal with the clan as a political field in itself by centering attention on the dynamics of the processes within the clan. Units (individuals or groups) of the clan that participate in clan processes and in, say, city-wide processes must be viewed as being involved in more than one political field; but, depending upon our interests at a particular time, we may limit our attention to only one of these.

The boundaries of a political field are determined by the processes that are actively carried out by the participants in that field, but the "givens" being manipulated by these active participants are part of processes that are going on in other fields. There is no a priori reason to devote our attention to one field rather than another, but our analysis will probably benefit from careful attention to whether we are centering our study on one field rather than another, or are dealing with several fields at once, why the field has been selected, and, most important, whether we have drawn the boundaries in terms of the processes with which we are most concerned.

FROM CONTEST TO COUNCIL: SOCIAL CONTROL AMONG THE ST. LAWRENCE ISLAND ESKIMOS [1]

Charles Campbell Hughes, MICHIGAN STATE UNIVERSITY

The Eskimos have provided authors in anthropology with many examples of groups in which social control was accomplished on the basis of informal and ad hoc interaction patterns rather than explicit judicial institutions. Quarrels were resolved by prowess, either in a wrestling match or in a public song contest which took the form of attempts to out-ridicule one's opponent. (The latter example refers, of course, to the famous "*nith* contest" of the central and eastern Eskimos.) At all times, in the background of social action, was the influence and threat of the strong and aggressive man, successful in hunting, whose reputation was an important factor in coercive control of behavior in the small band. Also, such men were often shamans, which added a supernatural element to their image of power. Finally, the elders were an important source of advice, restraint, and mediation.

Collective aspects of social control were exemplified principally in the support of one's nearest kin in blood vengeance and threat of reprisal if injury or insult should come to a relative. Less frequent but more dramatic was communal action by an entire group in disposing of a persistently troublesome sociopathic individual. But in no Eskimo society was there a superordinate social control structure that had the explicit task of adjudicating disputes, mediating among injured parties, and dispensing punishment. The nearest thing to this was the informal "council of elders," found both in the nomadic bilateral bands of the central and eastern regions, and in the more stable and more strongly unilineal extended family structures and clans of the Bering Sea region. An example from the latter area will be presented in this paper; and the discussion will range from social control mechanisms that are found in most Eskimo societies (such as wrestling matches) to those that evolved in response to pressures and suggestions from the white world. I will also appraise the successes and failures of these institutions with respect to questions of structure and situation.

[1] This paper was presented at the annual meeting of the American Anthropological Association, Detroit, 1964, and is based on fieldwork I conducted in 1954-55. I am grateful to Dr. J. M. Murphy for letting me use some of her field data.

255

The group of particular concern is the St. Lawrence Island Eskimos (Hughes, 1960). This island, part of the state of Alaska, lies in the north Bering Sea, a bit south of Bering Strait and just forty miles from Siberia. The St. Lawrence Eskimos are of interest in Eskimo studies because (as is true of some other Asiatic Eskimo groups) patrilineal clans are the most important structural feature of the social organization (Hughes, 1958, 1959; Fainberg, 1955; Menovshchikov, 1962).

The first long-term residence by Americans began in 1894, when a mission station was established in a village of some two hundred persons, later to be known as Gambell. Prior to that time, the politics of the group were the politics of interclan rivalries, alliances, threats of vengeance, and supernatural sanction. The most important economic activities were organized on the basis of clan affiliation: crews for the boats that hunted whales, walruses, and seals came from the lineages or extended families comprising the clan; and major patterns of sharing and mutual aid were normally extended only within the clan (except for some sanctioned sharing with those of one's matrilineal relatives who were members of the personal kindred). Religion was similarly structured along clan lines. Each person received the most important of his names, his "name-soul," from his clan; and he participated in a distinctive series of observances and rituals pertaining to death, sickness, and ensurance of or thankfulness for good hunting. In matters of social control the clan was again the most important group. As elsewhere in Eskimo culture, murder called for retributive vengeance, and the only sanction that could prevent a ceaseless round of such killings was the threat of overwhelming retaliation by another clan or open mediation by elders of the two clans involved. Lesser disputes were settled by public wrestling matches between the two litigants, the winner being awarded the verdict. The St. Lawrence islanders, like all Alaskan and Asiatic Eskimos, did not have *nith* song contests for deciding the justice of a dispute.

In settling controversies, the elders were motivated by the desire to keep the peace; Eskimo life was (and is) vulnerable to so many threats —from the weather, economic activities, and illness—that open hostilities between the clans within the village (or on other parts of the island) were not encouraged. This is not to say that pacifism was a positive virtue in all situations; indeed, prestige and acclaim went to the strong man, the man skilled with a lance, the man who through boastful arrogance could make others yield. Certainly a reading of the violent history of intervillage warfare on the western Alaskan coast belies any simple characterization of an amicable, peaceful people (Nelson, 1899). And the fortifications erected by the St. Lawrence people to defend themselves against raids by Siberians (remains of which can still be found) are further evidence of bellicosity.

In *intra*village relations, however, a delicate equilibrium was attempted between allowing individuals to assert and wrestle for individual claims and maintaining at least nonhostile relations among the clans as groups. One reason for trying to maintain good interclan relations, aside from that of keeping interpersonal tensions as low as possible, was the fact that most marriages were clan-exogamous. Open and continued hostilities could engender a profound conflict of loyalties for a person caught in a dispute between his patrilineal clansmen and matrilateral relatives, to some of whom he would have especially warm ties as members of his personal kindred (in a sense, the problem of "enemies and affines" [Brown, 1964]).

The year 1894 marked the beginning of the American presence on the island, and the possibility of disputes and punishment being arbitrated and administered by "outside" agents of social control. The missionary could call upon the captains of visiting coast guard or revenue cutters to judge disputes or to carry offenders off to jail on the mainland. In addition, the missionary himself appraised claims, held the *threat* of calling upon outside force, or used his (then weak) control over the supernatural beliefs of the villagers to influence conduct.

This pattern was maintained for the next thirty years or so. The basis of social control still lay in the clans and in the power relationships among them, with only an occasional intrusion of outside force by the missionary or the school teacher. There are instances of an assertive teacher or missionary openly contending with a shaman or strongman and of the cutter captain being called on to advise and adjudicate. There was also, during this period, increased activity by the federal government in economic affairs, for a reindeer herd was introduced onto the island and a program of herder training (under Laplanders) was initiated. But there was no development, at this time, of any coordinating social institution at the village level more embracing than the clan; community life during the first quarter of the twentieth century was formally patterned by interactions among clans, teacher, missionary, and cutter captain—each, for the most part, acting within a relatively autonomous sphere.

The first step toward a governing structure of greater scope than the informal grouping of clan elders occurred in 1925. In his annual report, the teacher at that time remarked:

The village has no centralized authority. Have discussed the idea of a village council. . . . They seem impressed but have not acted on the suggestion. I settle their small disputes to the best of my ability. . . . Any serious trouble . . . would be referred to the Captain of *Bear* [coast guard cutter], although nothing during the year warranted this action.

Despite the teacher's report of lack of enthusiasm, the idea of a village council was soon adopted, on a one-year trial basis. Its functional scope

was very wide, including matters that affected marriage, domestic harmony, family life, permissible limits on animal kills, regulations on fox
trapping, and ownership rights, in addition to judicial and punitive
duties. Illustrative excerpts from some of the early decisions of the
council are:

If a young man and his wife are living together and their parents try to separate them . . . they shall go to the village council before separating. If one side
did wrong he shall pay a fine according to how much wrong he did.
If any dog bites a person or child, the owner shall keep that dog tied. If the
dog bites the second time the owner shall pay a fine of one dollar for each
tooth hole bit in the skin.
The council decide that Ernest must take his whole family to his camp.
Because anybody who left some of his family is losing their time in coming
to see them.

Elected by the villagers, the council was apparently successful in
dealing with these and similar problems; and it continued to function for
the next ten years, at which time Congress passed the Wheeler-Howard
Act, giving a legal basis to village bodies of this type. Composed of
eight members, the council in the late 1930's continued implementing its
general mandate to act for the good of the village: by public sanction
and shaming it enforced legislative edicts affecting economic, social,
familial, recreational, political, educational, and hygienic affairs. The
only institutional area that was not touched by council deliberations was
religion.

Field notes from 1940 indicate an astonishing degree of compliance
by villagers with the council's edicts. This, moreover, was not simply a
grudging compliance; there was a high positive acceptance of the council's *legitimate right* to deal in matters that had for so long been the
province of the clan, settled through negotiations between clan elders
(Hughes, 1953). In the matter of arranging marriages, for example, the
council was explicitly on record as willing to mediate between the families of two young persons who wanted to marry. This is not to say that
the council usurped all of the clan functions or attempted too rapid a
change; rather, it channeled these functions through its own structure
and it selectively reinforced traditional customs. For example, one of its
bylaws supported continuation of "groomwork," work customarily required by the father of a prospective bride.

In summarizing the council's activities up to World War II, one may
say that it dealt with many of the problems formerly dealt with exclusively by the clans, and it did this with a greater degree of effectiveness
and acceptance. It did not supersede the clans, at least not directly and
immediately, but rather channeled many of their social functions—and
some of their leading spokesmen—into a new formal structure. This situation perhaps suggests a model of general applicability, so far as possi-

bilities for centralization of political authority in acephalous segmentary societies are concerned.

Diagrammatically, the relation between functions of the council and those of the clans during this period may be represented by two largely overlapping eulerian circles.

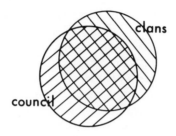

To what factors can one ascribe the council's apparent success? One was the guidance and implied coercion exemplified by the teacher, the formal agent of the U.S. government. A second factor was the representation of all major clans of the village in the council's elected membership; the council, it seemed, was a permanent adjudicative social mechanism analogous to the informal, evanescent council of clan elders that had for so long attempted to maintain the peace. A third element, of considerable importance, was the personality of the man who was council president for the first fifteen years of its existence—up to the time of World War II. This person, described by all as a man of common sense, vision, sensitivity, and justice, was recalled in warm terms—even two decades later—as one who had achieved the most difficult of tasks: keeping up with changing conditions, and accomplishing tangible social benefits with a minimum of interpersonal hostilities. It was under his imaginative administration that the native store chartered an airplane to take a cargo of fox furs to St. Louis in time for peak prices on the exchange; that the village installed a diesel electricity generator for public use; and that the council insisted on an annual spring cleaning of yards and houses to clear away the the accumulated winter debris.

Another factor, however, cannot be overlooked in this man's success as president: he belonged to one of the smallest and therefore weakest clans. Probably one reason for his success in governing was that, because of his clan origin, he had few nepotic ties among the villagers and could more easily be fair to most of them. Such an explanation suggests a problem for more systematic investigation: in a segmentary society with a central political authority, under what sociopolitical conditions does the leader come from a dominant group, as against one of the weaker groups? Whatever the more general social structural implications of this particular arrangement, the president of Gambell village at this time was obviously a remarkable man in his own right.

A related aspect of the council's activities must be mentioned at this point to complete the record. Since the early 1930's a welfare committee had operated in the community, performing tasks related to the general welfare: distributing food supplies to all households in the event of a sudden windfall; acting as a guardian to prevent children from being outdoors after the curfew hour at night; making arrangements for public entertainment, such as native dances; building caskets for corpses; keeping the community building in good repair, etc. Many of its functions clearly paralleled those ostensibly given to the council; in actuality, however, the committee served much more as the "operational arm" of the council—a group of men through whose actions the council's decisions were made to affect the community.

Beyond the considerations mentioned above, possibly the most important reason the council was largely successful in this early period was that it dealt with problems that were at least potentially solvable within the framework of skills and capabilities of its members. The fact that it did not alienate the clans is important; but equally cogent is that the *behavioral arena*, so to speak, in which it worked was localized and circumscribed, with its major parameters known to those who had to maintain order in the village, punish offenders, ensure social and economic justice, and transact affairs with the infrequent visitors from the outside world.

Two principal developments affected the functioning of the council between 1925-45 and 1945-55. The first is an enlargement of what I call the behavioral arena, the sheer situation of action—an enlargement that created problems for the later council that were solvable only with considerable difficulty (given the psychological characteristics of council members), despite the fact that the council's formal structure *qua* institution remained the same. For example, it still has a set of officers—president, vice-president, secretary, and treasurer—and four periodically elected members. Its scope of institutional concern for village affairs is as wide as before: health, marriage, economy, social welfare, recreation, social regulation and adjudication, and corporate contracts with the outside world. But the problems thrown its way by historical circumstances, the value framework in which they are perceived, the number and nature of conceived alternatives, and its structural ability to speak in a united voice as representing the village are all changed from the earlier period.

In short, the council's *problematic environment* and the gearing into that environment of the council's response have markedly restructured. Physical location or major attributes of habitat had not changed appreciably, but there had been shifts of a fundamentally ecological nature in other respects. Some of these differences were, for the most part, those of degree and not kind; for example, there had always been some contact with the outside world, but now this was greatly intensified, and it demanded new types of intellectual skills. There always had been emulation of and admiration for the white man; now, however, the white mainland had become the primary reference culture, and its values, instead of Eskimo values, legitimized many actions. Other differences were of kind and not degree; now the council had not only questions of *intra*village harmony to decide, it also had the problems of day-to-day relations between the village and powerful segments of the outside world: military, educational, public health, tourism, commercial interests, and petty bureaucracy. And it was attempting to cope with these problems in a framework of inadequate skills, of changing and partially disparaging self-identity.

The council was also attempting to cope with these problems in a context of structural conflict with the major bases of social action and personal loyalty, the clans (and this is the second principal development). Although still composed of elected members—and therefore structurally similar in basic form to the earlier council—the 1955 council no longer served as the structural analogue of the interclan council of elders. Most of its members were elected from one of the three major clans in the village, and, because clan affiliation was still the key ascribed feature governing interpersonal transactions, there were many charges and apparent instances of clan favoritism in village affairs. It now appeared that, instead of being the integrative locus in which clan rivalries were eradicated or channeled to the common good, the council had become a divisive element in interclan relations. Members of the disaffected clans without representatives on the council had, as it were, to "regress" structurally—had to look for their main basis of social support in the clan's power relationships and alliances. There was now much less overlapping between the concerns of the council and the clans, for the former was repeatedly charged with being an instrument of one clan and not a neutral meeting ground for all. In 1955 the relationship between council and clans could not be represented by the largely congruent eulerian circles of the earlier years; the area of common orientation was much smaller.

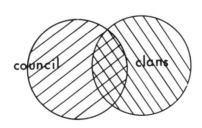

There had been changes in the welfare committee as well. For the first twenty years its membership had been unchanged; three men, from three different clans, had composed it. Then, in the 1954 elections, its membership was drawn from unsuccessful candidates for the council. Although sometimes criticized for its actions (such as seeing—as was its duty—that all soldiers left the village at curfew times), the welfare committee nevertheless exemplified a formal structure to which had been turned over activities that were understandable and acceptable in the framework for dealing with community problems that had been evolved up to the time of World War II. Thus its actions manifested the deeply held Eskimo values of sharing and concern for communal well-being when it distributed relief food supplies in a winter of scarcity, patrolled the village to ensure compliance with council edicts about children being in their houses at the proper time (to protect their health), and arranged for and cleaned up after public recreational events. There is much to suggest, in fact, that of the two structures—the welfare committee and the council—the committee had an easier time of it and received less ambivalent public acceptance in the 1950's, for most of its work had to do with problems which made sense to the villagers (although they might not always agree with the specific edict). Also, by comparison with the council, it had more than its share of activities that tangibly rewarded the public: food, entertainment, public service. Finally, it was not the body that exacted punishment for infractions (although such punishment might be a result of information it had provided; its chairman described it as the "eyes and ears of the council").

Any structure in nature—be it biological or social—develops and functions optimally in relation to a particular context of appropriate conditions. The context of human behavior is of course much more than geographic; it includes an assumptive social and psychocultural environment. Ecologists might speak of an "ecological niche" in this connection, and the philosopher Buchler might refer to a particular type of "proceptive domain" (1951), but, whatever the term, no pattern of structure-in-environment is functionally adequate for all times and circumstance; and a structural analysis that disregards environmental aspects in this set of interlocking ecological processes is abstracting only part of the dynamic transactions involved.

From my reading of the recent literature I infer that many of the factors I have discussed in the development of the Gambell town council have also played a part in the differential difficulties and successes of councils elsewhere in Eskimo Alaska (Hughes, 1965). I refer particularly to the lack of structural support between major units of the "indigenous" social organization, whether clans or merely extended families, and council membership; and especially to the nature of articulation between the capabilities of the council and major features of its ecological situation, conceived in psychocultural as well as geographic terms.

REFERENCES

BROWN, PAULA. 1964. Enemies and affines. Ethnology, 3, 4, 335-356.

BUCHLER, JUSTUS. 1951. Toward a general theory of human judgment. Columbia University Press.

HUGHES, CHARLES C. 1953. A preliminary ethnography of the Eskimo of St. Lawrence Island, Alaska. M.A. thesis, Cornell University.

———. 1958. An Eskimo deviant from the 'Eskimo' type of social organization. American Anthropologist, 60, 1140-47.

———. 1959. Translation of I. K. Voblov's Eskimo ceremonialism. Anthropological Papers of the University of Alaska, 7, 71-90.

———. 1960. An Eskimo village in the modern world. Cornell University Press.

———. 1965. Under four flags: recent culture change among the Eskimos. Current Anthropology, Vol. 6, no. 1, 3-69.

FAINBERG, L. 1955. K voprosy o rodovom stroe u eskimosov. Sovietskaya Etnografiia, 1, 82-99.

MENOVSHCHIKOV, G. A. 1962. O perezhitochnykh iavleniyakh rodovoi organizatsii u aziatskikh eskimosov. Sovietskaya Etnografiia, 6, 29-34.

NELSON, E. W. 1899. The Eskimo about Bering Strait. 18th Annual Report of the Bureau of American Ethnology, pt. 1. Washington: Government Printing Office.

CONFLICT RESOLUTION IN
CHANGING CHINESE SOCIETY: A TAIWANESE STUDY [1]

Bernard Gallin, MICHIGAN STATE UNIVERSITY

This paper is based on sixteen months of fieldwork during 1957-58 in a Chinese (Hokkien) agricultural community on the west-central coastal plain of Taiwan. The village was then composed of about 650 persons in 115 registered households, each an economic unit. The villagers are descendants of Chinese immigrants who came from the coastal region of Fukien province, on the mainland of China, some 170 years ago.

Although there are twelve different surnames in the village, four names comprise somewhat over 80 per cent of the village population. In most instances, families bearing the same surname consider themselves part of the same localized *tsu*, or lineage (frequently referred to as a "clan" in the literature). The village is therefore multi-*tsu*, each *tsu* being patrilineal and patrilocal, with a demonstrated common ancestor. Several related village families are not part of a lineage organization, and some families have no relatives in the village.

Within the village, two of the largest lineages are the most influential, probably because of their sheer size and their financial preeminence, which is due to several relatively well-off landowning member families. These well-off families are, in most cases, rather high in the village status hierarchy as well as that of their *tsu*. None of the village *tsu*, however, including the larger ones, have corporate landholdings that are significant either in material or symbolic value. Although the member families of each *tsu* are socially integrated, and although they form alignments within the village so that they can compete in exerting socio-political influence in village affairs for the benefit of their members, they nevertheless have very limited influence in matters that go beyond the village To a great degree this is due to the small size of the village *tsu* organizations and their lack of very wealthy families.

[1] I wish to acknowledge my gratitude to the Ford Foundation, which supported my fieldwork in Taiwan. This article is an expanded version of a paper first presented at the 63rd Annual Meeting of the American Anthropological Association, in Detroit, November, 1964. The original writing and expansion of this paper was supported by a grant from the Asian Studies Center, Michigan State University, to which I extend my thanks. I also wish to express my deep appreciation to my wife, Rita Schlesinger Gallin, for her participation in the fieldwork and her aid and encouragement in the writing.

Reinforcing the social integration and socio-political influence of these kinship-oriented *tsu* organizations are their several group activities, especially the ceremonial ones. These include group ancestor worship and various life cycle rituals, such as those that take place at marriage and death. In addition, the *tsu* organizations attempt to maintain internal order within their own ranks and also between themselves and the other village *tsu* groupings and nonaligned families.

The village is the nuclear type that is common both on the China mainland and in Taiwan, at least with respect to its living area. Each *tsu* organization or lesser kinship group of families lives pretty much in its own separate compound or neighborhood in the village. The very small kinship groups, made up of a few families, and the several unrelated small family units are interspersed throughout the village. These often look to the larger *tsu,* and sometimes to a particular *tsu,* for support or backing in case of trouble; and this is especially true of families that share the same surname with a large *tsu* but to which they are not related, being unable to trace *tsu* membership through a common ancestor. To further enhance their security, these families at times try to identify themselves with the *tsu* whose surname they share, and they sometimes manage to participate in some of the *tsu*'s secular activities.

Because the village is nucleated, its population lives in a rather small land area given over to houses. The house area is surrounded by many small fields, which in many cases are several miles away from the village proper. The villagers' small plots of land, both owned and tenanted, are most often adjoined by land that is operated by people from other villages—as well as from their own village.

The most important crop is wet rice, and the next is vegetables. Because rainfall is seasonal, the two annual crops of wet rice necessitate an elaborate network of irrigation dams, water gates, and waterways that covers the entire land area. The rice, and especially the vegetables (which have recently been increasing in importance as a cash crop), bring all of the villagers into contact with the government, and many of them into contact with the various market towns of the area—even nearby cities. In addition to this, and even more important, the recent great increase of the population on a limited land base has caused overpopulation and necessitated an ever-increasing migration of villagers to the cities, which offer growing opportunities for jobs and small commerce. At the outset, this migration is usually a temporary measure to supplement family income from the land; later, it often becomes a permanent move.

Recent years, then, have seen an increasing turning outward by the villagers, with a concomitant turning away from the traditional identification with the village—even, although to a far lesser degree, in the lineage or larger-kinship grouping. This affects the nature of the continuing relationships among people and groupings within the village and in the immediate area.

In this context, I shall examine one consequence of these recent developments: the change in means for resolving local social conflict in such a community. To do this, I shall discuss the breakdown in mediation, the traditional Chinese method for settling local disputes, and the accompanying increase in the resolution of internal conflict through external official agencies, especially the police and the courts. We shall see that increasingly significant socioeconomic extensions beyond the village and increased involvement with the national economy and urban forms of life have been instrumental in this development, and have disrupted the effectiveness of the traditional form of community social organization.

THE TRADITIONAL PERIOD

Mediators were most often educated persons of some wealth, usually in land, who could afford to devote time and effort to community service and could participate in most of the social and religious affairs of their village or area. Mediation was part of their community service; it helped create the image of a public-spirited local leader, and brought these persons much esteem. Mediation, then, was performed by respected leaders of a village, area, *tsu,* or even of a very small kinship group.

In resolving a conflict by mediation—if the disputants were members of the same *tsu*—the mediator would ideally be the *tsu* leader, or perhaps an honored matrilateral relative of a *tsu* member (usually from another village); if the disputants were not members of the same *tsu,* a notable village leader might be called in to mediate. Similarly, if the disputants were from different villages, a respected area leader would be asked to arbitrate. Thus the selection of a mediator was based on the relationships of the disputants (as well as on the nature of the conflict).

Conflict in the community, then and now, has resulted from several general causes, most frequently from internal disputes over water for irrigation, especially over its equitable distribution; land tenure disputes between landlord and tenant over rent or tenancy rights; and disputes over landownership and property boundaries. Another common source of conflict, especially in a multi-*tsu* village, has been power struggles between families—especially between *tsu* organizations—over such questions as village administration or the expenditure of funds by village or *tsu* for religious or festive activities. All of these types of conflict might also occur on the intervillage level.

In traditional and even in recent times, whatever the nature of a dispute or the level on which it occurred (within or between villages), mediation was almost always sought and applied because of two primary reasons.[2] The first was the desire to localize the scope and resolution of the conflict; the villagers preferred not to invite government intervention because the authorities tended to be extremely harsh with all concerned. At least part of the reason for this harshness was that the government also preferred not to be involved in local matters, if there was any way to avoid it; the bureaucratic corps in traditional China was too small to handle all potential and actual local conflicts. And an additional reason for the villagers' desire not to become involved in the government's legal system was that resort to the law usually proved to be financially devastating. The second reason for local mediation was the desire that the resolution might allow the parties to live harmoniously together. Villagers felt a great sense of permanence in their locale. Tied to their land and village, and tied by the particular kinds of relationships they had developed over the years with local people, both kin and non-kin, they had very few opportunities to leave the area, land, or kinship group to escape the repercussions of an ill-settled dispute.

Thus the manner in which a dispute was settled—that is, how well the "face" of each disputant was preserved—was far more important than any concept that "justice" be served. And, since it was both desirable and usual in traditional Chinese society to avoid interference from government or its official representatives (thus preserving local autonomy), local conflict was resolved on the local level by respected individuals whose "words would be heard" and respected. Mediation by men who were familiar with the conflict situation, as well as with its participants, increased the likelihood that a satisfactory solution would be reached with minimal residual bitterness. This, moreover, is reflected in the traditional Chinese view of the relative insignificance of formal law as opposed to *li* (propriety and reasonableness) as a guideline to action.

The effectiveness of mediation that was directed toward the preservation of local autonomy and harmony was possible, in large part, because of the society's acceptance of the hierarchical relationship system, in which all relationships—except, perhaps, personal friendships—are based on the positions individuals hold relative to each other. In kinship and family relationships, the kinship code itself, which clearly defines differences by criteria of sex, affinity, generation, collaterality, relative age, and bifurcation, serves to regulate relations between its members. Non-kin relationships also have a regulating code or concept—often referred to as *kan-ch'ing* ("sentiment" or "feeling"). As Fried pointed out (1953, pp. 226-227), the latter code facilitates interactions across class lines or between any two persons whose levels in the social hierarchy differ, such

---

[2] A description and discussion of rural forms of conflict and mediation in China can be found in Fei (1939), Freedman (1958), Gallin (1966), Hsiao (1960), Hu (1948), and Yang (1945).

as landlord and tenant. (Their relationship is mutually understood as a function of this differential placement, and if the position of each is respected by the other, the two are said to have good *kan-ch'ing*. If either fails to fulfill his tacit behavioral obligation to the other, bad *kan-ch'ing* is said to exist.) The social order was thus stabilized by a structure of mutual obligations that paralleled the established hierarchical system.

On this basis, then, the local mediators (usually the village landlords or *tsu* leaders) were extremely important in the community, and the successful resolution of conflict was in great part dependent on their willingness to assume the responsibilities of the codes. The mediators' success rested upon the respect the disputants and the community had for them; if they commanded respect, they were usually able to maneuver both sides into accepting a compromise solution.

RECENT DEVELOPMENTS IN A TAIWANESE RURAL AREA

In recent years, in rural Taiwan, the effectiveness of the mediator and of mediation as a principal means of conflict resolution has been diminishing. To a certain degree, this is a result of the deterioration of the accepted hierarchical relationship system—on both the kin and non-kin levels. On the non-kin level the concept or code of *kan-ch'ing*, and the quality of interpersonal relations governed by it, have weakened.

This situation developed, in part, when the traditional land tenure system was modified by Taiwan's land reform program of 1949-53. An important aspect of the reform was a rent reduction and limitation law, but even more important was the introduction of an official contract between landlord and tenant that secured the tenant's rights on the land despite his relationship—good or bad *kan-ch'ing*—with the landlord. This contract for the first time made it clear that the relationship between landlord and tenant, and their mutual responsibilities, were economic. Once their interaction was limited to an economic relationship, defined by an official contract, the traditional maintenance of good *kan-ch'ing* lost some of its former importance. In addition, for many villagers —landholder or tenant—the land and the local area have tended to lose their hold because of the many new opportunities for migration to urban areas, so that the many *kan-ch'ing*-oriented relationships that were formerly necessary for survival need no longer be maintained.

This deterioration in the basis for *kan-ch'ing*, and with it much of the prestige of the landlord class, has frequently meant that, unless the landlord had other means for sustaining his high status, he lost his usefulness as a mediator, being no longer capable of exerting influence and leadership in the community.

At the same time, the traditional responsibilities of landlords toward their tenants and the community have also been affected by the land reform.[3] The expropriation of much of their land has reduced the landlords' interests in the rural area by encouraging them to shift their investments to the level of urban or national industry and commerce. As a result, they have lost many of their traditional social and political interests in the local area.

This was very apparent during the period of my fieldwork; of the twenty-two villages in the district, five could find no qualified individual who was willing to devote his time and money to the job of being mayor. During almost the entire period of the fieldwork, these five villages were of necessity administered by a local official of the district's public office. It is increasingly apparently that in rural Taiwan many of the traditional local leaders can no longer be expected to assume a position of community responsibility, which includes mediation.

On the kinship level, the code that regulated relationships between individuals at different levels in the hierarchy has likewise been affected by change, thus lessening the community's ability to resolve local social conflict. This has occurred on the levels of lineage or *tsu*, and even in the family unit. The *tsu* leaders of the traditional kinship unit have always played an important role in settling any conflict by mediating among their own *tsu* members and between *tsu* organizations. Over the last several years, however, the prestige and authority of the *tsu* organization has decreased, which has limited its influence as a force in the resolution of social conflict. (Of course, under Japanese rule [1895-1945] the large and powerful *tsu* organizations had been divested of much of their power and authority to facilitate control over local areas.)

In more recent times, other forces have combined to increase the downgrading of the *tsu* organization as a generally effective local force for maintaining social order. Another result of land reform was that the *tsu* organizations lost much of their corporate landholdings by expropriation, and with this much of their remaining economic power, a main source of *tsu* prestige and authority. A *tsu* could no longer be depended upon to fulfill its traditional obligations and responsibilities, to its own people and to the local community (such as financial support for a *tsu's* needy members, educational assistance, support for a *tsu's* religious activities [maintenance of ancestral halls, and even the worship of *tsu* ancestors], etc).

As a result, the *tsu* has apparently also lost much of its ability to exert sanctions against its members or their opponents. At the same time, the land of the wealthy private landlord members of a *tsu*—who were usually of high status in the *tsu* hierarchy, and pillars of the *tsu* and its activities—was of course also expropriated by the land reform in Taiwan.

[3] For a more detailed analysis of the problem of the land reform and rural leadership in Taiwan, see Gallin (1963).

This, then, was an additional blow to the strength of the *tsu* organizations as conflict-resolving agencies.

It is perhaps worth noting that somewhat similar events have recently occurred on the Chinese mainland. Like the Japanese in Taiwan, the Chinese Communists sought (apparently with success) to win political control over even local areas by ending the influence of the large lineage organizations. A land reform in the early period of the Communist take-over, which expropriated the holdings of landlords, surely went far toward achieving this goal.

In Taiwan, *tsu* authority (and even that of the family itself) has also been weakened by the extension of the villagers' socioeconomic interests beyond the home area. The increased opportunities for earning a living in the urban centers has given the villagers increased economic and even social independence, not only from the village community and *tsu* but from the family unit itself. Now that villagers can easily go to the city to find work, neither *tsu* nor family can control their movements as they could in the past. A family, or one of its members, has a greater opportunity to behave unilaterally.

The village community, the *tsu*, and the family have lost much of their traditional ability to control the behavior of their members, not only when they have gone to the city but in the rural area as well. A growing individualism has become more and more evident among rural people. In traditional times villagers were frequently prohibited from disposing of their land without the permission of the community or kinship group. In recent years, however, villagers who have desired to leave the area have often sold their land to any buyer, and neither the community nor the kinship group can prevent it.[4]

All of these things have made it increasingly difficult to maintain the traditional relationships in rural society that were part of the kinship code and the code of *kan-ch'ing*. The weakening of the social hierarchy has been accompanied by a general inability to use the traditional respect for leaders of the landlord class or *tsu* as a force for settling disagreements.

It is not purely a matter of the weakening of the traditional hierarchical relationships between people, however, that has diminished the respect for traditional mediators. This trend has been intensified by the peasants' tendency toward a growing egalitarianism on the social and on the economic levels of life. This tendency was born of greater educational opportunities, the practice of electing officials, and land redistribution and land contracts, all of which have helped to equalize economic means and social relations. Although the peasants still recognize the former landlords' higher status and power, their willingness to accept

---

[4] For a discussion of changing traditional Chinese values toward the land in Taiwan, see Gallin (1964).

them as mediators has clearly diminished—as has this formerly powerful group's interests in such community service.

CONCLUSIONS

The loss of prestige and authority by the traditional mediators, and thus the decline of traditional mediation, has been accompanied by a questioning of a principal aim of mediation—that the goal of the resolution is to enable the persons in conflict to live harmoniously together.

Many villagers are no longer strongly wedded to their village. This is a result of several developments: the land reform, which has meant they can no longer expect to achieve wealth and status through the accumulation of land; the villagers' newly developing relations with the greater market economy; and increased economic opportunities and migration to the cities. The people no longer insist that disputes be settled in a way that preserves harmonious local relations. Although this is still very important for many people, it is no longer universal.

At the same time, several important developments have reduced the community's ability to enforce mediation on disputants as the principal means for conflict resolution. These are the growing independence from the village community and a growing individualism, evidenced by the atomization of tsu land ownership and kinship organization, coupled with the tendency toward some egalitarianism and a deterioration in the traditional hierarchical relationship system. Traditionally, whether or not a successful or satisfactory solution was reached, there had been little recourse beyond the decisions reached by mediation. In the interests of community life and organization, and of local autonomy, the threat of community censure served to keep in line those who might have sought to redress wrongs by bringing in outside elements, such as government officials. More recently, however, the possibility for such control has been limited and the effectiveness of mediation weakened.

The result has been a recent growing awareness among the villagers of the need for a more effective mechanism to serve justice and resolve the local conflicts that continue to occur. The alternative to mediation has been to turn to more official, extravillage means—the police and the courts. Although most often mediation is still first sought to settle differences, if a disputant feels that the mediator's decision is wrong or inequitable, now he need not feel bound by it, and may turn to an outside force in the hope of bettering the decision.

This change has further been made possible by another recent development. In traditional times there was a great fear of the authorities among the peasantry. This fear is still far from dispelled, but the villagers now have a modified image of the role and activities of the authorities and the government, so that there is a much greater willingness to appeal to government authorities in matters of local social conflict. This modification may or may not be due to a real change in government, but it is certainly strengthened by increased contacts between rural villagers and the government and the outside world, and by improved communications in general.

Unfortunately, however, the villager's faith in the ability of the government to redress injustices is not always supported by its actions nor by vindication of his claim. The Chinese government in Taiwan, faced with an increase in litigation, has not yet recognized the causal socioeconomic changes that are taking place in rural society. Often the government, following the traditional patterns, appears to discourage the courts and police from taking the necessary role in meting out justice, and these agents abdicate their authority by telling the Taiwanese peasant to have the dispute mediated locally. They do this even though the appearance of a case on a court docket or in a police station is usually an indication that local mediation was of no avail. Thus the agencies of the government still attempt to enforce recourse to the traditional forms of local conflict resolution, even though this means that many conflicts necessarily go unresolved, or are resolved unsatisfactorily from the point of view of preserving local harmony.

Ironically, it appears that the present Chinese government in Taiwan would like to have greater contact with and control over the local areas of Taiwan. However, the government is in a sense caught in a trap: it still tends to view the present changing society, with its rapidly changing needs, as if it were the traditional society with its preferred system of local autonomy. As a result, it is hardly able to visualize the possibility of moving into the local situation by taking advantage of the rural areas' need for a more centralized arbitrator of local social conflict.

REFERENCES

Fei, Hsiao-tung. 1939. Peasant life in China, a field study of country life in the Yangtze valley. London: Kegan Paul, Trench, Trubner.

Freedman, Maurice. 1958. Lineage organization in southeastern China. London: Athlone Press.

Fried, Morton H. 1953. Fabric of Chinese society. New York: Praeger.

Gallin, Bernard. 1963. Land reform in Taiwan: its effect on rural social organization and leadership. Human Organization, 22, 2, 109-112.

——. 1964. Chinese peasant values towards the land. Proceedings of the

1963 Annual Spring Meeting of the American Ethnological Society. University of Washington Press, pp. 64-71.

————. 1966. *Hsin Hsing, Taiwan: a Chinese village in change.* University of California Press.

HSIAO, KUNG-CHUAN. 1960. Rural China, imperial control in the nineteenth century. University of Washington Press.

HU, HSIEN-CHIN. 1948. The common descent group in China and its functions. New York: Viking Fund.

YANG, MARTIN. 1945. A Chinese village, Taitou, Shantung province. Columbia University Press.

LEADERSHIP AND THE DECISION-MAKING PROCESS

Arthur Tuden, UNIVERSITY OF PITTSBURGH

Flexibility and variation in leaders, and their various political functions in a political system, have not been amply documented. There is a tendency to assume political patterns are uniform within a society. Political systems, however, are complex, and to perform the requisite functions a multiplicity of leaders and sanctions and a variety of phases of political processes appear. To amplify this point, it is our aim to discuss the different phases of political processes, primarily conflict resolution and decision-making, in two societies, the Ila [1] and Swat Pathan. This paper will describe leaders, their recruitment patterns, and the cultural mechanisms that facilitate performance primarily in the decision-making process.

THE ILA

The Ila, a small cattle-keeping tribe, reside in the northwestern corner of Zambia. The territorial framework for political behavior was eighty autonomous or semiautonomous territorial divisions (*chisi*), which varied greatly in size. Some possessed as many as fifteen to twenty kin groups residing in close proximity, while the less populous territories were inhabited by only four or five kin groups. In each territorial division the basic structural unit was the *mukwaashi* or *chibuwe*, a small, exogamous-named group of agnatic relatives, three generations in depth, usually containing not more than fifteen or twenty males. The agnatic members with their wives, children, and slaves formed village cores. Matrilineal relatives—male and female—also resided in the villages, but rarely predominated numerically.

Solidarity of the *mukwaashi* was strong. Membership in the agnatic group permitted access to jointly owned cattle for bridewealth, aid in payment of fines, and cattle for milk and plowing. Membership in a *mukwaashi* also signified the right to farmland identified with the patrilineal kin group. Aid in herding cattle, the sharing of food during crop

[1] I thank the Ford Foundation, and the Program of African Studies of Northwestern University, for financial support for this field trip.

275

failures, and support during feuds were other functions of the residential group. Ceremonial beer drinks for ancestral spirits, funeral aid, and female puberty ceremonies drew on the local descent group for participants.

However, these localized patrilineal groups or villages were not autonomous; similar responsibilities and obligations were extended to matrikin. The dispersed matrilineal relatives contributed a portion of the cattle for bridewealth, debts and fines, and support in times of crisis. Property and spirit-names were also inherited matrilineally. Participation in ancestral rites was the joint responsibility both of matrilineal and patrilineal relatives.

Leadership was not fixed. In intragroup relations no kinship unit had a permanent, predominant political position. Ranking of the groups depended on temporary criteria, accessible to all local descent groups, and was related to the number of followers. Factors such as generosity in distributing property, friendship ties, and number of followers constantly served to reaffirm the ranking of kin groups in each territory.

The authority allocation in each *chisi* lacked well-defined patterns of superordination and subordination, and no descent group leader had clearly defined territorial, judicial, administrative, or coercive functions. Each group regulated the affairs of its members and defended their rights against other groups.

The leaders of the local descent groups, known as *musolozhi* ("head") or *mukaindi* ("large"), lived in egalitarian social surroundings. The criteria for recruitment of a kin leader was very broad. The qualities demanded of a *musolozhi* were generosity in dispensing property, competence to discuss court cases, ability to mediate between quarreling relatives, and lack of jealousy and envy. A kinship affilation or a quasi-kin tie usually existed between the leader and settlement members. In some cases, a sister's son, or a brother, or a son was disregarded and a distant relative or quasi-relative was elected as head of the kin groups. Achieved criteria, such as judicious use of wealth and a pleasing personality, could and did override close kinship ties in the election of the village head.

The primary function of the kin head was the care and protection of kin members. The *musolozhi* was primarily an administrator of communal property, both land and cattle. He was partially responsible for the allocation of cattle for bridewealth and for the management of the communal property. However, his position was not an enviable one. Affiliated kin members held property rights both to land and cattle, and demanded accounts of and participated fully in the disposal of goods and property.

The authority of the *musolozhi* was limited, and it derived from common interests. It was not based on any power inherent in his position. This kin leader, with the consent of other members, at times withdrew aid by not contributing to the bridewealth or payment of fines for well-known transgressors; but generally the kinship commitments prevailed. Ostracism or expulsion from villages was rarely practiced. (No information was obtained on ritual cursing of offenders or a withdrawal of the right to receive ancestral protection.) No ritual or religious paraphernalia was specifically associated with the office of the kin head. In general, relations between a village member and village heads were without authoritative overtones. Indeed, the incidence of actual physical conflict between village members and village heads was frequent, but the offending village member rarely received direct physical punishment. Witchcraft or malevolent magic is commonly practiced among the Ila, but did not appear to be used as an institutionalized support of authority.

In most instances the Ila villages were relative peaceful spots. Any conflict that emerged between villagers was held in check, or suppressed by the common interests, since unresolved conflict would eventually lead to a segmentation of village members. Therefore, such political processes as decision-making and the settlement of conflict was a delicate and slow process. Consensus was important. The pattern of decision-making in the kin group was designed to accommodate the needs of the entire group rather than the individual.

The conflicts between members of different kin groups were of a different order. In minor cases—those dealing with adultery or debts—the issues were settled by having representatives of the local kin groups meet with the kin members involved. There was no formally composed group for the adjudication of such disputes, and meetings to hear these cases were held in villages or fields. Such factors as economic ties, friendship, marriage bonds, and the acceptance of an internal code of values aided in the settlement of these cases. The settlement usually resulted in payment of cattle.

In more serious sources of conflict, such as theft and insults, kin group heads in a village convened with older members of the community in a council (*lubeta*). A decision was reached by interviewing witnesses and evaluating the evidence. Here again, the primary method of removing the source of conflict was the exchange of property. In many cases the decisions reached by the *lubeta* were unanimous, but collection of the fine was assigned to the kin head or kin group of the injured party.

A different series of sociocultural procedures was brought into play when the conflict had territorial implications, concerned a large amount of property, or blood had been shed. Such cases included miscarriages, which inevitably meant the payment of twenty head of cattle; killing, whether accidental or purposeful; altercations in which blood had been shed; fighting between kin groups in a territory; or an unresolved court case that held the threat of violence. These cases were settled by a village council composed of all local leaders, plus the assistance of a neutral leader.

Each territory was the home of a dominant spirit or *mushimo*. The *mushimo* was represented by a shrine, a shrinekeeper, and a male who was periodically possessed by the territorial spirit. An extensive portion of the sparse Ila mythology explained the importance and functions of the local deity. It was generally assumed that the local deity was responsible for the well-being of the territory. The spirit was partially responsible for the fertility of the soil and of women, and was instrumental in bringing rain and in removing cattle diseases.

The critical person for the operation of the spirit was the individual possessed by the deity—through whom the evil spirits' desires and wishes were made known. The recruitment of these spokesmen differed sharply from that of the kinship leaders. In one territory, two were of slave ancestry, and in two cases the spokesman was a stranger from a different territory. There was no trace of a hereditary principle, and the relationship between the spokesmen and the kin groups was kept to a minimum. These individuals were not members of any kin group, and usually wandered from village to village in a territory. Informants stated that the spokesman was chosen by the spirit solely because of his goodwill and good heart; conversely, the spokesman was rejected by the spirit—was no longer possessed—when he became evil or when the spirit no longer believed in his good intentions.

Many crimes did not automatically invoke the *mushimo* spokesman, but if (for example) two kin groups in one *chisi* were embroiled over the division of a newly killed deer, and physical violence spread to the entire *chisi*, the spokesman was possessed and stated that the fighting should stop; and, since the entire community was involved, no fines would be paid. The council of kin heads convened at the sacred ground of the territorial deity, where a black ox was slaughtered, and all male members in the territory shared the meat. Many court cases were settled without any intervention of the spokesman, but in three recorded instances of murder and in two outbreaks of violence in which kin groups refused to pay fines, the medium was possessed.

It was difficult to ascertain whether the litigants accepted the decision of the local deity as promulgated by the medium if they perceived the decision to be unfair or excessively harsh, but an appropriate decision plus the announcement of the medium was usually sufficient to suppress further violence between groups. For example, in the murder cases in which a black ox was sacrificed to the local spirit and later eaten by members involved in the altercation, a fine of twenty-two head of cattle was levied, of which eleven were given to affiliated kin members of the deceased; the remainder was divided among the kin heads who composed the council. There was no further open retaliation from the wronged kin group.

The sanction to enforce any decision reached by the local spirit medium was vaguely allocated to the supernatural realm. The Ila believed that death and illness resulted if individuals disregarded the decision of the medium. No power of punishment was attributed to the medium; it was thought to reside solely with the spirit. It was not possible to obtain a specific example of a group or an individual who had suffered after disregarding the advice or suggestion of a person possessed by the local deity. The appearance of the spokesman of the local deity at court trials appeared to be a mechanism for resolving or preventing the extension of conflict in situations where the parties were unwilling or unable to accept formal decisions.

In another sphere of potential conflict, the local medium played a role in preventing conflict before it occurred. Witchcraft was common among the Ila, and many deaths were attributed to this practice. When a number of deaths occurred in a community, it was usual for the spokesman to be possessed and summon the community to the local shrine. Here the putative practitioner was named (sometimes by actual name, but sometimes only by allusion) and threatened with immediate death, or told death was going to follow.

THE SWAT PATHANS

The social structure of the Swat Pathans is more complex and includes a wider variety of social groups than the Ila. Pathans are members of patrilineal descent groups, castes, and occupational and residential groups based on such territorial units as villages, wards, areas, and subareas. Although the territorial units are administrative units, they are not the framework on which political power and processes operates.

A duality of leadership and two bases of authority existed in the power structure. One focus is the chief, or khan. The power and authority of a khan depends to a great degree upon security the loyalty of followers, and competition for followers was great. A following requires control of land, money, and women—all necessary factors for leadership—and an unceasing struggle for them took place.

The political groups are created and maintained by individuals who are able to manipulate and mobilize them. In order to retain the loyalty of the followers, land is loaned or rented to individuals and crops are distributed as gifts. Services of the other followers are bought by gifts and by promises of more gifts; and in some cases the support is guaranteed—or compelled—by threats and force. The struggle for followers, and therefore political authority, is constant. Political loyalty of house tenants, for sale to the highest bidder, is bought by rewards and security (Barth, 1959, p. 73).

The following of a leader is never secure; the number can diminish almost without warning. Because leaders are permanently in competition, their conflict centers around the basis of their authority. Land is encroached upon, litigation involving landownership is constant, and murders of landholders are not uncommon. In cases of conflict, the following of a khan is clearly identified. The marshaling of forces behind a leader is a clear indication of support and loyalty. A successful leader has to be virile, aggressive, strong: a person who chose extreme positions rather than one who searches for compromises.

The focal point for loyalty is the men's houses, where the khan provides food, drink, and amusement for his followers. A leader, therefore, requires financial support to provide (or at least give the appearance of providing) sumptuous hospitality. A sign of defection or of a change of allegiance is the absention of a khan's follower from the men's house.

"Khan" does not indicate incumbency in a formal office; there is no recognized hierarchy—the title implies merely a *claim* of power over others. The relationship between the khans is one of endemic conflict and instability. (A further source of great conflict springs from a series of alliances that increase the potentiality of larger conflict between blocs within Pathan society.)

The second segment of leadership is composed of the saints, fakirs or *mullahs* (dedicated and propertyless men). Their authority is based on their reputation for morality and holiness—plus, in some cases, control of land (usually donated by the khans to remove it as a source of conflict when the land was hotly disputed by a number of khans). Because of their religious position, the *mullahs* cannot employ the violent techniques of land seizure practiced by the khans (Barth, 1959, p. 93).

The saints, respected and followed by most of the population, derive most of their ability to influence affairs from supernatural sources, control over the graves of saintly ancestors, and their legal and moral dedication; their claim of spiritual leadership supports their ability to mediate and give advice (*ibid.*, p. 100). These features enabled them to stand aloof from the mundane daily competition for power and make them particularly suited for a measure of political control apart from and above conflict. Not only do they stand above conflict over material possessions, or a striving for followers, they display moderation, piety, and indifference to physical pleasure and withdrawal from the petty and sordid aspects of common life (*ibid.*, p. 101). In essence, they shield themselves from the social groups by not partaking of the daily life in the men's houses or in gatherings at weddings and on holidays.

One of the major functions or roles of a saint is that of mediator. In a conflict between two khans over land and followers, both parties delegate their authority to one holy man. During this period of mediation the saint "held their fate in the hollow of his hand," and had considerable freedom in reaching his decision (*ibid.*, p. 97). His prime political function is to continually arrange compromises and reduce the tensions of conflict.

The holy man, or saint, has no institutionalized means of enforcing his decision; although the parties in conflict usually submitted, they could not be forced to adhere to his decision. The major power of the saints—as we have suggested—derives from their structural neutrality and their ability to suggest a compromise from a disinterested position. A major support in their ability to influence decisions is directly related to their function as mediator, which derives from the situation itself. When equally balanced forces neared conflict, acceptance of the compromise effected the necessary reduction of tension. In addition, because struggles between the khans were never-ending, the khans could not openly refuse to accept the saints' proposed compromises, for they knew they would have to turn to them eventually.

CONCLUSIONS

Although a controlled comparison that is based upon two societies is by no means conclusive, striking similarities in leadership recruitment and in the operation of the political systems is suggestive. In both cases, the leader's base and support is a relatively stable social group, and he is aided by economic and religious supports. These leaders and their followers are the focus of conflict; and kin or representational leaders seem to dominate the political processes—such as the mobilization of alliances—and to control the economic allocations. Variation in patterns of recruitment and in degrees of authority (as other writers have indicated) is heavily influenced by the economic levels and by the size and type of groups they head and represent (Sahlins, 1958; Fallers, 1946; Leach, 1954; Southall, 1956; Sutton, 1959).

However, in the processes of a total political system it appears that one function of a political system is to reduce conflict while facilitating the maintenance of the system. The political power for containing conflict within defined boundaries, in the two cases we have described, is wielded by another type of leader. This authority role, however, is without a stable following or body of adherents, and this narrowly limits its range of operation in the political processes.

These leaders do not command the authority to levy sanctions. They are able to influence individuals, but they can rarely initiate political processes. They are involved in the reduction or resolution of conflict that is particularly disruptive of society. The actions of these leaders are critical for the perpetuation of the major structural alignments of the society. In fact, these leaders appear to be instrumental in maintaining the overall structure of the political system, and without them—and their political impartiality—the system could not operate.

It is suggested that one organizational feature of some political systems is the allocation of authority to individuals who do not represent any one well-defined group. Some explanation for this has been touched on by other authors. Schneider (1957), in his discussion of supernatural incest and sanction among the Yapese, offers the suggestion that where the application of authority has the potential of disrupting a group it is assigned to supernatural deities or to political roles that are not clearly related to any member of the social groups. Harper (1957) concludes that when a society lacks strong power positions the resulting political equality precludes the possibility of strong localized authority, and political authority is assigned to supernatural authorities.

These explanations place too great a stress upon the supernatural features of political roles and ignore the specific content of the political processes. This type of allocation of authority, we suggest, is profitably viewed not in the light of decentralized political systems, or a lack of permanent roles within the community, but as a general characteristic of every political system. In all social systems it is likely that some conflicts emerge that a single group cannot resolve because it is completely identified with the struggle.

On-going political processes may require a great deal of impartiality in some cases of adjudication. The operation of adjudicative political roles is facilitated by great degrees of impartiality. Among the Ila and Swat Pathans, this was not achieved by recruiting on a group basis but by recruiting selectively, and by clothing the political role in impartiality. Thus the interlocking of social recruitment and cultural mechanism structurally removed the political leaders from the interwoven kin, caste, and territorial network. The cultural patterns of the political system had mechanisms, such as possession, selective recruitment, and ideology, that facilitated the assignment of authority to these roles. These cultural mechanisms increased the appearance of impartiality in the operation of the political functions. The political roles acted as intermediaries between groups, and their authority depended primarily upon their disengagement from the web of affilations.

REFERENCES

BARTH, FREDRIK. 1959. Political leadership among the Swat Pathans. London School of Economics, Monograph of Social Anthropology, No. 19.
EVANS-PRITCHARD, E. E., and FORTES, MEYER. 1940. (eds.), African political systems. Oxford University Press.

FALLERS, LLOYD. 1956. Bantu bureaucracy. Cambridge: W. Heffner.

GEERTZ, CLIFFORD. 1960. The Javanese kijaji: the changing role of a cultural broker. Comparative Studies in Society and History, 2, 2, 228-249.

HARPER, EDWARD B. 1957. Hoylu: a belief relating justice and the supernatural. American Anthropologist, 59, 801-816.

LEACH, EDMUND. 1954. Political systems of highland Burma. Harvard University Press.

OTTENBERG, S. 1958. Ibo oracles and intergroup relations. Southwestern Journal of Anthropology, 14, 3, 130-143.

SAHLINS, MARSHALL D. 1958. Social stratification in Polynesia. University of Washington Press.

SOUTHALL, AIDEN W. 1956. Alur society. Cambridge: W. Heffner.

SUTTON, FRANCIS S. 1959. Representation and the nature of political systems. Comparative Studies in Society and History, 1, 1-10.

SCHNEIDER, DAVID M. 1957. Political organization, supernatural sanctions and the punishment for incest on Yap. American Anthropologist, 59, 791-800.

TUDEN, A. 1958. Comments on the non-western political process. Journal of World Politics, 702-705.

SOME POLITICAL ASPECTS OF CLANSHIP IN A MODERN CHINESE CITY [1]

Morton H. Fried,[2] COLUMBIA UNIVERSITY

Before getting into the body of observations, a few comments of general nature will be useful. It would obviously distort the purpose of this article to include anything but the sketchiest discussion of the relationship between the culture of Taiwan and that of mainland China. Since certain aspects of that relationship are inescapably political, they cannot be avoided. For example, is Taiwan to be treated simply as another Chinese province? The Nationalist government, and the Communists who seek to displace it, are alike in maintaining that this is precisely the way in which Taiwan must be approached. There is a small contingent of separatists, at least partially in exile, that prefers not to consider Taiwan as Chinese, pointing to the Taiwanese absorption through the past several centuries of genes and cultural traits from aborigines, Europeans, and Japanese. In my own observation, Taiwan is no more deviant from abstract national Chinese norms than any other province I have visited. The kind and degree of non-*Han* ethnic penetration varies not only from province to province but also from county to county, and can easily accommodate Taiwan. This includes European contact and penetration, as well as that of the southern and northern "barbarians."

More serious is the relatively shallow history of Chinese settlement in Taiwan and its very late incorporation as a Chinese province. Though Chinese knowledge of the island is claimed from the sixth century, so little was done during the next millennium that the Ming rulers were quite pleased, in 1624, to offer Taiwan to the Dutch as a reward for leaving the offshore Pescadores. The Dutch foothold lasted less than forty years and made no significant impression. Of far greater importance has been the legacy of fact and legend left by Koxinga, the military genius

[1] By "political" I refer to all activities designed to secure optimum benefits from the structures of power in a society, where "power" is the ability to channelize the behavior of others through actual or threatened use of sanctions. By "clanship" I refer to all activities that comprise and that flow from membership in a corporate unilineal descent group whose constituents, as a whole, are related through stipulated ties.

[2] I wish to express my gratitude to the National Science Foundation and the John Simon Guggenheim Memorial Foundation for their support of the fieldwork upon which this paper is based. Needless to say, neither foundation is in any way responsible for any of the statements that follow.

285

who not only held out as a Ming loyalist against the Manchus, who had conquered the mainland, but struck (with varying degrees of success) against the coast on more than one occasion.

Born of a Japanese mother and a Chinese father (only the mother is honored in the recently restored Koxinga temple in Tainan; the father, Cheng Chih-lung, defected to the Ch'ing), Koxinga (Cheng Ch'eng-kung) is a dual political symbol in contemporary Taiwan. For the Nationalist exiles he represents an earlier honorable refusal to endure a barbarian conquest of China. For the Chinese born in Taiwan he represents the heterogeneous origins of the Taiwanese, and their strength and vitality.

If the Nationalists avoid seeing Koxinga's cause as lost, the Taiwanese seem to ignore his early death, which came only one year after his victory over the Dutch. Independent Taiwan was to endure some twenty more years, until, in 1683, the Ch'ing overran it—refusing to grant concessions to the boy-ruler, Koxinga's grandson. The Chinese population at that time is estimated by Professor Ch'en Shao-hsing (1962, p. 7) to have been about 34,000. It is significant that the growth represented by this figure, though partly natural, was spurred by continuous migration from the mainland, despite the most severe Manchu restrictions against such movements—restrictions that included the forced evacuation of all inhabitants from the Fukienese coast opposite the island, to a depth of one hundred miles in some regions.

After the Manchu conquest of the island, it was administered as a frontier extension of the province of Fukien. Most of the island was not originally included in the administrative structure, but, as the population grew and pushed back or acculturated or assimilated the aborigines, the area under nominal central control grew. A good portion of the growth continued to be attributable to migration. It is said that many of the earliest settlers were Hakka Cantonese, but by the early nineteenth century the pattern of dominance was already set.

The largest segment of the population, 82 per cent (Hsieh, 1964, p. 149), was Fukienese. Though some minor ethnic and linguistic differences separated them into at least two populations, the Hokkien and Hoklo, they were capable of joining together and making common cause —or at least of suppressing their rivalry—in favor of directing their hostilities against a third force. In most instances this was the Hakka population. A minority in terms of total island population, the Hakka concentrated in a few localities, where they exercised a high degree of control.

In boundary areas and in regions where, for various reasons, population fluctuated, there was endemic hostility. The villages in such areas were armed camps, often built and manned like fortresses. Conflicts usually started as purely local affairs, but at fairly frequent intervals they spread to neighboring villages, and sometimes threatened the peace of entire counties. On several occasions large scale wars, in the form of rebellions, shook most of Taiwan. Described as uprisings against the Manchus, they were almost invariably accompanied by a polarization of the population into Fukienese and Hakka armies. Despite the ideology of loyalism and rebellion, it is likely that most of the ordinary troops were most conscious of fighting the local ethnic enemy.

This situation was already well known on the mainland, and its effects on social organization are difficult to exaggerate. Maurice Freedman (1958) has given us an interesting analysis of the phenomenon; and a more detailed account relating to the struggles between the Cantonese and the Hakka of Kwangtung province is contained in an unpublished essay by Myron Cohen (1963). If anything, the situation was even more extreme in Taiwan. Physically, Taiwan was at least as remote from the central power as were the isolated valleys of Fukien and Kwangtung. Taiwan was also strongly subject to what Wittfogel has called "the law of diminishing administrative returns," as the main elements of imperial rule regarded the island as almost beyond the pale of civilization. The result was that much of the substance of actual government was left to nongovernmental associations. Playing a major role among these were localized lineages.

Taiwan continued to be administered as a frontier region of Fukien until 1887, when it was finally given provincial status and structure. Only eight years later the Japanese took over. Taiwan was now to experience fifty years as a colony. The period was one of profound change, compared with the previous 250 years.

Among the major alterations were several of particular relevance to this paper. The Japanese constructed highways and extended the insignificant railway trackage until most of the west coast, the area of population concentration, was brought within the range of rapid communications. Japanese administration penetrated into the villages and succeeded, more or less rapidly, in making armed group conflict a monopoly of the state. A number of changes in economic arrangements affected the older, financially based political power, and led to a revision of the channels of mobility. Though anticipating by only a few years the elimination of the imperial examination system in China, and its massive effects, the Japanese reform of the local educational system was sudden and sharp, and set in motion a train of changes that echoed for years in the Taiwanese social system.

Finally, although the Japanese created no new cities, they made considerable alteration in the ones that existed. Urban units increased in size and changed in relative importance; it is perhaps not an overstatement to say that the Japanese introduced the modern city to Taiwan; certainly they initiated the modernization of the cities. Supremely relevant for our immediate concern, this process was implicated in the sharp growth of an old institution, the clans.

Retrocession, as the Nationalist government calls the return of Taiwan to its authority in 1945, brought an even more accelerated process of change. Through the period of Japanese control, only a small Japanese population accumulated, and rather slowly. The total never went much above 400,000. By contrast, the mainlanders who came after the collapse of the Nationalist government did so in one main burst. It is not known how many came, but in addition to military personnel numbering about 600,000, the migrants are conservatively estimated to have exceeded half a million—and may have run more than twice that figure. Estimates of the proportion of mainlanders in present-day Taiwan range from a minimum of about 8 per cent to a maximum of 25 per cent. (The latter figure, which I believe is far too high, is from Latourette, 1964, p. 42.)

Many of these migrants, including the military, settled in the cities, which now grew at tremendous rates. Taipei is a metropolis of more than a million, excluding residential suburbs and industrial satellite towns that lift its population figure even higher. This growth is not the result of migration alone. One of the complex products of Japanese rule was a large and generally continuous decline in the death rate both in urban and rural areas. Furthermore, the Japanese had provided latent and sometimes manifest encouragement for the movement of rural folk into the cities. Both of these trends burgeoned after retrocession.

Aspects of change in Taiwan are numerous and interesting. In fairness to the topic stated in the title, however, only one more feature of change will be presented. Because of its profound effect upon the phenomena being considered, mention must be made of the program of land reform so successfully carried out in Taiwan. Although the focus has been on rural areas, there has been direct and immediate impact on the cities. Furthermore, though less publicized, a program of urban land reform combines zoning and restrictions on rents, and this also has had continuing effects on the associations we are discussing.

With regard to land reform, two things should be noted. It was not the first such effort in Taiwan, but it was undertaken in such a way, and with such efficiency, as to completely separate it from all previous attempts, including the abortive scheme of Liu Ming-chuan, the governor during the immediate, pre-Japanese period, and the very partial reforms carried out by the Japanese themselves. Secondly, it is a fact that the Nationalists were totally unsuccessful at carrying out any serious land reform when they controlled the mainland. That they were able to do so in Taiwan is clearly related to their total independence from, not to mention hostility to, the Taiwanese landlords.

Reluctantly circumscribing this rapid overview of the historical matrix in which the contemporary phenomenon of the clanship of Taiwan is rooted, we must turn our attention to clanship itself. As the description and analysis proceeds, it will be seen that each of the elements mentioned has played an important role in producing the current configuration. Far from being moribund, kinship retains a great deal of vitality as an organizing principle in the segment of Chinese society that continues in Taiwan; and much of this vitality is directed at political goals.

CLANS AND CLAN ASSOCIATIONS

The term "clan" would better fit most of the groups being discussed here, but some are "clan associations"—in the best sense. Most of the group memberships are comprised of persons of a single surname, some of whom can demonstrate their relationships to each other, but most stipulate relationship simply on the basis of common possession of the surname. Membership involves the assumption of common descent, sometimes from an ancestor only a few hundred years removed, more often from a mythical or quasi-historical figure. In some cases the ancestor is said to have lived in the remote past, as in the case of the Ch'ens, who claim descent from Shen Nung, a culture hero said to have lived 4,500 years ago (who has been deified as the spirit of agriculture). These, then, are clans; they fit remarkably well with a definition offered some years ago (Fried, 1957).

There are also associations that comprise members of more than one *hsing* or surname, a phenomenon well known to the overseas Chinese and well represented in the United States. For example, the Gee How Oak Tin brings together people of four surnames: Yüan, Yüan, Wu, and Ch'en.[3] Perhaps better known is the Lung-kong kongsi, which unites the surnames of the famous sworn friends of the Three Kingdoms: Liu, Kuan, Chang, and Chao. Several similarly structured sodalities in Taiwan should be distinguished by the designation "clan association" because they bring together into one organization two or more groups of people with discrete traditions of common descent. Sometimes, as in the Gee How Oak Tin clan assocation, there are stories that the component *hsing* are closely related; that the people now bearing one of the surnames formerly had one of the others but had it changed for some reason or another—perhaps to avoid persecution after the fall of a dynasty or after an abortive rebellion. Others, however, do not have myths of common origin but may simply attribute their association to some fortuitous event that had drawn their remote ancestors together.

Membership in clans and clan associations is sometimes ascribed, sometimes achieved. Actually, in contemporary Taiwan there are two types of formal structure for these groups, and a particular group may have one or both types of structure. One, the *tz'u-t'ang*, tends to be a tightly structured corporate unit with carefully apportioned rights, duties, and privileges. The other, known as *t'ung-ch'in hui*, is loosely organ-

---

[3] With the exception of Gee How Oak Tin and the Lung-kong associations, all Chinese words in this paper are given in standard Wade-Giles transcriptions of their Mandarin pronunciation.

ized, with a theoretically unbounded membership that comprises all people of the same surname, including those from different parts of China, of different languages, and even of different ethnic origins.

The former grouping, at least as far as Taiwan is concerned, has in recent years further distinguished itself by registering with the authorities as a *ts'ai-t'uan fa-jen*, or a nonprofit corporation. Such legal entities, which usually restrict membership and its privileges to those who have entered one or more ancestor tablets, or to the descendants of those who had, may exist side by side, in the same shared quarters, with the less restrictive type of group. What this amounts to is a throwing open of the temple, on the great ritual occasions, to all those of common surname who wish to come.

MEMBERSHIP IN CLANS AND CLAN ASSOCIATIONS

Membership in the *tz'u-t'ang* is symbolized and validated by ownership of one or more ancestor tablets in the clan temple. Membership in the *t'ung-ch'in hui* does not necessarily mean that one owns a tablet displayed in the clan hall; it is assumed that all participants are descendants of the founding ancestor, and they do not have to be specifically represented by any other, nearer ancestor. In the *tz'u-t'ang*, however, each member is represented by at least one tablet, which, for the purposes of membership, is associated exclusively with him and with no one else, not even his brother. Where two or more brothers may be considered members of a *tz'u-t'ang*, each will be associated with a discrete tablet or tablets.

No dilemma is caused by the fact that each tablet represents one and only one male ancestor, or by the fact that one individual's name appears on one and only one tablet in the temple. (In the clan temples of Taipei it invariably represents at least two people, since the wife's name is included. Some tablets also give the names of second wives.) The dilemma is avoided because a living individual can enter (*chin-chu*) his own tablet—that is, a tablet with his own name on it—during his lifetime. Such tablets are either covered with a fitted red cloth or have the names of the living persons covered with strips of red paper. They are known not as *tzu-p'ien*, ancestor tablets, but as *ch'ang-shou p'ien*, long-life tablets.

Although some persons enter their own tablets while alive, most prefer not to do so, apparently for a mixture of reasons, included fear of symbolically simulating death and the desire to avoid the expense, which is compounded of the costs of the tablet, the sacrifices at installation time, and the very large fee that must be paid to the temple for the seat, the spot that is occupied by the tablet. In a few temples there is no differentiation in the price of tablet-seats, but most have three ranks, designated by the usual Chinese *chia-i-ping* system. Prices fluctuate from temple to temple, and seem at least partially related to supply and demand. Accordingly, the highest prices are demanded by one of the oldest clan temples, which is also that of one of the most populous surnames in Taiwan. In this temple the only space available is in the lowest rank, which currently goes for NT$5000 (US$125).

Once a tablet is installed, many of the temples make no further demands for fees from the living person whose membership involves the tablet. Only a few temples ask for small amounts, paid annually, with which they purchase incense, ghost money, and other incidentals of worship, and pay for an annual or semiannual cleanup. Still others charge their members for the annual or semiannual banquets that conclude the one or two great ritual occasions of the year. Some rich and powerful temples charge nothing for maintenance, and give their entire memberships a free banquet, at which more than eight hundred people will be assembled.

SELECTED ECONOMIC ASPECTS

Unfortunately, the variety of circumstances of origination is too great to permit simple generalization about the source of real estate among clans with discrete and proper temples. However, common to almost all the relatively solvent temples is a time of past crisis when the "ownership" and/or management of the temple properties was wrested from the hands of a particular individual, who is often described as having been actively assisted and abetted by his immediate family. The forces that separated the "corrupt" old man from his "improperly obtained" estate usually comprised a coalition of persons active in the outside world, and of somewhat modern outlook, though this does not mean "westernized."

The stated and unstated reasons for the action were often quite complex, and cannot be analyzed here; suffice it to say that the coalition invariably identified itself as a formal body and adopted a euphonious name, such as the *Tun-mu hui*, "Committee to Promote Intimate Relationships." Though my sample is so limited as to make generalization dangerous, the main pivot of action was the committee's legal seizure of the estate—which seems to have been done with the tacit approval and perhaps even the active assistance of the Japanese during the 1930's. My own investigations of the activities of the period have been fragmentary, deriving from limited delving into the recent history of a particular clan, but there is a suggestion that the shift of managerial authority in the clans reflected the desire of the Japanese to eliminate traditional politico-economic strong points. Thus, it is not unusual to have an ousted manager described as an imperial degree-holder, whose successors were men who had achieved positions in the Japanese-dominated government or in commercial enterprises that were frequently under the control of the colonial rulers.

Before I go further, some clarification is necessary. Clans and lineages have existed on Taiwan for a long time; both go back to the earliest period of settlement, and can be traced even beyond, to previous groupings on the mainland. I have the impression that in Taiwan, as in southeastern China, clans have generally been weak and lineages have been strong. It was close to the turn of the present century that the balance shifted, and the coincidence of the Japanese seizure of the island and the decline of the lineage is not difficult to understand. The strength of lineages in Chinese society has varied greatly with time and place, so that any attempt at simple generalizations is more likely to mislead than inform. It is well established, however, that the adjacent area of southeastern China, particularly the home province of Fukien, has seen the greatest florescence of the Chinese lineage in modern times.

Constellating kin groups with tendencies to accumulate economic, political, and even military power have been found troublesome to central governments at various times in the long history of China. (Much interesting work could be done in this area; see, for example, Wang [1943].) Knowledge of the history of conflict between government and extended kin groups is not necessary to establish Japanese antagonism to such associations, if one realizes that lineages and clans definitely cut across class lines. In China this is common knowledge, accepted and acted upon with little conscious concern. Along with the scatter from wealth to poverty, however, is the common phenomenon of control vested in the wealthiest and most successful members. Simply put, organization heads, in return for favors, loans, patronage, and other kindly dispensations, reap loyalty and solidarity that may be turned to their political advantage. We will say more about this, in the forms it has taken in contemporary Taiwan, after a few more details about the economic foundations of lineages and clans.

The lineages, until fairly recently, were strongly based on fairly extensive holdings. While some strong lineages are totally rural, few (if any) have been strictly urban; many lineages found in the cities have significant portions of their total holdings in the countryside. Most estates are derived from the holdings of a single individual who, between 100 and 250 years ago, achieved a higher degree and appointment to a major office. Although this usually took him away from Taiwan for much of his career, the returns of office, both direct and indirect, appeared in the growth of real property held by his family and in the physical expansion of the house in which the family lived. A century or even fifty years ago, the holdings of some lineages, whose memberships comprised the demonstrated descendants of a successful scholar-bureaucrat, were of such size as to furnish a comfortable basis for life for several hundred people, most of whom lived as rentiers.

The Japanese gradually undercut these lineages by pursuing a moderate program of land reform and redistribution. I think it fair to say that the edifice of the lineage began to show cracks but still stood in fair repair. It took the land reform program of the present Nationalist government to produce the shock waves that seem to herald the collapse of these kin groups. Right now, in many places in Taiwan, the members of lineages hover like vultures above a dying animal, all attention, and determined not to lose *i fen,* a penny, of their share of the general inheritance.

The clans, meanwhile, are faring otherwise. Unable to offer a brief, specific capsule of the history of the clan as a Taiwanese institution, I would like to note that the clan temples in Taiwan in their present forms date back about 75 years or so. Most of them constructed such edifices as they have by raising contributions from wealthy "clan-brothers," taking pains to diversify the sources of this largesse so that no single lineage would assume total dominance. With the funds, land was purchased and construction begun. Originally, some of those in Taipei clustered around the old Confucius temple. When the Japanese took over the site to construct their offices of government, they compensated the clans that lost property by giving them land in another part of the city; the Confucius temple was also moved.

In these exchanges of land, I do not know how the various temples fared, nor have I seen anything about the negotiations that must certainly have preceded the final settlement. I can say, however, that each of the temples known to me found itself situated on a relatively large plot, only a portion of which was covered by the actual temple. Even after space was turned into ornamental gardens, there was still a surplus of land and with the developing pressure of urban land use, this area was ultimately covered with rows of shops or dwellings, so that rent returns became the largest single source of revenue for the clans. Additional sources of revenue can be quickly itemized: fees for entering tablets, fees for attending the nonexclusive nursery schools (an almost ubiquitous feature of clan temples in Taipei), and voluntary contributions of members and of nonmember "clan-brothers." (The nonmembers are almost entirely recruited from among overseas Chinese—particularly the most affluent of those who live in the Philippines.)

The organization of the economy of a clan temple is a welter of details from which certain facts stand out. The tedium of the balance sheets is periodically enlivened by conflict and controversy as factions form and fall out over the management of the enterprise. Though the amounts of capital handled tend to be small, they are equivalent to those that are turned over in a fairly large Taiwanese commercial enterprise. Some of these temples have a regular payroll and fifteen to twenty full-time employees; single contributions from wealthy overseas associations at the time of temple reconstruction may be more than $1,000 (U.S.).

The handling of funds is not at all familial but follows commercial practices. A temple has a board of controllers that supervises the handling of all receipts and disbursements. Some of the more prosperous clan temples have a professional staff that handles financial affairs on a day to day basis. They are responsible for the collection of rents, clan fees, school fees, and other receipts, and thely pay salaries, taxes, and other items of indebtedness. Even small purchases must be receipted, and every expenditure of consequence requires an officer of the temple to solicit three price estimates, from which he is obliged, other things being equal, to select the lowest. In spite of safeguards, suspicion of fraud is common, and sometimes erupts in nasty charges and countercharges.

CLANS AND POLITICS

Space does not permit discussion of the practical internal politics of a clan. (A later paper will examine the political structure of these clans, their methods of reaching and implementing decisions, and the relations between this internal political structure and the clan economy.) We will therefore consider the clan as a political form in the larger society of the present Republic of China. Even with this limitation, it is possible to concentrate on only a few aspects that may be of particular interest. Accordingly, I will deal briefly with four phenomena: (1) the political uses of clan rituals, (2) the uses of clanship in drawing together Taiwanese and mainlanders, (3) the uses of clanship as legal and quasi-legal functions, and (4) the uses of clanship in elections.

As each of these is treated, we should remember that we are dealing with the use of kinship in a politically sophisticated society, and, what is more, with its use in the most concentratedly urban sectors.

POLITICAL USES OF RITUAL

The word for religious rituals is *pai-pai*, and they seem more prevalent in Taiwan than anywhere else in China. That is to say, the Taiwanese seem to outdo their Fukienese ancestors in the pure frequency of their ceremonials, and that is quite a trick, because the Fukienese have long been outstanding in this regard. The very great development of ritual occasions among the Taiwanese has run afoul of the Nationalist government, which, stating that it is at war with the government on the mainland, has attempted to have the population of the province accept austerity as a way of life. This is extended to ceremonies, so that all sacrifices and banquets are supposed to be kept within bounds of moderation. Despite heavy propaganda, the government does not seem to be winning its point. It seems unwilling to use real sanctions to accomplish this end, and may feel that such an attempt would at the very least be branded hypocritical, for (despite some cases in which personal examples of austerity have been set) the government itself participates freely in a ceremonial complex that reaches a peak of display and expense in the Double-ten festivities commemorating the founding of the republic.

The ceremonial calendar of the clan temples is generally quite full, though the variations from temple to temple are extreme. Every temple has at least one major ceremony-cum-banquet a year, many have two, and some have more; the irreducible minimum is a celebration of either the spring or autumn sacrifices, but they are frequently paired. Hundreds of people gather for these occasions.

The basic ritual is a variation of that which can be seen once every year, in September, at the Confucius temple, as the "Birthday of the Master" is celebrated. There, a most important role is played by the ruler of the country, or by his surrogate, who is invariably of cabinet rank. Similarly, the semiannual commemoration of the ancestor in the clan temples is attended by a government official or by a surrogate.

Actually, most clan sacrifices of this kind are visited by two sorts of official representatives. A petty municipal official participates on behalf of the government and fulfills a legal requirement that such a functionary be present. Larger and more affluent clans are polite and proper in their dealings with this representative, but tend to eclipse him by inviting much more important figures. Thus when the Ch'en clan held a major sacrifice a few years ago to celebrate the extensive rebuilding of the temple, the chief guest was the late Ch'en Cheng, then vice-president and premier of the republic. (General Ch'en presented the temple with a large ceremonial plaque that now hangs over the main inner entrance to the temple.) The vice-president, a mainlander, was unable to attend subsequent sacrifices, but he usually delegated a younger brother to represent him.

The physical trappings in the temple at the time of a major sacrifice emphasize the ritual focus on ancestor worship. The carcasses of a hog and a goat (sometimes rented for the occasion) are prominently displayed, the altars literally sag beneath the heaped offerings of food and strong drink, and a heady aroma of incense saturates the air. But there are secular political touches, such as the national flag, pictures of Sun Yat-sen and Chiang Kai-shek (the latter sometimes missing), and slogans such as RETAKE THE MAINLAND! written on colored paper and pasted on the walls. In a real sense, the situation is used to demonstrate loyalty to the regime.

Important officials resist efforts to have them arrive early, and they appear only at the last moment. They are made comfortable in the guest parlor and are given refreshments, and the most renowned and wisest clan members (carefully chosen in advance) chat with them. It is at this time that relationships are made or reinforced, relationships that may be useful to the clan as a whole, when at a later date, eager to obtain easing of its tax burden or to obtain permission to increase rents, etc., the powerful figures will be approached for aid more directly. Simultaneously, individuals curry personal favor that they may be able to convert to advantage as situations arise in their lives and circles that can benefit from name-dropping, or somewhat more active use of powerful acquaintances.

TAIWANESE AND MAINLANDERS

The Nationalist government actively seeks to build an image of present-day Taiwan that features peaceful, pleasant accommodation as the mode of interaction between Taiwanese and mainlanders. There is ample evidence (which we shall not go into here) that the picture thus presented falls short of the reality—although overt antigovernment activity is subdued to the point that casual observers may be led to believe it nonexistent.

One of the main functions of clans in present-day Taiwan, both manifestly and latently, is to cement relations between these two sectors of the community. One way of doing this, as we have seen, is to involve mainlanders of high rank in the rituals of the clan, but other methods are also used, though none universally. The primary means, logically, is to incorporate ordinary mainlanders of common surname into the membership. Some clans, such as the Hsu, have had some success at this, though I cannot say much about the means by which it was accomplished. The great preponderance of members of the Hsu clan is Taiwanese, but there is a small but significant portion of mainlanders. What is more, some of the latter have risen to positions of leadership in the organization. (The mainlanders are not of homogeneous background but represent several provinces, and—though all whom I have met speak Mandarin—they have various dialectical backgrounds in terms of their mother tongue.)

Most of the clans for which data were gathered do not crosscut Taiwanese-mainlander distinctions as far as membership is concerned. This is most emphatically the case with the older, better-established local clans, which prefer to extend relations with mainlanders primarily through the institution of tsu-hsiung, "clan brotherhood," which admits a person to the circle of stipulated kin but not to the inner corporation. Similar treatment is accorded the huach'iao, or overseas Chinese.

The relations between the overseas Chinese and the clan associations are of great interest, but cannot be gone into here. It is in the realm of overseas Chinese activity that the national government makes one of its explicit uses of the clan, encouraging them to woo and involve the expatriates as a means of securing their loyalties to the country, and of course to the Kuomintang. Political functions in this arena are closely tied to economic ones: the involved huach'iao invest through contributions to clans and similar institutions, by direct contributions to the government (largely for the construction of schools), and by maintaining commercial relations with Taiwan through local investment or trade.

Individual *huach'iao* may go for years without setting foot in the clan temple, but their presence is continually acknowledged. Banners hang on the temple walls, commemorating the closeness of ties between the clan and its overseas analogues; physical testimony of the latest contributions is commonly displayed in the form of inscriptions on stone or metal, giving the exact sums and their kind provenance.

In return, the clan furnishes functions that run a gamut of subtlety. It should not be forgotten that many of the temples are physically impressive, though some are run-down. Overseas Chinese, particularly those who are most acutely aware of being cut off from the mainland, can feel that somewhere their own traditional functions of ancestor veneration are still being carried on, lending stability and continuity to an otherwise topsy-turvy world. Beyond the sacred and ceremonial lies a more diffuse collection of benefits: connections, a *pied-à-terre,* a potential protection for travelers.

With regard to the latter, an overseas Chinese merchant who had recently come to Taipei on business was found dead in a hotel room and was declared a suicide by the police. His relatives back home refused to accept this version of the death. They solicited the help of their clan association in Taipei, and its authorities went to great lengths to keep the matter before the police officials and in the press. After many months, there were sudden arrests, a trial, and two men were convicted of the murder of the clan-brother.

The national government seems to be in conflict about policy toward the clan associations. It supports their activities, particularly with reference to their wooing of overseas Chinese; on the other hand, it sometimes does petty things to reduce the clan's importance. Most importantly, it has failed to work out a clear-cut mechanism whereby the clans can escape the loss of their capital bases through the combination of high taxes and low, controlled rents. The ambivalence of the KMT in this matter is in contrast to the certainty of the mainland, where the communist government has rigorously, and apparently ruthlessly, suppressed the clan organization.

Mainlanders show little inclination to seek membership in existing Taiwanese clans, but many new clans have been formed in the last few years, and almost all of these, to my knowledge, have been formed primarily by mainlanders, though attracting some Taiwanese participation. When I was last in Taiwan, I attended two meetings at which such groups were being formed, and my assistant attended other such meetings. This activity is testimony to the role the clans play in contemporary urban Chinese life, and will bear continued investigation.

LEGAL AND QUASI-LEGAL FUNCTIONS

The case of the murdered clan-brother illustrates only one law-oriented function of the clans. From the variety of others, a few examples can be presented without much detail or analysis.

The clan serves as a semiformal forum for communicating messages from the government to the people, and vice versa. New laws, especially those relating to property and taxes, are formally discussed as they relate to the life of the organization and informally as they pertain to the personal fortunes of the members. In addition to circulating information, these meetings, both formal and informal, help place lay members in the company of persons of higher skills: officials and lawyers. Though most of this advice is available at firsthand only to the relatively small cadre of clan officials who meet with some frequency and regularity, it is not unusual for such a clan official to have someone else in mind during the discussion, which he manipulates so as to cover the points in which he is interested.

Less frequent is the use of the clan as an organ of mediation. Rarely, if ever, would an entire clan be used as such, though it *is* possible, since most of them meet in plenary sessions once a year, usually in conjunction with either the spring or autumn sacrifice. At such times it is possible to raise any issue that may be considered to relate to the clan. More frequently, matters at dispute are discussed informally by the directors, who advise the principals of their recommendations. Strictly informal, their advice is not coupled with formal sanctions and cannot be enforced.

Indeed, the clan appears to have only the most moderate of social control functions. Although most of the clans have clauses in their printed constitutions (all clans must have written consitutions and must register them with the provincial government) that state that members will be expelled for traitorous or similarly antisocial behavior, most members say that it is really impossible to evict a member. Certainly it is impossible to evict a tablet, even a *ch'ang-shou p'ien,* the long-life tablet of a living member. The main sanction is disapprobation, expressed through scolding, ridicule, and public accusation. It takes place mainly among the officials within the temple, but it can be employed more generally. In any case, it is not a major function of this aggregation.

This probably is an area of great change, for the clans formerly functioned as quasi-legal courts, keeping disputes out of formal courts. From a traditional posture of avoidance with regard to formal legal apparatus, the Chinese, at least those observed in Taiwan, seemed positively litigious. A great volume of cases is being taken to the courts, with a consequent atrophy of the clans' adjudicative functions.

CLANSHIPS IN ELECTIONS

While this study of clans was in progress, Taiwan held elections on the local level. Taipei elected a mayor, and the clans were beehives of activity and discussion. To my knowledge, each of the five persons who have served as mayor of Taipei during the post-restoration period has been an important figure in the clan association to which he belongs. This does not mean that active membership is indispensable to election, but it implies that politicians place some value on these things.

In fact, of the five candidates in the recent Taipei mayoralty race, the three who led the field had paid great attention to the clans. The campaign coincided (in part) with the season during which most of the clans hold their important sacrifices, and the candidates sent flowers and scrolls, and sought invitations—not only to the ceremonies but also to the subsequent banquets. They made speeches and drank toasts and made themselves as visible as possible.

At least two of the candidates identified themselves strongly with their own clans. The man who won the election, and is presently mayor, has for some time taken a major role in the affairs of his clan, and months before anything was said about his intention to run (he appeared to be a reluctant, last-minute addition to the list of candidates) I had seen him appear as Master of the Ritual at his clan's fall observances. Shortly before the election, at the spring sacrifice, he played the same role, but he left immediately after the ceremony, avoiding a formal plenary meeting that was marked by an acrimonious discussion of the condition of the temple.

One of the candidates vainly attempted to obtain the formal backing of the clan of the same name as his own. He was not a member, but could point to a number of tablets in the hall as those of relatives—though none, of course, were his. A special meeting was called, at which only a small portion of the officers of the clan assembled, the others sending regrets; and the candidate spoke to them at length, seeking to win their overt support, which would permit him to make a plea (on the clan letterhead) to the great number of persons of that surname living in Taipei. For a variety of complex reasons, he was unsuccessful. The clans conduct themselves with great seriousness in these matters.

CONCLUSIONS

Everyone knows that kinship does not "drop dead" in the face of modernization and urbanization, but there is certainly evidence that kinship plays a smaller share of the total role in the course of modernization and urbanization; and the attempt to rule it out completely is, to say the least, premature. In various other contexts I have stated and elaborated my opinion that mainland China under the communist regime has waged a war on extended kin units and not on the family per se, but I think it fascinating that one important kind of extended kin unit, the lineage, is in almost as much difficulty in Taiwan as it is on the mainland.

There is evidence, largely inferential, that some aspects of kin association on the supranuclear family level can be found reemerging in the Chinese People's Republic, particularly in the reassertion of nepotic privilege in communes or brigades. On the other hand, the overseas Chinese have long demonstrated, as do the present data from Taiwan, that the urban milieu presents new possibilities for extended kinship organizations. This is not peculiar to China or to the Chinese. The cousin-clubs in certain ethnic sectors of our own society are an equivalent phenomenon. The time is almost ripe for a comparative analysis of these associations.

When the comparative analysis is undertaken, one of its foci is sure to be the political functions of these groups, and they may be expected to vary in importance as well as content. In some instances, however, I think they will be found to have an unexpected potential, functioning not as anachronistic survivals of an older kind of society but as a new and dynamic part of modern political apparatus that seek to get more, for a carefully defined group of members, through a variety of means.

REFERENCES

CHEN, SHAO-HSING. 1962. The migration from Fukien to the Philippines under the Spanish colonization and to Taiwan under the Dutch colonization: an analysis of their patterns of development and their correspondences. Proceedings of the International Association of the Historians of Asia (Taipei), pp. 1-11.

COHEN, MYRON L. 1963. The Hakka or "guest people": dialect as a sociocultural variable in southeastern China. Unpublished essay for the degree of Master of Arts and for the Certificate of the East Asian Institute, Columbia University.

FREEDMAN, MAURICE. 1958. Lineage organization in southeastern China. London: Athlone Press. London School of Economics Monographs on Social Anthropology, No. 18.

FRIED, MORTON H. 1957. The classification of corporate unilineal descent groups. Journal of the Royal Anthropological Institute, 87, 1-29.

HSIEH, CHIAO-MIN. 1964 Taiwan—ilha Formosa, a geography in perspective. Washington: Butterworth's.

LATOURETTE, KENNETH SCOTT. 1964. China. Englewood Cliffs, N.J.: Prentice-Hall (Spectrum Books).

WANG, YI-T'UNG. 1943. The social, political, and economic aspects of the influential clans of the southern dynasties. Chengtu: The Institute of Chinese Cultural Studies, Chinling University. (In Chinese.)

INDEX

Abreu, J. C., 83
Acephalous societies, 137
Adjudication, 108 n.; in Bena society, 100-107
Administration, 28; attitude to Tonga witchcraft, 226-7
Administrative organization, 12
Adu Boahen, C. F. A., 129
Affiliation, 43
African Political Systems, 1-2, 9
Agnatic group, 275; *see also* Patrilineal groups
Agnatic succession, 132
Agrarian politics, 193, 205, 207, 209, 215
Algonkians, 62
Alien diviner, 221-7, 251
Alternative mechanisms to central political authority, 85
American Anthropological Association, 1964 Annual General Meeting, 1
Anarchy: Chimbu of New Guinea, 69; Kuikuru, 71-85
Ancestor tablets, 290-1, 298
Ancestor worship, 266
Anti-clericalism, 193, 204-5, 207; and factional politics, 211-4
Apinaye, 77, 82
Appointment of officers, 70, 124, 142, 176, 179, 182
Arbitration, 36
"Architectural" analysis of structure, 50-1
Arena, 2, 52-4, 249; behavioral, 260
Argument, 43
Arziyi beliefs: a self-validating theory, 14, 110, 134-139; compared to Calvinism, 134; and individual judgments about social roles, 135; as explanation of social structure, 135; distinguished from *baraka*, 136; similarity among Tallensi and Yoruba, 137; and witchcraft/sorcery, 137-8
Association, 43
Authority, 17-18, 29, 109-110; over the Cree, 64; among the Chimbu, 69; of Lugbara elder, 110; of Tolai "big man" through wealth, 109-110; and power, central to political system, 130; Kanuri obedience to, 131; Lugbara competition for, 147; of ritual office, 246
Authority code, 17-18, 109-110

Bailey, F. G., 34, 52, 54 n.; on concept of arena, 33
Bakunin, I., 206
Bales, R. F., 9, 37
Band chief: among the Cree, 62
Bands, 62, 174-5
Banfield, E. C., 9, 189
Bangala, 29
Banner, H., 82
Barama River Caribs, 84
Barnett, Paul, 175-85
Barnouw, V., 173-4
Barth, F., 53, 191, 279
Baraka: sacred power, 132
Beals, A., 52, 56, 58
Beals, R., 192
Bena of Tanzania, 89-108; psychological characteristics of, 91-8; social structure, 98-100; adjudication among, 100-107
Bierstedt, R., 9, 14 n.; on sources of power, 32-3
Big man: in New Guinea, 69; among Tolai, 109-110, 113-4, 122
Bingham, H., 157
Bornu of Sudan, 130-136
Bororo, 77, 82
Boundaries: of political fields, 247-53; conflict in, 286
Breach of the peace, 32-3
Brenan, G., 206
Breton, R., 81
Brown, P., 61, 69, 257
Buchler, J., 262
Bureau of Indian Affairs, 176, 180-1, 184
Butaritari, 157-8, 160-1, 167, 169

Carvalho, J. B. de, 83
Camaracoto, 81, 84